Realizing Africa's Potential

Praise for *Realizing Africa's Potential*

Realizing Africa's Potential: A Journey to Prosperity comes at the perfect time to act as a compass and a catalyst for businesses, both established and emerging, to navigate African markets and find success in the world's most promising region. It is with immense gratitude that we welcome this pivotal work by Professor Landry Signé, who shares the optimistic and practical vision that the private sector can unlock Africa's prosperity. Professor Signé's lifelong dedication to elevating Africa's presence on the global stage and improving livelihoods shines through this book as he inspires busi ness leaders and investors to be an active part in Africa's economic transformation. He not only inspires readers by analyzing opportunities and trends within different sectors, but also provides strategic advice based on his wealth of knowledge and future-oriented evidence that can help move investors from inspiration to action.

—*Børge Brende, President, World Economic Forum*

Realizing Africa's Potential is an essential and powerful guide for anyone committed to an integrated, resilient, and prosperous Africa, playing a strong role in the global economy. Given his worldwide leadership connecting the most influential business, political, academic, and societal stakeholders to solve global challenges, Professor Landry Signé is uniquely positioned to shape the future of African business—a future that focuses on partnership, industrialization, job creation, and meeting development goals. His work stands as a pivotal contribution to Africa's economic renaissance, promoting unity and solidarity among Africans for sustainable and inclusive growth. The continent remains infinitely grateful for the unique contributions of Professor Signé. As one of our most extraordinary and effective thought leaders, he has bridged the gap between powerful aspirations and transformational real-world outcomes, fostering progress and inspiring change across Africa. This book is a must-read for anyone looking to understand and engage with Africa's dynamic economic transformation.

—*His Excellency Wamkele Mene, Secretary General, African Continental Free Trade Area*

Realizing Africa's Potential is a bold, unique, and captivating masterpiece, a transformational guide to harnessing Africa's boundless potential. Our own Professor Landry Signé, the world's most authoritative and extraordinary thought leader on the topic, with unparalleled depth and transformative insights shines through, offering global leaders future-oriented perspectives on navigating African economies and realizing their potential successfully. This book is not only a powerful tool for entrepreneurs, business executives, and investors but also provides important insights for public sector leaders to better understand both the complexities of African business environments and critical sectors and strategies on how to effectively work together to transform economies for the benefit of all Africans.

—*Her Excellency Ameenah Gurib-Fakim, 6th President of the Republic of Mauritius*

Offering a rare blend of powerful wisdom and effective practicality, Professor Landry Signé provides a master class on the expanding business opportunities, trends, risks, and strategies for success in Africa for those poised to enter, expand, or succeed within the promising frontier, while accelerating inclusive prosperity. *Realizing Africa's Potential: A Journey to Prosperity* offers a holistic and nuanced view of various industries and sectors ripe for business and provides tangible steps for private and public sector leaders to successfully create high returns and generate general welfare in African economies.

—*John Olajide, Founder and CEO of Axxess, Chairman of Cavista Holdings, and Chairman of the Corporate Council on Africa*

Once again, Professor Landry Signé proves his leadership in the realm of African economies through his profound work, *Realizing Africa's Potential: A Journey to Prosperity*. The book provides insights into Africa's thriving and emerging business sectors, crafting a manual for business leaders that is both enlightening and actionable. As both a scholar and a pioneer, Professor Signé offers evidence-based expertise on the intricacies of African markets, providing a fresh take on how the private sector can thrive across one of the world's most promising regions.

—*Her Excellency Joyce Banda, First Female President of Malawi*

Professor Landry Signé's *Realizing Africa's Potential* is an essential blueprint that guides business leaders and policymakers through the continent's dynamic industries from mining to insurance and more. Leveraging his deep expertise in African business markets and economic development, Professor Signé, one of our most influential thought leaders, is leading the way in offering inspiration and a clear path to success for those who wish to master the continent's investment landscape, much needed to achieve Agenda 2063. It is a must-read for all those contributing to the continent's socioeconomic transformation and progress.

—*Ambassador Albert Mudenda Muchanga, African Union Commissioner for Economic Development, Trade, Tourism, Industry, and Minerals*

Realizing Africa's Potential
A Journey to Prosperity

Landry Signé

BROOKINGS INSTITUTION PRESS
Washington, DC

Published by Brookings Institution Press
1775 Massachusetts Avenue, NW
Washington, DC 20036
www.brookings.edu/bipress

Co-published by Rowman & Littlefield
An imprint of The Rowman & Littlefield Publishing Group, Inc.
4501 Forbes Boulevard, Suite 200, Lanham, Maryland 20706
www.rowman.com

86-90 Paul Street, London EC2A 4NE

Typeset in Minion Pro
Composition by Circle Graphics, Inc., Reisterstown, Maryland

The Brookings Institution is a nonprofit organization devoted to research, education, and
publication on important issues of domestic and foreign policy. Its principal purpose is to
bring the highest-quality independent research and analysis to bear on current and emerging
policy problems.

Library of Congress Control Number: 2024948323

ISBN: 978-0-8157-4097-1 (cloth : alk. paper)
ISBN: 978-0-8157-4098-8 (pbk. : alk. paper)
ISBN: 978-0-8157-4099-5 (ebook)

♾™ The paper used in this publication meets the minimum requirements of American National
Standard for Information Sciences—Permanence of Paper for Printed Library Materials,
ANSI/NISO Z39.48-1992

Contents

Foreword by Børge Brende

President, World Economic Forum

Africa is at the precipice of profound economic transformation backed by the world's largest projected youth population and accelerated by the ongoing full implementation of the African Continental Free Trade Agreement. As economic, social, and geopolitical dynamics are ever-evolving across the continent, *Realizing Africa's Potential: A Journey to Prosperity* comes at the perfect time to act as a compass and a catalyst for businesses, both established and emerging, to navigate African markets and find success in the world's most promising region.

It is with immense gratitude that we welcome this pivotal work by Professor Landry Signé, who shares the optimistic and practical vision that the private sector can unlock Africa's prosperity. With meaningful partnerships between the public and private sectors, civil society, and local communities, business success can transcend purely economic gains, leading to tangible improvements in sustainable development across the continent. Professor Signé's lifelong dedication to elevating Africa's presence on the global stage and improving livelihoods shines through this book as he inspires business leaders and investors to be an active part of Africa's economic transformation. He not only inspires readers by analyzing opportunities and trends within different sectors, but also provides strategic advice based on his wealth of knowledge and future-looking evidence that can help move investors from inspiration to action.

I am confident that the findings in *Realizing Africa's Potential: A Journey to Prosperity* will spark important dialogue—and, most importantly, action—among business leaders and policymakers alike, playing a pivotal role in accelerating Africa's path to industrialization and structural transformation. Professor Signé is an inspiration to all who will witness Africa's prosperity and destiny over the next few years, offering an invitation to anyone who wishes to play a part in Africa's remarkable story.

Foreword by His Excellency Wamkele Mene

Secretary General, African Continental Free Trade Area

By 2050, Africa's population is projected to reach 2.5 billion, with business and consumer spending expected to exceed $16.12 trillion. Achieving these impressive milestones through the African Continental Free Trade Area (AfCFTA) depends not only on the removal of trade barriers but also, more importantly, on the active engagement and commitment of both local and international business communities. Their involvement is crucial for accelerating industrial development and effectively integrating African markets.

In *Realizing Africa's Potential: A Journey to Prosperity*, Professor Landry Signé offers a comprehensive and systematic analysis of the continent's economic landscape. The book guides readers through critical sectors key to Africa's growth, from health care and mining to entertainment and capital markets. Professor Signé not only highlights the continent's economic potential but also details the significant roles that local and international businesses must play.

Grounded in Professor Signé's deep understanding of the economic environment, the publication provides nuanced insights into the opportunities and challenges facing business leaders, offering practical, actionable advice that extends beyond standard policy analysis. The recommendations aim to bolster industrial development and market integration, supporting the objectives of the AfCFTA.

While progress has been made in streamlining customs processes and facilitating seamless cross-border trade, substantial efforts are still needed to fulfill the visions of the AfCFTA and Agenda 2063. This endeavor demands active collaboration from all stakeholders. Professor Signé's latest work is crucial, signaling that Africa is open for business and calling for a more robust engagement that taps into the continent's vibrant economic opportunities.

Realizing Africa's Potential is an essential guide for anyone committed to an integrated, resilient, and prosperous Africa. Given his worldwide leadership connecting the most influential business, political, academic, and societal stakeholders to solve global challenges, Professor Signé is uniquely positioned to shape the future of African business—a future that focuses on partnership, industrialization, job creation, and meeting development goals. His work stands as a pivotal contribution to Africa's economic renaissance, promoting unity and solidarity among Africans for sustainable and inclusive growth.

The continent remains infinitely grateful for the unique contributions of Professor Landry Signé. As one of our most extraordinary and effective thought leaders, he has bridged the gap between powerful aspirations and transformational real-world outcomes, fostering progress and inspiring change across Africa. This book is a must-read for anyone looking to understand and engage with Africa's dynamic economic transformation.

Foreword by John Olajide

Founder and CEO of Axxess, Chairman of Cavista Holdings, and Chairman of the Board of the Corporate Council on Africa

Offering a rare blend of powerful wisdom and effective practicality, Professor Landry Signé provides a master class on the expanding business opportunities, trends, risks, and strategies for success in Africa for those poised to enter, expand, or succeed within the promising frontier, while accelerating inclusive prosperity. *Realizing Africa's Potential: A Journey to Prosperity* offers a holistic and nuanced view of various industries and sectors that are ripe for business, and it provides tangible steps for private and public sector leaders to successfully create high returns and generate general welfare in African economies.

As a Nigerian American who continues to engage on the continent after immigrating to the United States, I am well aware of this potential, and I have investments in African technology, agriculture, hospitality, and other sectors. I'm not alone. No other diaspora in the world matches Americans of African descent in economically engaging with their homeland.

Much of the world recognizes Africa's economic potential. Its governments and their businesses are drawn by Africa's large pool of talented and entrepreneurial youth, many excelling in high tech, the arts, and other innovative industries.

My own experience as the founder and CEO of a leading home health care technology company serves as a testament to the lessons shared by Professor Signé. Africa's leadership in leapfrogging and embracing new technologies allows for new business opportunities at the frontier of technological discovery.

In the health care industry, we are leveraging these capabilities to reach millions of people with high-quality health care services in their homes, revolutionizing how health care is delivered. This transformative power of technology, coupled with the entrepreneurial spirit inherent in African communities, illustrates how African entrepreneurs and their partners can spur global innovation and growth, which we are seeing not only in Nigeria but also across the continent.

As the first African-born Chairman of the Board of Directors for the Corporate Council on Africa, the premier business association promoting US investment on the continent, I am a strong advocate for rapidly increasing the quality and quantity of investment and engagement with African markets, and I share the book's conclusion that individual enterprises alone cannot lead to African prosperity—strategic partnerships and alignment between the private and public sectors will be the key accelerators of Africa's sustained prosperity. There needs to be a better understanding of each other's needs to align interests and come up with win–win opportunities. And both sides need to work hard to offer good propositions in a supportive environment if we want to see more investment and business.

The United States must be bold, aiming to be the most important commercial player in Africa. While our engagement is far from the level that most African leaders expect, Professor Signé's book offers a blueprint for understanding how to best make progess.

I applaud Professor Signé's lifelong efforts to transform African economies and make an impact on livelihoods, offering a vision of the future where the continent's youth have an opportunity to shape the world. His lucid optimism is contagious, leaving readers eager to explore the opportunities to deepen their relationships and footprints on the continent, inspiring leaders not only to see the promise of Africa but also to seize it. To be relevant on the continent of Africa, which will only become more important with its growing population and consumer spending power in coming decades, it's time for a reality check. This book provides it. Now it's time to get to work.

Acknowledgments

This book would not have been possible without the support of incredible people and institutions, for which and to whom I am extremely grateful: Cecilia Elena Rouse, president of the Brookings Institution; Brahima S. Coulibaly, vice president and director of the Brookings Global Economy and Development program; Yelba Quinn, publisher of the Brookings Institution Press; Michael Crow, president of Arizona State University; Charla Griffy-Brown, dean and director-general of the Thunderbird School of Global Management; Joel Cabrita, Susan Ford Dorsey Director of the Stanford University Center for African Studies; and Jonathan Sisk and Mikayla Lindsay of Bloomsbury.

I am also very grateful to His Excellency Wamkele Mene, secretary-general of the African Continental Free Trade Area (AfCFTA); Børge Brende, president of the World Economic Forum (WEF); Ngozi Okonjo-Iweala, director-general of the World Trade Organization; Her Excellency Professor Ameenah Gurib-Fakim, sixth president of the Republic of Mauritius; Her Excellency Dr. Joyce Banda, first female president of the Republic of Malawi and Africa's second female president; Ambassador Albert Mudenda Muchanga, African Union commissioner for economic development, trade, tourism, industry, and minerals; and Chido Munyati, Head of Africa at the WEF, for their special support. And I am very grateful to Aliko Dangote, the founder, chairman, and CEO of the Dangote Group; and to John Olajide, the founder and CEO of Axxess and chairman of the Corporate Council on Africa.

Writing a book requires the collaboration and unique contributions of many individuals. I would like to express my deepest gratitude to Chelsea Johnson, who has closely collaborated on this project, as she was my post-doctoral scholar during my tenure as an Andrew Carnegie Fellow, providing incredible support at many phases of the initial research. I am also grateful to Hanna Dooley and Alexandria Cordero for their substantial contribution to research and illustrations, as well as Zezhou Cai, Amy Copley, Hawa C. Coulibaly, Dhruv Gandhi, Bonnette Ishimwe, Ritika Iyer, Genevieve Jesse, Liona Muchenje, Nirav Patel, Anna Schaeffer, Wilfried Youmbi, and Nichole Grossman for research assistance on some chapters; and to Jeannine Ajello, David Batcheck, Christina Golubski, Joshua Miller, Nicole Ntungire, Esther Rosen, and Izzy Taylor for their editorial and design work on some chapters.

I am also grateful to my former students enrolled in my Stanford University's Continuing Studies course, Emerging African Markets: Strategies, Investment, and Government Affairs, where I have first taught many of the notions which were released in my book *Unlocking Africa's Business Potential* (2020), and on which this volume *Realizing Africa's Potential* builds. At Stanford University, Larry Diamond, Francis Fukuyama, Laura Hubbard, Richard Roberts, and Jeremy Weinstein have been incredible hosts and mentors.

I am very grateful to the Brookings Institution Press team—including Stephan Przybylowicz, the book's indexer; Circle Graphics, Inc., Reisterstown, Maryland; Alfred F. Imhoff, the book's editor; and Frederic King of the Brookings Bookstore. I am also thankful to anonymous reviewers as well as scholars who have provided valuable feedback on some chapters or the overall manuscript—including Belinda Archibong, Karim El Aynaoui, Hippolyte Fofack, Yves Jerouguel, Kasirim Nwuke, Aloysius Ordu, Witney Schneidman, and Eyerusalem Siba—and professionals including Nisrine Ouazzani Chahdi, Nada Drais, Mokhtar Ghailani, and Stephen Gardner.

The chapter on trade specifically benefited from the extraordinary support from multistakeholder collaboration organized by the WEF's Friends of the African Continental Free Trade Area, in partnership with the African Continental Free Trade Area Secretariat. Chido Munyati, Africa head at the WEF, and I—in my capacity as cochair of both the WEF Friends of the AfCFTA and WEF Regional Action Group for Africa—organized workshops and focus groups to collect data and excerpts from various companies within four high potential sectors for local and global business: automotive, agriculture and agro-processing, pharmaceuticals, and transportation and logistics. I am grateful to all the contributors involved in AfCFTA: A New Era for Global Business and Investment in Africa, including Oliver Alawuba,

Suhail Al Banna, Gilberto Antonio, Rita Babihuga-Nsanze, Sumeet Bhardwaj, Børge Brende, Sean Doherty, Hassan El Houry, Cynthia Gnassingbe-Essonam, Lutz Hegemann, Mohamed Hettiti, Philippe Isler, Anouar Jamali, Serge Kamuhinda, Fa-eez Karodia, Lutendo Khavhadi, Grace Khoza, Themba Khumalo, Youssef Lahmiti, Dom La Vigne, Fernanda Lopes Larsen, Shiletsi Makhofane, Walter Mandela, Esha Mansingh, Wamkele Mene, Racey Muchilwa, Patricia Obozuwa, Anu Paasiaro, Luis Alfredo Pérez, Michael Petrie, Mariam Soumaré, Matthew Stephenson, Supachai Wattanaveerachai, Candice White, and Geoffrey White. I thank all the contributors involved in the WEF's An Action Plan to Accelerate Global Business and Investment in Africa (2024), including Deeana Ahmed, Jason Blackman, Børge Brende, Rose Chilvers, Dave Coffey, Laurence Denmark, Andile Dlamini, Maximillian Effah, Tony Eneh, Cyntia Genolet, Cynthia Gnassingbe-Essonam, Chris Holden, Shazia Ijaz, Christine Irish, Philippe Isler, Faizel Ismail, Lutendo Khavhadi, Themba Khumalo, Nthabiseng Komane, Dom La Vigne, Fernanda Lopes Larsen, Siya Madikizela, Shiletsi Makhofane, Walter Mandela, Sarah Meinert, Wamkele Mene, Alex Moir, Edna Oduwo, Anu Paasiaro, David Paterson, Luis Alfredo Pérez, Steven Pope, Laura Raaen, Ravin Sanjith, Dirk Willem te Velde, Ashleigh Theophanides, Hannes van der Merwe, Noncedo Vutula, Jonathan Walter, Geoffrey White, and Andrew Whiting.

I am also grateful to my distinguished friends, experts, and the members of my network, who helped me choose a cover for the book through a vote on social media, given the beautiful design by Katie Merris.

I would like to thank my fantastic parents and siblings, whose unconditional support has been a constant source of motivation—Joséphine, Michel, Nadège, Carine, Gaël, Marcelle, and Ange. Last, but not least, I am grateful to my dearest love, Nadine, who not only provided invaluable moral support but also was so kind as to read the manuscript, and to my son, Landry Signé Jr., and my daughter, Lana Signé, spreading joy and happiness in our life every single day. I dedicate this book to my parents, Michel and Joséphine, my darling, Nadine, my son and daughter, Landry Jr. and Lana, and to everyone contributing to realizing Africa's potential. I want to celebrate here the memories of my grandparents; Martine, Fidèle, Joseph, and Djouonda; and the memory of Gigi.

This book was made possible in part by a grant from the Carnegie Corporation of New York and the Rubenstein Fellowship. The statements made and views expressed are solely the responsibility of the author.

One
Introduction
REALIZING AFRICA'S POTENTIAL—TURNING PROMISE INTO PROGRESS

Over the past two decades, the African continent has gone from being described as "hopeless" to being recognized as one of the fastest-growing regions of the world. The continent's success, however, has been neither linear nor consistent. While from 2000 to 2010, Africa experienced a series of achievements including an average annual real growth rate of gross domestic product (GDP) of 5.1 percent, the region's economic growth slowed in the following decade to 3.3 percent, only slightly higher than the pre-2000 average annual growth rate of 2.5 percent.[1] Yet the wide variation in economic performance across the continent reveals a more optimistic reality: nearly half of Africa's population lived in countries that exceeded the continent's average growth rate between 2010 and 2019.[2] The continent still holds tremendous potential, which can be unlocked and unraveled by pursuing challenging but rewarding business opportunities. As stated in my previous book, *Unlocking Africa's Business Potential*, companies seeking new markets to expand into with long-term investment perspectives will find opportunities for growth across the African continent.[3] Despite challenging economic conditions, companies have remained resilient and have continued to see growth in Africa.

Additionally, advancing trade, investment, and technology in Africa offers enormous potential for economic growth and increased prosperity, while increased political stability and the improvement of regional integration are helping to improve market access. Business expansion will also create new jobs for women and youth—two currently underserved majority groups in the population—which will contribute to social and economic development and the rise of a new middle class. In fact, before the COVID-19 pandemic, forecasts showed a positive outlook for the continent: by 2030, 43 percent of the region's population would enter the middle or upper class, with a market of 1.7 billion people; and by 2050, Africa would be home to an estimated $16.12 trillion in combined consumer and business spending.[4] While these estimates show positive trends for the continent, the world has changed since the pandemic, and recent geopolitical conflicts have created new dimensions that will shape key trends and change this potential.

Why should the world care? Why should countries or companies pay attention to the tremendous trade and investment potential across the African continent? Because there are tremendous mutual benefits for economic gain and prosperity for companies and countries alike through a market-based model of development.[5] Beyond economic gains, trade and investment also bring the peace, stability, and security that are critical for a sustainable and prosperous future.[6] In *Unlocking Africa's Business Potential*, I identify trade and investment trends, opportunities, challenges, and strategies that illustrate the tremendous potential of Africa, and I explain the complex competition between emerging and established powers on the continent.[7] In this book, I provide an update on these opportunities and take a deep dive into new sectors that are emerging as major industries on the continent, including health care and pharmaceuticals; mining; insurance; investment, private equity, and venture capital; international and intraregional trade; capital markets; and entertainment industries.

Africa's Tremendous Potential: Key Trends

To set the scene for the trajectory that will shape the future of these industries on the continent, it is critical to understand ongoing economic, geopolitical, social, and political trends and their implications for trade, investment, economic transformation, inclusive prosperity, and geopolitical dynamics in a time of competition between rising and global powers. It is also important to be cognizant of trends shaping Africa's future. These trends are highlighted in figure 1-1, and then are discussed.

First, Africa's economic transformation and business potential are more substantial than many think: Africa is the world's next growth market, with many growth narratives. Though it was considered a hopeless continent in 2000 by *The Economist*, Africa has seen the two best cumulative successive decades of its existence in the twenty-first century.[8] Trade in and with Africa

Figure 1-1. Key Trends

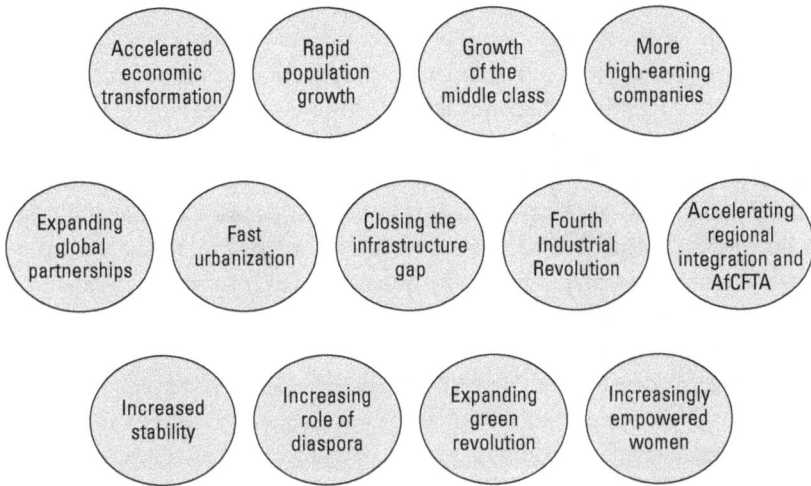

has grown 300 percent in the last decade, outperforming global averages (196 percent).[9] It has become home to many of the world's fastest-growing economies, offering unique opportunities for new investors. Moreover, Africa has a tremendous economic potential, and it offers rewarding opportunities for both local and global partners looking for new markets and long-term investments with some of the world's highest returns, as well as the potential to foster economic growth, diversification, job creation—including for women and youth—and improved general welfare.

However, aggregate estimates of Africa's growth can at times mask regional or country-specific differences. Across the continent, average growth in GDP has been 4.2 percent since 2000; however, each country has its own story. Some African countries experienced sharp declines, whereas others experienced accelerated growth, even during the slower growth decade between 2010 and 2019.[10] A 2023 McKinsey study breaks these different experiences down into four clusters. The first cluster, "consistent growers," is a group of thirteen countries, primarily in East and West Africa, that exceeded the 4.2 percent average growth rate from 2010 to 2019—and, even more impressively, in 2022, after the pandemic. This group has had a 3 percent annual growth in per capita consumption, has reduced the number of people living in absolute poverty, and has experienced above-average growth in urbanization, capital investment, and exports. The second cluster is the group of "recent accelerators," which is made up of eight countries, six of which are in West Africa. Comprising 9 percent of the continent's population and 7 percent of its GDP, this group has exceeded Africa's average growth rate in the past decade (2010–19), despite underperforming the decade before. The group has experienced growth in investment, exports, and urbanization, and, more recently, six out of the eight countries had above-average economic growth in 2022. The third cluster, the "recent slowdowns," is a group of thirteen countries, including some of Africa's largest economies—such as Egypt, Morocco, and Nigeria—that experienced growth in the first decade of the century but a slowdown in growth during the second. From 2010 to 2019, this group experienced slower-than-average investment and exports while maintaining the highest level of urbanization. The final group, the "slow growers," is made up of fifteen countries, representing 13 percent of the continent's population and 26 percent of its GDP, which have underperformed average growth, export, and investment rates over the past twenty years. Interestingly, this group is made up of the continent's large economies, such as South Africa and Algeria, as well as nine out of ten of its smallest economies.

These clusters show how diverse economic growth experiences have been across the continent, highlighting the fact that there is no "one Africa." Different national contexts mean that there is a wide and varied range of specific opportunities for business to take a leading role in particular growth narratives.

Second, rapid population growth on the continent could become either a threat to global prosperity and stability or an opportunity for demographic dividends. Africa's population is expected to nearly double by 2050,[11] at which point it will make up 26 percent of the global population (2.53 billion).[12] If Africa is not successfully integrated into the global economy, there could be a major threat to global prosperity and stability. Citizens could be further subjected to extreme poverty, fragility, violent extremism, illegal immigration, health challenges, and other maladies—challenges that many already face on the continent. However, if African economies continue to transform through meaningful investment and integration, the continent's growing youth population could be its key to success at a time when major economies are facing population stagnation or decline. Already Africa's youth are more connected than ever before, and they are quick adopters of mobile applications, leading to a strong and growing culture of tech-focused entrepreneurism.[13] Expanding formal employment and strengthening human capital overall will unlock this generation's immense entrepreneurial power to further compound development progress and investment goals.

Third, the continent's growing middle class is leading to growth in household consumption and business spending, representing a unique opportunity for trade and investment. The middle class across Africa has tripled over the past 30 years, reaching 313 million (34 percent of the population).[14] North African countries have the highest concentration of middle-class Africans, with Tunisia at almost 90 percent, Morocco at 85 percent, and Egypt at 80 percent, while other countries—such as Botswana, Ghana, Namibia, Mozambique, and Malawi—are also seeing growth. This growth is a driver of future business success on the continent. By 2030, 130 million new consumers will join African markets;[15] and by 2050, Africa will be home to an estimated $16.12 trillion in combined consumer and business spending.[16] Such growth will offer tremendous opportunities for businesses in household consumption ($8 trillion), in areas such as food and beverages, housing, hospitality and recreation, health care, financial services, education and transportation, and consumer goods, as well as business-to-business spending (construction, utilities, and transportation, agriculture and agro-processing, wholesale and retail, etc.). Considering different scenarios for the future if the current level of slow growth continues, the consumer market alone will exceed $600 billion by 2030 (with a total market of $2.2 trillion), but if consumption growth returns to the rates of the 2000–10 decade, consumption would grow by $1.3 trillion (total market, $3 trillion).

Fourth, high-earning companies are on the rise on the continent. Emerging economies with high growth rates have had, on average, double the number of large companies compared with other economies.[17] Already today across Africa, there are at least 345 companies with an annual revenue of more than $1 billion. This growth is expected to continue, with McKinsey reporting that the collective revenue ($1 trillion) from more than half these high-performing companies could increase by more than $550 billion by 2030 through increased productivity and expanded markets. Of the 345 companies, about 230 were started in an African country by an African entrepreneur. Among these locally created companies, about half are publicly traded, 30 percent are privately owned, and 20 percent are state-owned. Aside from homegrown companies, the remainder of the high-earning companies are foreign subsidiaries (37 percent publicly traded and the rest private), which have a disproportionate role in Africa compared with other regions.

South Africa is home to a disproportionately high number of these $1 billion+ companies—147, or 40 percent—while an additional 111 companies, or 32 percent, are located in slow-growth or recently slowed-down economies. A total of 60 percent of these companies are in Egypt, Nigeria, and South Africa, opening up opportunities for companies to flourish in smaller but faster-growing nations. Fifty-two of these high-earning companies are state-owned enterprises, with 70 percent of their revenue coming from oil and natural gas, retail and consumer goods, financial services, manufacturing, mining, and telecommunications. While state-owned companies are more involved in extractive industries, the large homegrown and foreign companies are more concentrated in services. The performance of these large companies varies greatly, with an average aggregate growth of 4.9 percent across the continent from 2015 to 2021. Growth rates in companies within each sector were more diverse, but average growth across sectors remained close. Looking ahead, estimates show that 60 percent of the revenue potential could be taken up by the services sector ($330 billion), one-third could be taken up by the oil and gas sector ($160 billion), and 12 percent could be taken up by mining and metals ($65 billion).[18]

Fifth, there is a rise in global partnerships and competition between traditional and new players. Partnerships and sources of foreign investment in Africa have significantly diversified in the past decade. In 2009, China became the region's prime trading partner, with trade surging between 2006 and 2016 (imports increased by 233 percent, and exports increased by 53 percent,[19] as they did for several other global players as well).[20] China's influence goes beyond the trade relationship; it is also Africa's top investor in infrastructure, and now is the first destination for English-speaking African students, ahead of the United States and the United Kingdom.[21] Despite declines in foreign direct investment, aid, and lending from the United States, the United States remains a critical player on the continent. Emerging economies such as Japan, South Korea, Russia, and Turkey, among others, are also becoming major trading partners, expanding the market for African goods and services, which is only expected to increase as the region continues to integrate. As I put it in a recent article, "The current era—and competition from other global powers—will require new ideas and a new approach to several key issues."[22] This competition for new ideas should increase the quality of partnerships, allowing African countries to diversify and raise their negotiating power on the global stage.

Sixth, rapid urbanization is being accompanied by rapid rural population growth. By 2040, Africa will be home to twelve cities of more than 10 million inhabitants, adding ten more cities to the current two: Cairo and Lagos.[23] Nineteen cities will have populations between 5 and 10 million, meaning that 31 cities in total will have over 5 million habitants across the continent, split evenly among all four growth clusters.[24] While city growth patterns also vary across the continent, cities within the consistent growers and recent accelerator clusters are expected to have the fastest-growing GDP and per capita GDP.[25] As the fastest-urbanizing place on Earth, Africa will see a migration of more than 500 million people from the countryside to cities by 2040.[26] Sub-Saharan Africa is home to some of the fastest-growing cities in the world, with the potential to become powerful economic centers, as is the case in the rest of Africa, with urban households earning and consuming more than twice as much as the rest of Africa between 2000 and 2019.[27] New investment opportunities specific to rural populations will continue to grow as well, given that Sub-Saharan Africa, along with the Middle East and North Africa, is the only region in the world with a growing rural population (57 percent of Africa's population lived in rural areas in 2019).[28]

There is also immense potential within secondary cities, which so far have grown at a slower pace than primary cities (2.5 percent vs. 3 percent between 2000 and 2019). Secondary cities have the opportunity to become economic centers as well, with targeted investment in enabling environments and partnerships with local governments, multilateral institutions, private financial institutions, and corporations. Two examples of thriving second cities are Cape Town, South Africa, and Kumasi, Ghana, which are in two different clusters—slow grower and consistent grower, respectively. Cape Town has attracted significant investment in its tech sector, now home to two hundred fintech start-ups and data engineering hubs, while also attracting millions of tourists each year. Meanwhile, Kumasi has focused on growing its manufacturing subsector through its partnership with Deutsche Bank. While there is much progress to be made, secondary cities are an area of opportunity for businesses to play a central role for investment as the continent continues to urbanize.

Seventh, Africa has made tremendous progress in mobilizing resources for infrastructure development, working hard to bridge gaps in information and communications technology, energy, water and sanitation, and transportation. Despite the remaining deficits, the Infrastructure Consortium for Africa reported that between 2013 and 2017, annual funding for infrastructure development in the region was $77 billion, about twice as much as the annual funding average for the first six years of the 2000s.[29] However, many gaps persist. In 2018, the African Development Bank found that Africa's infrastructure requirements are between $130 billion and $170 billion a year, leaving a financing gap of $68 billion to $108 billion.[30]

Africa's urban infrastructure varies greatly by region. A total of 100 million people living in African cities (18 percent of the urban population) do not have access to electricity. Countries such as Egypt, Morocco, and Tunisia have almost full electrification, whereas rates of electrification in countries such as the Central African Republic are less than 40 percent.[31] The required infrastructure investment across the continent is estimated to be about 8.6 percent annually, but every $1 invested is estimated to add 20 cents to GDP.[32] At the same time, Africa has one of the fastest-growing, and is the second-largest, mobile phone market in the world.[33] In Sub-Saharan Africa alone, there were 477 million mobile subscribers in 2019; by 2025, the region will host 614 million cellphone subscribers, and 475 million mobile internet users.[34] The internet is also expected to contribute to at least between 5 and 6 percent of Africa's total GDP by 2025.[35] While the information and communications technology sector is making incredible advancements, water and sanitation, transportation, and energy infrastructure development still need significant investment. However, this is indicative of positive and extensive investment opportunities that can be undertaken on the African continent, making urban infrastructure investment extremely valuable.

Eighth, the continent is experiencing rapid digitization, increased technological innovation, and an accelerated Fourth Industrial Revolution. The Fourth Industrial Revolution is characterized by the fusion of the digital, biological, and technological worlds, and technologies such as artificial intelligence, big data, 5G, drones and automated vehicles, and cloud computing.[36] As explored in my book *Africa's Fourth Industrial Revolution*, these advanced technologies can have beneficial spillover effects.[37] For example, in the health sector, countries such as Rwanda and Ghana are using the American drone company Zipline to deliver medications, blood, and medical supplies in record time to remote rural areas with limited road accessibility.[38] In agriculture, African farmers now have access to affordable precision farming tools that use sensors, satellites, smart devices, and big data technologies to inform every decision.[39] The lending, insurance, and e-commerce opportunities provided by the fintech industry are transforming the lives of all Africans, and not just those in urban centers. These advancements are just the beginning, as African entrepreneurs are increasingly seeking partners to bring transformative businesses to life. Recent research by the International Finance Corporation reveals that although 86 percent of African firms have basic or advanced access to digital technologies, only 63 percent adopt them and just 23 percent use them intensively for business purposes.[40] This means that firms have the potential to seize digital opportunities and boost business productivity, raise workers' wages, and create better jobs, which can ultimately accelerate inclusive economic transformation and prosperity. In fact, 24 percent (600,000) of Africa's firms with 5 or more workers and up to 40 million microbusinesses are estimated to have high potential to benefit from adopting digital technologies.[41] African tech start-up funding increased over 40 percent in 2020 to over $700 million, a fraction of what it is outside Africa.[42] Despite such progress, the digital divide remains significant, and it must be bridged to allow inclusive development. During the COVID-19 pandemic, for example, access to school and business on the continent became more challenging given levels of internet connectivity, among other limitations. Bridging the digital divide represents an opportunity to both advance global investment in Africa while addressing some of Africa's key priorities.

Ninth, fast regional integration and the African Continental Free Trade Area are opportunities for continental engagement. The African continent has historically had very low levels of intra-African trade, with only 10 percent of imports coming from other African countries and 17 percent of exports going to other African countries, meaning that more than 80 percent of exports leave the continent.[43] With the signing of AfCFTA in 2018, its ratification in 2019, and its official launch in January 2021, the continent is becoming more interconnected, and African growth prospects and business opportunities are being magnified. The continent is giving the world one more reason to invest in it, with the creation of the world's largest new free trade zone per number of countries since the creation of the World Trade Organization. AfCFTA will accelerate Africa's industrialization as well as drive incomes up, which will lead to increases in both household consumption and business spending, generating unique opportunities for US trade and investment. According to a World Bank study, AfCFTA has the potential to lift 30 million people out of extreme poverty, increase the incomes of 68 million Africans, increase Africa's exports by $560 billion, and generate $450 billion in potential gains for African economies by 2035.[44]

Tenth, the continent will be strengthened by the sustained demand for accountability, democracy, and stability of African citizens, and policy priorities aligned with investor interests. Per Afrobarometer surveys, seven out of ten Africans support democracy and accountable governance, and about two-thirds are opposed to a single party or military government.[45] In the past decade, thirty-four countries, representing 72 percent of Africa's population, have increased their governance performance, along with improvements in the rule of law, among others.[46] While challenges remain, there is an overall trend toward more accountable, stable, and democratic countries backed by a significant political will and citizen support.

Eleventh, the increasing role of the diaspora in fostering investment is a key factor. Formally recognized by the African Union as Africa's sixth region, the African diaspora has significant breadth and influence, which is being harnessed to propel business on the continent. The diaspora of African nations is a powerful engine for development: over $95 million in financial remittances were sent to and within Africa in 2021,[47] in comparison with the significantly lower $35 billion in official development financing in 2021.[48] In addition to remittances, and perhaps more crucial for development in the long run, the developing nations' diasporas may be a powerful force for development in their home countries by fostering trade, investment, research, innovation, and the transfer of knowledge and technology. Today's African governments face challenges in connecting with their diasporas, in according with relevant experience from both rich and developing nations. Some African nations are exploring initiatives to forge connections with Africans living outside Africa, either to entice them to return or to leverage their expertise, knowledge, and financial resources to support African development. Dual citizenship is being used by nations such as Ghana to strengthen relationships with their diaspora. Deeper knowledge of efforts—such as diaspora bonds and investments, contributions of skilled and unskilled diaspora members to knowledge transfer, analytical studies of return migration, and understandings of circular migration experiences—are all required in order to determine whether such endeavors can be scaled up or copied in other nations around the world. But it is already clear that the increasing engagement and prioritization of the diaspora signals the important role it will play in future investment.

Twelfth, Africa's green revolution potential is globally significant. Despite contributing less than 3 percent to global carbon emissions while having almost one-fifth of the world population, Africa is one of the most vulnerable regions for experiencing climate change consequences such as extreme weather, water stress, and reduced food production.[49] In fact, today, 36 percent of Africa's total population, 460 million people, is exposed to at least one climate hazard (droughts, heat, water stress, or flooding), and by 2050, this number will double. Yet as these challenges and consequences intensify, the pressure to innovate and finance new technologies to accelerate the global energy transition and to adapt to climate change around the globe is opening the door for significant investment opportunities. African countries need $2.8 trillion by 2030 to meet their Paris Agreement emissions goals, but they are only averaging about $30 billion in climate finance inflows annually.[50]

This urgent need could serve as a huge opportunity for global investors; according to a recent International Finance Corporation study, private investment to combat climate change through adaptation alone could amount to up to $100 billion by 2040.[51] These opportunities range from weather-resistant crop varieties to crop insurance for farmers, irrigation systems to protect against droughts, climate data and information systems, and building dikes to protect against coastal flooding. A recent McKinsey report found that eight manufacturing opportunities from off-grid and microgrid solar systems, electric two-wheelers, electric vehicle charging stations, and cross-laminated timber could yield up to $2 billion in revenue a year, creating 700,000 jobs by 2030.[52]

Opportunities abound beyond adaptation as well. Africa is also rich in the natural minerals that are critical for clean technologies. Home to 80 percent of the world's platinum, 50 percent of its manganese, two-thirds of its cobalt, and a significant portion of its chromium, Africa is and will continue to be a key global player in the clean energy market. Clean energy was only a small portion of demand in mineral markets up until the mid-2010s, but now, due to the ongoing energy transitions in developed and emerging economies alike, it has become the fastest-growing segment of demand for minerals.[53] Africa has the potential to be a provider of carbon credits, a supplier of green hydrogen, and a hub for manufacturing green technologies.

Thirteenth, empowering women has the potential to increase economic output by up to 50 percent. Africa can achieve a significant growth dividend if it accelerates its efforts to eliminate gender gaps. According to new analysis from the McKinsey Global Institute, equal advancement might improve African economies by the equivalent of 10 percent of their total GDP by 2025.[54] Women are key players in innovation, entrepreneurship, and labor market participation. One study found that if countries with lower female-to-male labor market participation rates had rates similar to those of advanced countries in 2018, Africa would have gained an additional 44 million women in its labor market.[55] Given Africa's growing population, the potential of adding more women to the formal labor market will only become more important. Nine out of ten employed women in Sub-Saharan Africa are employed in the informal sector.[56] Opportunities such as local value chains and increased intra-African trade open an opportunity to formalize many of these jobs, especially given that women are three times more likely than men to be employed informally in nonagricultural employment.[57] While there is a long way to go to reach gender parity and unlock this powerful entrepreneurial force on the continent, Africa is moving in the right direction, having closed 67.8 percent of its gender gap as of 2022.[58]

Yet the potential of all these trends is not without challenges. It is impossible to speak of Africa's immense potential without recognizing and addressing some of the ongoing challenges that slow economic performance, regional integration, returns for businesses, and welfare for citizens.

The Opportunity to Address Key Challenges

Realizing Africa's potential requires overcoming challenges faced by various stakeholders, despite the diversity of experiences (Signé 2020). Key challenges include productivity, structural transformation, economic diversification, governance effectiveness, peace and security, infrastructure, regional integration, climate change, financing, and corporate issues. African leaders are increasingly dedicated to solving these challenges, despite contrasting outcomes across countries and regions.

Productivity, Structural Transformation, and Diversification

Foreign observers remain optimistic, but productivity in Africa has not yet taken off, having slowed in the second decade of this century, from 2.2 percent from 2000 to 2010 to 0.8 percent from 2010 to 2019.[59] Productivity also varies greatly between clusters, with productivity in slow-growing and recently slowing down clusters being higher than in consistently growing and recently accelerating clusters; however, within-cluster productivity also varies significantly. Across all sectors, productivity has risen only modestly and is low relative to other regions. Greater investment returns would be possible in industries like manufacturing and agriculture, for instance, with more efficient output.

The lack of structural transformation typically prevents big companies from working together effectively to accomplish infrastructure projects and an industry-wide adoption of technology, which hinders efficiency and productivity improvements. Due to its propensity to draw managerial and technological know-how, foreign direct investment must play a significant role in the development of an industrial state by ensuring promotion, adaptation, and access to global and regional value chains, as well as increased efficiency, significant investment flows, and increased productivity. Macroeconomic resilience is a sign that a structural transformation has been achieved. The continent has made progress in developing its service industry, which contributed 56 percent to GDP in 2019 compared with 50 percent in 2000, but there is still a long way to go. Overall, if Africa could match Asia's productivity in the service industry alone, it would add $1.4 trillion to its economy, doubling its value added today.[60] African countries must overcome the lack of economic diversification that has led to higher volatility, higher risk perceptions, and a deceleration of structural transformation.

Governance Effectiveness, Accountability, and Transparency

Too frequently, dysfunctional governance mechanisms remain in place, fostering environments where political and administrative elites behave unscrupulously and embezzle limited public funds that could be allocated to infrastructure, farm-to-market roads, water treatment facilities, education, health care, or technology. When the rewards from investment are sufficiently great or are ensured, as in the case of Africa's natural resource sector, many international investors have shown a readiness to tolerate public sector corruption. However, it is more challenging to promote investment in industries where returns are less attractive or assured, such as manufacturing and services, where similar patterns have become entrenched.

Any study or analysis of how to conduct business in African markets is likely to emphasize how legal ambiguity, bureaucratic red tape, and corruption frequently impede investment growth. Less than one-third of businesses operating in the region believe that administrative and regulatory procedures are handled effectively or that the national policy environment is typically proinvestment. Only 4 African nations made it into the top 50 nations in the world according to Transparency International's Corruptions Perceptions Index: Botswana (35th), Cabo Verde (38th), and Mauritius and Rwanda (tied at 50th).[61]

Improving the harmonization and rationalization of trade and investment regulation is one of the objectives of integrating Africa's regional economic communities; however, unsuccessful implementation at the national level and the inability of smaller nations to enforce compliance or penalize officials who act in a rent-seeking manner has slowed the process. However, with the ongoing implementation of AfCFTA, this process is likely to accelerate, leading to reduced regulatory uncertainty.

Peace, Security, and Geopolitics

The first step for advancing human development in Africa must be wealth generation, which calls for a strong entrepreneurial class and sustainable investment. Peace and security are essential for achieving these objectives, particularly for the peaceful cohabitation of the many ethnocultural groups that make up each African nation. Unfortunately, many African nations are still unable to establish and maintain favorable conditions for cohabitation, entrepreneurship, and wealth development because of weak and dysfunctional government systems. In fact, the absence of administrative mechanisms supported by the rule of law has failed to stop ethnically motivated violence in nations like Cameroon, the Democratic Republic of Congo, and South Sudan.[62]

These nations' economic development and entrepreneurship are being hampered by this violence. Without the establishment of inclusive and participatory governance systems, these nations are unlikely to experience the restoration of peace and security, which are essential for economic growth and wealth creation. The African Union has petitioned for more sustainable and predictable financial support for its African-led peace operations, which have seen both successes and challenges in preventing or stopping violent conflict in the region.[63] The relationship between peace and security and investment is far from linear, but the two will likely have to come in tandem. Similarly, recent global disruptions such as the COVID-19 pandemic and the Ukraine-Russian war have illustrated just how interconnected the global economy is, presenting unique challenges for African economies that struggle to remain resilient in the wake of external shocks, especially when trade and commerce are disrupted.

Human Capital, Skills, and Labor Market

Despite impressive progress in the Human Capital Index, there are still important challenges to overcome when it comes to human capital, especially in the context of business. Sub-Saharan Africa has reached only 40 percent of its productive potential, and health and education factors have worsened since the COVID-19 pandemic.[64] As the internet continues to spread across the continent, the types of skills needed for the upcoming workforce are changing, as they are in the rest of the world. Digital skills will continue to rise in demand, and forecasts show that about 230 million jobs in Sub-Saharan Africa will require digital skills by 2030.[65] Businesses have noted the lack of skilled labor to be a challenge within the continent across various sectors, from logistics to health care, information technology, and finance.[66]

Also critical to understand are the role and breadth of the informal sector in Africa, which will be critical, considering the staggering number of young people in informal jobs, representing nearly 83 percent of employment in Africa and 85 percent in Sub-Saharan Africa.[67] This reality—while bringing challenges related to productivity, wages, and job security—also has the potential to be leveraged as an asset for entrepreneurship. At 22 percent of its population, Africa's entrepreneurship rate is high.[68] Compared with the rest of the world, Sub-Saharan Africa has the most positive attitude toward entrepreneurship as a desirable career choice.[69] Significant effort is needed to make sure that informality does not remain or turn into a vicious cycle, by increasing access to credit and improving conditions for entrepreneurs. Investment in human capital, especially the production of a critical mass of scientists and engineers, and technological endowment are the most important and catalytic drivers of development to drive the process of industrialization.

Infrastructure and Energy

The quest for industrialization that will put the continent on an irreversible path to prosperity hinges on overcoming the physical and digital infrastructure deficit to enable growth and economic transformation. The African Development

Bank estimates that Africa needs to close an annual $402 billion gap by 2030 to "fast-track its structural transformation," including investments in key areas of education, energy, productivity, and infrastructure.[70] Perhaps the most pressing gap to close is addressing the energy crisis, which has been a major constraint on growth and structural transformation and requires investments of $200 billion annually through 2030.[71] The chronic deficit of energy is widespread, affecting both smaller and larger economies across the region. Unless investments in both human and physical capital are sustainably undertaken to lift this constraint, energy poverty will continue to drive intergenerational poverty, and prosperity will remain elusive across the region.

Although the $30 billion in annual investments in power and energy required in Africa may appear to be a risky, glass-half-empty situation, it represents a vast opportunity to fulfill unmet demand.[72] Similar to this, the boundless energy of youth portends a dichotomous action—for either good or bad. Infrastructure is another challenge that could represent an opportunity when it comes to supply chains. Mobility between countries can be unreliable and disrupt the supply chain due to transportation barriers; however, with the onset of AfCFTA, logistics and transportation are becoming a main priority to help businesses become more efficient.

Financing Deficits

To reap the benefits of the business opportunities across the continent, African countries must overcome significant financing deficits. In order to meet the UN Sustainable Development Goals, Africa faces a $4 trillion annual financing shortage.[73] In terms of climate financing, only $29.5 billion (12 percent) of the $2.8 trillion needed between 2020 and 2030 to implement Africa's Nationally Determined Contributions has been mobilized so far, leaving a significant gap between $118.2 billion and $145.5 billion per year in climate financing alone.[74] Insufficient climate financing is being directed toward Africa. In fact, Africa only received 20 percent of global adaptation finance flows—less than half of the flows to East Asia and the Pacific region.[75] The private sector has also contributed only 14 percent of total climate finance in Africa, compared with 37 percent in South Asia, 39 percent in East Asia and Pacific, and 49 percent in Latin America and the Caribbean.[76] Financial gaps in areas such as infrastructure (estimated to be about $100 billion a year) threaten the ability of African countries and investors to manufacture locally and hinder innovation. African institutional investors such as pension funds and insurance companies are also an undertapped source of capital. Africa, in partnership with the private sector and the global community, will need to rapidly accelerate financing efforts in order to meet the demand of its growing population and the untapped business potential. This includes mobilizing more resources at an affordable cost, as high-risk perceptions have led to higher costs of financing for African countries. Overall, it will be critical for African countries to overcome the challenges of accessing affordable financing in order to maximize the potential impact of increased business and investment on the continent.

Corporate Challenges in Africa

Beyond the business environment, companies have faced specific challenges in African countries. These challenges can be divided into three causes of failure: management, marketing, and financial. Management causes of failure include a lack of strategic management, including vision or operational plans; a lack of efficient leadership style and structure; unethical business practices; and a focus on immediate profit rather than an investment in long-term success. Marketing causes of failure include a lack of understanding customer needs and the actual potential market; the lack of ability to create a sustainable comparative advantage for a market; the inability to develop a customer-driven strategy; the lack of reliable partnerships, infrastructure, and information; and competition with informal sectors. Finally, financial causes of failure include limited access to credit, poor cash flow management, poor spending habits and redistribution, limited budgeting skills, inability to create a sustainable financial strategy or forecast system, and fraud or corruption. Capital from African banks can have high interest rates, making it especially difficult for homegrown companies to scale up or expand.[77]

Looking Ahead

These challenges are neither universal nor mutually exclusive, and they will vary greatly within each country and industry; however, having a better understanding of how these challenges manifest in Africa specifically can help companies manage risk, including political, country, legal, sectorial, stock market, currency, corruption, scams, portfolio, payment, private equity, and venture capital risks. In many cases, the perceived danger is greater than the actual risk, and the economic environment is rapidly improving in many nations. Nations like Mauritius, Rwanda, Botswana, Nigeria, South Africa, and Kenya all offer increasing ease in doing business through supportive environments and incentives, and there has also been work done on reforms to improve the business environment. Having moved up from 49th to 25th place in the Doing Business rankings, Mauritius continues to be the top-ranked economy in Sub-Saharan Africa. South Africa is ranked 82nd, followed by Botswana, Kenya, Rwanda, and Kenya.[78] The World Bank claims that Rwanda is among the top nations in the world for getting credit (ranked 2nd) and for registering property (ranked 6th).[79] The political resolve to secure and promote regional integration and backward integration must, however, triumph over policy uncertainty and regulatory inconsistencies. While these challenges must be reckoned with, it is still clear that the future will hold immense opportunities for business across the continent in industries from health care to entertainment.

Perhaps an even more powerful signal that these opportunities are lucrative is the real experience of African and international companies that are already finding success across Africa. Such companies, from Novartis in the pharmaceutical industry, to UBA in the financial industry, have recognized these opportunities and have created specific strategies for their engagement in African countries, ultimately contributing to Africa's prosperity. While each company has its own unique strategies based on its goals and strengths, some common themes have emerged as pathways for success, including developing strong partnerships with African governments and communities; aligning the needs of companies, governments, and communities where possible; leveraging digital tools; and understanding local needs. Further exploration of such specific strategies can be found in the conclusion to this book, chapter 9.

Conclusion

Ongoing global and local trends have created a unique momentum for greater engagement with Africa. Global investors should seize this momentum to strengthen their engagement with Africa, drawing on consultations with African partners and multilaterals to develop and successfully implement cutting-edge strategies. By acting swiftly and forging transformative partnerships aligned with African values, global investors have the opportunity to contribute to the transformation of the continent that will constitute nearly 40 percent of the world's population by 2100, as well as the opportunity to build a more prosperous, democratic, secure, and stable world. As William Schurz has put it, "Borders frequented by trade seldom need soldiers."

This book builds on my work *Unlocking Africa's Business Potential* by highlighting the new trends, challenges, and, most importantly, opportunities within key industries and sectors that have unprecedented potential to trans-form African economies and African livelihoods.[80] This new book also provides readers with a future-oriented and cutting-edge understanding of Africa's key emerging industries, underscoring the nuanced connection between private sector investment and Africa's prosperity. It therefore offers power-ful insights and actionable strategies for private sector leaders interested in effectively investing and doing business in Africa while creating high values, returns, and impact for various stakeholders, and for public sector and global leaders who are interested in leveraging Africa's economic potential to achieve development goals.

Each chapter discusses the major trends, relevance, opportunities, players, challenges, and strategies within specific industries, starting with chapter 2 on Africa's trade and industrial potential under the African Continental Free Trade Area, featuring high-potential sectors such as automotive, agriculture and agro-processing, pharmaceuticals, and transportation and logistics—followed by chapter 3 on entertainment and cultural and creative indus-tries; chapter 4 on health care and pharmaceuticals; chapter 5 on mining; chapter 6 on insurance; chapter 7 on investment, private equity, and venture capital; and chapter 8 on capital markets. Chapter 9 concludes with an in-depth presentation of the specific strategies for both the private and the public sectors that will help usher in an era of African business and prosperity.

Notes

1. My recent books provide systematic accounts on various aspects of the evo-lution, transformation, and prospects of African economies: *Africa's Fourth Industrial Revolution* (Signé 2023); *Unlocking Africa's Business Potential* (Signé 2020); *African Development, African Transformation: How Institutions Shape Development Strategy* (Signé 2018); and *Innovating Development Strategies: The Role of International, Regional, and National Actors* (Signé 2017).

2. Kuyoro et al. (2023).

3. Signé (2020).

4. Signé (2020).

5. Signé (2021b).

6. Signé (2021b).

7. Signé (2020).

8. *Economist* (2000).

9. Signé and Heitzig (2022).

10. Kuyoro et al. (2023).

11. Kuyoro et al. (2023).

12. UN DESA, Population Division (2019).
13. Palladium (2020).
14. AFR-IX Telecom (2022).
15. Kuyoro et al. (2023).
16. Signé (2020).
17. Kuyoro et al. (2023).
18. Kuyoro et al. (2023).
19. Signé (2021a).
20. Chen and Nord (2018).
21. Signé (2021a).
22. Signé (2021a).
23. Kuyoro et al. (2023).
24. These cities include Casablanca, Morocco; Algiers, Algeria; Alexandria, Egypt; Cairo, Egypt; Khartoum, Sudan; Addis Adaba, Ethiopia; Kampala, Uganda; Mogadishu, Somalia; Nairobi, Kenya; Dar es Salaam, Tanzania; Antananarivo, Madagascar; Lusaka, Zambia; Johannesburg, South Africa; Cape Town, South Africa; Lubumbashi, DRC; Mbuji-Mayi, DRC; Kinshasa, DRC; Luanda, Angola; Douala, Cameroon; Onitsha, Nigeria; Lagos, Nigeria; Accra, Ghana; Abidjan, Côte d'Ivoire; Kumasi, Ghana; Ibadan, Nigeria; Bamako, Mali; Dakar, Senegal; Ouagadougou, Burkina Faso; Kano, Nigeria; Abuja, Nigeria; and Yaoundé, Cameroon.
25. Kuyoro et al. (2023).
26. Kuyoro et al. (2023).
27. Kuyoro et al. (2023); Signé and Heitzig (2022).
28. Kuyoro et al. (2023); Signé and Heitzig (2022).
29. Lakmeeharan et al. (2020).
30. African Development Bank Group (2018a).
31. Kuyoro et al. (2023).
32. Kuyoro et al. (2023).
33. GSMA (2020).
34. GSMA (2020).
35. African Development Bank (2021).
36. Ndung'u and Signé (2020).
37. Signé (2023).
38. Lewis (2020).
39. Ekekwe (2017).
40. International Finance Corporation (2024a).
41. World Bank (2024).
42. Jackson (2021).
43. Kuyoro et al. (2023).
44. World Bank (2020b).
45. Gyimah-Boadi, Signé, and Appiah-Nyamekye Sanny (2020).
46. Signé and Gurib-Fakim (2019b).

47. Ndwaru (2022).
48. African Development Bank (2022b).
49. IEA (2022).
50. Galma (2022).
51. International Finance Corporation (2022).
52. Kuyoro et al. (2023).
53. IEA (2021).
54. Moodley et al. (2019).
55. African Development Bank (2019b).
56. Woldemichael (2020).
57. Woldemichael (2020).
58. Owusu-Gyamfi (2023).
59. Kuyoro et al. (2023).
60. Kuyoro et al. (2023).
61. Transparency International (2022).
62. Mbaku (2020).
63. United Nations (2023a).
64. Brixi, Rawlings, and Koechlein (2021).
65. International Finance Corporation (2019).
66. Workpay (2022).
67. International Labour Organization (2024).
68. Exchange (2023).
69. International Monetary Fund (2017).
70. African Development Bank (2024c).
71. IEA (2024).
72. Dangote (2019).
73. African Development Bank (2024b)
74. African Development Bank (2024a).
75. Ijjasz-Vaquez, Jamal Saghir, and Morgan Richmond (2024).
76. African Development Bank (2022c).
77. Sodiq (2022).
78. Dangote (2019).
79. Dangote (2019).
80. Signé (2020).

Two

Africa's Trade and Industrial Potential Under the AfCFTA High-Potential Sectors
Automotive, Agriculture and Agro-Processing, Pharmaceuticals, and Transportation and Logistics

By 2050, the African Continental Free Trade Area (AfCFTA) will connect 2.5 billion people (25 percent of the global population),[1] for combined consumer and business spending of $16.12 trillion,[2] expanding African economies by $29 trillion, and offering tremendous opportunities for unlocking business potential across Africa and the world.[3] Historically, Africa's foreign direct investment, as well as its regional and global value-chain participation, have been consistently low, hampered by barriers to trade and competitiveness. AfCFTA removes many of these barriers and unlocks opportunities for Africa to join regional and global value chains and integrate with international businesses. In its private sector engagement strategy, AfCFTA identifies four sectors with the highest potential to both accelerate manufacturing and trade: automotive, agriculture and agro-processing, pharmaceuticals, and transportation and logistics.[4] All these sectors add value in different ways, including through job creation, inclusivity, contribution to gross domestic product (GDP), and the potential for increasing local value added.

This chapter updates and improves excerpts from three key publications.[5] The first is my testimony to the US Congress, "Understanding the African Continental Free Trade Area and How the US Can Promote Its Success," published by Brookings.[6] The two others are the strategy ("AfCFTA: A New Era for Global Business and Investment in Africa," 2023),[7] and the action plan ("An Action Plan to Accelerate Global Business and Investment in Africa," 2024),[8] released by the World Economic Forum (WEF) in collaboration with AfCFTA, and of which I am the lead author,[9] which have benefited from multistakeholder collaboration.[10]

This chapter first presents the importance of African trade. It then presents the trends and players within African trade, followed by the unique trends, players, and opportunities for local and global businesses within the four sectors chosen in the WEF's Private Sector Engagement Strategy within the era of AfCFTA. Finally, it discusses the challenges and risks and the strategies for investment that can be used to overcome these challenges, including the various operational tools the private sector can use to capitalize on these opportunities, with a specific focus on facilitations by the AfCFTA Secretariat, the WEF, and strategic tools.

The Sector's Importance

AfCFTA's significance cannot be overstated. It is the world's largest new free trade area since the establishment of the World Trade Organization in 1994. It promises to increase intra-African trade through deeper levels of trade liberalization and enhanced regulatory harmonization and coordination. Moreover, it is expected to improve the competitiveness of African industry and enterprises through increased market access, the exploitation of economies of scale, and more effective resource allocation.

As shown in figure 2-1, Africa's share of global trade has not kept pace with its population growth, remaining under 3 percent since the 1980s.[11] The economies of scale promoted by AfCFTA can help drive the commodity-based industrialization model by strengthening both forward and backward linkages in the commodity sector to help build regional value chains on the continent.[12] By opening up new opportunities for adding value to exports within the region, export diversification can help lead to structural change within African economies.[13] Export diversification is critical for African development, given the strong correlation between higher diversification/sophistication of products and higher incomes per capita and faster economic growth rates.[14]

My research has shown that AfCFTA—and its accompanying increased market access—can significantly grow manufacturing and industrial development, tourism, intra-African cooperation, economic transformation, and the relationship between Africa and the rest of the world. In fact, under a successfully implemented AfCFTA, Africa will have a combined consumer and business spending of $6.7 trillion by 2030 and $16.12 trillion by 2050, creating a unique opportunity for people and businesses—and meaning the region can be the next big market for American goods and services.[15]

Figure 2-1. Africa's Contribution to Global Trade Compared with Population Growth, 1960–2022

Millions of dollars

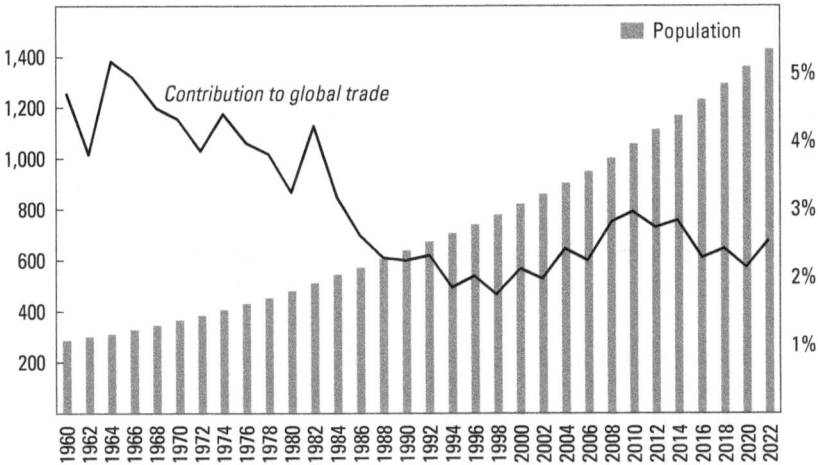

Source: Fofack (2024).
Note: Africa's contribution to global trade is falling despite its growing population. Africa's population has grown at a constant rate over the past sixty years and is expected to reach 2 billion by 2050. However, Africa's contribution to trade is not reflective of this growth trend. The continent's contribution to global trade has remained below 3 percent since the 1980s, and in recent years has trended closer to 2 percent.

The UN Economic Commission for Africa (UNECA) has predicted that by 2040, implementation of AfCFTA will raise intra-African trade by 15 to 25 percent, or $50 billion to $70 billion.[16] The World Bank estimates that AfCFTA will lift 30 million people out of extreme poverty and substantially increase the income of 68 million people who are just slightly above the poverty line by 2035.[17] The International Monetary Fund similarly projects that, under AfCFTA, Africa's expanded and more efficient goods and labor markets will significantly increase the continent's overall ranking on the Global Competitiveness Index.[18]

UNECA has calculated that AfCFTA has the potential to increase African economic output by $29 trillion by 2050.[19] Business-to-business spending ($4.2 trillion) will be about $915.3 billion in agriculture and agricultural processing; $666.3 billion in manufacturing; $784.5 billion in construction, utilities, and transportation; $665.1 billion in wholesale and retail trade; $357.6 billion in resources; $249.3 billion in banking and insurance; and $79.5 billion in telecommunications and information technology.[20] Consumer spending ($2.5 trillion) will be about $740 billion in food and beverages, $397.5 billion in education and transportation, $390 billion in housing, $370 billion in consumer goods, $260 billion in hospitality and recreation, $175 billion in health care, $85 billion in financial services, and $65 billion in telecommunications.[21] These numbers are important for understanding how spending patterns will change. It is also important to note that by 2030, more than half of Africa's population will reside in seven countries: Nigeria, Ethiopia, the Democratic Republic of Congo, Egypt, Tanzania, Kenya, and South Africa.[22]

AfCFTA will also allow countries to seize the opportunity offered by the Fourth Industrial Revolution, in what is called "industries without smokestacks." These largely services-based industries provide three key benefits of traditional manufacturing—exportability, higher productivity, and the tendency to absorb large numbers of low-skilled labor. The ongoing revolution in such industries—such as tourism, agro-industry, and some services based on information and communications technology—can serve as a development escalator.

AfCFTA is also capable of securing longer-term prosperity for Africa by spurring investment in manufacturing. Indeed, a majority of the projected $560 billion increase in exports resulting from AfCFTA's implementation will be in manufacturing.[23] Increased manufacturing will steer Africa away from a volatile, commodity-dependent model of trade, which many of its economies currently follow.[24]

Much of the immediate benefit of AfCFTA will come from the reduction of tariffs on AfCFTA imports (the majority of which are destined to be phased out over the next five years) as well as the elimination of nontariff barriers (NTBs) as a result of harmonizing trading frameworks. Projected reductions in tariffs vary substantially by sector.[25] Producers of chemical, rubber, and plastic products are expected to see an 85 percent reduction in tariffs by 2035, the largest of any sector. Additionally, wood and paper products, textiles and wearing apparel, and many subcategories of manufacturing are all projected to experience tariff reductions upward of 75 percent. Tariffs on processed food and petroleum and coal products are projected to fall by 64 percent and 60 percent, respectively. Tariffs on agricultural products and fossil fuels are expected to fall by 55 percent and 40 percent, respectively. The tariff reductions in other sectors will be more modest but still sizable. Natural resources and minerals are not projected to experience a reduction in tariffs over this period.

In the medium and long terms, however, tariff reduction will likely play a small role in spurring trade across Africa. Instead, if achieved, the reduction of NTBs will play a major role in driving intraregional trade. Projected NTB reductions display less variation across sectors, with most sectors projected to experience a reduction between 35 and 50 percent. The only sectors that are projected to experience a smaller degree of reduction are natural resources (34 percent) and services (21 percent).

The greatest benefit of AfCFTA, however, could come from enhanced trade facilitation with African and global partners alike.[26] Expected and realized gains from trade could attract investment in physical infrastructure (e.g., new plants, new ports, and transportation terminals) and digital infrastructure (software to facilitate transactions, improved internet connectivity, the development of digital processes, etc.). These investments could improve Africa's trade prospects vis-à-vis the rest of the world. A decade from now, Africa could develop new comparative advantages vis-à-vis the world, and it will be in a better position to facilitate trade in these areas thanks to investments made possible by AfCFTA.

Key Trends and Dynamics within African Trade

AfCFTA—which was signed in 2018, ratified in 2019, and officially launched in 2021—unifies the small, fragmented markets of 55 separate African states into a single market that, by 2030, would represent 1.7 billion people and $6.7 trillion in consumer and business spending.[27] If AfCFTA is fully implemented, it could increase real incomes by 7 percent, or nearly $450 billion.[28] A total 47 of the 54 signatories had ratified AfCFTA as of August 2023, and 31 countries have started trading under the Guided Trade Initiative as of 2024.[29] As of 2023, 48 tariff concessions, which make up 87 percent of African Union (AU) membership, have been submitted, and 46 have been approved by the Council of Ministers.[30] Rules of origin have been agreed upon by negotiating partners for 92.3 percent of traded goods.[31]

Since AfCFTA has become operational starting in 2022, intra-African trade has already seen a rise in volumes, having increased to $189.3 billion in 2023 (up from $185.1 billion in 2022 and $169.9 billion in 2021).[32] This rise is expected to continue, as Africa is the region predicted by the World Trade Organization to have the fastest-growing export volume in 2024.[33] African trade dynamics have already shifted and evolved over the past decade, in part due to gradual changes, such as ramped-up trade activity by certain players, and in part due to global shocks that have affected the global economy, commodity prices, and geopolitical dynamics.

The EU and Asia

European countries and the European Union have long been Africa's leading trade partner; but over time, emerging economies in Asia, specifically

China and India, have increased their share, from 4.5 percent in the 1990s to 26 percent between 2013 and 2023,[34] especially as European countries have reduced their demand due to geopolitical tensions, sovereign debt crises, and other shocks.

African exports to Asia reached $171.9 billion in 2023, 63.7 percent of which went to China, making China Africa's single largest trading partner.[35] Combined, India and China represent 24 percent of Africa's total exports to the world.[36] Asia is also the biggest importer of African goods, having surpassed the EU in 2015, and it is continuing to widen the gap, currently at 32.9 percent of all African imports as of 2023.[37]

The Middle East

As of 2019, the Middle East overtook North America's third-place spot for Africa's top export destinations. North America's share has steadily declined, especially due to the lower demand for African oil in the United States. Meanwhile, the Middle East became third in exports as cooperation between the regions increased.

The United States and the African Growth and Opportunity Act

The African Growth and Opportunity Act (AGOA), which was enacted in 2000, has been the cornerstone of United States–Africa trade. Thirty-two African countries, as of 2023, are eligible for AGOA, which provides duty-free access to the United States for more than 1,800 products.[38] Africa's exports to the United States under AGOA reached $9.7 billion in 2023, down from $10.2 billion in 2022, but up from $6.8 billion in 2021.[39] The year 2023's AGOA exports to the United States were made up of petroleum products ($1.3 billion), motor vehicles ($1.2 billion), natural gas and components ($1.2 billion), and motor vehicle parts ($861 million). Non–crude oil exports under AGOA contributed $5.5 billion of the $10.2 billion, increasing its share over the past few years.[40] Nigeria was the top exporter under AGOA, dominated by oil, followed by South Africa, Kenya, Ghana, Madagascar, and Angola. AGOA continues to be a key player in African trade. Its current authorization expires in September 2025 and is expected to be renewed.

Intra-African Trade

Already, AfCFTA's implementation is helping to keep intra-African trade more resilient despite global macroeconomic shocks. Intra-African trade grew by 3.2 percent in 2023, after an impressive 10.9 percent in 2022. Yet despite the slower overall growth, intra-African trade accounted for 14.9 percent of total

Figure 2-2. The Top Ten Contributors to Intra-African Trade, 2023 (percent)

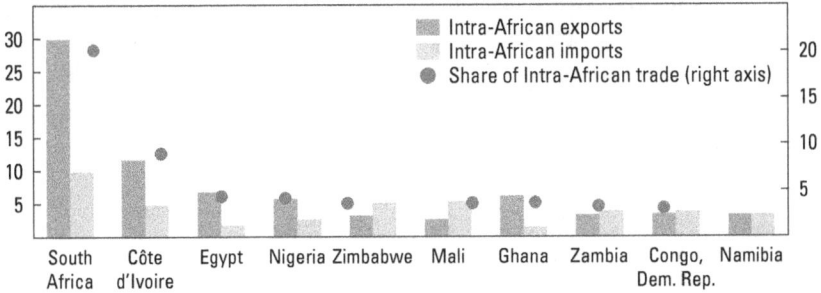

Sources: International Monetary Fund Direction of Trade Statistics, Afreximbank Research.

Figure 2-3. Africa's Export Destinations (percent)

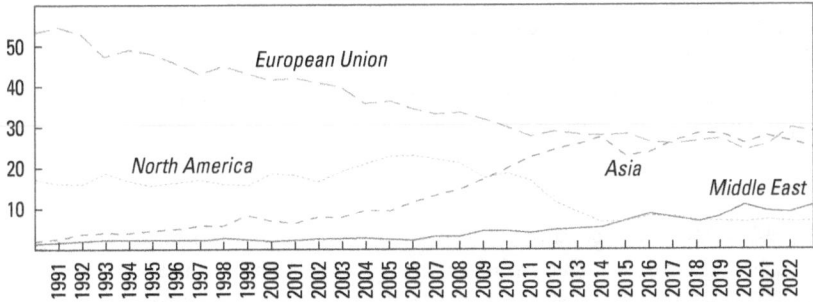

Source: Afreximbank (2024).

African trade in 2023, which was an increase from 2022.[41] Southern Africa accounted for the largest proportion of intra-African trade in 2023 by a significant margin (41.4 percent of intra-African trade), largely driven by South Africa's import activity from the continent and even bigger export activity, followed by West Africa (25.7 percent).[42] A total of 29.6 percent of South Africa's total exports in 2023 were to other African countries (figure 2-2).

Intra-African trade remains low compared with other regions of the world (67 percent in intra-Asia trade and 72 percent in Europe),[43] but AfCFTA is a catalyst for rapidly increasing these volumes. Looking ahead, an Afreximbank analysis finds that Southern Africa has the largest export potential, followed by Eastern Africa and Western Africa, North Africa, and Central Africa (figure 2-3).

With incomes, connectivity, dynamic youth populations, and trade integration on the rise across Africa, it is clear that the private sector is becoming increasingly aware of the transformative opportunities for business across the African continent. As intra-African trade increases, AfCFTA's implementation is bringing new opportunities to create local value and strengthen supply chains.

Background Facts, Trends, and Opportunities within the High-Potential Sectors

The World Economic Forum has recognized four sectors that demonstrate how much of an impact AfCFTA will have on new and existing businesses to accelerate its footprint in Africa. The four sectors identified in the AfCFTA Private Sector Engagement Strategy as having high potential for investment (automotive, agriculture and agro-processing, pharmaceuticals, and transportation and logistics) have been selected as opportunities to focus on in this section on the basis of their potential to meet African demand through local production as well as their potential value as exports to the rest of the world. Together, these four sectors represent $130 billion in goods and services imports.[44]

Automotives: Key Trends

By 2035, Africa will require 5 billion units of vehicles, per recent estimates.[45] In 2021, the automotive industry in Africa was valued at $30.44 billion, and it is predicted to grow to $42.06 billion by 2027—an almost 40 percent increase in value.[46] Across the continent, there is an average annual demand for 2.4 million motor cars and 300,000 commercial vehicles. Currently, this domestic demand—rising due to the continent-wide increase in disposable income, the strong growth of the middle class, and rapid urbanization—is met mainly by imports of used vehicles. Imported vehicles account for 85 percent of Africa's total vehicle fleet in 2021.[47] However, domestic production has been growing in the past few years at a rate of 7 percent a year on average. At present, domestic production across Algeria, Egypt, Morocco, and South Africa exports about 56 percent of its production outside Africa.[48] With domestic production already growing, there is a strong opportunity to apply domestic production to local demand.

The Automotive Sector: Key Players

Today, Morocco and South Africa are leading the way as major players in the automotive sector, making up 80 percent of African exports, with Algeria experiencing rapid growth. AfCFTA will likely increase the competition and interest in North Africa as a nearshoring destination for European countries and as a manufacturing hub for local demand.[49] Major private sector players include the African Association of Automotive Manufacturers (AAAM) and several global companies that have expanded their operations across the continent. AAAM has been a major player for the sector, working directly with governments in Egypt, Ghana, and South Africa, among others, and directly with the AfCFTA Secretariat to help shape the vision and strategy for the automotive sector under AfCFTA. Specific global companies are also recognizing the opportunity for industrialization in Africa through the automotive sector. For example, Volkswagen has recognized the potential and need for new, modern, and safe vehicles to be produced in African countries to meet African demand rather than the continent continuing to rely on imported used cars. So far, the company has successfully established local assembly operations in Kenya, Rwanda, and Ghana, and two wholly owned subsidiaries in Rwanda and Ghana.

Automotives: Opportunities under AfCFTA

The automotive industry's unique characteristics of having high product complexity and high potential for meeting local demand make it a key sector to accelerate intra-African trade. AfCFTA will help amplify these strengths, providing opportunities for domestic and global businesses alike to invest in the automotive sector.

AfCFTA unlocks several opportunities for African and global businesses in the automotive industry to seize. *First, the unified market under AfCFTA enhances the competitiveness of local assembly and local sourcing partnerships.* This means opportunities for local and global businesses to enter or expand their operations in the automotive industry in Africa. The common market is a much more attractive dynamic for investors than fifty-four smaller economies, especially in a sector that requires economies of scale.[50] It will allow companies to plant assembly locations in one country while being able to both target a greater consumer base across the region and take advantage of reduced tariffs on local inputs (e.g., aluminum in Mozambique and rubber in Côte d'Ivoire). As companies relocate production steps and supply chains in African countries, these countries will be able to avoid losing out on revenue from value added as they do when raw materials are exported.[51] Currently, many regional economic communities apply a 25–35 percent value-added threshold for locally originated products.[52] AfCFTA's rules of origin will help to set common thresholds for value-added levels. If these common thresholds are progressively harmonized across regional communities, these more general and coequal rules will help stimulate trade.[53]

Second, there is significant political will among numerous African governments and private sector players to develop automotive regional value chains because of the sector's historic contribution to knowledge-intensive industrialization, and leadership is actively working toward improving the investment environment for the automotive sector specifically. For example, the African Export-Import Bank (Afreximbank) and AAAM are working together to support the industry by helping to harmonize automotive standards, developing a focused training program for the public and private sectors, and providing financing to industry players across the value chain. In addition, Afreximbank has committed $1 billion to supporting the industry through direct financing and partnerships.[54]

Third, current and future demand is pointing to opportunities for new markets in electric vehicles and motor vehicles. Africa could be an important region for local and global companies to promote sustainable mobility and harness renewable energy. The electrical vehicle (EV) market is a key target for the continent, as the global market for EVs is projected to be $7.7 trillion by 2025 and $46 trillion by 2050. Meanwhile, Africa holds 19 percent of the world's critical minerals and metals required for building EVs,[55] such as copper, platinum, cobalt, bauxite, and lithium. Electric vehicles make up less than 1 percent of sales in South Africa, but demand is growing across the continent as some of Africa's main trading partners have banned internal combustion engine vehicle sales as early as 2035.[56] Already, there are pilot projects for sustainable vehicles in Rwanda, Egypt, and South Africa, and e-mobility start-ups have emerged across the continent.[57] There is also a huge market for motorcycles in Africa (especially in West, East, and North Africa), with the potential for more domestically produced inputs and domestic production. There is opportunity, too, for the electric two-wheeler to become more of a player as the technology for electric motorcycles is simpler than it is for electric vehicles.

Agro-Processing: Key Trends

Agro-processing has important implications for economic growth, food security, job creation, and poverty reduction.[58] While African countries have accelerated their focus on agro-processing as a result of food insecurity caused by trade disruptions from global shocks, it will also be important as a way to transform economies from the current export of raw materials, which has much less benefit for a country's economy.

Of Africa's 51 million farmers, 80 percent are smallholders engaged in subsistence farming on land of less than 1 hectare (2.2 acres), earning about $2 a day.[59] The continent's land surface is 60 percent arable land, but about 20 percent of Africa's soils are degraded and suffer from the worsening effects of acute climate change. As a result, Africa's agricultural yields only reach 25 percent of full potential. Agriculture and agro-processing have high potential for economic growth, employment, and inclusivity, and could spur an increase in intra-African trade. Currently, the continent imports about $50 billion in agricultural products a year;[60] but, by 2030, intra-African agricultural trade is projected to increase by 574 percent if import tariffs are eliminated, compared with a scenario without AfCFTA.[61]

In particular, the fish and meat industries have great potential for investment. The majority of demand for both fish and meat is met by local production that is not traded, and only 16 percent and 10 percent of demand, respectively, is met by imports.[62] They are both expected to see an increase in overall demand given rising incomes, which means there is a tremendous opportunity to scale up production and increase the trade in processed goods. Demand for fish is exceeding local supply, growing at about 4 percent annually for the past ten years,[63] and demand is also accelerating for meat.[64] Production of beef is widely fragmented across the continent, but meat processing is concentrated in a few countries.[65] This means there is a major opportunity to scale up the production of processed meats, such as sausages and canned meats, to meet rising local demand.[66] Southern Africa is more connected via trade relationships within the beef industry, but AfCFTA will unlock opportunities for Northern and Western African countries to join.[67]

Agro-Processing: Key Players

Ghana is an example of a country that has taken steps to boost agro-processing by attracting foreign investment and investing in infrastructure for preserving, storing, and transporting harvest yields.[68] Ghana intends to process more of its cocoa domestically, rather than exporting raw cocoa beans, so that it can reduce dependence on raw material exports and shift its status and strengths toward the top of the value chain—becoming a top trader of processed goods.[69]

Agro-Processing: Opportunities Under AfCFTA

Agro-processing was named a key sector for AfCFTA's Private Sector Engagement Strategy because of its exceptional potential for increasing intra-African trade, meeting local demand, accelerating GDP growth, creating jobs, and improving inclusivity due to its upstream and downstream linkages. AfCFTA will expand participation in value chains and trade since countries will no longer have to rely on exporting only agricultural intermediaries with little value added.[70]

According to the African Development Bank, the continent's food and agriculture market could increase from $280 billion a year in 2023 to $1 trillion by 2030.[71] Important opportunities for the private sector here include adding value to an already-competitive agriculture sector, using regional differences to develop food value chains, and meeting input and infrastructure needs.

Agro-processing is a way to add value to an already-competitive agriculture sector. Africa's wide range of climates, high percentage of arable land, and counterseasonality to the Northern Hemisphere all contribute to the competitiveness of the sector. Agro-processing specifically has *unique strengths* for investors and African countries alike. It is described as the most important subsector of manufacturing because of the greater stability of world prices for processed agricultural products compared with raw products. It is also significant for its effect on the generation of new companies, its diversification of rural economies, and its creation of new job opportunities.[72] Scaling up agro-processing also has important inclusivity effects, given that women make up 70 percent of employment in the overall agricultural sector and the majority of the domestic agro-processing workforce is female.

The common market can use regional differences in the strengths and competitiveness of African countries in food value chains.[73] Increased intra-African trade through AfCFTA will help reduce dependency on foreign agricultural inputs with positive effects for continental food resilience. Each region has natural advantages that, if better coordinated to benefit African partners, can help create full regional value chains. For example, South Africa's integrated value chain—from inputs, equipment, packaging, and specialized logistics to marketing and retail—is an example for other African countries, and it showcases the great potential for investment in this sector in conjunction with AfCFTA.[74]

There is also a great opportunity for new businesses to meet the input and infrastructure needs of the agricultural sector. Major barriers to scaling agro-processing include the need for more local production of inputs. For example, a major barrier to scaling fish production are the high costs and high dependency on foreign trade for fish feed.[75] Regional hubs can help increase intra-African trade of fish feed and allow for scaling up within what is now a highly fragmented market made up of small producers.

For agriculture more broadly, there is also a significant need for inputs and infrastructure to sustain higher levels of exports. According to a McKinsey report, Africa's agricultural potential will require an 800 percent increase in fertilizer application for main nutrients, a $65-million-plus investment in irrigation, and more than $8 billion in investment for storage through local warehouses.[76] Companies are already finding these areas to be lucrative opportunities to develop value chains across the continent. The common market will help reduce dependency on exports, leading to stronger and more sustainable domestic development. OCP, for example, has recognized the potential of AfCFTA to develop unifying standards for fertilizer regulation and to increase inter-African trade for agricultural goods and supplies, as well as the significant potential of investing in these value chains.

Pharmaceuticals: Key Trends

Africa's high fertility rates and increase in life expectancy are leading to new pharmaceutical demands. The prevalence of noncommunicable diseases is on the rise and is predicted to be the cause of 50 percent of deaths in Africa by 2030, compared with 28 percent in 2003.[77] For example, diabetes patients across the continent are expected to double, from 24 million in 2021 to 55 million in 2045.[78] The pharmaceutical industry is projected to grow at 5.13 percent compound annual growth rate for 2022–27 in Africa.[79] The UN Industrial Development Organization has identified four important factors that are leading to high projected growth in Africa's pharmaceutical market specifically. These are increased expenditures; expanded provision; a maturing business environment; and increased genericization.[80]

Within pharmaceuticals, packaged medicines and medical instruments[81] make up the largest import shares for the continent (65 and 12 percent, respectively, of the $17 billion[82] pharmaceutical import market).[83] Packaged medicines represent the biggest opportunity, given their high percentage of imports and the sourcing and manufacturing stages of the value chain. Some 40 percent of the disease burden on the continent is due to HIV/AIDS, tuberculosis, malaria, diarrhea, and respiratory diseases. To treat these, packaged medicines typically come in the form of either solid oral pills or liquids and gels that have simpler manufacturing processes than other types of drugs such as injectables. Total demand for all packaged medicines in Africa is about $18 billion annually, of which 61 percent is imported and 36 percent is locally produced and not traded. Only 3 percent of demand is met by intra-African trade. This lack of intra-African trade is leading to a high dependency on imports (e.g., seven times more than India), even though local production is possible.

Meanwhile, local production is concentrated in generic medicines (70 percent) with simple production processes. The processes, which are concentrated downstream in formulations and packaging, have little upstream research and development and limited production of intermediates and active pharmaceutical ingredients, which require complex chemical and biological processes.[84] There are currently about six hundred manufacturers of packaged medicines on the continent, and they are highly concentrated in eight countries (80 percent), with North Africa leading the way. Only four countries have more than fifty manufacturers, while 22 countries have none.[85]

Pharmaceuticals: Key Players

South Africa, Egypt, Algeria, Morocco, and Nigeria lead the way with the largest pharmaceutical market size, with South Africa having the highest per capita spending as of 2023.[86] Seven African countries make up 75 percent of pharmaceutical sales, and eight account for 80 percent of the production on the continent; meanwhile, 40 African countries have a registered demand of less than $1 billion, meaning there is much to be done to deconcentrate the market.[87]

Private companies are already leading the way to meet African demand. More than $4 billion has been committed across private and public sources to vaccine production in Africa.[88] Three of the top five destinations (Kenya, Ethiopia, Lesotho, Morocco, and Uganda) for greenfield pharma investments in 2021 were in East Africa, indicating its leadership in the development of pharmaceutical manufacturing.[89]

Some African countries are leading the way, leveraging digital technologies to find innovative health care solutions. South Africa has been leading in telemedicine and electronic prescriptions; meanwhile, Rwanda has been a global leader in medicine delivery via drone technology. Projections for the pharmaceutical industry suggest (figure 2-4) that Egypt will remain the largest pharmaceutical market through 2027, followed by Nigeria and South Africa, with West African countries growing more slowly than the African average.[90]

Pharmaceuticals: Opportunities Under AfCFTA

Pharmaceuticals is one of the four sectors seen to have the highest potential, due to the feasibility of addressing barriers to trade and production in a short time frame, as well as the strong potential for meeting demand locally. Pharmaceuticals also have high product complexity, which can lead to greater opportunities for high local value-added production. AfCFTA has a unique opportunity to help enhance internal trade and supply routes, remove tariff and nontariff barriers, and ensure the free movement of workers and professionals. It can create a stable business environment that respects business ethics and incentivizes local innovation and entrepreneurship, including through intellectual property. And it can help build sustainable health care

Figure 2-4. The Top Ten African Countries in the Pharmaceutical Market: Past and Future Growth (exclusive of COVID-19, billion dollars)

Future growth (2022–27), CAGR (%)

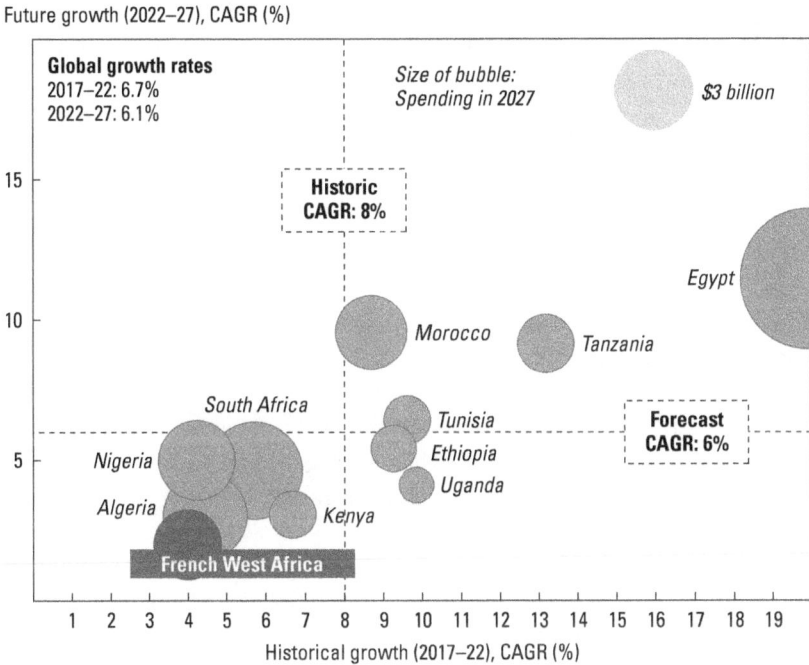

Global growth rates
2017–22: 6.7%
2022–27: 6.1%

Size of bubble:
Spending in 2027

$3 billion

Historic
CAGR: 8%

Egypt

Morocco

Tanzania

South Africa

Tunisia

Forecast
CAGR: 6%

Nigeria

Ethiopia

Uganda

Algeria

Kenya

French West Africa

Historical growth (2017–22), CAGR (%)

Source: Rickwood and Lutzmayer (2023).
Note: CAGR = compound annual growth rate.

systems and provide opportunities for the development of the pharmaceutical sector across the value chain.[91]

The pharmaceutical industry in Africa presents unique advantages for the private sector to pursue both profit-driven and impact-related interests. These opportunities are growing, thanks to the mitigation of regulatory challenges and the acceleration of new manufacturing. Wider opportunities are also arising within the pharmaceutical industry for products that can be produced locally.

Regulatory challenges that have long hindered the growth of the pharmaceutical industry in Africa are already being mitigated by AfCFTA. For example, the lack of regulatory alignment and weak regulatory frameworks have been addressed through the Africa Medicine Regulatory Harmonization (AMRH) initiative. The AMRH initiative was created in 2009 to address challenges faced by national medicine regulatory authorities (NMRAs) that were leading to poor access and overpriced medicines.[92] Thanks to this initiative, the marketing approval time has been reduced from more than a year to between seven and eight months in the East African Community (EAC) and the Southern African Development Community regions.[93] It has also successfully achieved appropriate standards for four of the seven East African NMRAs and five West African NMRAs. Most importantly, the AMRH paved the way for the treaty to establish the African Medicines Association (AMA) in 2019, which has been ratified by twenty-four countries to date. The AMA will promote the adoption and harmonization of medical products' regulatory policies and standards, as well as provide scientific guidelines and coordinate existing regulatory harmonization efforts in the African Union. The AfCFTA can help scale these efforts by acting as a liaison between local manufacturers and the AMA, as well as supporting other countries that are not covered so that they are also able to align standards and regulatory practices. Such regulatory harmonization will be a great enabler for innovation, for regional as well as international companies, and the reduced fragmentation of the market can also help reduce the prices of imported medicines (e.g., by eliminating the need for custom-made packaging).

AfCFTA will help to overcome the challenge of small, fragmented markets to create a positive cycle of increased regional manufacturing, research, and local talent. Small and isolated markets made it impossible for African countries to compete with Asian manufacturers. With a continental market, it will be possible to sustain greater economies of scale, which will help businesses achieve higher production volumes that will save money.[94] Regional markets will allow for specialization, which ultimately will enable regional procurement markets that are beneficial for investors. Frannie Léautier, chief executive officer of Southbridge Investments, explains how local manufacturing contributes to stronger local health systems for the mutual benefit of investors and countries: "There is a positive cycle, where you go from detection and diagnosis to research and development to treatment. This creates an ecosystem of experts who work together on different dimensions of the problem. The missing link in all of that is the manufacturing side. If you can tighten that link, and improve the medical products that are available, you attract qualified doctors and nurses. Then more people come down for treatment, so you have longitudinal studies that offer results. Manufacturing has been very important in all the countries that have succeeded in building pharmaceutical centres of excellence—it has helped them retain talent."[95]

AfCFTA will open a wider range of opportunities for the types of activities that can be executed and sourced within the continent. Beyond packaged medicines, there are several opportunities in the pharmaceutical industry for investment, including building quality health care infrastructure and increasing the capacity for vaccine manufacturing.[96] The Africa Investment Forum has facilitated investments since the onset of the pandemic, including five transactions, valued at $484 million total, spanning the creation of a multinational health fund to a mobile telemedicine product.

Transportation and Logistics: Key Trends

The transportation and logistics industry has an important role to play in enabling the acceleration of intra-African trade and increasing investment and export activity overall. Demand for logistics and transportation is skyrocketing as trade barriers and import costs are lowered, particularly as small and medium-sized enterprises are increasingly integrated and connected to the larger continental market.

A majority of intra-African exports are transported over land (60 percent of automotive exports, 56 percent of pharmaceutical exports, and 60 percent of agro-processing product exports). As for maritime trade, this is projected to increase from 58 million to 132 million tons by 2030 with the implementation of AfCFTA.[97] Road and maritime freight transportation therefore offer, at present, the biggest opportunity, as the infrastructure for air and rail transportation is still being developed. Transportation and logistics barriers have historically held African countries back as they have faced higher custom delay periods, lower percentages of paved roads, and a higher loss of goods due to limited cold chains compared with other regions in the world. All these challenges are being addressed through AfCFTA. The establishment of AfCFTA is projected to increase intra-African freight demand by 28 percent, leading to demand for almost 2 million trucks, 100,000 rail wagons, 250 aircraft, and more than 100 vessels by 2030.[98]

Transportation and Logistics: Key Players

Large logistics companies have historically been too expensive for African companies to use, but that is changing with the rise of new digital logistics companies. China and Southeast Asia have been major players in the sector, with competitive transit times for companies connecting Asia and East Africa. An example of this is Hapag-Lloyd, which successfully entered the market to connect landlocked East African countries with inland connections.[99]

Transportation and Logistics: Opportunities Under AfCFTA

Transportation and logistics represents a high-potential sector due to its role as an important enabler of the trade of goods and the fact that it is the largest contributor to imports (the value of imports of freight transportation to African countries—from within and outside the continent—is $36.8 billion annually).[100]

Transportation and logistics includes passenger and freight transportation, third-party logistics, freight forwarding, and courier express and parcel services.[101]

As AfCFTA increases intra-African trade and eliminates burdensome customs and costs, there is an opportunity to help close the urban/rural divide, develop digital logistics, and fulfill the logistics needed to ensure long-term increases in both business-to-business and business-to-consumer commerce.

The overwhelming demand and need for logistics and transportation services will only increase as AfCFTA is implemented and intra-African trade increases. Unlocking intraregional trade will skyrocket the demand for logistics, with more small and medium-sized enterprises needing logistics providers to connect to bigger markets. If commodities prices are lower due to the removal of trade barriers and import costs, consumption and demand will increase, to the benefit of African manufacturers and the logistics and transportation sector.[102] This will also open the door for digital logistics companies to step in and reduce costs, as well as improving the quality of services while promoting sustainability.[103]

Closing the urban/rural divide also presents significant opportunities in the logistics sector. Rural areas are increasingly reliant on regional supply chains rather than megacities, but they are often isolated due to the inadequate road infrastructure. Start-ups have begun to address these issues, with innovative solutions to integrate rural and city markets.[104] Infrastructure gaps, especially those that take a long time to fix, such as road issues, have prompted companies to create innovative, new solutions, including cargo drones, inland waterways and ports, and other means of transportation.

Business-to-business (B2B) logistics is expected to dominate the sector in the short to medium terms, but business-to-consumer logistics will continue to increase as consumer spending rises, e-commerce becomes more prevalent, and urbanization increases.[105] African companies spent $2.6 trillion on B2B transactions in 2015, with spending expected to reach $3.5 trillion by 2025.[106] Building upon these already existing trends, AfCFTA will accelerate opportunities for companies providing B2B services, including companies specializing in digital logistics.

Challenges and Risks

These four high-potential, high-impact sectors demonstrate the power of AfCFTA to accelerate business opportunities. Despite the impressive progress made by AfCFTA's implementation, challenges remain to get

AfCFTA to be fully implemented and operational for companies to take advantage of.

Macroeconomic Instability

Although the region has exhibited substantial improvements across macro-economic indicators over the past two decades, the novelty and rapidity of change still lead most analysts to view Africa's macroeconomic climate as volatile and uncertain. The continent is witnessing a period of rapidly rising income levels and the emergence of a middle class, which increases consumption. This, in turn, increases the demand for imported goods, which, in the short-term, can outpace growth in exports. Moreover, those countries that have continued to experience relatively high inflation rates in recent years, by regional standards, are more likely to face a decrease in current accounts caused by reduced foreign demand for their exports.[107]

Government policies can have a significant impact on macroeconomic conditions and, therefore, on a country's balance of trade. Some African countries, like Rwanda, have started to subsidize priority sectors and industries, which can improve the price competitiveness of exports. Rwanda also had targeted reforms that led to major success in areas such as opening a business, insolvency regulation, a labor code, trade facilitation, and taxation. While global shocks and issues are widespread and sometimes uncontrollable, government policies committed to stabilizing economies and diversifying exports have proven to bring positive trade outcomes.

Harmonization of Fragmented Markets

There are currently eight regional economic communities (RECs) recognized by the AU that are working to facilitate regional economic integration. Each African country is a member of three different RECs, on average,[108] meaning that integration can be challenging as one country can be operating within three different RECs with different rules of origin. By opting into the establishment of AfCFTA, African countries are delegating trust, which can be tricky to sustain. Yet having reached an agreement on a high percentage of goods, there is positive momentum to continue to defragment the different individual markets and RECs.

Barriers to Trade

Despite efforts in the developed world to encourage Africa's integration into the global economy by improving its terms of trade, emerging African countries continue to face higher tariff barriers on the world market than do middle- and high-income producers. Beyond tariff liberalization, AfCFTA's impact will rely on other factors, including improving customs cooperation, transit, and trade facilitation, and reducing nontariff barriers such as technical barriers to trade and sanitary and phytosanitary measures.[109] African countries have not performed as well as other regions when it comes to trade facilitation. For example, Sub-Saharan Africa has the highest cost-to-export ratio of all regions and outperforms only Latin America and the Caribbean in cost of imports, based on border compliance, and South Asia, based on documentary compliance.[110] Nontariff barriers have been estimated to be equivalent to an import tariff of 18 percent on average across the continent, which is also raising costs for trade in Africa.[111]

Trade Infrastructure Gaps

Many African countries struggle to fill physical and human capital gaps that are needed to fully seize the opportunities for increased trade under AfCFTA. Physical and digital infrastructure, although having made progress, still lags behind other regions, with major gaps (a $100 billion gap in physical infrastructure financing,[112] and 600 million people without access to electricity),[113] creating challenges for businesses to operate efficiently. For example, gaps in road infrastructure increase production and transaction costs for companies, adding an estimated 30–40 percent to the costs of goods traded among African countries,[114] while also making it more difficult for consumers to access goods and services. On average across Africa, roads carry 80 percent of goods and 90 percent of passenger traffic, yet only 43 percent of the population has access to an all-season road.[115] Progress is being made to address these challenges, though substantial finance gaps remain. The African Development Bank has financed 25 transportation corridors, and has constructed over 18,000 kilometers of roads, 27 border posts, and 16 bridges for $13.5 billion, as of 2022.[116]

Environmental and Demographic Changes

The population of Sub-Saharan Africa is growing faster than that of any other region in the world, generating rapid growth in demand for imports such as energy sources, construction materials, and manufactured goods. Most countries in the region have failed to grow the value of their exports at a rate that keeps pace with that of imports, resulting in a growing deficit, mounting central government debt, and dwindling reserves of foreign currencies.

The growth of populations and extractive industries has also generated pressures on land and habitats. Deforestation has become a major threat to agricultural production in the Sahel region, and grew at an alarming rate in 2022 in the forests of the Congo Basin—the second-largest tropical forest in the world—which already experienced a degraded area of 23 million hectares from 2000 to 2016.[117] Africa's oceans are the most overfished in the world, which poses a significant threat to tourism-based economies of island nations like Mauritius and the Seychelles. Moreover, most fishing is done by either foreign or unregistered vessels, making it very difficult to regulate.[118]

Strategies for Investment

Understanding the key trends, opportunities, challenges, and risks associated with specific sectors is fundamental for deciding the destinations of trade and investment in African economies. But to really succeed, it is critical to develop business and investment strategies that leverage unique tools, including supporting initiatives from AfCFTA and the WEF, to create value and high returns on investment.

The WEF's Five Pillars to Ease Physical, Capital, and Digital Flows in Africa

As AfCFTA continues to progress through the different negotiation periods, the World Economic Forum has developed five pillars that give an insight into the support it offers throughout the process. These supporting initiatives can provide companies with clearer information and allow them to take advantage of better coordination processes throughout the implementation stage (table 2-1).

Operational Tools

As both local and global companies seek to capitalize on the immense opportunities in the various sectors that have been accelerated by AfCFTA, operational tools exist to help them navigate the implementation period and beyond:

1. *The AfCFTA Guided Trade Initiative.* Though trade under AfCFTA officially commenced in January 2021, commercially meaningful trade under the agreement was delayed due to disruptions arising from the COVID-19 pandemic, prolonged negotiation periods, administrative issues, and overlaps with other existing customs unions.[119] Therefore, the AfCFTA Secretariat organized the Guided Trade Initiative, which was launched on October 7, 2022,[120] as an exercise to demonstrate that AfCFTA is truly operational. Countries that have ratified the agreement and submitted their schedules of tariff concessions are able to trade preferentially among themselves.[121]

Table 2-1. Five Pillars to Ease Physical, Capital, and Digital Flows in Africa and Grow Inclusive and Sustainable Development

Pillar	AfCFTA	World Economic Forum supporting initiatives
Pillar 1: Facilitating trade in goods	Phase 1 negotiations: AfCFTA trade-facilitating provisions	The Global Alliance for Trade Facilitation: a public-private partnership led by the World Economic Forum, International Chamber of Commerce (ICC), Center for International Private Enterprise (CIPE) and the German Agency for International Cooperation (GIZ), which has been working with Cameroon, Madagascar, Malawi, Morocco, Mozambique, Senegal, Tunisia, and Zambia to implement trade-facilitation projects. These projects cover various aspects of trade facilitation such as digitizing border processes, digitizing phytosanitary and rules of origin certificates, modernizing customs broker arrangements, establishing advanced rulings, and facilitating imports of vaccines and HIV/AIDS test kits.
Pillar 2: Facilitating services and investment	Phase 1 and 2 negotiations: Protocol on Trade in Services, already in force	Enabling Action on Sustainable Investment (EASI) initiative: to be launched in Sierra Leone and Ghana in 2023. EASI projects will bring a public-private approach to implementing investment measures that will facilitate the flow of sustainable investment and grow a larger continental market, thereby attracting greater FDI from outside Africa. EASI projects can also help support the implementation of the WTO Investment Facilitation for Development Agreement, where this is requested by host governments participating in the Agreement, and work to maximize the benefits of trade and investment opportunities brought about by the AfCFTA protocols. EASI projects will help operationalize the provisions of the AfCFTA investment protocol once the text is agreed to.
Pillar 3: Facilitating digital trade	Phase 2 and 3 negotiations: The Protocol on Digital Trade is advancing	TradeTech: a concept that reflects different Fourth Industrial Revolution technologies in the trade space. The WEF has identified opportunities and proposed policy recommendations associated with TradeTech, which are ready for deployment in Africa.
		Digital Economy Agreements Leadership Group: this provides an impartial space for information exchanges and debate concerning digital economy agreements.
		Trade Finance Frontiers: a multistakeholder group to explore and analyse where public-private cooperation can help the growing trade finance gap.
		Digital Economy Agreements Leadership Group: this provides an impartial space for information exchanges and debate concerning digital economy agreements.

Table 2-1. Five Pillars to Ease Physical, Capital, and Digital Flows in Africa and Grow Inclusive and Sustainable Development (Continued)

Pillar	AfCFTA	World Economic Forum supporting initiatives
Pillar 4: Facilitating inclusive trade	Phase 2 negotiations: Protocol on Women and Youth	Inclusive Trade Initiative: the Forum aims to improve the societal outcomes of trade. Its Trade and Labour Programme and Trade and Indigenous Peoples Programme aim to identify how trade tools and mechanisms can better serve workers and increase access to trade benefits for Indigenous businesses and communities.
Pillar 5: Facilitating environmentally sustainable trade	Phase 2 and 3 negotiations	Green Trade and Investment pathways: for African governments and businesses to lead a just transition by preparing for the new competitiveness needs of a carbon-constrained global economy.
		This includes a guidebook of investment facilitation measures for developing countries to attract FDI aligned with climate action.
		The World Economic Forum has worked with national stakeholders in Ghana and South Africa to identify opportunities for trade policy to contribute to a circular economy for plastics. More of these studies at the national and regional levels are being planned.

Source: World Economic Forum (2023, 20).

Eight countries—Cameroon, Egypt, Ghana, Kenya, Mauritius, Rwanda, Tanzania, and Tunisia—participated in the first round in 2023, which then expanded in 2024 to add an additional twenty-four countries.[122] In collaboration with their respective ministries of trade and national coordination offices, the AfCFTA Secretariat matched businesses and products for export and import among interested state parties. For the first time ever, African goods were traded with preferential duties and simplified documents under AfCFTA. The initiative helped members of the private sector learn how to use the agreement practically and also helped the Secretariat note avenues and areas that require further intervention. Members of the private sector can currently take full advantage of all of the trade-facilitating aspects of the agreement now that it is fully operational. As the AfCFTA Guided Trade Initiative continues, there is a great opportunity for interested companies to gain experience in trading under AfCFTA with direct support from the initiative, giving them a head start and competitive advantage. The private sector should be engaged in monitoring the outcomes of this initial trading period as it may provide valuable, specific lessons in terms of implementation. This initiative is a powerful signal to the private sector locally and globally that trade under AfCFTA has begun and that there is a tremendous opportunity for the private sector and the AfCFTA Secretariat to converge on their mutual interest of developing strong value chains by building on the lessons learned from this first period of trading.

2. *The Pan-African Payment and Settlement System (PAPSS)* is a centralized financial market infrastructure enabling the efficient and secure flow of money across African borders. This is an African Union plan developed in collaboration with the African Export-Import Bank (Afreximbank) to complement trading under AfCFTA, and it enables users to make near-instant payments (within 120 seconds) in their local currency, without converting to a foreign currency or using a third-party institution/bank. As of the end of 2023, the PAPSS network consists of 13 central banks, 114 commercial banks, and 10 switches.[123] All central banks are to sign up by the end of 2024 and all commercial banks by the end of 2025. The instant nature of payments, in local currency, provided by PAPSS will help African businesses avoid the delays in confirming payments that have long been a barrier to trade. This new platform will lead to increased trust and time capacity to increase trade volumes.[124] Overall, PAPSS will remove the payment bottleneck for companies, reduce the dependency on foreign currencies and improve the efficiency of cross-border trade across the continent.[125]

3. *The AfCFTA Adjustment Facility Fund.* AfCFTA will create significant general and long-term benefits across the continent, including stimulating structural transformation. As with any major trade liberalization program, AfCFTA may introduce near-term disruptions, as tariff revenues by state parties are reduced, industrial sectors are disordered, businesses and supply chains are reorganized, and employment is dislocated—often in ways that cannot be anticipated. The estimated requirement for uninterrupted implementation of AfCFTA and elimination of the adjustment cost is $7.7 billion over the next six to ten years.

To combat the adverse effects that may arise from implementation of AfCFTA, Decision Ext/Assembly/AU/Decl. 1 (XII) of the 12th Extraordinary Session of the Assembly of July 2019 committed to provide an Adjustment Facility (the "Facility") and to "collaborate with international financial institutions to mobilize short term financing to assist State Parties meet their liberalization commitments in the AfCFTA with minimum adjustment costs."[126] Decision Assembly/AU/Dec 751 (XXXIII) further requested the development of a statute and resource mobilization plan.[127]

Afreximbank and the AfCFTA Secretariat were mandated by the AfCFTA Council of Trade Ministers and the African Union Heads of State and

Government to establish and operationalize AfCFTA Adjustment Funds, which consist of the base fund, the general fund, and the credit fund. The base fund will be used to mobilize grants to address tariff revenue losses and to support AfCFTA state parties to implement the various protocols under AfCFTA. The Afreximbank board also approved grant funding in the amount of $10 million as seed funding to kick-start the establishment of the base fund.

The general fund will be used to mobilize concessional funding, while the credit fund will mobilize commercial funding to support the public and private sectors, including small and medium-sized enterprises as well as youth and women, to adjust to the new trading environment arising from AfCFTA. These funds will be critical in enabling the private sector to address the short-term disruptions through financing, technical assistance, and grants and compensation funding. Specifically, the funds will support companies to undergo changes in skills, tools, and capabilities in line with the development of regional value chains that add value to goods and services.[128] The credit fund will enable factories that previously produced primarily for local demand to retool and reorganize their operations for different types of production that will be traded within the region. The benefits for countries themselves should also give investors confidence that AfCFTA is committed to offsetting potential losses, allowing smaller countries that were previously dependent on tariff income also to become important players participating in AfCFTA.

4. *The AfCFTA Private Sector Engagement Strategy.* The AfCFTA Secretariat has developed an engagement plan to guide its efforts in collaborating with the private sector and other important stakeholders to boost intra-Africa trade and production. The engagement plan is the outcome of extensive consultations with industry players and associations in the priority value chains, development finance institutions, and African Union institutions. The plan can help companies better understand the initiatives and policy recommendations associated with each of the four value chains discussed above (automotive, agriculture and agro-processing, pharmaceuticals, and transportation and logistics) and their impact. The recommendations are based on on-the-ground experience that will provide practical advice and a better understanding of the links between company and continental goals. AfCFTA has also outlined other important value chains that will be the focus of future reports.

5. *The AfCFTA Rules of Origin Manual and E-Tariff Book* sets out guidelines on the operationalization of Annex 2 on Rules of Origin to accord tariff preferences to goods that meet the origin rules and are traded among the AfCFTA state parties. Flexible rules of origin regimes will be vital to unlocking the potential of AfCFTA, and the manual can help provide transparency

and consistency among trading partners. The manual spells out in detail the application of the rules used in determining the origin status of goods, the procedures for administering the rules, and the institutional framework for the implementation of the AfCFTA Rules of Origin. This manual can help provide clarity for countries and businesses so they can understand how an economic identity will be assigned to goods. In the future, its annual review will help simplify, clarify and enhance the rules. The *Rules of Origin Manual and E-Tariff Book* is another milestone—by publishing information on the rates of duty under AfCFTA state parties—and makes searching and comparing easy. Companies will be able to use it to close any information gaps.[129]

Operational tools such as those mentioned above can help businesses close information gaps, facilitate payments more efficiently, and provide practical insight into the progress of the implementation of AfCFTA in various industries and value chains. Some companies, both local and multinational, have already found success in African countries by building local partnerships, trust, and relationships with communities, and using AfCFTA accelerators and synergies in a way that is beneficial to both their company goals and the overall country goals.

Conclusion

By leveraging the operational tools, following the supporting initiatives highlighted here, and adapting strategies deployed by existing companies that have already found success operating across Africa, new and existing businesses can seize the opportunities across industries that are being unlocked by AfCFTA and its effects on greater intra-African trade. As AfCFTA continues to become fully implemented and integrated, it is a great opportunity for companies to enter African markets and take advantage of the enormous and growing market size, enhanced payment features, and ease of flows that can help add more value to the continent. Doing so will help strengthen local value chains, which will in turn help to diversify African economies, create jobs, increase incomes, and improve livelihoods. Through strategic partnerships and thoughtful leadership between the public and private sectors, AfCFTA's promise can be realized.

Notes

1. Stanley (2023).
2. Signé (2020).
3. UNECA (2021).

4. World Economic Forum (2024).

5. The chapter builds from direct excerpts, updated and improved as needed, from these three publications.

6. Signé (2022a).

7. World Economic Forum (2023).

8. World Economic Forum (2024).

9. Contributing author: Chido Munyati, Head of Regional Agenda, Africa, World Economic Forum.

10. Along with the Africa Head at the World Economic Forum (WEF), we organized workshops and focus groups to collect data and excerpts from various companies within four high-potential sectors for local and global business: automotive, agriculture and agro-processing, pharmaceuticals, and transportation and logistics. The contributors involved in "AfCFTA: A New Era for Global Business and Investment in Africa" include Oliver Alawuba, Suhail Al Banna, Gilberto Antonio, Rita Babihuga-Nsanze, Sumeet Bhardwaj, Børge Brende, Sean Doherty, Hassan El Houry, Cynthia Gnassingbe-Essonam, Lutz Hegemann, Mohamed Hettiti, Philippe Isler, Anouar Jamali, Serge Kamuhinda, Fa-eez Karodia, Lutendo Khavhadi, Grace Khoza, Themba Khumalo, Youssef Lahmiti, Dom La Vigne, Fernanda Lopes Larsen, Shiletsi Makhofane, Walter Mandela, Esha Mansingh, Wamkele Mene, Racey Muchilwa, Patricia Obozuwa, Anu Paasiaro, Luis Alfredo Pérez, Michael Petrie, Mariam Soumaré, Matthew Stephenson, Supachai Wattanaveerachai, Geoffrey White, and Candice White. The contributors involved in the WEF's "Action Plan to Accelerate Global Business and Investment in Africa" include Deeana Ahmed, Jason Blackman, Børge Brende, Rose Chilvers, Dave Coffey, Laurence Denmark, Andile Dlamini, Maximillian Effah, Tony Eneh, Cyntia Genolet, Cynthia Gnassingbe-Essonam, Chris Holden, Shazia Ijaz, Christine Irish, Philippe Isler, Faizel Ismail, Lutendo Khavhadi, Themba Khumalo, Nthabiseng Komane, Dom La Vigne, Fernanda Lopes Larsen, Siya Madikizela, Shiletsi Makhofane, Walter Mandela, Sarah Meinert, Wamkele Mene, Alex Moir, Edna Oduwo, David Paterson, Anu Paasiaro, Luis Alfredo Pérez, Steven Pope, Laura Raaen, Ravin Sanjith, Dirk Willem te Velde, Ashleigh Theophanides, Hannes van der Merwe, Noncedo Vutula, Jonathan Walter, Andrew Whiting, and Geoffrey White.

11. Fofack (2024).

12. Nubong (2021).

13. Nubong (2021); Freire and Slany (2023).

14. Nubong (2021).

15. Signé (2020).

16. Signé and van der Ven (2019).

17. World Bank (2020b, 2020c).

18. Signé and van der Ven (2019).

19. Signé and Gurib-Fakim (2019).

20. Signé (2018a); Signé and Gurib-Fakim (2019).

21. Signé (2018b).

22. Signé (2018a).
23. World Bank (2020a).
24. Rodrik (2016); UNECA (2020a); Fofack (2020).
25. Calderon et al. (2020).
26. World Bank (2020a).
27. Signé (2020).
28. World Bank (2020c).
29. TRALAC (2023).
30. Afreximbank (2024).
31. Afreximbank (2024).
32. Afreximbank (2024).
33. Afreximbank (2024).
34. Pan African Chamber of Commerce and Industry (n.d.).
35. Afreximbank (2024).
36. Afreximbank (2024).
37. Afreximbank (2024).
38. United States Trade Representative (2024).
39. United States Trade Representative (2024).
40. United States Trade Representative (2024).
41. Afreximbank (2024).
42. Afreximbank (2024).
43. Afreximbank (2024).
44. AfCFTA (2021).
45. Augustine (2024).
46. Agarwal et al. (2022).
47. UNCTAD (2023c).
48. World Economic Forum (2023).
49. Zhang (2021).
50. Agarwal et al. (2022).
51. IndustriALL Global Union (2020).
52. Agarwal et al. (2022).
53. Signé and Madden (2020).
54. Oramah (2021).
55. UNCTAD (2023b).
56. Agarwal et al. (2022).
57. EBCAM (2020).
58. Hackman (2021).
59. World Economic Forum (2024).
60. AfCFTA (2021).
61. Africa Legal Network (2022).
62. AfCFTA (2021).
63. AfCFTA (2021).

64. AfCFTA (2021).
65. Mainly South Africa, Egypt, Morocco, and Nigeria.
66. AfCFTA (2021).
67. iAfrica (2019).
68. Hackman (2021).
69. Hackman (2021).
70. Africa Legal Network (2022).
71. African Development Bank (2023a).
72. Owoo and Lambon-Quayefio (2018).
73. Fusacchia, Balié and Salvatici (2022).
74. investSA (2020).
75. AfCFTA (2021).
76. Goedde, Ooko-Ombaka, and Pais (2019).
77. Rickwood and Lutzmayer (2023).
78. Rickwood and Lutzmayer (2023).
79. Sharma (2022).
80. UNIDO (2018).
81. AfCFTA (2021).
82. AfCFTA (2021).
83. AfCFTA (2021).
84. AfCFTA (2021).
85. World Economic Forum (2023).
86. AsokoInsight (2023).
87. AsokoInsight (2023).
88. AsokoInsight (2023).
89. AsokoInsight (2023).
90. Rickwood and Lutzmayer (2023).
91. World Economic Forum (2024).
92. African Union Development Agency (n.d.).
93. AfCFTA (2021).
94. Byaruhanga (2020).
95. Léautier (2021).
96. African Development Bank Group (2022c).
97. UNCTAD (2021a).
98. UNECA (2022).
99. *Global Trade* Staff (2018).
100. AfCFTA (2021).
101. AfCFTA (2021).
102. Cooperative Logistics Network (2021).
103. Léautier (2021).
104. EHS Africa Logistics (n.d.).
105. EHS Africa Logistics (n.d.).

106. Boughin et al. (2016).
107. Chand (n.d.).
108. Afreximbank (2023).
109. UNCTAD (2019a).
110. UNCTAD (2019a).
111. Fofack (2024).
112. African Development Bank (2023c).
113. IEA (2022).
114. Green (2023).
115. African Development Bank (2023b).
116. African Development Bank (2023b).
117. Cavallito (2022).
118. United States Trade Representative (2016).
119. Nzimande, Shafrir, and Bhugwandeen (2022).
120. Rao (2022).
121. Rao (2022).
122. Ecofin Agency (2024a).
123. Afreximbank (2024).
124. Ogbalu (2022).
125. Peter (2022).
126. Assembly of the African Union (2019).
127. Assembly of the African Union (2019).
128. Afreximbank (2022).
129. Dundee & Angus Chamber of Commerce (2022).

Three
The Potential for Entertainment, Cultural, and Creative Industries in Africa
TRENDS, OPPORTUNITIES, CHALLENGES, AND STRATEGIES

The cultural and creative industries (CCI) represent a highly influential sector and one of the fastest growing sectors of the global economy, generating about 3 percent of global gross domestic product (GDP) (over $2 trillion in revenues annually) and employing roughly 50 million people, about half of whom are women.[1] By 2030, the creative industry is projected to grow by 40 percent,[2] accounting for 10 percent of global GDP.[3] While the economic and social importance of CCI is widely accepted, definitions of this term vary, as do definitions of an important subsector of the CCI, entertainment and media (E&M).[4] When referring to the creative industries, the United Nations Conference on Trade and Development (UNCTAD) highlights that the CCI "are at the crossroads of the arts, culture, business and technology . . . [and] comprise the cycle of creation, production and distribution of goods and services that use intellectual capital as their primary input."[5] Figure 3-1 and table 3-1 provide an overview of the major subsectors in the CCI and their respective characteristics.

Economists have determined that there is little to no impediment to entering the entertainment market.[6] Considering these low barriers to entry, developing countries have the unique opportunity to harness the CCI to drive sustainable, high economic growth. In particular, African countries have excess potential for growth, especially considering the continent accounted for only 1.5 percent of the global creative economy and 2.9 percent of global creative exports,[7] and that it generated 5 percent of the global cultural and creative jobs (2 million) as of 2022, as estimated by UNCTAD.

Figure 3-1. The Cultural and Creative Sector

CIRCLES	SECTORS	SUBSECTORS	CHARACTERISTICS
CORE ARTS FIELD	Visual Arts	Crafts, Paintings, Sculpture, Photography	• No industrial activities • Outputs are prototypes and potentially copyrighted works (i.e., these works have a high density of creation that would be eligible to copyright but they are, however, not systematically copyrighted, as is the case for most craft works, some performing arts production and visual arts, etc.)
	Performing Arts	Theater, Dance, Circus, Festivals	
	Heritage	Museums, Libraries, Archives, Archeological Sites	
CIRCLE 1: **CULTURAL INDUSTRIES**	Film and Video		• Industrial activities aimed at massive reproduction • Outputs are based on copyright
	Television and Radio		
	Video Games		
	Music	Recorded music market, live music performances, revenues or collecting societies in the music sector	
	Books and Press	Book publishing, magazine and newspaper publishing	
CIRCLE 2: **CREATIVE INDUSTRIES & ACTIVITIES**	Design	Fashion design, graphic design, interior design, product design	• Activities are not necessarily industrial and may be prototypes • Although outputs are based on copyright, they may include other intellectual property inputs (trademarks) • The use of creativity (creative skills and creative people originating in the arts field of cultural industries) is essential to the performances of these noncultural sectors
	Architecture		
	Advertising		

Source: Hivos (2018).

Table 3-1. The Nine Cultural Industries

—Traditional cultural expressions: arts and crafts, festivals, and celebrations
—Cultural sites: archeological sites, museums, libraries, exhibitions, and the like
—Visual arts: paintings, sculptures, photography, and antiques
—Publishing and printed media: books, press, and other publications
—Design: interior, graphic, fashion, jewelry, and toys
—Performing arts: live music, theater, dance, opera, circus, puppetry, and the like
—Audiovisual: film, television, radio, and other broadcasting
—New media: software, video games, and digitized creative content
—Creative services: architectural, advertising, creative research and development, and cultural and recreational

Sources: Alaoui M'Hammdi and Jaïdi (2023); UNCTAD (2008).

While these rates remain low, they are on the rise, with UNCTAD reporting a 13 percent increase in the industry in 2018 and a rise of 4 percent in CCI exports between 2010 and 2020, Africa now ranks fifth in the world for its creative industries market.[8] The rise in mobile telephones and internet connectivity across Africa has only served to transform the CCI, and in particular the E&M sector, to factor in the production and distribution of cultural goods and services through mobile devices, social networks, and other digital platforms, further driving growth potential.[9] By 2050, Africa will be home to one-third of the world's youth with the fastest growing creative industry,[10] and consumer spending in hospitality and recreation could reach $1.2 trillion,[11] leading to incredible opportunities within the entertainment sectors.

Countries such as Mali, Morocco, Mozambique, Senegal, and the Democratic Republic of Congo have robust creative industries, from visual arts to music. Meanwhile, Nigeria, Kenya, and South Africa have outsized potential, especially in their E&M sectors, which are projected to grow at significantly faster rates than the rest of the world.

Through 2027, Nigeria, Kenya, and South Africa's E&M revenues will continue to increase, with Nigeria projected to grow E&M revenues the most, more than doubling from $6.6 billion in 2022 to $12.9 billion in 2027.[12] Kenya's E&M sector has experienced strong growth in the past decade, including 9.8 percent growth in 2022, achieving $2.3 billion in revenue.[13] Kenya, unlike South Africa and Nigeria, will also experience growth in all E&M segments, with internet advertising and over-the-top (OTT) video with the highest growth. South Africa's E&M market experienced high growth in 2021, bouncing back from the pandemic, when it still outpaced the global average.

From Nigeria to Kenya to South Africa, the growth of E&M sectors is proof of Africa's potential to expand and strengthen existing markets to mutually benefit private business and overall society. In particular, formalizing the CCI could unlock this sector and bring tremendous growth to Sub-Saharan African economies, especially considering the large role that the informal economy currently plays in the E&M sector. Many of Africa's CCI activities are primarily concentrated in the informal economy, with 53.3 percent of the cultural industries in Senegal, 51.7 percent in Namibia, and 80 percent in Kenya found to be dominated by the informal sector in 2020.[14] While South Africa is an exception to this trend, the country still has 35 percent of its cultural industries represented by the informal economy.[15] Since the informal sector accounts for 55 percent of Sub-Saharan Africa's GDP, bringing CCI into the formal economy has the potential to reap high returns for investors and create positive socioeconomic development on the continent.[16]

With these opportunities in mind, this chapter first expands on the history and trends of the CCI in Africa before delving into the current driving factors in its growth and the sector's major players. Then, opportunities for commercial enterprise and economic growth are contrasted with the challenges and risks related to entering this market on the continent. The chapter concludes with strategies by which investors in Africa can intelligently tap into opportunities in the CCI and capture future growth prospects in the present.

Background Facts and Trends

Adopted in 1969 by the Organization of African Unity, the Pan African Cultural Manifesto represents the first attempt to create a consolidated cultural policy framework to promote arts and culture development in Africa, linking this development to broader socioeconomic growth.[17] Since then, African nations and transnational organizations have introduced various proposals to promote CCI development. More recently, in 2018, the African Union introduced the Plan of Action on Cultural and Creative Industries to harness the potential for member states to promote their creative economies to further boost economic and social development.[18] In 2020, twelve heads of state in Africa committed to playing a leadership role in facilitating arts,[19] culture, and heritage during the Thirty-Third Assembly of the African Union.[20]

However, growth in the CCI has stagnated in many African countries, hindered by a lack of support and funding. According to the United Nations, global trade in creative goods and services has grown substantially in the last decade, with global exports of creative goods increasing from $419 million in 2010 to $524 million in 2020 and global exports of creative services increasing from $487 billion to almost $1.1 trillion in 2020.[21] However, this trend has not been as evident in Africa for the same period due to the only recent uptick in mobile technology and entertainment subindustries as global players. In fact, according to a 2022 UNCTAD report, Africa represented less than 1.5 percent of the global creative economy.[22] At the same time, there has been growth in certain sectors of the industry in selected regional markets, as described in this section.

Before 2011, Egypt hosted a globally renowned film industry. Among Arabic-speaking countries around the world, Egypt accounted for 75 percent of all films produced, and it developed a deep market for original content production.[23] The Arab Spring set this particular industry back, as local production became impossible amid growing political instability and violence. However, film industries in South Africa, Morocco, Nigeria, Kenya, and Ghana grew in its stead. These countries have offered cheaper production costs, tax credits for international film companies, and improving infrastructures that have led to an array of international movies being produced in them.[24] In 2023, for instance, the Moroccan film industry achieved record profits, in large part due to the increase in foreign investment over the past decade. After a reduction of foreign investment of about 50 percent from 2019 to 2021 due to the COVID-19 pandemic, Morocco introduced a rebate system that attracted foreign companies to film in the country, leading to its record profits in 2023.[25]

African countries' music industries followed a trajectory similar to their film industries. The West African archipelago has the highest concentration of musicians per square mile in the world, and the region's various carnivals and festivals attract tourists in large numbers (or at least they did before the pandemic).[26] Before the period of independence, African-made music was barely known off the continent. After 1960, Nigerian artist Fela Kuti's inspired genre of Afrobeat, a mix between West African jazz and funk music, became popular among activist-minded artists in North America and Europe, as many of his lyrics focus on universal themes like challenging unjust authority and brutality.[27] In the 2000s, as broadband connections spread throughout the continent, African and global musicians and listeners alike entered a more equitable arena. Recently, famous musicians, including Drake and Beyoncé, have brought attention to African musicians through mutually beneficial collaborations with them, promoting their music on their own global platforms. The local music market was projected to be $1.7 billion in South Africa, $33 million in Nigeria, and $30 million in Kenya in 2023.[28] African music's growing popularity earned itself a new category at the Grammys—"Best African Music Performance"—as of 2024.[29]

Although still in its beginning stages, international interest in African cultural goods is increasing, representing a massive opportunity for countries to grow their creative economies and investors and companies to achieve significant returns. Aside from collaborating with Western-based artists like Beyoncé, African artists are also gaining international recognition on their own, as evidenced by the fact that South African musician Master KG's 2020 Song of the Year Award at the NRJ Music Awards, where he beat well-known Western artists like Nicki Minaj, Jason Derulo, and Dua Lipa to take home the title.[30] Singers like Angelike Kidjo, Burna Boy, and Wizkid, but also Ayra Strarr and Tyla more recently, have entered the American mainstream.[31]

Despite the continent's fifty-four countries and nearly 2,000 local languages, the Western music industry has a tendency to view it as a monolithic region. US artist-and-repertoire representatives find that their strategies do not always work in other African countries. There may be universal access to the internet, but music streaming has lagged, which means there is a lack of listener data. Instead, artist-and-repertoire representatives in Africa continue to place a strong emphasis on personal connections and intuition. In today's environment, which is heavily influenced by analytics, Watson argues, "That's scary." However, major label collaborations are assisting in supplying the analytical tools to quicken the process of talent discovery.[32] Nollywood—Nigeria's answer to Hollywood—has gained global recognition for its film productions and surpassed Hollywood in 2009 to become the world's second-largest film producer.[33] Likewise, there is an increasing interest in African cultural traditions, particularly in the fashion sector, via the burgeoning demand for colorful, vibrant pieces from domestic designers.[34] Even African art is gaining more international interest, with Bonhams, the London-based auction company, setting twenty-one world records for prices in its 2013 Africa Now auction, which featured works from sixty-six African artists.[35]

As new technology is being developed, the creative industries are following the trends in innovation and, as a result, are continually changing. For example, advertising within the cultural and creative industries has had to weather the transition from print media, to television promotion, and now to internet advertising. As of 2016, global internet advertising surpassed revenue from TV advertising. Terrestrial TV advertising is expected to further contract globally through 2024 due to the continued diversification of TV watching habits and the ongoing effects of the COVID-19 pandemic.[36] This decline in TV advertising follows a similar decline in DVD and Blu-ray, although these physical home video formats remain influential in some African countries like Nigeria due to poor broadband infrastructure that limits the growth of streaming services.[37] At the same time, revenue from OTT video, which delivers content via the internet without requiring a subscription to a traditional cable or satellite TV provider, was forecasted to grow significantly through 2023. Even countries with current deficits in broadband infrastructure are projected to see growth. For instance, Nigeria's OTT market was projected to experience a compound annual growth rate (CAGR) of 17.9 percent through 2023, the highest growth rate out of all sectors of its television market,[38] while video-on-demand services are projected to have a 9.75 percent CAGR through 2027.[39]

While the numbers given here tell the story of global trends within the entertainment sector, a biennial study by the market research and consulting firm Ipsos of Africa's affluent populations indicates how these trends are playing out on the continent. The study calculates the media use and consumption behavior of the top 15 percent of income earners in Cameroon, Ghana, Kenya, Morocco, Nigeria, South Africa, and Uganda.[40] While the study includes the three largest domestic entertainment markets, the authors consider international media goods and services that are consumed by this population, diversifying the averages of entertainment usage and growth among Sub-Saharan African countries. The study reveals that over 95 percent of Africa's affluent population watches international television networks on a monthly basis. Two-thirds of this group report using devices other than a TV to watch television networks, a higher proportion than a similar socio-economic group in Europe.[41] Social media and mobile technology are also dominating the statistics of this group's reception of international media, international and domestic news, and domestic digital entertainment. The Ipsos study is important for understanding the changing trends within the E&M sector, which no longer relies on physical attendance at entertainment events or on the consumption of local media. With the rise of online networks for sharing film, music, art, and other cultural and creative goods, the African continent's CCI and its entertainment subsector are growing.

The Sector's Importance

One of Africa's greatest challenges is its growing population. Over the next twenty-five years, Africa is expected to see its population double, and it is the only region of the globe where the working-age population is expected to continue growing beyond 2035.[42] In fact, Africa's burgeoning young workforce is expected to reach over 600 million by 2030, adding 11 million new workers every year.[43] This growing workforce is going to need employment, but there is no automatic link between population growth and job creation. Currently, Africa suffers from high levels of unemployment and underemployment, especially in its youth population, and failing to address this issue risks social and political instability.[44] Consequently, it is essential to recognize that the CCI activities are capable of generating economic growth and also can be important mediums for educational development and political communications at the state and local levels. At the same time, the CCI are often born out of or are developed as a way to reconcile, remember, and harbor history and national identity, which plays an important role across the continent. The preservation of archeological sites, for example, can be a driver for creative industries, and meanwhile, digital museums and displays of history (e.g., the

Unboxing Mayibuye–Access to Digital Heritage project in South Africa) can be a powerful way to grow in the market while having positive spillover effects for culture and belonging.

The CCI represent an avenue to address youth unemployment on the African continent and promote socioeconomic equality for underrepresented populations. In particular, forecasted revenue increases that accompany a rise in internet access on the continent present an opportunity to expand the job market in the E&M sector to meet rising demand. For instance, Nigeria's E&M sector rose 26.6 percent to achieve total revenue of $4.4 billion in 2018.[45] The CCI tend to employ more young people than other sectors of the economy and are more open to a diverse group of participants. In Europe, for instance, the CCI tend to employ more workers in the fifteen- to twenty-nine-year age group than any other sector of the economy. Likewise, women tend to participate at higher rates in the CCI compared with the workforce average for other sectors.[46] Since 60 percent of Africa's population is under twenty-five, and 51 percent is female, there is the opportunity to leverage this growth in the CCI to provide employment to these traditionally underserved populations.[47] Due to its connections with other industries, music production fosters entrepreneurship and offers prospects for youth employment.[48]

Aside from creating employment, the CCI can drive overall economic growth and development on the African continent. The performing arts have been shown to have direct, positive effects on social progress and economic growth, along with potential positive indirect effects on areas like tourism, nation branding, and environmental stewardship.[49] Research also has shown empirical evidence linking the creative industries to positive economic development in South Africa.[50] Likewise, the South African government has determined that CCI accounted for about 3 percent of jobs and 1.7 percent of GDP in 2016, noting that the growth rate of CCI was significantly faster than the rest of the economy.[51] This amounted to 2.97 percent of GDP in 2019. At 6 percent of jobs, there were about 1 million people employed. The number of jobs is up from 2017, when it was 5.9 percent (965,000 jobs).[52]

South Africa's CCI activities are still made up of relatively small firms; yet, growth in the sector and national plans to increase its development will allow firms to grow and fulfill employment needs in the country. Likewise, there is evidence that promoting growth in the creative industries can have spillover effects that benefit the development of sectors like tourism and even manufacturing. An example of the role of the CCI in augmenting growth can be found in Nigeria's film industry, Nollywood. Nigeria produces about 2,500 films a year, with total box office receipts expected to reach $14.82 billion in 2025, increasing at a 16.5 percent CAGR over the next five years.[53] At a 13.4 percent CAGR, total music sales were projected to increase to $73 million in 2021.[54] About a million people were employed locally as of 2021, and the sector contributes more than $8 billion to the economy. As of 2021, the music industry made over $2 billion in revenue in Nigeria, which is home to over five hundred music producers, a thousand record labels, and over fifty radio stations.[55]

Fashion is another subsector of the CCI that represents an opportunity to catalyze economic growth and employment. In 2015, the African Development Bank (AfDB) launched the so-called Fashionomics initiative to promote job creation, regional integration, entrepreneurship, industrialization, and equality by growing the textile, apparel, and accessories (TA&A) sector in Africa.[56] The AfDB has projected that further developing the TA&A sector has the potential to create 400,000 new jobs through 2025,[57] and since a large percentage of its workforce is composed of women, such as nearly 80 percent in Ethiopia, this development has the potential to advance gender equality in employment as well.[58] Promoting the development of the TA&A also can promote further development of the secondary sector in Africa. In South Africa alone, 2.5 percent of total manufacturing output was represented by the clothing, textile, footwear, and leather sector as of 2020.[59] Already, the combined apparel and footwear market in Sub-Saharan Africa has reached an estimated value of $31 billion. While Ethiopia, South Africa, Mauritius, Madagascar, and countries in North Africa have all seen growth in their TA&A sectors, other African countries are lagging behind.[60] Since about 90 percent of fashion businesses in Africa are in the informal sector, formalizing this sector has the potential to reap significant rewards for both investors and general society.[61]

The CCI also can help bolster efforts to address structural deficits in training and education on the continent. While Africa has a rapidly growing labor force, the World Economic Forum's Human Capital Index found that Sub-Saharan African countries only capture an average of 55 percent of the human capital potential of their workforce, 10 percent lower than the global average.[62] This dearth in skilled labor is compounded by gaps in the current education system, which only has been exacerbated in the wake of the COVID-19 pandemic and resulting school closures.[63] However, the CCI can provide nontraditional ways to promote education and early childhood development. Buckingham and Scanlon have coined the term "edu-tainment," defined as a "hybrid genre that relies heavily on visual material, on narrative or game-like formats, and on more informal, less didactic styles of address," showing how educational entertainment materials can be disseminated by the CCI.[64] Although researchers recommend avoiding television exposure for children under two,[65] a study of the US children's program *Sesame Street* found that it improved school performance among preschool-age children in the country, illustrating how the CCI have the potential to augment education outcomes in Africa as well.[66] Researchers also have explored using digital games to enhance learning in the classroom,[67] and in South Africa, the publishing sector is dominated by educational materials.[68]

Ogunmilade even argues that television and radio programs are the "prime movers" of national development because television can disseminate large volumes of information to a diverse audience rapidly and raise public awareness of economic activities.[69] In fact, South Africans reportedly spend a total of 7 hours per week listening to the radio.[70] Television and radio are but two mediums through which the E&M sector distributes content in Africa. As these mediums transition with new technology, the potential for creating entertaining educational materials must adapt. The entertainment sector should not be overlooked within the field of education development and social reforms because many movements of change are built and expanded through it. With the increasing adoption of mobile phones and digital technology and the increased interest in virtual learning due to the COVID-19 pandemic, the E&M sector may be at the forefront of political conversations on the continent, buttressed by its significant potential effects on economic growth and education.

Key Drivers

The uptake in technology on the continent is a very broad driver of growth within the CCI and in particular the entertainment and media sector. Internet access increasingly allows more consumers to participate in media creation and sharing, and expands the rate of consumption. Likewise, technology has led a transition from physical to digitally enabled goods and services in many sectors. While there always has been a demand for cultural and creative entertainment, the digital revolution on the continent has transformed the way consumers can access this content. The most visible drivers of the sector in Africa are digital payment platforms, infrastructural access to technology, general consumer market growth, and the subindustry of advertising.

Infrastructural Access to Technology

Increasing access to technology infrastructure is allowing businesses in Africa to leapfrog over previously impenetrable barriers to expansion or facilitation,

Figure 3-2. Mobile Connectivity Map, 2023

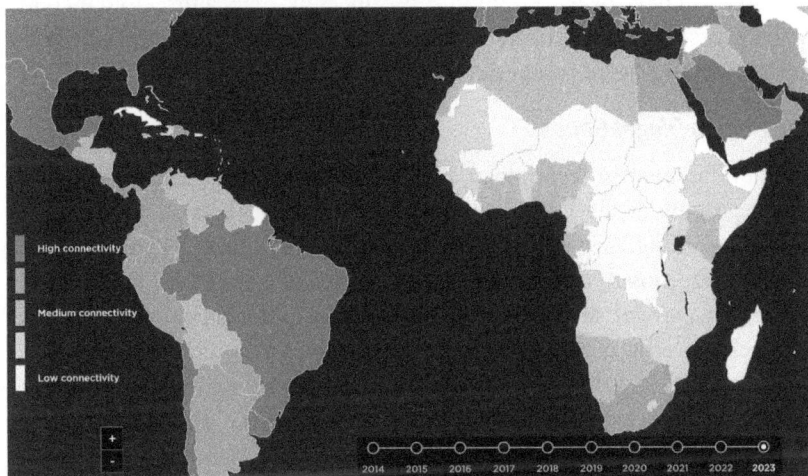

Source: Global System for Mobile Communications Association, "Mobile Connectivity Index," https://www. mobileconnectivityindex.com/index.html. Printed with permission.

fueling the growth of the CCI and in particular the E&M sector in Africa. There are rising rates of mobile penetration and internet access in Africa, though mobile phone penetration on the continent still lags behind that of every other region in the world. By 2025, Africa is expected to have 120 million new subscribers, leading to a total of 615 million.[71] In 2020, the Alliance for Affordable Internet, which measures the affordability of mobile broadband globally, found that Africa saw the greatest policy advances in achieving greater internet affordability compared with 2019.[72] The availability of information and communications technology (ICT) has already expanded the CCI in large economies like South Africa and Nigeria, but other countries are gaining ground and becoming better able to accommodate budding digital media and entertainment products. For instance, Ghana now has the highest mobile penetration in West Africa, at 55 percent of the population,[73] and its E&M market also has a higher projected CAGR relative to that of South Africa, Kenya, Nigeria, and Tanzania through 2023.[74] Figure 3-2 shows the degree of mobile internet penetration on the continent, where a total of eight countries are characterized as "transition" countries, or at the 3rd level of development on a scale of 5, as of 2019.[75] According to Conviva's research, the third quarter of 2021 saw a 273 percent increase in demand for streaming services in major African regions like South Africa, Nigeria, Egypt, and Kenya.

Dataxis, a global media and business analytics company, predicts that the industry will have over 15 million subscribers by 2026, a threefold increase in five years, after doubling between 2018 and 2021. The company attributes this growth to a fierce competition for viewers.[76]

The Shift to Digital Goods

The development in technology and internet access has opened up whole new segments of the CCI, including e-publishing, video streaming, and music streaming. Growth in these sectors has become the primary driver of many traditional industries. In South Africa, the electronic books sector represents a growth area, while the distribution of traditional printed books has declined, especially as schools and universities transition to using online publications.[77] In 2019, digital publications accounted for over half the revenues from imported professional books in the country.[78] The music and film industries also are becoming more reliant on technology, as music and movies are increasingly distributed via streaming platforms and online downloads. In fact, streaming revenues accounted for more than half of global recorded music revenue for the first time in 2019, illustrating the growing importance of streaming technologies.[79] The reliance of the film industry on digital platforms was compounded by the COVID-19 pandemic, which drove many studios to release new movies via streaming platforms in the wake of cinema closures.

In general, COVID-19 has accelerated the shift to digital goods, even in sectors of the CCI that traditionally would not be associated with the digital landscape. For instance, Africa's largest multiarts festival, the Grahamstown National Arts Festival in South Africa, shifted to hosting an eleven-day online event in 2020, selling tickets on a pay-per-view platform to view live and prerecorded performances, films, and even physical art. Ultimately, the rise of digital goods necessitates an integrated knowledge of technology and creativity in order to thrive within this sector. At the same time, the existence of creative goods and services on digital platforms allows for their near permanency and global distribution, thus increasing the overall potential for returns. For instance, the song "Jerusalem" by the South African artist Master KG boasted 143 million Spotify streams from 18.5 million listeners in ninety-two countries by the end of 2020.[80] Another music streaming service owned by the Chinese technology and media company Tencent, Joox was a success that greatly benefited from an increase in demand during COVID. Since its initial success, Joox is now trying to expand into more African markets.

Increasing competition among digital content providers has enabled the development of improved goods and services for consumers, creating a dynamic market that is highly responsive to consumer demand. One area that exemplifies this consumer market transition is the TV and video sub-industry. The reliance of this industry on new technology has created a niche market to which consumers have quickly adapted, leading developers to provide products and services that better fit their demands. In particular, individuals are seeking mobile viewing options that allow for more preferential, customized consumption, instead of the traditional focus on subscription services that offer access to a fixed range of content that may not align with a consumer's unique interests.[81]

Companies will need to innovate and create new products and user experiences that ensure their place in the market, while continually engaging with production and distribution partners in the E&M sector. African firms are on the precipice of developing integrated businesses with mobile technology, presenting opportunities for innovative investors to capitalize on this nascent market.

Digital Payment Platforms

The digital revolution in Africa has brought change to the CCI sector, and internet access has become just one instigator of this transformation. In terms of real economic growth, the introduction of digital payment platforms, by which consumers can immediately pay for media content from anywhere with internet access, is the new reality that businesses can take advantage of for greater revenue. Digital revenue compared with nondigital revenue has significantly different growth rates, with digital tending to have a significantly higher rate in major E&M markets on the continent.[82] For instance, as of 2023, the total share of entertainment and media revenues attributable to internet access in Nigeria was predicted to exceed 80 percent.[83]

The new digital payment reality opens an array of commercial opportunities for smaller firms that are intent on expanding their market access and consumer base. Digital payment is possible in almost every subindustry of the CCI, including music, film, physical art, video games, social media applications, and news, among others. In Kenya, the M-PESA digital payment platform allows for single-use payments to entertainment and media producers, as well as digital subscriptions to applications, streaming services, or other digital mediums of distributing creative and cultural goods. These mobile payment platforms also can reduce the need for consumers to curtail their purchases of cultural goods in the wake of economic hardships.

For instance, M-PESA mobile money was found to help families better cope with financial shocks like an unexpected illness without having to reduce their consumption, since they were able to borrow and transfer money from friends and family via the electronic platform.[84]

Consumer Market Growth

Consumer market growth and the rise of the middle class are primary drivers of the CCI, particularly in the context of E&M production. In Africa, the middle class has tripled, to 313 million (34 percent of the total population) over the past thirty years,[85] and the number of high- and middle-income consumers is projected to grow by 100 million by 2030. This growth will be accompanied by an increase in consumer spending, as Africa is expected to have an average growth rate of 5 percent, higher than the average 3.8 percent growth rate projected for the rest of the developing world.[86] In fact, by 2030, total consumer expenditures on the African continent are expected to reach a remarkable $2.5 trillion.[87] Membership in an income group has been found to be strongly correlated with spending on entertainment, even outstripping factors like age in determining spending.[88] Africa follows this trend, with cultural goods like African fashion expected to become increasingly in demand as the domestic middle class expands.[89]

As its consumer market grows, Africa is becoming increasingly powerful in shaping the landscape of the global CCI, as more companies seek to capitalize on this burgeoning market and appeal to local tastes. Netflix has increased its investments in producing original content on the continent, especially in the Nigerian and South African movie industries.[90] In 2020, the largest music label in the world, Universal Music Group (UMG), launched a stand-alone label, Def Jam Africa, to develop hip-hop, Afrobeats, and Trap music from African artists.[91] Aside from appealing to Africa's burgeoning consumer market, this focus on promoting local content has galvanized the spread of African CCI globally, as evidenced by the growing popularity of Nollywood films, the rising demand for African fashion prints, and the burgeoning interest in African art and music. In fact, South Africa saw its cultural goods exports grow a remarkable 14.6 percent a year between 2015 and 2018, a rate that is significantly faster than exports of other goods.[92]

The creative economy saw a large overall decline in 2020 (−6.6 percent, compared with −5.9 percent for the economy as a whole), after reaching a peak year-over-year growth rate of 3.4 percent in 2017. This decline was evident even before the pandemic. In 2020, CCIs directly contributed 2.97 percent, or about 3 percent of South Africa's GDP.[93] Ultimately, this globalization of African art and media encourages investment and further builds the consumer base to which African artists and media producers can market their products. The highest-grossing superhero movie of all time is the 2018 Hollywood blockbuster *Black Panther*, which featured African actors, music, and design influences. It earned more than $1.3 billion worldwide. The three biggest record companies in the world—UMG, Sony Music, and Warner Music Group—have all increased their presence in African markets over the past four years through the signing of African artists, purchases of African record labels, or the establishment of new offices there. In April, Apple Music expanded to thirty-seven additional African nations, and in May, Universal introduced its hugely popular Def Jam label to the continent. In the meantime, Netflix has been attempting to purchase and encourage the creation of African content.[94]

Advertising

Advertising revenue is a critical aspect of the CCI, particularly in the E&M sector. While access revenue through digital adoption is limited to first-time use, advertising has multiplying factors that increase revenue with both the initial and continued use of digital media. Where the rate of movement toward internet access revenue slows, consumer use and advertising potential increase, presenting opportunities for unlocking nascent revenue sources. Internet advertising represents a significant subsector for growth, controlling a steady 13 percent CAGR until 2022.[95] As of 2020, Africa's total annual advertising investment was over $10 billion, 40 percent of which was digital advertising. In the digital advertising market, 71 percent of total ad spending will be generated through mobile sources in 2026.[96] In 2018, TV and video represented the largest advertising segment in South Africa, Nigeria, Kenya, and Ghana, while radio was the largest segment in Tanzania.[97] Advertisers across the continent are gaining access to multiple platforms of consumers within the E&M sector, thus increasing the inherent persuasiveness of their campaigns and the potential for acquiring revenue. Internet advertising surpasses TV advertising in absolute growth, but both are critical for the sector due to linking to mobile devices.[98] The development of mobile applications on the continent is leading consumers to integrate media products into their everyday lives, through music streaming, and the consumption of cultural content on social media. Content generators are also increasingly able to access consumer data, gain insight into consumer demand, and generate new opportunities for revenue.[99] Since nearly half of African consumers have indicated that marketing messages have a significant impact on their

Figure 3-3. Entertainment and Media Market Growth in South Africa, Nigeria, and Kenya, 2022–27

Compound annual growth rate (%)

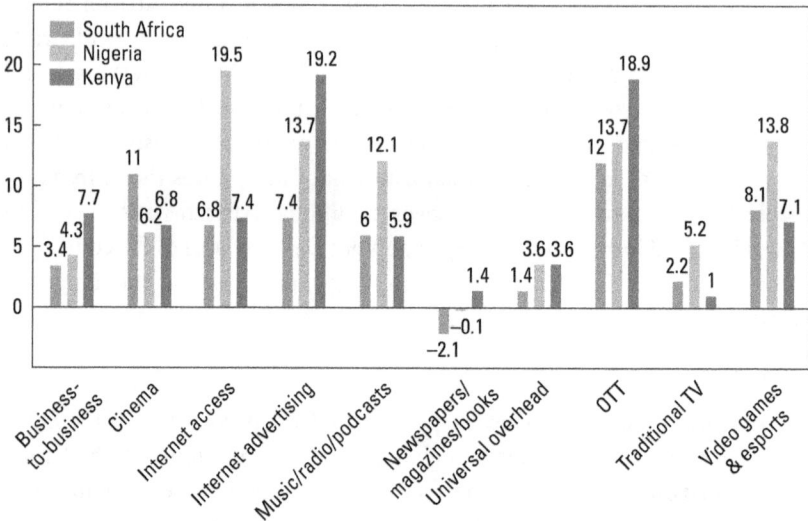

Source: Data are from PwC (2023).

purchasing behavior, companies looking to reach and influence consumers should increasingly demand advertising services.[100] Advertisers must become more adaptable to changing trends to tailor entertainment and cultural products to growing consumer classes (figure 3-3).

Key Players

The production of media and entertainment often requires high start-up capital. Films, music, and art are generated and distributed now in an era of high-cost technology, and their production is dependent on investments. Likewise, technology investments are key to shaping connectivity on the African continent, a crucial factor in the growth of streaming platforms and sectors like gaming. In 2020 just $22 million, or 1.1 percent of African start-up investment funding, was allocated to the entertainment sector.[101] We expect this to decrease, given the level of capital flight from the continent and the shift in investment priorities since the COVID-19 pandemic. To close these gaps and help creatives get a head start on building long-lasting careers, the HEVA Fund was established. It is the first fund on the continent devoted to extending the CCI. In order to help businesses survive the epidemic, it made investments in fifty enterprises, directly helped over ten thousand creative professionals. The fund works to offset foreign investors' risk aversion and disconnection from some aspects of the African economy.

International Media Companies

International media companies are increasingly looking to Africa and African artists as an opportunity for investment. Vivendi—a French media conglomerate that has operations in music, television and movies, publishing, and video games—is particularly active on the continent. As previously noted, the largest music label in the world, Vivendi's UMG, already is very active on the continent. The company already has divisions in Nigeria, Kenya, South Africa, Côte d'Ivoire, Senegal, Cameroon, and Morocco, and it has announced plans to expand further in Africa. Aside from targeting domestic consumers, UMG is moving toward marketing music by African artists globally, announcing a strategic partnership between Nigeria's Aristokrat Records and Universal Music France.[102]

Often, international media companies have to leverage partnerships and work creatively to bridge the gaps in infrastructure when operating in Africa. Vivendi's CANAL+ Group also represents the market leader in pay TV in Francophone Africa, boasting more than 4 million subscribers and reaching about 40 percent of households in 2018. Through its partnership with the data connectivity company SES, the company offers the largest amount of high-definition programming in Africa. [103] Vivendi also has one of the largest networks of theaters and live event venues in Africa with the CanalOlympia network, which span fourteen venues in ten countries and hosts films, live events, and even escape rooms.[104] By partnering with Bluestorage, CanalOlympia's cinemas are self-powered through solar, which allows a more reliable and accessible energy source compared with existing infrastructure, and the company's success has led to a planned expansion to fifty venues total.[105]

While there are challenges, international companies can have significant success when entering Africa, as evidenced by the case of Boomplay. Owned by the Chinese media company Trassnet Music Limited, Boomplay launched in Nigeria in 2015 and had grown to over 68 million users and 20 million songs in its catalogue by January 2020. In 2018, UMG was the first major international label to license its catalogue to Boomplay, which had become the largest streaming platform in Africa.[106] In the book publishing industry in South Africa, Pearson has captured the largest market share in the educational publishing segment, another success story considering that the book publishing market in the country largely is composed of educational materials.[107]

Netflix is another international giant looking to deepen its presence in Africa. In 2018, Netflix acquired its first original Nollywood film. In 2020, the streaming giant represented 57 percent of Africa's subscription video-on-demand subscribers. While its market share is projected to fall to 44 percent by 2026, its aggregate customer base will be 6.26 million subscribers, or triple its 1.99 million subscriber base in 2020.[108] It also recently announced a partnership with Africa's largest pay TV company, MultiChoice, to offer streaming services through MultiChoice's new decoder, alongside the company's own streaming platform Showmax.[109] Netflix is increasingly tailoring its subscription plans to the unique needs of the African consumer. As of 2020, Netflix was testing two cheaper, mobile-only subscription plans in most markets in Africa, acknowledging both the limitations of fixed broadband availability and the increased adoption of mobile phones on the continent.[110]

The demand for digital material was intensified by COVID-19 to the point where Netflix announced in April 2021 that it would reduce its bandwidth for African members by 25 percent in order to relieve and alleviate the strain on network infrastructure. The number of subscribers to this medium will rise as data prices in Africa continue to drop. Aside from Netflix, other streaming services are looking to enter the African region and capitalize on its large and growing customer base. In March 2019, Google's YouTube Music service entered the market, competing against other international companies like Spotify and Apple Music that had already entered the market.[111] Disney+ also entered the African market in 2022 and is projected to grow to 3.13 million subscribers by 2026.[112]

Government Cultural Ministries and Agencies

While the involvement of government is typically crucial to shaping the development of the CCI, government cultural ministries and agencies in Africa suffer from a dearth of financial support. The African Union declared 2021 to be the "Year of Arts, Culture, and Heritage," and the African Union champion for the year, transition president of Mali Bah Ndaw, highlighted the fact that most African countries make insufficient budgetary allocations to the culture sector, arguing in favor of allocating at least 1 percent of national budgets to the CCI.[113] According to UNESCO, insufficient funding significantly hinders the potential of the CCI to create beneficial growth and development on the continent.[114] In Kenya, for instance, the 2020 budget only allocated 0.16 percent of total national government expenditures to the Department for Culture and Heritage.[115] In Ghana, the numbers were similar in 2021, with the Ministry of Tourism, Culture, and Creative Arts having projected expenditures of about 0.17 percent of the total federal government budget.[116]

While many ministries suffer from a lack of sufficient funding, there is still progress being made on the continent. South Africa is one African country that has shown an increased interest in the potential of the CCI for contributing to long-term economic growth and job creation. In 2014, the South African Department of Sports, Arts, and Culture (DSAC) launched the South African Cultural Observatory (SACO) as part of its Mzansi Golden Economy Strategy, which promotes the arts, culture, and heritage sectors and CCI in order to stimulate the economy. In particular, SACO undertakes research on the specific impact of these industries on the overall economy, helping to provide a greater justification for their support.[117] In the wake of the COVID-19 pandemic, DSAC, in collaboration with the Department of Small Business Development, also established a fund to provide relief to the craft, design, audiovisual, and visual arts sectors.[118] In keeping with its growing interest in CCI, South Africa is one of the countries that has stepped up to support its struggling arts sector in the wake of the pandemic. For instance, DSAC has offered relief money for productions and live events that were disrupted due to the pandemic.[119] However, while South Africa is more aware of the socioeconomic benefits of the CCI, the country still allocated only about 0.3 percent of its national budget to DSAC in 2021/22.[120]

In order to be better equipped to promote the growth of the CCI in their respective countries, African governments' culture ministries and agencies ultimately need to receive greater financial support. At the same time, more African governments in countries like Burkina Faso, Cabo Verde, Côte d'Ivoire, Kenya, Mauritius, Nigeria, Senegal, South Africa, and Zimbabwe have stepped up to help the struggling arts sector in the wake of the COVID-19 pandemic, with some offering aid for the very first time. The ramped-up support as a result of the pandemic should be continued as a new reframing for how African governments allocate support to the CCI.[121]

Domestic Media Companies

Domestic media companies also play a powerful role in the E&M market in Africa and are valuable partners for international companies when entering the market due to their trusted brand names and local knowledge. For instance, domestic companies represent a large portion of the local music streaming market. A 2020 study of music streaming platforms found that of the over twenty-five companies in Africa, 72 percent were homegrown and only 28 percent were international companies.[122] Radio Audience Measurements estimated that South Africa, which has more than 100 radio stations, had an adult radio reach of 89 percent at the end of 2018, compared with Tanzania's 83 percent and Zambia's 85 percent. Because radios are more portable and significantly less expensive than televisions, rural areas in Africa vastly outpace urban areas in these statistics.[123] Naspers of South Africa is the largest and probably most famous African media company. Naspers is colloquially known as "Africa's SoftBank," for its wide-reaching global investment portfolio, with its most famous investment probably being its early stake in the Chinese media giant Tencent. However, Naspers' role in the CCI in Africa extends beyond its international investment activities. In particular, Naspers operates Media24, the largest publisher, printer, books and magazines distributor, and newspaper publisher in Africa.[124] As of 2020, Media24 was responsible for publishing about thirty magazines and eighty newspapers and has a robust digital media presence, generating nearly 17 million average daily page views across its digital platforms.[125] Within South Africa's book industry in particular, Media24's NB Publishers is an influential player and was the market leader in the general books segment in 2019.[126]

Naspers also was an influential player in the development of MultiChoice Group, with the pay TV company just gaining independence in 2019. MultiChoice group has seen significant growth in recent years, with the company adding 1.2 million 90-day active subscribers between September 2019 and 2020. Although challenged by COVID-19-induced lockdowns, the company made significant investments in filming local content, producing 1,870 hours in 2020 and growing its domestic content archives to nearly 59,000 hours.[127] The company's Showmax platform is actually projected to increase its paying subscriber count by 1 million by 2025, driven by its new Pro platform, which offers online sports streaming, and lower prices for mobile subscribers. Likewise, Showmax is able to extend its reach to additional households as a free extension for pay TV subscribers.[128]

Domestic players are increasingly partnering with international media companies, which recognize their influence in reaching the African consumer, and MultiChoice Group is a prime example. Aside from its aforementioned partnership with Netflix, MultiChoice has also announced plans to offer Amazon's streaming content through its Showmax platform, seeking to create a one-stop shop for African consumers and relieve pressure from competition from international streaming services by making them partners rather than adversaries.[129] Vivendi's Canal+ Group currently has a 31.7 percent stake in MultiChoice Group and has made an offer to fully acquire the group in 2024, acknowledging the rising demand for local content by consumers.[130]

Technology Investors

A key trend shaping the E&M market in Africa is the investment of technology companies in improving internet connection and access on the continent, which in turn enhances the ability of African consumers to obtain media products. Increased investment in technology infrastructure is crucial, since internet and mobile phone penetration have been shown to have an impact on foreign direct investment, producing positive effects on both GDP growth and GDP per capita, which in turn improves consumers' ability to purchase entertainment products.[131] The digital operator MTN is a big domestic player in investing in technology on the continent. Headquartered in South Africa, MTN operates in traditional telecommunications, digital infrastructure, and fintech, and it had over 288 million customers in eighteen markets in Africa and the Middle East in 2024.[132] Naspers also ranks as one of the largest technology investors in the world, and within South Africa, the company has established the Naspers Foundry to invest over $93 million in local tech start-ups.[133]

Investments in the cloud are increasingly driving the growth of the gaming sector in Africa. In May 2019, Microsoft was the first major cloud provider to open a data center in South Africa, leading a pack of companies entering the region that included Huawei and Amazon. Intel and Nvidia also have augmented investments in cloud gaming, illustrating the increasing competition in this sector on the continent. These investments should lead to fewer instances of service lags, which can benefit the growth of the gaming sector by ensuring that local gamers will no longer be hindered by these lags when competing.[134] Since the current online gaming market is fragmented but is expected to grow due to the increasing penetration of mobile applications, enhanced investments in the cloud will only help to drive this growth path.[135]

In general, tech investors are becoming increasingly interested in Africa as an investment target. Figure 3-4 shows the sustained increase in tech venture capital equity rounds between 2015 and 2020. In 2020, these 359 equity rounds led to total funding commitments of $1.4 billion, which was 29 percent lower than the previous year due to the effects of COVID-19.[136] As the impact of the pandemic lessens, this number has the potential to significantly

Figure 3-4. Africa Technology Venture Capital: Total Number of Equity Rounds, 2015–20

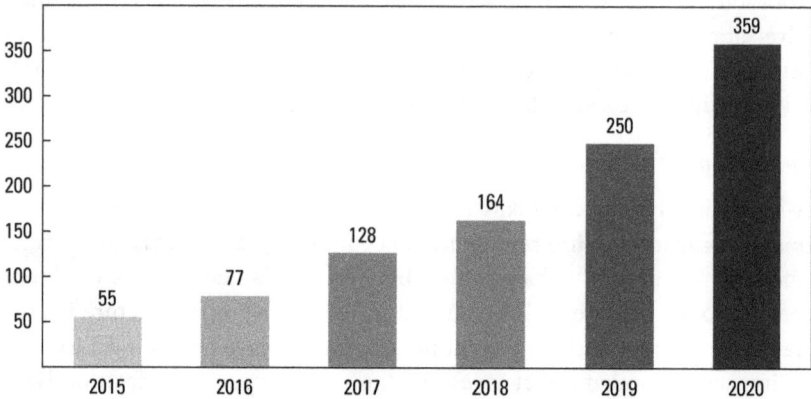

Source: Partech (2020).

increase. Since an investment of $109 billion is estimated to be necessary to ensure universal access to affordable, high-quality broadband internet, which consequently enables access to and growth of a plethora of subsectors of the CCI, technology investment will be crucial in shaping the growth of the CCI in the coming years.[137]

Opportunities

There are numerous opportunities on the continent for investors, firms, and individuals to capitalize on the growing importance of the CCI. While Africa's largest and most globally integrated economies are also more visible in this sector, giving South Africa and Nigeria the largest platform, other countries also are cultivating growth in their CCI, leading to opportunities throughout the continent. In particular, the E&M sector presents critical opportunities for investors and firms seeking visibility on the continent and in global markets. As of 2022, there are already an estimated 1.4 million subscribers in Sub-Saharan Africa, and by 2026, that number is expected to increase to 2.4 million.[138] Total OTT revenue outpaces the global projections in all three countries (Nigeria, Kenya, and South Africa; figure 3-5).

The CCI in South Africa has exhibited remarkable growth over the past few decades, becoming an increasingly important source of employment and economic development in the country. In 1995, South Africa's film industry employed only 4,000 people. As of 2017, the industry had grown to employ more

Figure 3-5. Total Over-the-Top Revenue (annual growth, 2019–27, global vs. selected African markets)

Global versus selected African markets, total OTT revenue, annual growth, 2019–27 (%)

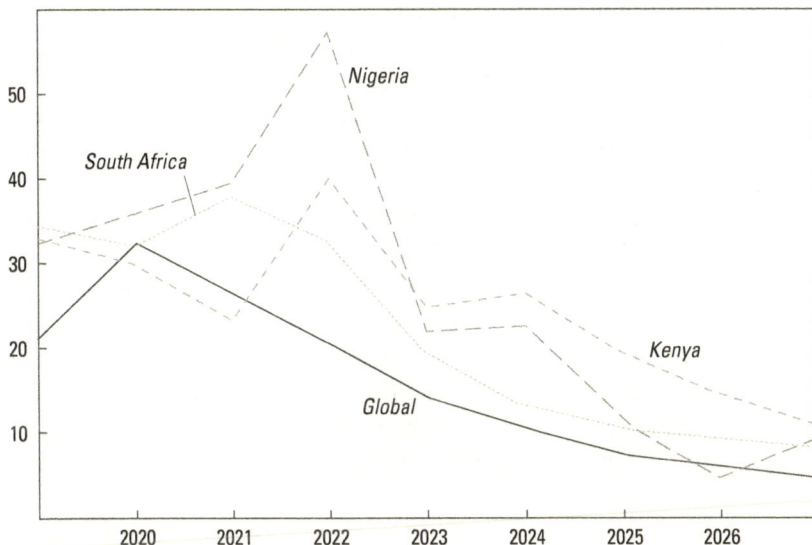

Source: PwC (2023).
Note: OTT = over-the-top video services.

than 21,000 people and contribute roughly $89 million to the country's GDP.[139] In 2018, the CCI as a whole directly accounted for 1.7 percent of South Africa's GDP, and in 2017, creative economy employment represented 7 percent of all jobs, over 0.8 percent higher than numbers in 2015.[140] The film business had 31,444 full-time employees before the COVID-19 pandemic, but 60 percent of those positions were lost as a result of it.[141] When considering direct, indirect, and induced effects of the CCI, 69 percent of GDP impact was found to result from multiplier effects, illustrating how growth in the CCI have spillover effects that benefit other parts of the South African economy as well.[142] This growth is projected to continue, as South Africa's E&M sector is estimated to reach about $12.9 billion by 2027, buoyed by increasing levels of internet access.[143] The South African Broadcasting Corporation's radio station Ukhozi FM has more than 7.7 million listeners, making it the biggest radio station in Africa.[144]

South Africa has become a hub for cultural events and festivals on the content. The country hosts the largest music festival in Sub-Saharan Africa, the Cape Town International Jazz Festival, which has affectionately become known as "Africa's Grandest Gathering," due to its large size and portfolio of well-known international and local performers.[145] This is relatively understandable, considering that South Africans were ranked as some of the most enthusiastic music consumers in the world based on a consumer study conducted by the International Federation of the Phonographic Industry in 2019.[146] The country also boasts the largest multiarts festival in Africa, the National Arts Festival (NAF) in Makhanda. Held for a period of eleven days, NAF typically attracts over 200,000 visitors to view over 2,000 performances, contributing about $24.7 million to the Eastern Cape Province in 2016.[147] In recent years, NAF has expanded to feature diverse subsets of the CCI, including music, dance, theater, and craft markets.[148]

Visual arts and design also represent an important area of growth and development. The South African government estimates that about 17,000 people work in the visual arts sector.[149] The country is now considered to be the leading arts market on the continent, with over ten auction houses and dozens of notable art galleries.[150] In 2017, the country saw the opening of the largest contemporary art museum in Africa, the Zeitz Museum of Contemporary African Art in Cape Town, a project that arose from a $38 million renovation of a grain silo complex,[151] and welcomed nearly 300,000 visitors in its inaugural year.[152] South Africa also is home to two of the top 100 architectural firms in the world, with local companies SAOTA and Boogertman + Partners being ranked 90 and 98, respectively, based on the number of fee-earning architects they employ.[153] Architecture should represent a growing opportunity, with the South African construction industry, reaching $25.5 billion in 2022,[154] driven in part by growth in residential sector construction due to competition between mortgage lenders and more favorable loan terms offered by banks.[155]

In the E&M market, revenue growth in South Africa can be attributed to internet access and changes in consumer demand. As the largest TV market on the continent, South Africa's economic growth is affected by TV market revenue from advertising and content production. Pay TV is one subsector that is projected to continue growing; it was at about 9 million households in South Africa as of 2022, and is projected to grow by 18 to 20 million by 2027. South African TV consumers are leading pay TV companies like MultiChoice to make deals with international sports and entertainment providers to air events, such as games for the UEFA Champions League and the English Premier League. Through this, the companies can provide consumers with desired content and strengthen their hold on the market.[156] This becomes increasingly important with the rising popularity of OTT services, with Netflix, MultiChoice's Showmax, YouTube Premium, and Amazon Prime Video all representing major players in the South African market.[157]

At the same time, a recent study found that OTT TV services were complements to rather than substitutes for pay TV services, with consumers of various socioeconomic backgrounds preferring different combinations of services, which indicates that both subsectors represent opportunities for growth.[158] In 2018, TV advertising remained a smaller proportion of total revenue, at just 24.5 percent, as internet was on the rise in its stead, increasing 24.2 percent from 2017 to 2018.[159] Public broadcasting is losing out against private providers in terms of financial gain; however, the South African Broadcasting Corporation has the highest all-day and prime time ratings, even with the entry of streaming services like Netflix and Amazon Prime Video.[160]

South Africa's film industry presents steady opportunities for investors and firms seeking high potential for growth. Box office sales and cinema advertising are two areas that bring in consistent revenue, although both have been hurt by the effects of the COVID-19 pandemic.[161] In addition, South African films are becoming more popular on the international stage. South African films and individuals have received some of the highest recognitions at global cinema awards shows, such as the drama *Inxeba*, which was nominated for an Oscar for a foreign language film. The film industry is dually important for infrastructure development and tax revenue for social services, contributing about $464 million in employment, taxes, and inward investment between 2016 and 2017.[162] In fact, the audiovisual and interactive media segment of the CCI in South Africa accounted for 11 percent of CCI's contributions to GDP, boasting the highest growth rate of all subsectors, at 5.9 percent a year.[163]

Nigeria

Within the larger CCI in Nigeria, mobile and internet access growth has had profound effects on the country's domestic entertainment and media sector's revenue, with ICT contributing three times the amount of revenue as oil and natural gas in Nigeria.[164] Data consumption was projected to hit a compound annual growth rate of 44.9 percent by 2023, as smartphones allow consumers to stream music, videos, and other media-sharing platforms.[165] Internet access and TV and video, in particular pay TV platforms, are the most profitable in Nigeria.[166] In fact, Nigeria will overtake South Africa in subscriber growth in the pay TV market on the continent by 2026, adding 11 million subscribers.[167] However, the market remains susceptible to decreases in oil prices—which can have serious, wide-reaching negative effects on the economy and reduce the funding available for infrastructure investments.[168] As a result, this fluctuation has limited the development of the country's broadband infrastructure, and its broadband access has not exceeded its high of 48 percent in 2023. Thus, the internet broadband area represents a significant opportunity for first movers to capitalize on a limited market and build the infrastructure necessary to expand broadband services and meet consumer demand.

Fashion represents a portion of the CCI in Nigeria that is an opportunity for growth and investment. Nigerian fashion has been gaining international recognition in recent years, especially since high-profile figures like Michelle Obama and Lupita Nyong'o have chosen to wear and promote Nigerian fashion designers.[169] Estimates from Nigeria's minister of information and culture indicated that the Nigerian fashion industry was worth $5 billion as of 2020, encompassing about 1,000 businesses that employed over 30,000 individuals.[170] Overall, the textile, apparel, and footwear sector has seen an average growth of 17 percent since 2010, with events like Lagos Fashion Week helping to attract international attention and drive demand.[171] At the same time, there are significant opportunities to grow the influence and profitability of the sector, as Nigeria still does not rank in the top ten apparel exporters in Sub-Saharan Africa.[172] While Nigeria was home to Africa's largest textile industry in the 1970s and 1980s, most of these firms have since closed, creating a dependence on imported fabrics and hindering sector growth.[173] Ramping up textile production through investments in Nigeria will help to address this barrier to growth in the fashion industry and present an opportunity for investors to achieve significant returns.

Infrastructure in Nigeria's film industry is another opportunity for investors and companies looking to expand an already-growing market. Projections indicate that if Africa as a whole were to invest broadly in cinema infrastructure, the continent has the potential to achieve annual box office revenues of $1.5 billion to $2 billion, with both Nigeria and South Africa making up about $500 million of this revenue.[174] Per 2021 estimates, Nigeria had only 1,653 cinema screens, which translates into 1 screen per 781,402 people, indicating the immense opportunity to enter this market or expand existing firms in the physical media sector.[175] According to UNESCO, 77 movie theaters were needed to accommodate a 200-million-person population in 2020.[176] Nollywood will continue growing as its films become more popular on the international stage, with the 2016 release of *The Wedding Party* noted for its success, even grossing a record $11.5 million domestically during an economic downturn.[177]

Films and broadband access growth are also indicators of the potential within the video game industry, as many video games are created based on already-existing cultural media and entertainment products. Nigeria's video game market is already sizable and was poised to reach a value of $483 million in 2023, with social/casual gaming becoming the largest and most important sector.[178] These industries hold enormous opportunities for employment generation, revenue growth, and general success compared with countries with less-established video-producing and distributing sectors. The Banker's Committee and the Central Bank of Nigeria collaborated in May 2019 to offer N22 billion to investors and entrepreneurs in the information technology and creative industries.[179] Uncoordinated value chains, underinvestment, antiquated rules, and lax enforcement of intellectual property laws need to stop draining Nigeria of much-needed funds. Nollywood movies were seen by 90.2 percent of Ghanaians and 65.4 percent of Beninese, according to a recent poll by Oluyemi Fayomi. This demonstrates how Africans' appetite for entertainment is expanding. This high percentage of viewers in these two nations may be related to the importance of Nollywood movies in Africa.[180] In February 2020, Netflix created "Netflix Naija," a Twitter account that details the company's plans for showing off its expanded investment in Nollywood. The existence of Netflix increases awareness of African films and, most crucially, lessens the negative effects of movie piracy in Nigeria.[181]

Kenya

Within the E&M sector, Kenya's business-to-business market overtook Nigeria's in 2018 to become the second-largest business-to-business market in Sub-Saharan Africa behind South Africa, boasting the fastest rate of expansion among all global economies.[182] This market encompasses business information services, directory advertising, trade magazines, and trade shows, and its projected growth creates a positive outlook for Kenya's E&M sector, particularly as the country integrates new technological innovations with its cultural promotion through art and other goods and services. From 2017 to 2022, Kenya's entertainment and media industry grew from a value of $1.6 billion to $2.7 billion.[183] Internet access is again the largest driver of growth, along with TV and radio providers, and these subsectors will continue to dominate advertisers' choices in the near future. Figure 3-6 illustrates Kenya's entertainment and media sector growth.

A lack of finance and the fragmented character of the cultural and creative spheres have been problems for Kenya. Although there have not been many artist-friendly policies, there is a lot of promise.[184] In each of its three

Figure 3-6. Kenya's Entertainment and Media Revenue, 2014–23 (millions of dollars)

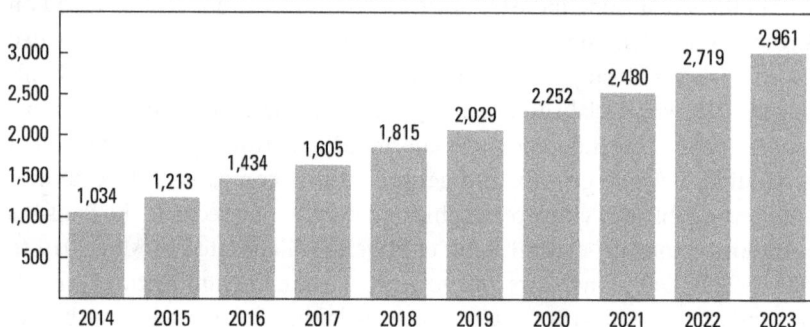

Source: PwC (2023).

cycles since 2015, Nairobi-based HEVA, Africa's first fund devoted to products and services of the creative and cultural kind, raised between $200,000 and $500,000 as of January 2019. Over 8,000 creative professionals have received direct help from it, and it has invested in 40 start-ups. This fund will assist in addressing the issue of artistic livelihood and commercially viable ventures that might make Kenya a popular destination for international art and entertainment.

Challenges and Risks: Intellectual Property Rights and Piracy

Research has shown that copyright protections are a necessary ingredient to foster viable growth in CCI sectors like music in developing countries.[185] However, recent bills have raised questions about the security of intellectual property rights on the African continent. The International Intellectual Property Alliance (IIPA) returned South Africa to its watch list in 2018, citing three problematic bills in recent years that have had a detrimental impact on copyrights and moved the country further away from international norms.[186] As of 2021, South Africa's growing intellectual property risk had caused the country to be placed on IIPA's priority watch list, while Kenya had entered its regular watch list.[187]

Across the CCI in Africa, piracy and copyright infringements represent a significant threat, but there is a lack in institutions and procedures to address this issue. One of the primary challenges facing music streaming start-ups in Africa is piracy, as their music catalogue often becomes a prime target for pirates.[188] While Nollywood is a driver of the Nigerian economy and employment, its impact is also severely limited by piracy. After its release, a new Nollywood film automatically hits a so-called revenue ceiling, when pirated copies begin to circulate, and this often occurs a couple of days after its official release.[189] In fact, the World Bank has estimated that for every legitimate copy sold of a Nollywood film, nine others are pirated copies; and UNESCO estimates that 50 to 75 percent of movie revenues from African producers are lost to piracy.[190] Piracy also affects the publishing industry, with writers less motivated to write when the royalties they see are lessened by sales of pirated copies. In fact, Nigerian publishers lose over 40 percent of their revenues to pirated sales.[191]

Strategies and Risk Management

The CCI in Africa represent a significant opportunity for governments and businesses alike to drive socioeconomic development and high returns, and strategies can be put in place to mitigate the current barriers to growth and risks in the sector.

Embracing Online Channels

To address the threat of epidemics, African businesses need to invest in building up their online capabilities to be able to flexibly reach consumers through a plethora of different sales channels. This will ensure steady revenue streams, even when consumers cannot access creative economy products and services in person, as during the COVID-19 pandemic. Likewise, online channels can augment sales by providing consumers with another avenue to purchase products, even when in-person options are available. During the COVID-19 pandemic, many sectors of the CCI utilized online channels to mitigate the economically disastrous effects of the pandemic. For instance, the Nigerian apparel and footwear market saw a negative impact on sales due to distribution challenges during lockdowns at the beginning of the pandemic. In response to the challenge, retailers shifted to using e-commerce channels, innovatively using third-party e-commerce sites to reach consumers and reduce the calamitous impact of lockdowns.[192] In the visual arts sector, the Circle Art Gallery set a record in October 2020 by holding Kenya's first online art auction, achieving a 90 percent sell-out rate and raising over $128,000 in sales to provide needed relief to this struggling sector.[193] As Africa emerges from the pandemic, the rising influence of online sales channels is expected to continue, further necessitating a strong response by businesses in the CCI. In South Africa, a survey by Deloitte found that two in three respondents planned to shop more online in 2021, with fashion being one of the most popular products for online pur-chases.[194] As a result, investing in online channels is necessary, not only to address the risks associated with epidemics but also to address changing con-sumer purchasing habits.

Improving Government Policy and Protections for Intellectual Property

African governments need to take action to cultivate a business environment that encourages the development of and investment in the CCI. The lack of a cohesive policy for the music industry limits its role in the continent's eco-nomic development.[195] Previous research has found that while there are poli-cies in place in Sub-Saharan Africa to protect intellectual property (IP), they are ineffectual, with many innovators not using IP protections because they are not aware of their existence or because enforcement is inadequate.[196] The African Union's revised Plan of Action on Cultural and Creative Industries includes a focus on protecting IP rights, and this is a step in the right direc-tion.[197] However, individual African countries need to strengthen the institu-tions in place that enforce IP law and combat piracy, along with codifying clear IP guidelines into law that creators can understand and easily use.[198]

Aside from strengthening IP protections, African governments need to devote more funding to building the infrastructure needed to support the CCI. Considering the fact that many governments do not allocate even 1 percent of their annual budgets to the CCI, there needs to be a reevaluation of budget-ary priorities to support the CCI, especially considering its role in promoting job creation and socioeconomic development and the challenges many CCI sectors faced during the COVID-19 pandemic.[199] Additionally, governments need to institute business-friendly policies and regulations that promote inno-vation and development and consider the needs of entrepreneurs, investors, and other stakeholders.[200]

Looking to the Future

The renaissance of the CCI in Africa can only continue, presenting oppor-tunities for businesses, governments, and private citizens alike. By 2030, Africa's growing consumer market will reach over 1.7 billion consumers, with a pocketbook of $2.5 trillion.[201] This burgeoning consumer market is increasingly demanding creative products, especially as infrastructure improvements allow them to access the CCI via diverse channels. Afreximbank, the African Export-Import Bank, established a $500 million loan facility for African cultural and creative items in January 2020 as the financial infrastructure developed.[202] The internet economy has the potential to add $180 billion to Africa's GDP by 2025.[203] As technology adoption accelerates on the continent, the CCI will be transformed, with new, nascent industries coming into the forefront.

The animation, gaming, and visual effects sector is an area of the CCI that can only grow. While globally valued at $264 billion in 2019, the sector is just beginning on the African continent but has great potential, as evidenced by the fact that two African-made animation movies have become the third- and fourth-best-grossing films in South African history.[204] The rising young population of Africa, coupled with increasing access to technology like the multifunctional gaming console, also is expected to drive a 12 percent CAGR in the African gaming industry through 2026.[205] With the rise in 5G technology, mobile gaming and in particular mobile e-sports also will increase their influence.[206]

Africa also is poised to retake power over its heritage, enriching the museum and visual arts sectors of the CCI. Roughly 90 to 95 percent of African heritage is housed outside the continent, a legacy of colonization that resulted in the plundering of artifacts and artwork by colonizers.[207] Now, however, there is a growing movement to repatriate this heritage, especially in the wake of the spread of the Black Lives Matter social justice protests in the summer of 2020.[208] In April 2021, Germany became the first national government to set a timeline for returning some of this looted art, the Benin Bronzes, which were pillaged during a 1897 British raid in what is now the country of Nigeria. Repatriating these artifacts will grow the number and quality of museums on the continent, as evidenced by the fact that the repatriated Benin Bronzes are set to be housed in the newly designed Edo Museum of West African Art in Benin City.[209]

In the end, if governments and businesses take action to support the CCI in Africa, its growth has the potential to support wide-reaching, equitable socioeconomic development on the continent. Since the CCI tends to employ more young and underrepresented populations like women than other sectors, the CCI can promote equality and the creation of high-quality jobs for Africa's growing young workforce.[210] Likewise, developing the CCI can have spillover effects that benefit other areas of the economy, especially the secondary sector.[211] While there are challenges and risks that represent barriers to growth, there are strategies that businesses and policymakers can use to overcome these challenges, including diversifying the ways businesses reach consumers via online channels and improving the business environment for CCI companies. Ultimately, if leveraged correctly, the CCI represent an opportunity for businesses, governments, and consumers alike to promote development and reap significant benefits from the expansion of the creative economy on the African continent.

Notes

1. UNCTAD (2019b, 2021b). International Finance Corporation (n.d.).
2. Deloitte (2021).
3. International Finance Corporation (n.d.).
4. McKee (2014).
5. UNCTAD (2008).
6. Andersson and Andersson (2006).
7. UNDP (2023).
8. M'Hammdi and Jaïdi (2023).
9. Manyika et al. (2013).
10. Bonsundy-O'Bryan and Bonsundy-O'Bryan (2024).
11. Signé (2020).
12. Nex Media (2023).
13. Nex Media (2023).
14. Buse (2020).
15. Buse (2020).
16. Slavova and Okwechime (2016).
17. Reis et al. (2008).
18. African Union (n.d.).
19. These countries are Morocco, Namibia, Kenya, Ethiopia, South Africa, the Democratic Republic of Congo, Egypt, Cabo Verde, Ghana, Nigeria, Congo, and Equatorial Guinea.
20. See the Connect for Culture Africa site: https://cfcafrica.org/project-brief/.
21. UNCTAD (2022b).
22. M'Hammdi and Jaïdi (2023).
23. EY (2015).
24. Hruby (2018, 5).
25. Erraji (2023).
26. Koigi (2021).
27. IFPI (2016); Pareles (2020).
28. Adams & Adams (n.d.).
29. Enos (2023).
30. SACO (2020a).
31. Cirisano (2020).
32. Cirisano (2020).
33. United Nations (2009).
34. AfDB (n.d.–a).
35. African Business (2014).

36. PwC (2020b).

37. PwC (2019, 74).

38. PwC (2019, 75).

39. See the statistics at https://www.statista.com/outlook/dmo/digital-media/video-on-demand/nigeria.

40. Ipsos (2018).

41. Ipsos (2018).

42. World Economic Forum (2017a).

43. World Economic Forum (2017b).

44. World Economic Forum (2017a).

45. PwC (2019, 23).

46. EY (2015).

47. African Union (2021a).

48. Solutions for Youth Employment (2021).

49. Kabanda (2014).

50. Abisuga-Oyekunle and Sirayi (2018).

51. Department of Sports, Arts, and Culture (2020, 33).

52. SACO (2022).

53. Onu (2023).

54. PwC (2017).

55. Augoye (2023).

56. AfDB (n.d.–a).

57. AfDB (n.d.–a).

58. AfDB (2018b).

59. Department of Trade and Industry and Invest South Africa (2020).

60. AFDB (n.d.–b).

61. Dakora (n.d.).

62. World Economic Forum (2017c).

63. Signé (2022b).

64. Buckingham and Scanlon (2000); Okan (2003, 1–2).

65. Anderson and Subrahmanyam (2017).

66. Kearney and Levine (2019).

67. Subrahmanyam and Renukarya (2015).

68. Business Wire (2020).

69. Ogunmilade (1979); Ajayi-Dopemu (1985).

70. IFPI (2019).

71. FurtherAfrica (2022).

72. Alliance for Affordable Internet (2020).

73. Omondi (2020).

74. PwC (2019).

75. See the GSMA Mobile Connectivity website: https://www.mobileconnectivityindex.com/index.html.

76. Onyango (2022).
77. Business Wire (2020).
78. Business Wire (2020).
79. IFPI (2020).
80. SACO (2020a).
81. PwC (2017).
82. PwC (2017).
83. PwC (2017).
84. Hattingh, Leke, and Russo (2017).
85. AFR-IX Telecom (2022).
86. Aykut and Blaszkiewicz-Schwartzman (2018).
87. World Economic Forum (2017a).
88. Lobaugh, Stephens, and Simpson (2019).
89. AfDB (n.d.–b).
90. Kazeem (2020).
91. Universal Music Group (2021).
92. SACO (2020a).
93. SACO (2022).
94. Hruby (2020).
95. PwC (2016a).
96. Nwora (n.d.).
97. PwC (2019, 7).
98. PwC (2019, 7).
99. PwC (n.d.).
100. Nielsen (2014).
101. Gachara (2020).
102. Gachara (2020).
103. SES (2019).
104. See CanalOlympia's citation at https://www.canalolympia.com/en/about/.
105. Bluestorage (n.d.).
106. See Bloompay's site: https://www.boomplay.com/about/.
107. Business Wire (2020).
108. Digital TV Research (2021a).
109. Bloomberg (2020).
110. Kazeem (2020).
111. PwC (2019).
112. Digital TV Research (2020).
113. African Union (2021b).
114. UNESCO (2021).
115. National Treasury of Kenya (2020).
116. Government of Ghana (2021).
117. SACO (n.d.).

118. Department of Sports, Arts, and Culture and Small Business Development (2020).

119. Department of Sports, Arts, and Culture and Small Business Development (2020).

120. National Treasury of the Republic of South Africa (2021).

121. Joffe (2021).

122. WT Research (2020).

123. Grange (2020).

124. Reuters (2020).

125. Naspers (2020).

126. Business Wire (2020).

127. MultiChoice Group (2020).

128. Digital TV Research (2021a).

129. Bloomberg (2020).

130. Goodfellow (2024).

131. Asongu and Odhiambo (2020b).

132. MTN Group Limited (2020).

133. Naspers (2020). Author's calculation using an exchange rate of R1 = $0.067 (the spot exchange rate on March 26, 2021).

134. PwC (2019, 105).

135. Mordor Intelligence (n.d.).

136. Partech (2020).

137. Broadband Commission (2019).

138. Roxborough (2022).

139. Urban-Econ Development Economists (2017); calculated using an exchange rate of $1 to R13.65 (the rough spot rate on December 31, 2016).

140. SACO (2020b).

141. News24 (2021).

142. News24 (2021).

143. PwC (2023).

144. See Ukhozi FM's statistics at https://www.ukhozifm.co.za/ukhozifm/about-us/.

145. See the Cape Town International Jazz Festival's page at https://www.cape townjazzfest.com/about-us/.

146. IFPI (2019).

147. See the website https://nationalartsfestival.co.za/about-us/.

148. SACO (2018); calculated using a spot rate of R1 = $15.23 (the rough spot rate in 2016).

149. South African Government (2010).

150. Mutu (2020).

151. Katz (2017).

152. Zeitz Museum (2019).

153. Building Design (2021).

154. See the data at https://www.globaldata.com/store/report/south-africa-construction-market-analysis/.
155. PR Newswire (2020b).
156. Business Wire (2023).
157. Udoakpan and Tengeh (2020).
158. PwC (2018).
159. PwC (2019, 19).
160. PwC (2018).
161. PwC (2020b).
162. PwC (2018).
163. SACO (2020b).
164. Jaiyeola (2023).
165. PwC (2019, 66).
166. PwC (2019, 24).
167. Digital TV Research (2021b).
168. Adedokun (2018).
169. Ndukwe (2020).
170. APA (2020).
171. Akinsola (2019).
172. AfDB (n.d.–b).
173. Isaac (2019).
174. 234 Media (2018).
175. Esther (2023).
176. Akan (2022).
177. Vourlias (2017).
178. Ayo-Odewale (2022).
179. Koigi (2021).
180. Fayomi (2015).
181. *Ventures Africa* (2021).
182. PwC (2019).
183. PwC (2019).
184. *Ventures Africa* (2021).
185. Andersen, Z. Kozul-Wright, and R. Kozul-Wright (2000).
186. IIPA (2018).
187. IIPA (2021).
188. WT Research (2020).
189. Paulson (2012).
190. Mgbolu (2024); Moudio (2013).
191. Tagholm (2019).
192. Euromonitor International (2021).
193. Mutu (2020).
194. Schaefer and Bulbulia (2021).

195. Solutions for Youth Employment (2021).
196. Adegoke (2011).
197. African Union (2021a).
198. Adegoke (2011).
199. African Union (2021b).
200. Wolken (2020).
201. World Economic Forum (2017a).
202. Afreximbank (2020).
203. Google and IFC (2020).
204. African Union (2021a).
205. Mordor Intelligence (n.d.).
206. PwC (2019).
207. Sarr and Savoy (2018).
208. Gbadamosi (2020).
209. Marshall (2021).
210. EY (2015).
211. Department of Trade and Industry and Invest South Africa (2020).

Four
Africa's Health Care and Pharmaceuticals Potential
TRENDS, DRIVERS, OPPORTUNITIES, AND STRATEGIES

Africa's health care and pharmaceutical industries are poised for profound transformation as the continent seeks to meet the health demands of its surging population, strengthen the resilience of their health systems, and drive health care innovation and discovery, given their critical importance for well-being and economic performance.[1] By 2030, Africa will be home to 14 percent of the world's health and well-being business opportunities,[2] second only to North America, with a total market value of $259 billion.[3] By 2050, household spending on health care could exceed $623 billion.[4]

Many countries have primarily tropical climates, which only increases the incidence of infectious disease, particularly malaria, tuberculosis (TB), and other outbreaks of cholera, hepatitis, yellow fever, and influenza. Thus, where countries face a high risk of disease outbreaks, recent upticks in economic growth suggest a corresponding increase in lifestyle diseases, such as cardiovascular disease, diabetes, and cancer.[5] By 2050, people over 60 years of age will make up 13 percent of the total African population, or 163 million people, and this trend—combined with ongoing lifestyle changes—is exacerbating the rapid rise in noncommunicable diseases (NCDs) like diabetes and cardiovascular disease, which already constitute 21 percent of the region's disease burden. Projections show that by 2030, NCDs will account for half of all deaths on the continent and will double again by 2060, when the region's life expectancy is expected to surpass seventy years.[6] Thus, Africa's expanding, urbanizing, and aging middle class will continue to push for reliable access to good-quality health care.[7]

Africa's health sector requires significant investment—both financial and political—as countries' economies start experiencing a surge of interest from investors, development organizations, financial institutions, and global entrepreneurs. WHO estimates that the investment gap in Africa's national health systems stands at $140 billion, with demand already vastly outstripping supply.[8] Many African countries have been working to scale up their infrastructure and institutional systems to better provide for persistent health care challenges. The region carries 25 percent of the global disease burden, despite having only 17 percent of the world's population.[9] There has been an obvious increase in the amount of health care and pharmaceuticals, as well as government capacity to provide health care as an essential human right. Improved health leads to better life expectancy, educational performance, increased savings and investment, decreased debts and health care expenditures, and increased productivity. A healthy population is an important investment for African governments, and international investors would be wise to capitalize on this growing market.

Africa's vaccines and medicines market is worth $50 billion annually.[10] The need for imported pharmaceuticals represents a real opportunity for investment in domestic manufacturing and distribution across the continent. Uganda is one example of the market potential to fulfill the high demand for pharmaceutical products, of which 90 percent are imported into the country for NCDs and long-term illnesses that are becoming more prevalent.[11] The challenges experienced during the COVID-19 pandemic, from inadequate health infrastructures to fragmented regulatory systems, have been a catalyst for Africa to accelerate the development of sustainable health care ecosystems. While the pandemic set the continent, and the world, back from achieving the UN Sustainable Development Goals (SDGs) related to health, it also renewed much-needed attention on the importance of investing in health, which has led to new business opportunities on the continent. The continent's growing business environment and the harmonization of regulations accelerated by the implementation of the African Continental Free Trade Agreement (AfCFTA) is contributing to the rapid growth of the health care sector, showcasing that it is possible to overcome market constraints with harmonized regulation, increased investment in production and supply chains, and more private sector involvement.

There are investment opportunities in both the public and private sectors, as governments will need to develop drug volume monitoring systems to track pharmaceutical production quality and distribution procedures. Kenya and Nigeria are two of the largest growing pharmaceutical markets in Sub-Saharan Africa, while other African countries will benefit from greater production, particularly with increased continental and regional trade and the growth of local production of medicines and vaccines which is one goal of AfCFTA.[12] By overcoming challenges to local production, AfCFTA will help unlock opportunities for investment in local value chains in areas with high-value-added potential, including vaccines, medical instruments, and packaged and unpackaged medicines.[13] Health and pharmaceutical firms and investors should look to the continent to capture market potential.

Background Facts and Trends

Substantial progress has been made on several health indicators in Africa over the past fifty years, yet challenges remain to reach the SDGs related to health. Africa experienced the greatest growth in healthy life expectancy in the world from 2000 to 2019, rising from 46 to 56 years, while also making progress in the under-five mortality rate and other health indicators due to investment in access to care and disease prevention services.[14]

There has also been noticeable improvement in the burden of communicable diseases in the region as a result of its more robust health and pharmaceuticals sector. Despite seeming to reach a crisis point in the early 2000s, there has been substantial progress in combating the HIV/AIDS epidemic over the past decade. In 2010, Eastern, Southern, Western, and Central Africa accounted for 68 perent of global HIV infections, but significant investment reduced their share to 50 perent as of 2022.[15] HIV fell from the leading cause of death in Africa in 2000 to the fourth leading cause in 2019.[16]

Meanwhile, the incidence of malaria and TB in Africa has decreased significantly since the 1990s. From 2010 to 2019, the malaria incidence cases per 1,000 people decreased from 363 to 225, yet in 2019, 94 perent of global malaria cases were found in Africa.[17] Many other preventable and tropical diseases—like polio, leprosy, guinea worm, and river blindness—have been all but been eliminated. Moreover, in response to the Ebola outbreak that shocked the world in its intensity and geographic spread, the regional-level Integrated Disease Surveillance and Response strategy was effectively implemented to improve the detection of, reporting of, and coordinated response to emergency diseases.[18]

Although Africa's health figures are currently improving more rapidly than those of any other region in the world, the continent still lags far behind other world regions across a range of indicators, including other developing countries. Africa remains the region with the highest neonatal mortality rates (26 deaths per 1,000 live births) and the highest under-five mortality rate (70 deaths per 1,000 live births).[19] In 2022, Africa accounted for over half of the global under-five deaths, despite accounting for only 30 perent of global live births.[20] According to WHO, just half of all live births in Africa are attended by skilled health personnel, and far fewer women than that receive antenatal care coverage.[21] Although all but six African countries met the goal of reversing the incidence of HIV by 2015,[22] Southern and Eastern Africa are home to 53 perent of the global population living with HIV, and 15 countries have an HIV prevalence above 3.5 perent.[23]

While population growth, violent conflict, epidemiological emergencies, and especially the HIV epidemic have all exacerbated these disappointing patterns, much of the global comparison masks variation within Africa. The regional average tends to be pulled down by poor performers, such as Zimbabwe, Lesotho, and Swaziland, where mortality rates are actually increasing, and places where progress has lagged substantially due to the heavy disease burden, especially in Central Africa.[24] The Democratic Republic of Congo (DRC), the Central African Republic (CAR), and Cameroon, for example, have all exhibited less than 5 percent improvement in infant mortality since 1990. This region also exhibits some of the lowest numbers for life expectancy: in 2023, just 53.8 in Nigeria, 55.4 years in CAR, 53.67 in Chad and DRC, 54.9 in Lesotho, 59.5 in Guinea, and 56.5 in South Sudan.[25] In contrast, people born in North Africa and the island nations—including Mauritius, Seychelles, Cabo Verde, Algeria, Egypt, Libya, Morocco, and Tunisia—can expect to live more than 70 years—about equal to the global average.[26]

In fact, within Africa, the most significant progress in health to date has been made in North Africa. Over the last twenty-five years, North Africa's maternal mortality rate has decreased by 66 percent, compared with 44 percent in Sub-Saharan Africa, while the under-five mortality rate has improved by 50 percent. Other impressive performers in Africa include Sierra Leone, where the maternal mortality rate (MMR) decreased by half between 1990 and 2015, from a global high of 26.3 per 1,000 live births to 1,360, as well as Eritrea and Mozambique, where the MMR declined by roughly 75 percent over the same period.[27] In Ghana, the MMR has fallen by almost one-third since 1990, from 5 deaths per 1,000 live births to less than 3.4, as a result of the national policy exempting women from delivery-care fees.[28]

Africa also lags behind the world in the average bed-to-population ratio with all countries except for South Africa falling below the global average.

This will only continue to rise if not met with significant investment as the population grows. For example, in Nigeria, it is estimated that $82 billion is needed to meet the global average bed ratio to keep pace with current population growth.[29] Similarly, Africa struggles with health human capital, as it is the region with the lowest density of skilled health professionals in the world.[30]

In 2001, African Union member states committed themselves to raising government spending on health to 15 percent of national budgets, but most countries still fall short of this target, many allocating less than 5 percent. Only South Africa and Cabo Verde met this target in 2021, leading the African Union to recommit to this target in 2023.[31] As a result, health care access in Africa is heavily dependent on assistance from international donors and aid agencies, along with out-of-pocket payments for services, which places a significant strain on low-income households. Yet, despite decades of foreign aid, few countries in the region meet the minimum $34–$40 a year per capita in spending considered necessary by WHO to provide basic health care.[32] Meanwhile, nearly half the population of Sub-Saharan Africa lacks access to clean water or sanitation services, which is an increasingly pressing health concern considering the rapidly expanding populations of the region's urban slums.

As a result of the remaining gaps in infrastructure and government spending, a consensus is emerging that the private sector will be key to the region's ability to overcome remaining health challenges and meet future development targets.[33] Although Africa's health sector has historically been neglected by private investors in favor of industries like telecommunications and oil and mineral extraction, private health companies are being increasingly integrated due to the implementation of AfCFTA, deregulation of the industry, tax exemptions and other government incentives, technological innovation, and supply chain development.[34] A domestic pharmaceutical industry designed to serve local needs is on the rise in countries like Kenya and Nigeria, with many other emerging markets likely to follow suit.

The Sector's Importance

Recent studies have begun relating measures of individual and societal health to changes in economic growth. WHO estimates that for every $1 invested in health, the return is about $9.[35] As African countries' economies grew from high prices in export commodities, an explosion of natural resources, and improved governance, Africa's development outlook improved, particularly regarding global health standards. However, when world prices for oil and minerals collapsed in 2016, overall growth in Sub-Saharan Africa declined to

1.5 percent—the lowest since the 1980s.[36] The resulting health crisis, based on poor incumbent systems and then a lack of available financing for overall health care throughout the continent, have only been exacerbated by natural disasters, disease outbreaks, and armed conflict that have dismantled health infrastructure. Among Africa's diverse economies, different approaches have been taken to address existing health challenges. Some reforms take a "vertical" approach, which target specific disease outcomes and intentionally address the factors that spread disease and impediments to treatment.[37] Other governments and health care practitioners implement "vertical" programs that are intended to improve the entire health system, from the factors that increase disease prevalence to the prevention of future illness.

African countries have made strides to modernize and elevate their health sectors to a priority for policymaking, investment, and innovation. However, data on viral disease prevalence, rising percentages of NCDs, and stories about incomplete health care systems all reveal the extent of work that is still necessary to better treat patients across the continent. Risk factors for NCDs are steadily increasing, based on surveys done in Cameroon, the Republic of Congo, Eritrea, and Mozambique, which counteract improvements in treatment as a result of an increasing number of consumers.

External risk factors are also affecting the health sector's development, such as in Uganda, where injuries from road traffic collisions cost the economy $84 million each year, or 5 percent of the country's gross domestic product (GDP).[38] Inefficiencies are also leading to lost potential. As of 2024, Africa's health systems are only 77 percent efficient, according to WHO, meaning that $1 of $5 spent on health is lost due to inefficiencies such as technical or workforce challenges.[39] As the continent faces growing population and economic changes in the globalized world, the health sector has immense potential to benefit from technological, political, social, and economic transformation.

The continent's overall economic growth is driving investment and business opportunities in every sector. Health care companies are increasingly looking to Africa as a place for future investment because it is one of the few places that can still achieve double digit growth. Life science logistics, encompassing the pharmaceutical and medical device supply chain, has changed significantly within the last five years. Import hubs are growing, particularly in Kenya, which then distributes shipments throughout East Africa and South Africa, as well as other countries that have the new capability to receive shipments directly.[40] As the infrastructure sector changes, there will be greater opportunity to incorporate the health sector into broad economic policies that prioritize efficient health care for all levels of society.

General economic growth is said to increase the demand among all sectors of society for health care.[41]

The health sector is critical for economic growth, just as the sector benefits from improvements in other sectors. A healthy society is essential for stability and economic improvements because improved health can lead to a greater life expectancy, increased productivity, better educational performance, and less debt within the health care system.[42] The health sector is also being considered more and more as a productive sector with the potential to create a significant number of jobs. The health and pharmaceutical sector on the continent could provide about 2 to 3 million jobs for young Africans.[43] Increased investment in health could translate into hundreds of billions of dollars a year of additional income, which could be redistributed to address external factors that have an impact on the health of citizens throughout the continent. Achieving the SDGs related to health care on the continent would save about 47 percent of the lost productivity from health burdens, amounting to about $796 billion, which could be reinvested in other priorities.[44] The health and pharmaceuticals sector is part of the transformation of Africa's emerging markets, providing opportunities for research and development, manufacturing, sales, and distribution, in addition to professional services in hospitals, health insurance markets, and medical education.

Key Drivers

There are six key drivers in the health and pharmaceuticals sector. These drivers include endogenous factors that are transforming the sector from within, such as education and social determinants of patients, including their nutrition and social factors. The exogenous factors driving the growth of the health sector—such as infrastructure changes, urbanization, and changing demand—are responsible for creating new access points for patients to the health services and pharmaceuticals sector. These external factors have the potential to transform the sector in exponential proportions to enable African industries to make the transition to maturation, development, and sustainable innovation. Figure 4-1 outlines the development stage of domestic pharmaceutical industries and notes the progress of Sub-Saharan African industries thus far.

While figure 4-1 specifically refers to the pharmaceutical industry, the stages of development it shows reflect the factors that have driven African markets to their current stage of development. Amid changing factors, these markets are growing and indicate the potential of the health and pharmaceutical sector.

Figure 4-1. Stages of the Pharmaceutical Industry's Development in Sub-Saharan Africa

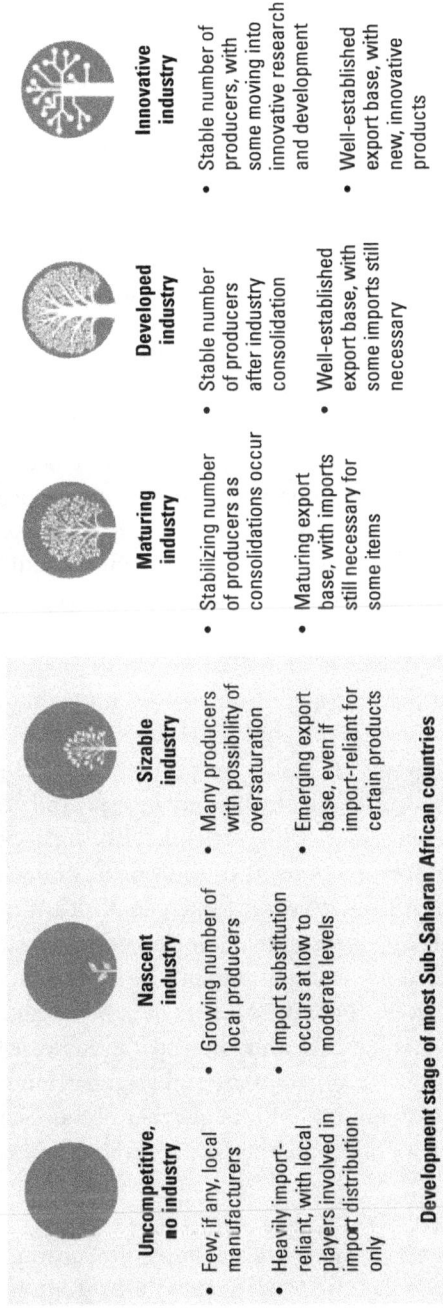

Uncompetitive, no industry
- Few, if any, local manufacturers
- Heavily import-reliant, with local players involved in import distribution only

Nascent industry
- Growing number of local producers
- Import substitution occurs at low to moderate levels

Sizable industry
- Many producers with possibility of oversaturation
- Emerging export base, even if import-reliant for certain products

Maturing industry
- Stabilizing number of producers as consolidations occur
- Maturing export base, with imports still necessary for some items

Developed industry
- Stable number of producers after industry consolidation
- Well-established export base, with some imports still necessary

Innovative industry
- Stable number of producers, with some moving into innovative research and development
- Well-established export base, with new, innovative products

Development stage of most Sub-Saharan African countries

Source: Conway et al. (2019).

Demand

Shifting demand patterns within Africa's health sector are prioritizing private provision and consumption of health and pharmaceutical services. Private health care expenditures roughly doubled between 2009 and 2016, to $35 billion a year.[45] The emphasis on private health care is continent-wide, as numerous surveys have documented the public's preferences for private providers instead of public ones for the differences in convenience and quality of care. Private institutions have generally become better supplied and staffed to serve the public than government health centers. However, there are still risks of inconsistent care and corruption within the private health sector that challenge the notion that private health provision will become the sole or primary supplier within the health sector. Private health care and private pharmaceutical production are two of the fastest-growing industries in the sector. Consumers are seeking low-cost health solutions and medicines, which could have the ultimate benefit of improving public health for people of all classes. It is important to note that the private sector cares for people of all economic classes; 40 percent of people in the lowest economic quintile in Ethiopia, Nigeria, Kenya, and Uganda received health care from private providers.[46]

Urbanization

Changing demand patterns among consumers hinges on the rapid urbanization happening throughout the continent. General health services and disease control programs are still in the process of coordinating immediate care and long-term care, while growing urban areas and general population growth further challenge the existing systems. It is estimated that Sub-Saharan Africa is home to only 1.3 percent of the world's trained health personnel and the shortage of health care workers in Africa is predicted to reach 6.1 million by 2030.[47] More recently, estimates of urbanization indicate that 37 percent of Africans live in cities, with this figure set to reach 53 percent by 2030. Three out of every four city-dwellers in Sub-Saharan Africa currently live in slums, and this figure is only projected to increase as cities struggle to accommodate growing populations and stagnant infrastructure. At the beginning of the millennium, only 58 percent of Sub-Saharan Africa had access to safe water supplies and only 31 percent had access to sanitation.[48]

Infrastructure Changes

Despite the numerous challenges throughout Sub-Saharan Africa to accommodate growing populations and increased urbanization, growing investment in the infrastructure and architecture of health systems is driving the transformation of the health sector. Improved infrastructure that incorporates new technology and new models of domestic and private financing can improve rapid-response programs to monitor, contain, and treat frequent disease outbreaks on the continent. While most African countries have local companies that make pharmaceutical products, infrastructure improvements are driving the potential for larger companies to move into the market and fulfill demand for cheaper products.

Social Determinants

Social determinants of Africans' health are affecting the future of the health sector, and are driving investors, health providers, and policymakers alike to adapt to changing health needs. Social determinants—such as food, nutrition, and the physical environment where people live—are important for health. As infrastructure changes and urbanization affects people's living situations, their health challenges and resilience against malnutrition, viral disease, and NCDs changes. These circumstances are shaped by political, social, and economic policies, and these policies then inform the health care decisions of providers and the public.[49] It has been proven that higher income levels also affect health, improving access to food, water, sanitation, and education.[50]

Education

Education is an important factor in the health sector because it affects both the provision of health through better-educated workers and the number of people, particularly children, who can receive education because of improved health standards and care. African governments have started to divest from the education sector, leaving room for doubling the impact of investments in training and certificates for individuals to create opportunity for innovation within the health and pharmaceuticals industries. Improved health also affects education by allowing students to remain in school for longer periods and improves their cognitive ability and learning. Education has a twofold effect on the future of the health sector by reducing mortality rates and increasing incentives for investment in education and health services. At higher levels of education, Sub-Saharan Africa has the potential to transform the health sector with better-trained workers and individuals who may be incentivized to stay on the continent to build the health education sector.

Key Players

The key players here include private sector suppliers, international investors, domestic manufacturers, and investors. Let us briefly consider each one.

Private Sector Suppliers

Most of the private sector suppliers to African markets are international firms that supply both products and education to domestic workers to operate imported equipment and sell imported health care goods. For example, Siemens Healthcare, headquartered in Germany, sells diagnostic equipment to several African countries; and Phillips Health Systems, headquartered in the Netherlands, sells medical devices adapted to rural use where electricity is erratic or nonexistent, as in Nigeria and Kenya.[51] These types of international suppliers have the capital to innovate and manufacture specialty products that can accommodate infrastructure and educational challenges in some Sub-Saharan African regions.

International Investors

The International Finance Corporation is one of the largest multilateral investors in health and pharmaceuticals worldwide. International investors are critical for the growth of Africa-based start-up companies that are fulfilling the need for adapted health solutions. In Kenya, Penda Health has received investments of about $100,000 from international investors to develop its social enterprise providing health services for low- and middle-income women.[52]

Domestic Manufacturers and Investors

Domestic manufacturing companies of pharmaceutical processes and medical devices constitute only a small portion of the African market, with 99 percent of Africa's vaccine needs and 70 percent of Africa's essential medicine supply needs being met by imports.[53] However, with pharmaceuticals being a key industry for accelerating the implementation of AfCFTA per the World Economic Forum, domestic manufacturers are increasingly attracting both international investment and public sector support through training and policies. South Africa's burgeoning health and pharmaceuticals sector has also produced large manufacturers that are slowly reaching other markets throughout the continent. The driving factors of growth in the health and pharmaceuticals sector are affecting the roles of investors, manufacturers, suppliers, and health care professionals in contributing to sectoral development.

Opportunities for Investment

Africa's overall health care sector is expected to be worth $259 billion by 2030, opening up incredible opportunities for companies to enter and scale up across the continent.[54] As AfCFTA becomes fully implemented and integrated, the health care sector is becoming increasingly more lucrative, given the harmonization of regulations. Instead of navigating 54 different regulatory environments, AfCFTA is acting as a liaison between health companies and the African Medicines Association, which was created in 2019 to promote and coordinate regulatory harmonization in the African Union.[55] Companies are already recognizing the value in these efforts, leading to increased investments in areas such as packaged medicines, health care infrastructure, vaccine manufacturing, and health technologies.

For example, by 2040, the African vaccine market is projected to reach between $2.8 billion and $5.6 billion,[56] which has led to significant investment in the industry from domestic and international companies, with support from an initiative established in 2021 between the African Union and the African Centers for Disease Control and Prevention called the Partnerships for African Vaccine Manufacturing, which has a goal of enabling Africa to meet 60 percent of its vaccine demand locally by 2040.[57]

Overwhelmingly, coverage of Africa's health care system tends to focus on daunting challenges and negative statistical trends and outcomes, which has exacerbated negative perceptions about the potential for returns on investment. However, this approach has masked the remarkable opportunities in the sector, especially looking to the near future. A large proportion of existing consumer demand remains unmet in most African countries, with thousands of wealthy citizens traveling abroad every year to seek medical care and medications. In general, however, Africa's political and economic climate is continuing to improve, thus stabilizing the underlying conditions for investment, while positive macroeconomic projections over the next decade point to rising incomes and, therefore, growing demand.

To fill the supply gap, roughly half of needed investment will likely focus on health care provision, which currently tends to be the domain of the social enterprises and nongovernmental organizations working in the region. Yet, with the other half of investment needs split across pharmaceutical production and storage, distribution, retail, risk pooling, and technical training and education, there are also enormous opportunities for for-profit enterprises.[58] Morocco, Kenya, South Africa, and Botswana are examples of countries that are ripe for health care business investment given their unique dynamics.

Morocco

By African standards, Morocco's health system is relatively stable and well developed, though with substantial opportunities for future investment. Currently, the government is the main provider of health services, reaching

$2.3 billion in 2022, up 19 percent from 2021.[59] This allows 70 percent of the population to receive care via public hospitals. Though the demand for private health care is at 15 percent of all demand for health services, this private market is growing rapidly.

Since 2005, the Moroccan government has espoused the principle of quality and affordable access for all citizens, especially for the neediest. Many development organizations have supported Morocco in recent years in achieving this goal. In 2013, the African Development Bank approved a loan of roughly $130 million to fund the government's plan to reform medical coverage, Programme d'Appui à la Réforme de la Couverture Médicale, PARCOUM III.[60] Other projects include the construction of four hospital university centers in 2018, and the development of emergency and mobile service units.

Since Morocco lacks a domestic, medical manufacturing sector beyond disposables, these projects represent substantial opportunities for foreign producers of medical equipment and supplies, particularly imaging and scanning equipment, X-ray machines, emergency aid equipment, monitoring and electrodiagnostic equipment, computers, and information and communications technology (ICT), such as e-medicine and related software. The United States, Germany, and France have been the top suppliers to date, although there is increasing demand for cheap Chinese and South Korean products.

The primary barriers to market entry in Morocco are in the regulatory environment, which is especially burdensome, and inconsistently applied customs procedures. It generally takes six months to obtain a certificate of registration to begin importing medical projects, although it is often advisable to work in partnership with a locally based distributor to gain essential knowledge about contacts, regulations, and relevant opportunities, as business in Morocco is largely based on mutual trust and reciprocity.[61]

Morocco is becoming a leader in vaccine production. For example, partnering with a Swedish company called Recipharm, Morocco has received between €400 million and €500 million in investment for a vaccine plant that aims to produce 116 million doses, meeting 70 percent of the country's vaccine demand and 60 percent of the continent's vaccine demand. [62]

Kenya

The average life expectancy at birth in Kenya has increased significantly, from 53.9 years in 2000 to 66.1 years in 2019, an increase of 12.2 years.[63] It now has one of the highest rates of antiretroviral therapy coverage in the Africa region, at 79 and 59 percent for adults and children, respectively, in 2021, a signal that the international development community has invested heavily in meeting the supply gap for health services in the country.[64] Interventions by the African Development Bank, for example, have improved sanitation and clean water supply in cities like Nakuru, contributing to a reduced incidence of water-borne diseases and prevention of disinvestment of industry.

Yet, with a maternal mortality rate of 3.1 per 1,000 live births (compared with the global average of 2.23) and a relatively high burden of communicable disease, there is still substantial room for improvement in Kenya's health sector. The gap between urban and rural coverage is particularly stark—just 30 percent of the rural population has a health center within 4 kilometers of their home, while this figure increases to 70 percent among the urban population. The most developed facilities tend to be in Nairobi and the Central Province, while facilities in other provinces and rural areas tend to be less developed and suffer from shortages of staff, medical equipment, and pharmaceuticals. Meanwhile, NCDs like cancer are placing a growing strain on the health system. The lack of equipment for diagnosis and treatment often creates patient waiting times of up to two years, even in developed urban areas.

Most health services in Kenya are provided by the public sector, with policies and investment coordinated by the Ministry of Health (MOH). Nearly three quarters of all health services centers—from general hospitals to district hospitals, health clinics, and dispensaries—are operated by the MOH, with remaining demand met by nongovernmental organizations, faith-based organizations, and private companies. Since 2000, Kenya's Medical Supplies Agency has handled the logistics of meeting the government's National Health Strategic Plan to provide public health facilities with the "right quantity and quality of drugs and medical supplies at the best market value." Under its $404 million program launched in 2015, the Medical Supplies Agency has sought to ensure that at least two public hospitals in each of the country's forty-seven counties are fully equipped with modern medical equipment and that every constituency has at least one modern health center, which would make Kenya's hospital system the best-equipped in all of Sub-Saharan Africa.

Currently, however, Kenya's market for medical devices relies almost exclusively on imports. According to current projections, the market is expected to grow by an annual rate of 8.2 percent in the next few years, leading to a value of $197.9 million by 2026.[65] Following a competitive and transparent bidding process, Kenya's MOH has already signed contracts with five multinational medical equipment manufacturers from China,

India, Italy, the Netherlands, and the United States to supply its modernization program.[66]

South Africa

As one of the largest economies in Africa with one of the region's largest middle classes, South Africa has large demand for modern health care, reaching $1.26 billion in 2022.[67]

The medical import market is currently mostly made up of by-products from the United States, yet the changing economic climate is increasing demand for less expensive Asian sources; China's market share has increased by roughly 10 percent in recent years. Domestic production of medical supplies in South Africa tends to focus on disposables, like bandages, and on beds. There are indications that technical manufacturing is on the rise, as with the successful production of the full-body X-ray machine by Lodox Systems, which has proved to be competitive against imports. Still, the gap between supply and demand is stark, with just a few MRI and CT scanners present in all public hospitals in the country.

Conversely, South Africa's private health sector is the most sophisticated in Africa, and it supports significant demand for imported, innovative medical devices, especially dental equipment and mobile patient aids and monitoring devices. Depending on the macroeconomic trajectory over the near term and whether the spending power of the government improves, an overhaul of hospital infrastructure is under consideration, which would provide a substantial boon to the market both for imported products and for domestically manufactured pharmaceuticals and equipment.[68]

Botswana

In comparison with other African countries, Botswana has received criticism for its initial handling of the HIV/AIDS epidemic. By the turn of the century, prevalence rates had soared to above one-quarter of the population.[69] Since then, however, in addition to generous assistance from the United States' President's Emergency Plan for AIDS Relief program, the government of Botswana has committed to translating tax revenues into substantial investment in the health of its citizens. In 2020, at $363 per capita, government health expenditures in Botswana were significantly higher than the regional average, and the country now has one of the region's lowest levels of out-of-pocket spending on health care.

Much of the focus on government spending has been to improve health care infrastructure, modernize medical and surgical equipment through imports, and introduce telemedicine as a means of reaching remote populations. It has also attempted to address the remaining shortage of trained health professionals in the country both by seeking to outsource some services and constructing a 450-bed teaching hospital at the University of Botswana. One of the other major remaining challenges is in the procurement and distribution of medications, especially since the country lacks domestic production capacity for pharmaceuticals or medical equipment. However, many foreign producers have already shown interest in establishing production operations in Botswana.

In light of the government's willingness to incentivize investment in key areas and its high degree of political stability and transparency, Botswana has one of the region's prime opportunities for investment in key areas such as medical manufacturing, storage and distribution of medication and medical supplies, and technical, supportive services for the treatment of infectious diseases, such as malaria, TB, and HIV/AIDS.

Challenges

According to Deaton and Tortora, African citizens have some of the lowest rates of satisfaction with their health care system for any region in the world.[70] Despite heavy investment by both foreign donors and African governments over the past two decades, the sector is still characterized by a lack of access and infrastructural gaps, shortages of medications and medical staff, and mismanagement and corruption. As a result, health outcomes on the continent continue to be among the worst in the world. The authors also find that most Africans fail to prioritize health care as a policy matter, which has only exacerbated problems of accountability in the sector. If these challenges are not adequately addressed, and without increased private sector investment in the health industry, the current demographic patterns on the continent point to additional stress on its already-overburdened and underdeveloped system.

Human Capacity and the Brain Drain

The shortage of trained, professional personnel is a significant exacerbator of the gap between supply and demand in Africa's health sector, along with the poor management of health care facilities. In general, there is a dearth of health care workers and research on improving health systems across Africa. African countries account for 40 out of the 55 countries included in the 2023 WHO's Health Workforce Support and Safeguards List that represents the countries that face the most pressing health workforce challenges related to universal health coverage.[71] By 2030, WHO estimates that Africa's shortage of health workers will reach 6.1 million, a 45 percent increase from 2013.[72]

Lacking sufficient domestic courses for medical education and training, many countries pay for doctors and nurses to be trained abroad. However, once accredited, many professionals are incentivized to remain abroad due to the better working conditions and higher salaries offered in other regions, resulting in a brain drain away from Africa's health sector, one of the areas where skills and expertise are perhaps most needed.[73] According to data collected by the Center for Global Development, Angola and Mozambique have more doctors working in foreign countries than in their home country; in Liberia, there are two doctors working abroad for every one working at home.[74] A financing gap of 37 to 43 percent is in the way of employing enough health workers in East and Southern Africa.[75] To combat this problem, some Western countries, such as the United Kingdom, have begun to implement policies preventing the recruitment of medical staff from Sub-Saharan Africa, even those who attend British medical schools, while many African countries—including Ethiopia and Malawi—are funding domestic training programs to increase the quantity of local medical staff members.

Weak Infrastructure

The greatest current challenge for health care delivery in Africa is access, especially the lack of health facilities and gaps in pharmaceutical availability and affordability. The hospital-to-patient ratio is exceptionally low in Sub-Saharan Africa, where fewer than 50 percent of people have access to a modern health facility. Even where they are considered "reached," patients are often forced to walk half a day or more to reach the nearest clinic, and some clinics serve more than 20,000 patients.[76] The health facilities that do exist tend to lack diagnostic equipment—such as X-ray machines, ultrasounds, and chemistry analyzers—causing medical staff to rely on conventional diagnostics and often delaying diagnoses until diseases are more advanced and difficult to treat. Moreover, many vital preventive medications are not available in most health centers, especially dispensaries and government clinics.[77]

Beyond the deficiency of staff, facilities, and equipment, the health system is also threatened by the broader infrastructural gaps that threaten all economic sectors in Africa, especially in basic utilities and ICT. For example, hospitals and clinics—particularly those in rural areas—often face power outages, which pose a significant risk for surgical patients and limit the ability to store vaccines and other pharmaceuticals. Moreover, one of the greatest current health challenges in Africa stems from the lack of infrastructure for clean water and sanitation. Roughly two-thirds of the population lacks access to improved sanitation facilities and roughly 319 million people in Sub-Saharan Africa lack reliable access to safe water,[78] which exacerbates the incidence of communicable diseases.

Finally, the absence of mass internet connectivity and the lack of ICT-related skills among health personnel limit the capacity of national health management and information systems to generate, coordinate, store, analyze, and disseminate data relevant to health crises, as well as that relevant to patients' long-term health.[79] Where such technologies do exist, they have usually been donated by a nongovernmental organization for communal use and are therefore prone to a lack of maintenance and upgrading.[80]

Government Spending and Inefficiency

In 2001, leaders of the African Union's member states committed themselves to increasing health-related spending to 15 percent of their national budgets.[81] However, while the average share of government expenditures on health increased markedly between 1995 and 2004, they have remained relatively constant, at about 11 percent since then.[82] Just two countries met the 15 percent benchmark agreed to in the Abuja Declaration as of 2021—Cabo Verde and South Africa.[83] In per capita terms, however, government health expenditures have continued to increase steadily since the mid-1990s, with the average African country now spending roughly $110 per person, in purchasing power parity, every year, compared with just $40 in 1995. Some countries spend an impressive $400 per capita or more, including Gabon, Swaziland, Mauritius, Namibia, Botswana, South Africa, Algeria, Seychelles, and Equatorial Guinea. With these countries substantially skewing the regional average upward, however, nearly half of all countries in the region are still spending less than $50 on the average citizen's health each year.[84]

Perhaps most significantly, the public health sector has been one of the most negatively affected by waste and inefficiency, with corrupt practices often diverting resources away from health care delivery and reducing access and affordability for patients. With bilateral and multilateral assistance flowing into Africa to attempt to reduce the out-of-pocket payments households face in seeking health care, reports have compounded over the past decades of public officials and medical staff directly diverting aid money, trading bribes for drug registration or health inspections, or selling medications meant to be provided free. Corruption and mismanagement have created a situation of uncertainty and a lack of coordination in the sector. In some countries, the tenure of health ministers has averaged just six months; in 2009 alone, the Gambia had four health ministers in office.[85]

The amount of official development assistance given to health care in Africa, which was already declining after the 2007–8 global financial crisis, is further threatened by perceptions about corruption and wasteful expenditures. Meanwhile, many observers have argued that the failure to meet public spending goals has itself been exacerbated by the large amount of donor funding flowing into the sector to fill resource gaps.[86] Governments have become highly reliant on donor aid, particularly in the area of disease control—such as HIV, TB, and malaria—which leaves the health system vulnerable to further decreases in official development assistance in the future.

Future Risks

Given that Africa is the continent most affected by the consequences of climate change,[87] WHO has warned that Africa is particularly at risk for climate-related health hazards like extreme weather events, high temperatures, rising sea levels, air pollution, changes in vector distribution and ecology, water scarcity, and reduced food production, which negatively affect health outcomes.[88] While much of the current focus of health interventions is on highly visible diseases like HIV/AIDS and malaria, rising incomes on the continent are extending people's lives and causing lifestyle changes that will make NCDs—such as cancer, diabetes, and cardiovascular disease—much more prevalent in coming years. As in the developed world, Africans are consuming more processed, high-sodium foods, as well as alcohol and tobacco, and are engaging less in physical activity.[89] Thus, there is a growing imbalance between general health services and disease control programs, and while the vast majority of donor funding has focused on infectious diseases, there has been little attention given to other critical areas likely to be affected by these patterns, including reproductive health.[90]

Strategies for Effective Investment

Merrill Lynch recently named health care as one of the top five sectors primed for investment in Africa—even higher than infrastructure—while the global logistics company DHL has termed Africa as the "next frontier for health care."[91] Current investment in African infrastructure is at an all-time high, and it includes direct government interventions, which indicate enormous potential for improving supply chains and closing the gap between supply and demand in Africa's health sector.

Public–Private Partnerships

A number of African countries are beginning to offer incentives for private investment in health, as well as vital sectors considered linked to the health system, such as in infrastructure and education.[92] While ministries of health are likely to maintain their central role in managing and coordinating health policy, the need for private funding signals leverage for private industry to use its expertise in assisting African governments in areas such as logistics and distribution, such that prioritized programs are best able to reach target populations, especially in rural and remote locations.[93]

By locating fixed assets in countries that have more developed political regulations and business structures, and by outsourcing supply chains to local, third-party operators—such as Eurapharma in West Africa—foreign pharmaceutical companies are better able to manage the logistical challenge of distribution in Africa.[94] Local businesses often have a wealth of knowledge about specific markets and consumer demand, as well as existing brand recognition and marketing opportunities, but they tend to lack technical capacity and capital.[95] In Nigeria and Kenya, for example, GSK works with pharmaceutical production and packaging companies to offer products that range in size and pricing, in order to be competitive in a wide variety of markets. In fact, considering the current reticence of large multinationals to get involved in Africa's health sector, many analysts have suggested that private investment in the near future is likely to be driven by small- to medium-sized enterprises with investments of $3 million or less, often provided by foreign investment banks or venture capital firms.[96]

Local Engagement and Traditional Healers

One of the primary criticisms of previous health interventions in Africa is the failure to incorporate local communities into the processes of implementation, monitoring, and evaluation. The success and sustainability of all health programs are now understood to be intrinsically tied to local ownership, such as through the use of local volunteers and community health workers, but also in specialized training to build up the supply of medical staff at the local level.[97] Pharmaceutical companies, for example, can work to overcome the deficiency of skilled and educated workers in Africa by building capabilities in house and training their own managers. In Morocco, Pharma5 has trained a seventy-strong sales team from the Sub-Saharan region in just four years, putting its top sales representatives in charge of the recruitment and training process.[98] While this strategy has required a substantial and time-consuming initial investment, it should also help companies remain flexible and responsive to the demands of local markets.

Moreover, trust in and uptake of health programs, especially in remote villages, is often dependent on the incorporation of traditional healers, who are integral to African cultures in various ways. This strategy proved highly effective in combating the HIV epidemic in Uganda, where traditional healers proved willing to translate and implement national-level health policies in ways that included local beliefs and practices. Moreover, since traditional healers are often more available in rural areas than health practitioners trained in Western medicine, integrating them for nonvital, preventive procedures helps to free up doctors to concentrate on diagnosis, treatment, and disease control.[99]

Maximizing Efficiency

The value-for-money factor is one of the primary avenues for improving health services without the need for substantial additional investment. Inefficiencies in the public sector are evidenced by the fact that different countries seem to achieve divergent health outcomes with similar spending levels—the proportion of births attended by a skilled health worker, for example, varies from 20–80 percent at the same national level of expenditures. With the poorest quintile of Africans benefiting from only 13 percent of allocated funds, the need for strong and coordinated governance and improved accountability is clear. However, the improved skills, management, and performance incentives of the private sector suggest substantial opportunities for maximizing efficiency through private investment.[100]

E-Health

In a variety of ways, incorporating ICT into the health sector can help to enhance efficiency and access to health services, improve knowledge and skills among the workforce, and disseminate important information. Several e-health solutions have already been introduced by both the public and private sectors and have proved to help overcome the unique challenges facing Africa's health care system, including national health observatories, distance learning, telemedicine, and mobile health (m-health) services. In fact, these interventions have been especially effective where infrastructure gaps are most acute. While many patients had previously traveled long distances to reach clinics and then find that needed medications were unavailable, a mobile health system in Uganda called mTRAC now provides information about medicine stocks in clinics across the country. Another m-health program in Kenya is helping to improve the efficiency of the supply chain by using SMS surveys to redistribute medicines to clinics where they are most needed.[101] As the wave of mobile phones and internet connectivity sweeps across the continent, and especially as the ICT gap between urban and rural areas is bridged, these innovations are likely to become even more relevant in coming years, helping health services to access even hard-to-reach populations, like the nomadic populations in the Sahel.[102]

Looking to the Future

The COVID-19 pandemic laid bare the inadequacies of the health care system in Africa along with the great need to move production of medical equipment and vaccines onto the continent. The lack of vaccine production on the continent and the supply chain shocks felt across the world significantly affected the continent and slowed down the distribution of the vaccine. Meanwhile, only 600 manufacturers of packaged goods are located on the continent, concentrated across 8 countries (representing 80 percent).[103] The pandemic mainstreamed the urgency required to meet demand and be better prepared for future global health shocks.

This increased attention is leading to investment acceleration within the pharmaceutical industry and the vaccine manufacturing industry, which is expected to grow to between $2.8 and $5.6 billion by 2040 with a goal of meeting 60 percent of the vaccine demand by 2040 through local production driven by public–private partnerships.[104] AfCFTA is a key driver for localizing production not only in vaccine manufacturing but also in packaged medicines and other medical devices. Since the start of the pandemic in 2020, the Africa Investment Forum has facilitated over $484 million worth of investments in the health sector.[105] These opportunities will continue as increased attention and pressure have led to action by public and private sectors alike on the continent.

Governments, donors, and international stakeholders in Africa's health care systems must consider the impact that the private sector's rejuvenation can have on rebuilding African societies into healthy, innovative populations. The health and pharmaceuticals sector is already on a trajectory of strong growth. Still, African countries will need sustainable investments in health care infrastructure and domestic pharmaceutical manufacturing to avoid the real human consequences of another global recession. Africa's health sector would benefit substantially, as would investors and firms, from the greater participation of private sector actors.

The typical perspective of Africa's health challenges requires a coordinated approach by policymakers, business leaders, international institutional investors, local actors, and civil society. African economies' emergence on the global level necessitates a combination of vertical and horizontal reforms that are designed to create a sustainable industry with the capacity to handle both long-term illnesses and short-term disease outbreaks. Growing demand for high-quality, affordable pharmaceutical products must be met by domestic producers and distributors that will have the long-term investment to become securely established in markets. A growing trend toward intra-African trade and continental trade through the African Continental Free Trade Area should be incorporated into plans for supply chain development and infrastructure improvement.

Africa's vaccines and medicines market is worth $50 billion annually,[106] and its overall health care sector is expected to be worth $259 billion by 2030.[107] The expanse of this market—in addition to the persistently growing needs of patients with new communicable diseases, like Ebola, or persistent illnesses, like TB—presents numerous opportunities for investment and entrepreneurship. The potential for diseases like Ebola to spread to a large city is an incentive for innovation and technology adoption for the eradication of such diseases that can disrupt entire communities or societies. African innovators are in tune with the needs of their societies and present a good case for an increase in venture capitalism in the continent's health and pharmaceutical research-and-development industry. The increase in technology available on the continent will only facilitate the expansion of health solutions to rural communities and regions still facing infrastructure challenges. Each stakeholder in the sector must tackle the remaining policy, institutional, and investment challenges, and thus transform the health and pharmaceuticals sector into a sustainably profitable sector that can both facilitate economic growth and generate high returns that will continue to encourage innovation.

Notes

1. Signé (2023); Weil (2014); Bloom et al. (2019); UNECA, GBC Health, and Aliko Dangote Foundation (2019).
2. Virginia Economic Development Partnership (2021).
3. Virginia Economic Development Partnership (2021).
4. Signé (2020).
5. Frost and Sullivan (2016).
6. WHO (2014, 17); African Development Bank (2013, 17).

7. Breedon (2016); African Development Bank (2013); African Business (2016); Frost & Sullivan (2016).

8. Katrina (2015).

9. Gouda et al. (2019); WHO (2022).

10. Torkington (2024).

11. Torkington (2024).

12. Frost and Sullivan (2016).

13. Frost and Sullivan (2016).

14. Ossé and Krönke (2024).

15. Global HIV Prevention Coalition (2023).

16. Global HIV Prevention Coalition (2023).

17. Niohuru (2023).

18. WHO (2014, 18).

19. WHO (2024a).

20. WHO (2024a).

21. WHO (2016).

22. All except Uganda, Equatorial Guinea, South Sudan, Mali, Cabo Verde, and Algeria. In the case of Uganda, this is likely due to the substantial progress that was made in reversing the prevalence of HIV in the 1990s.

23. Alcorn (2024).

24. WHO (2016, 44).

25. UNICEF (2023).

26. WHO (2016, 26).

27. WHO (2016, 32).

28. African Development Bank (2013, 20).

29. Prosper Africa (2023).

30. Virginia Economic Development Partnership (2021).

31. Parikh (n.d.)

32. International Finance Corporation (2016, 7).

33. International Finance Corporation (2016).

34. International Financial Corporation (2007); Breedon (2016).

35. WHO (2024b).

36. Russo, Bloom, and McCoy (2017).

37. Bryan et al. (2010).

38. Okillong (2024); conversion using 2024 rate.

39. WHO (2024b).

40. Breedon (2016).

41. International Finance Corporation (2007, 9).

42. Kaseje (2006).

43. African Development Bank (2013, 20).

44. WHO (2019).

45. Grigorov (2009).

46. Grigorov (2009).
47. Amref (n.d.).
48. Banerjee and Morella (2013).
49. WHO (2014, 87–88).
50. Bloom and Canning (2008).
51. Katrina (2015).
52. Mulupi (2012).
53. IFPMA (2023).
54. Manlan (2019).
55. World Economic Forum (2023).
56. Gavi Vaccine Alliance (2022).
57. World Economic Forum (2024).
58. International Finance Corporation (2000, 11, 38, 50).
59. International Trade Administration (n.d.–b).
60. The national health care system is divided into Mandatory Health Insurance (AMO)—both private (La CNSS) and public (La CNOPS)—as well as a social assistance program for low-income citizens and a separate system for military personnel.
61. The US Commercial Service in Morocco also provides counseling about market entry for US companies, including forging joint venture partnerships.
62. Mansouri (2024).
63. WHO (2022c).
64. Masaba et al. (2023).
65. International Trade Administration (2022).
66. International Trade Administration (2022).
67. International Trade Administration (2024).
68. Export.gov (2019a).
69. Allen and Heald (2004).
70. Deaton and Tortora (2015).
71. WHO (2024a).
72. WHO (2022b).
73. Awases et al. (2004).
74. Center for Global Development (2012).
75. WHO (2023c).
76. Clausen (2015).
77. Conway (2019).
78. Kwakwa (2024).
79. Kirigia and Barry (2008).
80. Ajayi (2015).
81. Kaseje (2006, 4).
82. It is worth noting that this ratio is higher than for some other WHO developing regions, including Southeast Asia and the Eastern Mediterranean.
83. Human Rights Watch (2024).

84. WHO (2016, 83).
85. African Development Bank (2013, 14).
86. Kaseje (2006, 4).
87. Trisos et al. (2022).
88. Integrated African Health Observatory and World Health Organization (2024).
89. Clausen (2015).
90. African Development Bank (2013, 14).
91. Breedon (2016).
92. African Business (2016).
93. Kaseje (2006, 10–11).
94. Holt et al. (2015, 8–9).
95. African Business (2016).
96. International Financial Corporation (2000, 38).
97. Kaseje (2006, 11).
98. Holt et al. (2015, 7).
99. Chatora (2003); Kasilo (2003); Kaseje (2006, 10–11).
100. African Development Bank (2013, 14).
101. Kirigia and Barry (2008).
102. WHO (2014, 128).
103. Munyati and Signé (2023).
104. World Economic Forum (2024).
105. World Economic Forum (2024).
106. Torkington (2024).
107. Manlan (2019).

Five

Africa's Mining Potential

TRENDS, OPPORTUNITIES, CHALLENGES, AND STRATEGIES

Emerging economies in Africa are at the forefront of the reinvestment of natural resource rents for the sustainable growth of the overall economy. Africa has immense natural resource endowments, especially in minerals used for technological development and manufacturing. Mining contributes significantly to African economies—in fact, in 15 of Sub-Saharan Africa's most mineral rich countries, mining contributes to 8 percent of government revenue.[1] As concerns about global climate change continue to fuel transitions to renewable energy, Africa is poised to benefit since the continent is endowed with many of the metals and minerals critical in clean energy production. Africa has 19 percent of the world's metals required to produce electric vehicles[2] and 30 percent of the world's green mineral reserves.[3] Africa is home to 92 percent of the world's platinum group metals and diamonds, and more than 50 percent of the world's manganese and cobalt.[4] Over 70 percent of global cobalt output is in the Democratic Republic of Congo (DRC), meanwhile over 60 percent of global manganese production is in South Africa, Gabon, and Ghana (table 5-1).[5]

Demand for these minerals is expected to increase substantially in the near future because they are required for the production of batteries, wind turbines, and solar energy.[6] Demand for battery minerals will triple by 2040 and increase sixfold by 2050.[7] This demand will come from the global community but also from within Africa—mineral resources have the second-greatest intra-African export potential, behind machinery and electricity.[8] By 2050,

Table 5-1. Availability of Green Minerals in Africa

Mineral	Clean energy technology	Share of global reserves in Africa	African countries with reserves
Platinum group metals	Green hydrogen	92%	South Africa, Zimbabwe
Cobalt	EVs	56%	DRC, South Africa, Zambia, Madagascar
Manganese	EVs, wind	54%	Gabon, South Africa, Côte d'Ivoire, Ghana
Chromium	Geothermal, solar, wind	36%	South Africa
Bauxite	Wind, solar	24%	Guinea
Graphite	EVs	22%	Madagascar, Mozambique, Tanzania
Zirconium (ores and concentrates)	Green hydrogen	15%	South Africa, Senegal, Mozambique
Vanadium	Steel, batteries	13%	South Africa
Copper	EVs, wind, solar	6%	DRC, Zambia
Lithium	Batteries	4%	DRC, Zimbabwe, Mali
Nickel	EVs, wind	4%	Madagascar, South Africa
Tellurium	Solar	3%	South Africa
Rare earth	Wind	1%	Tanzania, South Africa, Madagascar, Burundi

Sources: Zero Carbon Analytics (2024). Data are from UNCTAD, Critical Minerals and Routes to Diversification in Africa, 2023; USGS, Mineral Commodity Summaries, 2023; UNEP, Environmental aspects of critical minerals in Africa in the clean energy transition, 2023; and IRENA, Geopolitics of the Energy Transition: Critical Materials, 2023.
Note: DRC = Democratic Republic of Congo.

the demand for nickel will double, the demand for cobalt will triple, and the demand for lithium will increase tenfold.[9] Even though global climate change presents some challenges to the mining industry, it also creates an opportunity for investors to benefit from increased global demand for minerals required for clean energy production.[10]

In 2023, Africa's exploration budget totaled $1.27 billion,[11] yet the potential to reap global revenues is growing rapidly. By 2050, the combined global revenues from copper, nickel, cobalt, and lithium are projected to reach $16 trillion and Sub-Saharan Africa could capture over 10 percent—raising the region's GDP by 12 percent or more.[12] Opportunities abound for business leaders and policymakers given these projections, offering Africa the opportunity to move beyond extraction toward processing and value added, which can create jobs, increase tax revenues, reduce poverty, and contribute to Africa's prosperity.[13]

Background Facts and Trends

Africa is the world's top producer of a range of valuable resources, and it is also thought to have some of the largest remaining untapped reserves.[14] Because of a lack of systematic geological mapping and exploration, the full extent of the continent's mineral base remains unknown,[15] even though the race for its mineral wealth has been raging for over two centuries. In the postcolonial period, African leaders and international development organizations have become increasingly interested in building linkages between the mining sector and broader processes of economic and social development. In the 1960s and 1970s, the dominant ideology was nationalization, resulting in large, state-owned mining companies in countries including Ghana, Zambia, and Zaire (now the DRC). After stagnation of the industry, however, a process of privatization since the 1990s has led to the diversification of the mining sector in most countries.[16] Today, mineral exploration and production are helping to redefine geostrategic relationships between Africa and the rest of the world, as the major emerging markets—namely, China, Brazil, and India—are increasingly investing in Africa's resources.[17] Chinese investment, in particular, has increased substantially since 2000, with Africa accounting for 75 percent of all Chinese foreign mining investment as of 2011.[18]

Much of the international narrative on Africa's natural resource reserves has been dominated by the notion of the "resource curse," which fails to recognize countries like Botswana that have managed their resources well. The notion of the resource curse, which is also called the "paradox of plenty," often arises when a nation-state has a major revenue-generating natural resource sector but the resulting revenues ultimately lead to negative development outcomes, including political tensions, economic stagnation, social grievances, and ecological destruction.[19] The existence of natural resources in tandem with corrupt institutions, individuals, and policies is usually the ultimate driver of the resource curse. Once the idea of the resource curse is applied to a country, it can be difficult to perceive the positive economic effects of mining. However, a recent focus on mining and natural resources in some emerging markets—where key commodities including copper, bauxite, iron ore, and precious metals are available for mass production—is highlighting Africa's potential to generate well-managed revenues from

Figure 5-1. Changes in Commodity Prices, January–April 2020

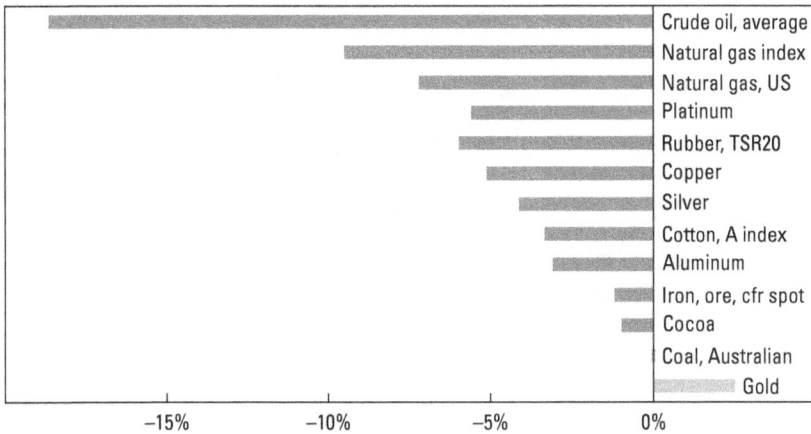

Source: Gajigo and Ahadjie (2020).

the mining sector and support economic transformation. Since 2003, several countries have adopted the Extractive Industries Transparency Initiative (EITI), which has established a common standard of transparency and accountability for extractive industries by requiring implementing countries to publish comprehensive government and corporate reports, including revenue flows, to ensure the good governance of natural resources.[20] The fact that twenty-seven African countries have joined the EITI demonstrates their commitment to improving transparency across the extractive industry value chain, and to reducing illicit practices.[21]

Over the past decade, Africa's mining sector has proved resilient to adverse conditions in the global economy, such as the financial crisis of 2007–8 and the decline in world commodity prices since 2014, even if the COVID-19 pandemic has recently exacerbated the forward pressure on commodity prices. Most base metals and precious minerals have experienced sharp price declines because of demand-side shocks when pandemic-related shutdowns started. The only exception was gold, the price of which has increased because of its perceived value as a safe haven asset. Figures 5-1 and 5-2 show the changes in the prices and production of different commodities between January and April 2020 and from 2020 to 2022.

In 2008, the mining sector was bolstered by the African Union's Africa Mining Vision, which seeks to build capacity, improve transparency and management of revenues, confront environmental and social challenges, and develop linkages

Figure 5-2. Declining Production Rates since 2000 Only in Europe: Change from 2000 to 2020

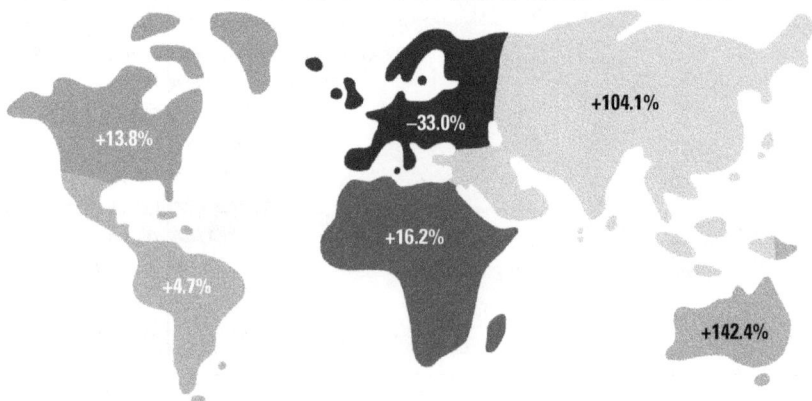

+13.8%
−33.0%
+104.1%
+16.2%
+4.7%
+142.4%

Source: World Mining Data (www.world-mining-data.info), various years.

with other productive sectors, especially manufacturing.[22] Africa accounts for a substantial share of global production of bauxite, chromite, cobalt, industrial diamonds, gold, iron ore, lead, copper, manganese, phosphate, and uranium.[23] Mining now makes up a significant portion of many of Africa's national economies, with ores and metals accounting for 20 percent, on average, of total merchandise exports.[24] However, there is a substantial variation in the significance of mineral production across the continent, which tends to be driven more by differences in structural endowments than by the investment climate. For example, the mining sector accounts for more than half of total exports from countries including Zambia (75.6 percent) and the DRC (83.1 percent), while others remain high, including Guinea (25.8 percent), Mauritania (39.5 percent), and Mozambique (30.5 percent) as of 2022.[25] In such places, mining accounts for a significant concentration of economic production and a significant amount of foreign exchange earnings—in the DRC, Botswana, and Guinea, for example, mining represented more than one-fifth of total fiscal revenues in 2015.[26] Conversely, many countries in North Africa and Central Africa produce less nonfuel minerals, largely depending instead on oil extraction and agriculture respectively, although Morocco represents an exception to this rule as a world leader in phosphate reserves.[27]

Despite the seemingly contradictory relationship between mining and development, there is some evidence that the sector has been an important source of employment and infrastructural development in some of Africa's most poorly managed economies. During Zimbabwe's period of relative stability at the turn of the century, mining accounted for roughly half of all foreign currency earnings and provided jobs for up to 60,000 people. The sector also stimulated construction of roads, railways, telecoms, and other infrastructure projects in rural mining towns such as Hwange and Kadoma.[28] In postconflict Sierra Leone, an increase in iron ore production accounted for 93.4 percent of export revenues in 2013 and—combined with indirect spill-over effects in agriculture, construction, and business services—contributed to 20.1 percent growth in real gross domestic product (GDP) that year.[29]

Recognizing the potential for resource wealth to drive economic growth, most African governments are investing heavily in infrastructure to support the sector. This contributes to the sector's continued expansion, despite the recent decline in world commodity prices. In Namibia, for example, Project 2050 seeks to build barriers along the coastline to provide a protected area for mining. In South Africa, roughly 220 billion rand was committed to new mineral projects by the public and private sectors in 2018.[30] One main challenge for the mining sector in Africa is that the clear majority of resource exports leave the continent unrefined. However, some countries are ratcheting up efforts to build linkages between mining and manufacturing, such as by constructing cement factories. Roughly 12 percent of the new investments in South Africa are targeted to processed minerals.[31]

Across the continent, 50 new, significant mining project investments started in 2020. While much of this investment was concentrated in the traditional mining powerhouses—especially South Africa, the DRC, Mauritania, Namibia, Zimbabwe, Zambia and Guinea—analysts predicted that the fastest growth in mining would likely occur in West Africa because of the size of its untapped reserves, improving business climates and making infrastructure improvements. In 2023, Ghana initiated the construction of its first lithium mine (Barari Dv Ghana's Ewozaa).[32] This is partly due to West Africa's perceived favorable mining regulations. When it comes to specific minerals, the best investment opportunities were perceived to be gold, cobalt, copper, diamonds, and rare earth metals.[33]

This situation is brought on by a lack of socioeconomic infrastructure, bribery, and the meager or nonexistent legal system. As African nations have attempted to utilize the advantages of extractive resources, problems have emerged. Resources are often a source of violent conflicts, environmental degradation, escalating gender inequality, and threats to democratic government, despite the fact that many countries fail to gain from them.[34]

The Sector's Importance

The mining and natural resource sector is just as critical to human development as to economic growth. The stabilization of mining industries can be a necessary step to curtailing detrimental inflation, national debt, and outsized shocks to commodity prices. Political stability is a critical aspect of the mining industry's success, because it gives positive assurance that countries can avoid the resource curse, and it encourages greater foreign investment.

The export of raw materials—particularly oil, diamonds, and platinum—has been a key source of revenues on the continent for decades, but many African countries have been unable to receive the full economic benefits associated with their natural resources because of the so-called resource curse, which is discussed in greater detail below. Gold also has been a key resource, although its economic contribution varies based on whether its extraction is sourced from small-scale, artisanal mines or larger industrial mines that are subject to regulations that typically require the payment of royalties and other taxes to the federal government.[35] Likewise, many regions remain underexplored, suggesting there is a high probability that the continent hosts natural resource wealth that, if leveraged correctly, could pull countries out of economic stagnation and into an era of emerging market growth. Protecting and expanding access to natural resources is also an important method of supporting pro-poor growth. Preventing the privatization of resources on which the poor depend encourages wealth distribution and inclusive economic activity.[36] In addition to the potential for inclusive growth in the mining sector, there is a major potential for adding value to minerals before exporting. In general, rising exports contribute to higher government finances, which provide the funding needed to build human and physical capital.

Natural resource abundance may lead to weakened private and public incentives to grow human capital and redistribute wealth, because of the prevalence of nonwage income, including dividends, social spending, and low taxes.[37] Countries need strong institutions to overcome the challenges of managing natural resource discoveries, investment from foreign extractive and development companies, and domestic production. In Africa, where countries still struggle to adjust to diversity within their societies, good governance and the rule of law are essential to prevent the benefits from natural resources from becoming a source of ethnic or identity-based conflicts.[38] These types of preventive policies and intentions were not adopted proportionally to the discovery of natural resources in Africa. However, in 2008, the African Union adopted the Africa Mining Vision with the goal of using Africa's mining growth to meet the United Nations' Millennium Development Goals through socioeconomic development.[39] Increasing trade liberalization across the continent supports the mining and natural resource sector and supports the push for more equitable, sustainable growth in countries with new natural resource wealth.

Key Drivers

The mining industry has been a key driver of growth throughout history—first, in the iron and bronze ages; then, during the Industrial Revolution; and now, in the infrastructure of the modern information era.[40] Research on and analyses of the mining and natural resource sector are often focused on the macroeconomic effects of the sector. Well-managed resources can be fundamental to overall economic growth, while also contributing to employment growth and income generation. Research shows that the number of direct jobs created by the mining sector is usually minimal, ranging from 1 to 4 percent, at most.[41] However, the mining sector creates a lot of indirect employment through the linkages between the sector and other industries; but these indirect jobs are difficult to measure.[42] There are several major drivers of the mining industry in African countries. Due to the varying degree to which states have adopted new technologies, legislation, and incentive structures, the drivers of the mining sector are not necessarily uniform to all resource-rich African countries. These drivers can be divided into three categories: macroeconomic, governance, and operations.

Macroeconomic Financing and Tax Incentives

African governments have discovered a fortuitous balance between incentivizing exploration and gaining revenue from new mining projects within their borders. Despite the global trend of rising mineral royalty taxes, most African countries have maintained a stable tax system on which mineral companies can rely for future planning.[43] This provision of revenue then effects the quality of education and social services available to local workers seeking employment in mineral extraction jobs that require increasing technical skills to operate and maintain more digitally advanced equipment. In most regions, local workers fill more than 90 percent of gold-mining jobs. This job creation has an important twofold effect on increasing the distribution of real wages to local populations and creating a workforce with the necessary skills to manage the growth of the sector. To decrease profit shifting in the mining industry and prevent losses in tax income, Sub-Saharan African countries will need to implement focused regulatory interventions. Governments may be able to recoup some of this desperately needed tax revenue with targeted policy measures to combat tax evasion. New staff research by the International Monetary Fund reveals that governments in Sub-Saharan Africa are losing between $450 million and $730 million a year in corporate income tax revenues as a result of profit shifting by multinational companies in the mining sector.[44] These governments are currently under enormous pressure to increase public spending in response to the COVID-19 pandemic. Governments might collect some of this desperately needed tax revenue to aid in the recovery and meet the UN's Sustainable Development Goals with the help of targeted legislative efforts to limit tax avoidance.[45]

Macroeconomic International Investment

Of the twenty-nine major mining projects identified by Deloitte as being in development in 2015, more than half met their investment needs through international stock exchanges:[46] "The Toronto Stock Exchange is funding 28 percent of projects, followed by Hong Kong stock exchange funding 17 percent and the National Stock Exchange of India funding 10 percent of these projects."[47] The London Stock Exchange, the Australian Stock Exchange, Euronext Paris, the Russian Trading System, and the Johannesburg Stock Exchange are also important investors in the continent's various mining projects. These international stock exchanges drive the exploration and transition of projects to online platforms, and ongoing extraction thanks to their access to capital and their ability to market Africa's mineral opportunities to interested global parties.

An Effective Fiscal Plan

Royalties, corporate income taxes, and, occasionally, taking a noncontrolling ownership position in projects where they get dividends from corporate earnings are how the majority of African nations raise money from the mining sector. The pattern and magnitude of the revenues received are influenced by the structures that exist at the mines in a certain region. Fewer revenues have resulted from the decrease of corporate income taxes by many governments in the mining sector as a tactic in the competition to draw investment and efforts to enhance economic development. As an incentive in at least one resource agreement with investors, at least nine governments lowered their ad hoc corporate income tax rates as of 2021.

Playing the Shell Game

A recent IMF study found that collected revenues are significantly affected by global profit shifting. By moving profits to nations with lower tax rates, multinational corporations can minimize their tax obligations in jurisdictions with high tax rates. Underpricing minerals or utilizing subcontractors to transfer profits to foreign countries are two examples. According to this study, multinational mining corporations' tax dodging causes African nations to lose an estimated $450–$730 million in corporate income tax revenue annually.[48]

Staunching the Flow

Targeted policy initiatives can aid nations in reducing tax evasion in the mining industry and promoting revenue generation. It could be beneficial to make a concentrated effort to block present profit-shifting methods. Transfer pricing protection should be strengthened and made simpler. Interest deductions should also be restricted. Tax treaty procedures should also be improved. Investment negotiation procedures should also be strengthened.

This study discovered that the responsiveness in profit allocation by multinational corporations due to differences in international tax rates was reduced by half when interest limitation rules were implemented. When it comes to combating profit shifting in the mining industry, several nations have already had success. Nine of the 15 resource-intensive economies have alternative minimum taxes that can ensure at least some corporate taxes are paid each year, and Kenya added an antitreaty shopping clause to its tax treaty policy. Guinea, Liberia, and Mali strengthened their transfer pricing protection, and South Africa and Nigeria limited interest deductions. Sierra Leone's new fiscal system moved the country away from negotiating fiscal terms mine by mine. It is promised that the mining industry will generate more cash and that these nations will receive compensation on par with it. However, recent international tax developments demonstrate that change is achievable. Improving tax policy and combating tax avoidance involve deliberate planning and stronger capacity, which take time, resources, and political commitment.

Governance: Accountability

Initiatives and policy movements, such as the Extractive Industries Transparency Initiative, are critical to growing and improving the natural resource sector. The EITI represents a broader push for public disclosure of natural resource revenues—globally, 70 percent of developing countries within the top thirty gold-producing countries have implemented the EITI.[49] Reducing corruption in the natural resource and mining sector has the potential to create substantial growth in both national and local economies. Transparency and accountability are the first steps in revolutionizing the sector to avoid the resource curse, or the negative externalities of a booming natural resource sector, such as deindustrialization, the underdevelopment of other sectors, and state fiscal dependence on resource rents.

Governance: Efficiency

A growing focus on citizens' rights as workers and inhabitants of areas near mines or natural resource deposits has created pressure to "secure the social license to operate."[50] Mining companies are increasingly pushed to make heavy investments in the socioeconomic conditions of host communities, covering areas such as health care, education, training, and sanitation. Mining affects local communities positively because of this political pressure, including increased employment and income, improved infrastructure, better worker training, and stronger management.[51] These localized investments help to offset the benefit to national government revenue, and governments facilitate these investments through efficient handling of licensing and permit issuance. Private firms and investors are aided in their pursuit of ownership and operative control of extractive activities and employment by the increased efficiency of governments. Efficiency offsets many of the costs of doing business. For example, in South Africa, mining companies face rising electricity costs, which have risen at double the rate of inflation over the past few years.[52] This is making it necessary for mining companies to invest in innovative ways to achieve energy efficiency.

Operations: Infrastructure Development

A global decline in mineral exploration has left Africa to advance its ongoing extractive projects and fund supporting infrastructure projects, such as the development of roads, ports, and electricity grids. These projects reinforce the economic reliability of investing in African mineral projects and lower costs for firms. Between 2003 and 2030, Deloitte estimates that over 830 infrastructure projects will be undertaken, and about $50 billion will be invested in mining projects during the same period.[53] This comparison indicates the potential level of simultaneous development of roads, bridges, railways, power grids, and water systems with the mining sector, suggesting mutual growth for mutual gain.

Operations: A Faster Transition from Exploration to Online Projects

The speed with which firms transition from their initial investments into establishing the infrastructure and operational capacity to begin extracting minerals is not necessarily correlated with the potential revenue success of these activities. However, perceptions of mineral quality can influence firms to transition more quickly to the production stage. Africa's mineral deposits, particularly in Zambia and the DRC, are becoming globally known for the grade and quality of ore deposits.[54] Higher-grade deposits encourage increased investment and make it more urgent to capitalize on the mineral's potential, even during periods of commodity price declines, as in 2016. The speed of projects' transition is also critical to increasing competition between investors and firms.

Key Players

The mining sector in Africa has evolved in recent years, between large multinational mining companies and the emergence of players such as China, although activities remain focused in key countries in Africa. Let us consider the various key players.

Multinational Mining Companies

Multinational companies have been at the forefront of the sector's growth. Most mining companies in Africa are internationally operated, with headquarters and stock listings in Johannesburg, London, Toronto, and Sydney. Examples include African Copper Plc, Aquarius Platinum, Anvil Mining, Rio Tinto, Oando Energy Resources, the De Beers Group of Companies, Kinross, Kumba Iron Ore, and Cardinal Mining Services. Uranium has attracted numerous multinational companies to explore and produce exports for Europe, the Americas, and Asia. Australia has recently shown a keen interest in investing in the extractive sector in Africa, and the number of Australian companies involved in the exploration and production of minerals has steadily increased over the past two decades.[55] The Australia–Africa Minerals and Energy Group is one particular body that facilitates the trade relationship between Africa and Australian mining companies operating in Africa. The African mining sector is therefore composed of various interconnected local and global players.

Emerging Economies and New Players—China, India, and Brazil

Emerging economies are catching on to Africa's resource boom of the past decade and to the continent's potential to remain dominant in the global market. India, Russia, and Brazil are expanding in Africa's mineral resource sector, increasing their investments and becoming more competitive for rights to known-resource-rich land and unexplored land. Africa still offers low costs of production, and the continent's growing workforce provides a further incentive to expand operations. In about 2012, more multinational companies—the BHP Group, Rio Tinto, Anglo American, and Xtrata—started moving from high-cost projects, such as in Australia, to Africa.[56] India has increased its investments in the continent's metals and minerals sector, offering the potential to incentivize infrastructure development, increase mineral production, and create an entrenched system of value-added processing.[57]

China in particular has demonstrated a formidable presence in Africa. Between 2005 and 2015, China's investment in African mining industries multiplied by a factor of twenty-five.[58] A 2007 loan from China to the DRC totaled $5 billion, indicating to Western countries China's serious intentions to invest in African resource extraction.[59] In 2017, Chinese demand for base metals composed 40 percent of the global market.[60] In order to establish a stable source of commodities to fuel economic expansion, China has continued to develop deals ranging from infrastructure projects to resource extraction, joint ventures, indirect investments, and a diverse array of other agreements. Meanwhile, concerns over Chinese mining in Africa have been a prominent feature of United States–China trade negotiations.[61]

Key Countries and Companies

Some African countries—including South Africa, Niger, Guinea, Ghana, Tanzania, Zambia, the DRC, Namibia, and Mozambique—are endowed with more mineral resources than others. For example, Botswana accounted for 35 percent of Africa's total diamond supply in 2022.[62] Debswana, which is a 50/50 joint venture between the Government of Botswana and the De Beers Group of Companies, is the leading diamond producer and employer in the country.[63] The DRC also supplies a significant amount of diamonds, but it is widely known for having large reserves of copper and cobalt.[64] The DRC is increasingly becoming important in the extractive sector because of its production of two-thirds of the world's supply of cobalt, which is required in renewable energy production.[65]

One of the key players in the country is Gécamines, which is the largest state-owned cobalt and copper-producing company in the DRC.[66] Gécamines entered into joint venture agreements with Chinese companies under the Sicomines agreement, which allows the DRC to obtain infrastructure projects support in exchange for giving Chinese companies some mining rights.[67] First Quantum, a large Canada-based copper producer in Zambia, which accounted for 44 percent of Zambia's total revenue from minerals, is also partially owned by Chinese companies. Gold production in Africa is dominated by Ghana and South Africa.[68] Ghana recently overtook South Africa and became Africa's leading gold producer.[69] Ghana is home to key companies, including Gold Fields, Asanko Gold, and AngloGold Ashanti.[70] The largest gold producer in Ghana is the United States–based Newmont Mining Corporation, which operates Aykem mine and Ahofa mine.[71] The second-largest gold producer in Ghana is Gold Fields, a subsidiary of South Africa's Gold Fields company, which operates Tarkwa Mine, the largest gold mine in Ghana.[72]

South Africa led global gold production for a century, but its gold output is shrinking as a result of increased mining difficulty, as its gold deposits now tend to be much deeper.[73] South Africa is now the second-largest gold producer in Africa, and its largest gold-producing company, Sibanye Gold Ltd, has diversified into platinum production to counter the rising costs of gold extraction in South Africa.[74] For similar reasons, the Anglo Gold company in South Africa began shifting its focus to other countries with lower-cost mines, including Ghana, Mali, and Guinea.[75] In 2018, West Africa received the largest portion of mining investment (oil, natural gas, and gold), followed by Southern Africa (gold, platinum, nickel, and cobalt).[76] East Africa and Central Africa received the least amount of mining investment because of political instability, especially in Central Africa, which limits exploration activities.[77]

Opportunities

Despite the presence of significant challenges and risks within the Africa mining sector, several opportunities for investors are still available for exploration. Table 5-2 summarizes some of the key opportunities and risks within the extractive sector in Africa.

The Availability of Underexplored Mineral Resources

Africa is home to many mineral resources, a significant portion of which are unexplored or underexplored. West Africa as a region is endowed with underexplored mineral resources, especially in Burkina Faso and Côte d'Ivoire, which are the least-explored countries that are part of the Birimian Greenstone Gold Belt, which stretches across Ghana, Côte d'Ivoire, Guinea, Mali, and Burkina Faso.[78] Burkina Faso has recently begun shifting its focus from agriculture by incentivizing investment in its underexplored mining sector.[79] Roxgold, one of the first companies to invest in exploration

Table 5-2. Opportunities and Risks within the African Mining Sector

Opportunities	Risks
New technology (digitization and automation)	COVID-19 pandemic
Growing demand for minerals and metals used in renewable energy production	Fluctuating commodity prices
Availability of underexplored mineral resources	Global trade tensions
Increasing urbanization	Rising extraction costs
Need for mineral processing plants	Inadequate infrastructure
African Continental Free Trade Agreement	Local content policies
Localization	Negative externalities
	Inadequate mineral exploration
	Falling productivity
	Increasing input costs
	Inadequate and often weak industrial base to supply mining inputs

Sources: KPMG data; author's calculations; Global Business Reports & Mining Indaba (2019); Cassim, Goodman, and Rajagopaul (2019).

in Burkina Faso, has grown dramatically in just five years since the drilling of its first mine.[80]

A variety of other companies in Burkina Faso have also recently benefited from new, lucrative gold deposit discoveries. These companies include IAM-GOLD, Teranga Gold, B2Gold, NordGold, and SEMAFO.[81] Côte d'Ivoire and Senegal are currently on the radar for investors because of their under-explored geological potential and stabilizing political situations.[82] Guinea also has gained attention, as the country boasts the largest amount of untapped iron ore reserves globally, with the Mount Simandou region in particular having an estimated 2 billion tons of high-quality iron ore.[83] While underexplored regions offer significant investment opportunities, investors should be prepared to overcome infrastructural challenges: the reason why some of these countries are largely unexplored tends to be poor infrastructure. In fact, the development of mining activities in the Simandou mountain range has been delayed both by difficulties accessing the region and legal challenges.[84]

Zambia

For more than twenty years, Zambia has received significant investment from foreign mining companies because of its favorable geology, its political and macroeconomic stability, its competitive tax environment, and the progressive privatization of its state-owned mines.[85] In addition to a recent series of new laws that seek to rationalize regulations across mining subsectors, and to coordinate and centralize decision-making in the presidency, a new mining fiscal system came into effect in January 2015 to standardize taxes at 8 percent for underground operations, 20 percent for open-cast operations, and 30 percent for income earned from the tolling or processing of minerals. These are relatively low and clear rates by regional standards.[86]

Coal has been produced in Zambia since 1967, and although it is currently one of the smallest producers of coal in the Southern African region—output fell from 214,000 short tons in 2000 to 1,000 short tons in 2010—Zambia's coal output grew rapidly before the commodities market decline in 2016, and there are still at least 50 million metric tons of proven coal reserves to be exploited.[87]

Zambia is currently the sixth-largest copper producer in the world, with 4.4 percent of global output in 2011. In light of the high quality of its copper deposits and a number of substantial expansion projects already under way—especially those by First Quantum in Sentinel and Kansanshi—it was the world's eighth-largest producer of copper as of 2022 and is likely to break into the top five global producers in the near future.[88] Other key deposits in Zambia include emeralds (20 percent of global supply in 2013), copper-cobalt ore (an estimated 2 billion tons in remaining reserves), iron ore (900 metric tons in estimated remaining reserves), gold, and uranium. There is also an abundance of industrial minerals—including feldspar, talc, sands and clay, limestone, dolomite, apatite, and barite—which have the potential to contribute to future growth in manufacturing and agriculture in the region, as well as in mining.

Since Zambia is a landlocked country, its transit infrastructure and port access remain primary constraints on returns on investment. However, there has been impressive investment in Zambia's infrastructure from both public and private sectors in recent years, and several significant new mining projects have been launched as a result. Four major new mines have started operating in recent years—in uranium, gold, copper, and iron ore—contributing to substantial increases in government revenues and export earnings in 2015 and 2016.[89] With $8 billion in investment between 2008 and 2013 alone, figures that are continuing to accelerate, Zambia is expected to become one of Africa's most competitive destinations for future mining projects.[90]

Ghana

Under British colonial rule, Ghana was known as the Gold Coast—an illustration of its historical status as a cradle of valuable resources. In the decades after independence, investment in its extractive sector suffered from political instability, state-led protectionism, policy reversals, and macroeconomic crises caused by an overreliance on cocoa exports.[91] Several positive developments since the mid-1980s have improved its investment climate and, combined with rising gold prices, have resulted in impressive growth in the mining sector. As early as 1995, Ghana was rated among the world's top ten emerging markets for mining—the only African country to be included—in an international survey.[92]

Today, Ghana is Africa's second-largest gold producer, after South Africa. Gold contributed 41 percent to Ghana's total export revenues and more than 5 percent to its overall GDP in 2015.[93] Unsurprisingly, its gold subsector is relatively well saturated, with at least six large mining companies operating ten major gold mines.[94] With 142.2 tons, Ghana is currently the top producer, accounting for 37 percent of all exports and 90 percent of mineral exports. It is crucial to remember that gold reserves accounted for about 1,000 metric tons.[95] Although gold accounts for 95 percent of all Ghana's mineral revenues, there are also operative mines producing bauxite, manganese ore, and diamonds. In total, The country's mining sector contributed roughly $1.6 billion to its annual government revenues in 2016—a 23 percent increase from 2015 levels.[96]

Since 2006, licensing and tax regulations facing Ghana's mining sector have been further liberalized and streamlined through its Minerals and Mining Act. This act allows renewable thirty-year mining leases across subsectors, while ensuring that the state receives an automatic 10 percent stake and that new leases obtain approval from local, traditional authorities as well as from the national Minerals Commission.[97] Although this represents an important step in addressing concerns about the lack of linkages between mining companies and local communities and the broader national economy, a debate rages on in Ghana about the best way to ensure that the population benefits from the country's resource wealth. Potential investors should consider whether the norms or policies that emerge in the future in response to this debate are likely to make an impact on returns on investment. In 2008, for example, members of Ghana's Chamber of Mines spent more than $12 million on voluntary social responsibility projects, and industry players also paid for the University of Mines and Technology to create opportunities for locally generated capacities. Moreover, significant challenges remain in Ghana in the capacity of, and coordination between, the commissions that exist to oversee the industry. These commissions lack adequate funding, which heightens uncertainty about the way tax laws are interpreted and implemented.[98]

South Africa

The South African government has taken major steps to prioritize the mining sector as an engine of economic growth for the country. The government has debated several measures in the past decade to determine the best configuration to enable companies to lower costs, raise revenues, and mitigate labor grievances. Though the country and the mining industry suffered a heavy blow from the 2012 Marikana massacre, investors have still determined that South African gold is a safe bet and have increased their market capitalization, from 22 percent in 2014 to 48 percent in 2016.[99] Platinum mining companies also improved their market capitalization, increasing from 155 billion rand in 2015 to 178 billion rand in 2016, although platinum prices declined between 2014 and 2018 as diesel vehicle production slowed.[100] South Africa's coal industry has seen a significant increase in market share, and it has proven to be a steady investment in recent years. Total revenue in the coal industry increased by 1.3 billion rand from 2015 to 2016, and global prices rose through 2018.[101]

Iron ore extraction in South Africa showed real production growth over the last ten years. Infrastructure development in transportation aided high production levels, which have been maintained despite mid-2010s drops in commodity prices. Iron ore has also sharply decreased in price.[102] In 2019, however, iron ore prices increased to the highest levels since early 2017, due in part to a dam collapse in Brazil that spurred the shutting down of ten other dams connected to iron ore production.[103] In 2020, the trajectory of production and prices was unclear, though Africa's considerable reserves offer long-term potential for higher production levels.[104]

On the benefit side, the mining production process—the revenue (or value added) that mining produces—resides in the forefront. The return on the production elements—such as salaries (i.e., the return on labor) paid to employees, profits (the return on capital) paid to investors, and tax income to the government—are all included in value added. In mining, the "economic rent," or the return on the resource itself, is given particular attention. These rents are frequently unnatural mining profits, or the discrepancy between the value of mining sales and costs. Since costs are generally constant, the magnitude of the rent is determined by the price of the commodity, with high prices translating into high rents. In a way, mining is done so that societies can profit from the commercialization of national-asset-quality natural resource deposits. This analysis pays particular attention to the multipliers mining generates through backward and forward linkages with the rest of the economy, which can range from local communities supplying mines to highly complex technical inputs sold by local companies or imported from foreign firms, in addition to value added. Many of the externalities that the production process creates, such as health or pollution costs, are internalized by the mining industry; this compensation must also be taken into account under benefits, offsetting costs.[105]

Kenya

The Kenyan economy is booming, with mining currently considered by industry analysts to be one of the key opportunities for investment. In 2018, the mining sector contributed less than 1 percent to Kenya's total GDP, but the Kenyan government is working to grow the mining sector's GDP to as much as 10 percent by 2030. This suggests that the sector will likely experience a favorable investment and regulatory climate.[106] Kenya already has a well-developed mining subsector focused on industrial materials—including limestone, marbles, soda ash, fluorspar, and dolomites—that help to support growth in manufacturing and construction. Growth in domestic cement production, which requires supplies of gypsum and limestone, is expected to increase rapidly in the near future to support the government's "Vision 2030," which has dedicated substantial investment to infrastructure and construction projects.[107] In addition to the wealth of nonmetallic commodities already being exploited, recent discoveries of rare earth deposits along the coastal region, which are relatively cheap and easy to distribute to seaports, are valued at about $62.4 billion, placing Kenya among the top five countries in the world for such reserves.

Participation of the community in decision-making procedures has long-term effects on the community's social, economic, and environmental conditions. This bottom-up strategy for environmental democratization encourages local residents to take part in decision-making. Environmental peace builds the framework for environmental justice, according to environmental democratization. Conflicts in resource zones are decreased by promoting local community involvement. The mere mention of some multinational corporations (like Shell in Nigeria and Lonmin in South Africa) currently causes animosity and unrest among the communities that housed these businesses in the majority of African states.

Relying on environmental democratization paradigms precludes the central government from making choices about the management of natural resources in a unilateral manner and, consequently, from exercising power in a unilateral manner. Because of the enormous governance gap created by an unregulated globalization drive, indigenous communities that host extractive projects are more vulnerable to being denied their rights. The international community has developed a number of voluntary projects to address this problem that could act as a baseline for states, businesses, and stakeholders. Voluntary initiatives, such as the UN Guiding Principles on Business and Human Rights, describe the key building blocks for mainstreaming human rights in regulations and legislation in a way that delivers more effective protection for persons and communities, as the UN's statement reads. If the stress and disputes in resource regions are to be addressed by the government, environmental democratization should be a regulated process and be given proper consideration.[108]

Mozambique

Mozambique's mining sector has experienced a recent increase in nationalization. The nation's new Mining Law, which was introduced in August 2014, states that mineral resources found within the country's boundaries are considered to be state property. This policy has demonstrable effects on the participation of the local population in the mining industry, given that there must be between 5 percent and 20 percent local shareholders in each major mining project or concession that lasts up to twenty-five years.[109]

These laws and stipulations reflect the government's awareness of the country's vital natural resources. Mozambique hosts some of the world's largest untapped coal deposits—both high-quality coking coal and thermal coal—and deposits of graphite, iron ore, titanium apatite, marble, bentonite, bauxite, kaolin, copper, gold, and tantalum.[110] Other major investment projects in Mozambique include the mining and processing ventures of its heavy sand deposits. The Moma Heavy Sands and Corridor Sands projects, operated by Kenmare Resources and the BHP Group, respectively, require investments of more than $1 billion.[111] These projects highlight the vast investment and revenue potential of Mozambique's natural resources.

Challenges and Risks

The challenges of investment and growth in Africa's mining sector depend, to a large degree, on the type of mining activity pursued. For example, deposits that tend to be located in landlocked areas, such as ferrochrome and cobalt, are liable to face higher distribution costs, while subindustries that have longer histories on the continent, especially coal, tend to face more barriers to accessing commercial credit and higher interest rates due to legacy debts.[112] As in any economic sector, investment risk and operating costs also vary depending on the target country, especially as several African countries attempt to overhaul their regulatory and tax structures that apply to mining companies.[113] In general, however, common challenges can be identified across the sector—along with the risk of uncertainty in the demand for natural resources that are being mined.

The COVID-19 Pandemic

The COVID-19 pandemic and its associated business disruptions are having both immediate and long-term implications for the mining industry. Because countries implemented quarantine measures and restrictions on movement of people to curb the spread of the coronavirus, many businesses shut down and the mining industry experienced immediate demand-side shocks.[114] Demand contracted because construction projects and industrial production, especially of nonessential goods, almost came to a halt.[115] Commodity prices tanked as a result of contraction of demand globally, and aluminum and copper initially took the hardest hit within the mining sector.[116] Some companies had to shut down nonessential mining operations in response to new regulations to control the pandemic.

The most affected region in Africa was Southern Africa, primarily South Africa, which had the highest number of COVID-19 infections in the region.[117] In response to COVID-19, South Africa initially ordered all underground mining activities to be halted temporarily to protect workers.[118] In April 2020, the South African government mandated that mining companies operate at a "reduced capacity of not more than 50 percent" and to provide rigorous testing and quarantine facilities for employees at mining sites.[119]

Other African countries were also subjected to labor restrictions, but the severity of this disruption's impact on operations largely depended on different factors, including the level of automation. Some industry players, especially large-scale and labor-intensive mine sites, were more affected than others.[120] For example, while the Rio Tinto mine in Mongolia was temporarily forced to shut down nonessential operations, leading to a slowdown in production,[121] Syama mine in Mali, a fully automated mine equipped with self-driving vehicles and drills, continued to operate at near maximum capacity through its already-established remote operation center.[122] These outcomes could potentially accelerate the adoption of automation technology in mining in the near future.

One of the biggest disruptions of COVID-19 was the economic slowdown in China, which is a key driver of global commodity demand growth and the main trading partner of many African countries.[123] Commodity-dependent

African countries were more vulnerable to the external shocks presented by COVID-19.[124] Disruption of global supply chains could drive up costs of operation as mining companies are forced into longer delays or to source raw materials locally. Localization can result in higher costs in the short term but also has the potential to benefit companies in the long run in the form of less vulnerability to global supply chain disruptions, lower transportation costs, and shorter delivery times. Due to the evolving nature of the COVID-19 pandemic, it was difficult to predict the future impact of the pandemic on the mining industry; therefore, mining companies faced high levels of uncertainty, which held back investments in new projects and operations.

Numerous economies around the world were affected by the COVID-19 outbreak. According to an evaluation of the pandemic's effects in Ghana, Mali, South Africa, and Zambia, there were effects on government revenues, employment, and output. The pandemic's consequences led to supply and demand shocks that decreased prices for most minerals, with the exception of gold.[125]

Resource Curse / Dutch Disease

In developing countries, where institutions tend to be weaker and economies are less diversified, resource wealth can often have adverse effects on the potential for future growth and good governance. Investment in human and physical capital is often hampered by the fact that revenues generated by resource extraction are finite, and that they create opportunities for public officials to engage in rent-seeking behavior. In these conditions, both the public and private sectors are prone to corruption and are less likely to invest in the development of broader infrastructure, strong institutions, or public goods that would contribute to a productive workforce and encourage entrepreneurial behavior. These public goods include education, health care, and legal mechanisms for enforcing contracts and protecting property rights.[126] Meanwhile, competition over resource wealth, particularly in the absence of gainful employment opportunities—since the mining sector tends to employ a disproportionately low share of the local workforce—enhances the likelihood of violent conflict between identity groups whose members feel a sense of ownership of the land, along with the political elites who become entrenched in lucrative networks of corruption.[127]

In macroeconomic terms, countries also become more susceptible to boom-and-bust cycles, especially as they increasingly rely on resource exports.[128] The high value of resources during boom periods tends to strengthen the local currency, which discourages investment in other productive sectors of the economy and thereby enhances dependence on resources to generate export revenues. A subsequent decline in the world market price of commodities causes rapid and unpredictable losses in state revenues and trade deficits, resulting in central government debt and inflationary pressures on the currency, and thereby further hampering investment—a vicious cycle known as Dutch disease.[129]

Many African countries are already highly dependent on resources, with two of the continent's fifty-four countries generating more than 75 percent of their annual export earnings from mineral products.[130] Under these conditions, the potential for economic diversification and development is especially low, since foreign and domestic companies are unlikely to invest in nonextractive sectors, such as manufacturing or agriculture. Much of the minerals produced in Africa are actually exported without processing, illustrating the absence of effective linkages between mining and other productive economic sectors. As a result, resource-dependent economies have already been negatively affected by the decline in global commodity prices since 2014, especially those with substantial exports of coal, metals, and diamonds.[131]

Negative Externalities

Beyond the well-established negative correlation between resource wealth and economic indicators, mining exploration and extraction have been shown to make an impact on local environments and populations in several ways.[132] Despite increasing attempts to combat pollution and climate change through regulation at national and international levels, the sector continues to exacerbate environmental degradation—a problem that is especially pronounced at the local level. Mining exacerbates deforestation and land degradation, generates substantial volumes of industrial waste, creates large-scale surface disturbances, and releases potentially harmful noxious gasses into the atmosphere, even when complying with current best practices.[133] For example, the heavy machinery used to extract minerals such as gold generates large amounts of dust, which often destroys surrounding vegetation and is associated with respiratory problems, especially among children and the elderly.[134]

Thus, social dislocation is not only a product of people being forcibly relocated to make room for mining concessions. Negative spillovers of water, soil, and air pollution also reduce the agricultural productivity of remaining farms, while the sector generally fails to provide alternative employment opportunities or health services for people whose livelihoods have been affected.[135] The inability of the public sector to address these social issues has often resulted in conflict—for example, several labor strikes at South Africa's platinum and gold mines have resulted in deaths.[136] There is variation across countries, however. In some countries, the local population's health indicators actually appear to improve near mining sites, possibly because of higher incomes and more available infrastructure, such as electricity and clean water. In Mali, areas surrounding mining sites have lower infant mortality rates, less stunted growth, and lower incidences of respiratory disorders.

Infrastructure

The relative logistics-related cost of mining in Africa is estimated to be 250 percent of the world average because of infrastructure gaps, especially in transit and energy networks.[137] Only 10 percent of the land on the African continent is within 100 kilometers of the coastline—compared with 27 percent in Latin America, for example—and there are few navigable rivers connecting the high plateau inland to seaports. This often means that many of Africa's resource reserves are stranded inland, in part because individual mining projects are unable to absorb the full cost of the infrastructure development that would be necessary to access and export the minerals.

Energy supply tends to be expensive and unreliable in Africa, which is a challenge for mining ventures in gold, aluminum, platinum, and copper. Depending on the extractive sector, electricity accounts for between 15 and 40 percent of operating costs for mining companies working in the region, with supply fluctuations having substantial effects on profitability.[138] As a result, self-supply has increased substantially, from 6 percent of mining projects in 2000 to an estimated 18 percent in 2020. At the same time, demand for power in the mining sector was expected reach 23,443 megawatts per year by 2020—roughly 150 percent of the volume of demand in 2012—and account for up to 35 percent of total grid supply in the region.[139]

Access to Finance

In the current commodities market, it is likely to be difficult for any mining company to secure adequate or favorable financing, and not only those working in Africa. There has been a dramatic decline in the world market prices of hydrocarbons, copper, and other minerals since 2014, and Chinese demand for minerals has decreased markedly in recent years, because of the deceleration of domestic economic growth in China. In the future, the global shift to renewable energy is likely to undermine the prospects for thermal coal ventures, in particular. As a result of these conditions, however, many mineral producers have attempted to ratchet up existing operations to reduce costs per unit or to capture market share, which is likely to give heavily invested corporations an advantage over future competition if commodities markets rebound. In the meantime, further mineral exploration and market entry are likely to be impeded unless companies are willing to accept unfavorable credit terms.[140]

Sustainable cost reductions can be achieved by balancing short-term advantages and long-term value. Demand is rising as a result of the COVID-19 pandemic, but so are input, shipping, labor, and decarbonization program expenses. For miners, cutting costs and increasing productivity requires striking a balance between securing short-term profits and generating long-term value. Variability has a significant impact on the output of miners. Improved geological modeling to reduce uncertainty, asset performance analytics to enable predictive maintenance and increase reliability, operational discipline to deliver consistent results, and integrated operating models that are aligned with markets to enable quick response to change are all necessary for managing this.

Local Content Policies

Local content policies refer to the requirements put in place by communities directly adjacent to extraction projects, usually requiring specific benefits to be guaranteed to local populations and the national economy at large. About 9 out of 10 resource-rich nations implement some sort of local content policies in employment, domestic involvement in material processing, or other forms of economic investment.[141] For instance, South Africa's 2018 Mining Charter has local procurement requirements mandating that 70 percent of total mining goods procurement spending be on domestic manufactured goods.[142] Though designed to ensure protection for those most directly affected by mining sites and to enhance education, infrastructure, and incomes, among other benefits, local content policies have often been poorly executed and even detrimental to those involved.[143]

In fact, of the average national contributions of mining in low- and middle-income countries in 2016, only 1 to 2 percent went to job creation.[144] In some cases, these requirements have demanded unrealistic levels of local employment that assume training and skill sets that could be better found in other regions of the nation, resulted in supply-and-demand bottlenecks, and leading to more expensive projects that benefit the local community less.[145] This type of agreement can and has affected positive change in numerous contexts but must be carefully designed to avoid unintended consequences.[146] For instance, in Nigeria, a recent study evaluating the impact of local content policies found that while Nigeria's policies had a positive, significant impact on local value creation, the value created was lower than the expected target.[147] To enact effective local content policies, it is essential for governments and firms to consider available capacity, practicality, evaluation tools, and inclusivity.

Jihadism—Threats to Mining

On June 4, 2022, extremists on motorbikes rode into Solhan, Burkina Faso, a major hub for gold mining in the region, and killed 130 people. It was the bloodiest attack in the nation's history and a graphic illustration of how extremists are deliberately targeting the nation's thousands of artisanal mines, which are said to collectively produce up to 30 tons of gold annually, in search of rich funding sources. The Sahel area of Burkina Faso put a ban on all artisanal mining after the incident, in response to the growing correlation between gold and terrorism. Contrary to valuable gemstones, gold still lacks traceability. This is partially because it is more difficult to chemically link one piece of gold to another specific mine, making the task more difficult to control.[148]

The artisanal mining of gold can be a dangerous activity, with numerous health and environmental risks. Furthermore, children frequently labor in these small-scale mines. Another problem is that every year, other countries get billions of dollars' worth of gold that is smuggled out of Africa, breaking trade laws and depriving African countries of much-needed tax money.

Investment Strategies

The development benefits of mining can be measured in numerous African countries, and more countries that capitalize on their resource potential will enjoy these benefits. The distribution of wealth, the reduction in poverty, and the accumulation of capital that can result from a booming natural resource sector must be facilitated by sustained investment. Partnerships are key to unlocking the potential of the mining industry across Africa. Where countries have succeeded with heavily state-regulated industries, others can tout the benefits of private participation and even management. In gold-producing countries, evidence suggests that gold-mining companies can be reliable, growth-inducing development partners.[149]

Public–private partnerships imply greater coordination of regulations, strategies, and information sharing for the overall benefit of the sector. Government bodies must adapt their technical processes and regulations surrounding private ownership and management of extractive mining industries, to free up capital and debt issuance for these privately owned industries. Private firms should take the lead in conducting research on the socioeconomic effects of mining in individual countries. Social development is a critical area in need of significant investment from private corporations that have the floating capital to provide education, health, and social services for the benefit of host communities—where many workers are likely to be employed. The mining industry can lead directly to socioeconomic benefits for African countries, whose governments would greatly benefit from domestically based development assistance.

Countries with confirmed natural resource endowments—including Botswana, the DRC, South Africa, Namibia, and Tanzania—are reliable locations for investment because of the availability of infrastructure and technical support for mining operations, in addition to current extraction projects. Other countries—including Ghana, Zambia, Mozambique, and Kenya—require substantially higher sums of investment but offer the potential for higher returns for first movers. Buying stock in resource companies is important for the continuation of ongoing projects and mineral extraction, while direct investment in exploration or mining projects is important to influence the direction of mineral extraction in a country.

Many researchers advocate for investment to go to long-term infrastructure projects that can underpin the extractive industries and support an array of sectors that will bring capital to local economies and elevate the business environment.[150] The African Union contends that "such stabilization or future funds would also go some way in providing 'intergenerational equity' over non-renewable resource extraction, as future generations would be the beneficiaries of the investments into improving the national infrastructure platform."[151] This long-term strategy requires the maintenance of strong partnerships between African stakeholders and foreign investors or firms.

While the mining sector does not always provide for equitable growth or wealth distribution, it presents an opportunity for foreign and multinational investors to engage in development and economic growth plans with the potential for higher profits than in other less-resource-rich regions of the world. These revenues can be injected back into host communities, assuming effective, accountable governance, and thus can improve the value chain of firms entering a country's mining sector. The International Council on Mining and Metals (ICMM) is in favor of revenue transparency among governments to ensure that companies are accountable to their shareholders. African governments' adherence to ICMM recommendations should be a signal to investors of the levels of accountability within countries. Mining companies currently operating across Africa are also responsible for adhering to ICMM commitments to transparency, for the sake of elevating Africa's mining sector to a level of global competition. Investments in the sector should target long-term infrastructure projects that will catapult mineral extraction industries to the forefront of economic development and growth.

Looking to the Future

Collaboration among mining companies, governments, civil society, and other stakeholders is the key to unlocking the potential of Africa's mining and natural resource sector. Each of these stakeholders must avoid disputes and ensure equitable sharing of opportunity, wealth, and decision-making. The mining sector has suffered from fluctuations of conflict, commodity price booms and busts, corruption, and a lack of accessible capital, but there is significant potential to overcome these challenges and ensure that the mining sector is a revenue-generating stalwart for future decades. The COVID-19 pandemic exacerbated the challenges faced by the mining sector, but some opportunities remained for companies to explore. Africa is set to emerge as a key supplier of the minerals and metals required in the production of clean energy globally.[152] Energy transitions are creating new opportunities for a set of mineral resources, including cobalt, lithium and platinum.[153] The rising demand for these minerals shows that investing in their exploration and extraction has the potential to bring in sustainable revenue and profits. It is difficult to make accurate predictions of actual economic growth or contraction figures as a result of the COVID-19 pandemic.

The challenge of rising costs faced by mining companies can be mitigated by the adoption of artificial intelligence, automation, and big data. Such technologies can help companies reduce operational costs, boost productivity, and increase profit margins.[154] For example, drones can be used to significantly shorten surveying time, while improving accuracy. Smart protective devices are also a good option for companies to increase worker safety. In 2018, the Syama mine in Mali launched its autonomous mining operation, which consists of self-driving trucks, drillers, and loaders.[155] OptiMine, the technology used to power autonomous mining at the Syama mine, is capable of providing descriptive and predictive insights that can be used to optimize production processes.[156] Other mining companies are exploring the effectiveness of this digital solution for potential implementation. The Chamber of Mines in South Africa has set up the Digital Mine Laboratory at the University of Witwatersrand to explore innovative digital solutions to improve productivity and safety in mining operations.[157] Another opportunity mining companies can utilize is applying advanced analytics to optimize mine planning, increase yields, and reduce equipment downtime. A thirty-year-old gold processing plant in South Africa applied advanced analytics across key processes and managed to improve its processing efficiency by up to 2 percent.[158] Continued adoption of new technologies and strategies can help extractive companies to remain competitive.

To address the priorities of productivity, safety, and environmental, social, and governance standards, miners are driving innovation. The use of technology and innovation has been crucial in assisting miners in increasing production. In order to facilitate more flexible cost decision-making, an EY study anticipates seeing an even higher use of data science, modeling, and scenario planning. The enormous potential of digital to enhance onsite health and safety was also underlined by COVID-19. The 2022 EY poll found that businesses intend to expand investment in automation and remote operation centers because these technologies helped miners survive the pandemic. Technology is another tool that miners are using as part of their environmental, social, and governance standards strategy. Diversification into greener products and more reporting transparency are both possible thanks to digital innovation.[159]

Another important technological advancement that mining companies can utilize is the adoption of renewable, energy-efficient systems. Globally, at least forty-one mining sites have installed renewable capacity, including the Essakane gold mine in Burkina Faso, which installed 130,000 photovoltaic solar panels to reduce its reliance on fossil fuels and to lower its carbon footprint.[160] Similar plans to adopt efficient renewable energy systems are under way in many other mines but are at different stages of execution.[161] While the adoption of new innovative technologies can mean high initial costs for companies, it provides an opportunity to cut costs in the long term, with long-lasting benefits in productivity and safety, which are essential for the resilience of the extractive sector in Africa.

The UN's Sustainable Development Goals place additional responsibility on mining companies to ensure that they are development partners, contributing to a positive presence in local economies and creating socioeconomic benefits for the countries from which they are sourced.[162] A study of the impact of mining in various African countries concluded that while Tanzania reduced extreme poverty from 84 percent to 67 percent between 2000 and 2007, Ghana and Mali experienced little to no reduction in poverty during the same period.[163] These figures indicate that political and regulatory changes must occur for African countries to transition, and for multinational corporations to move from transactional relationships to mutually beneficial partnerships. Policy recommendations that should be espoused are:

1. Increase and ensure appropriate use of government revenues.

2. Implement strong support to the artisanal and small-scale mining sector (this field is roughly 12 million people).

3. Encourage automation technologies in the mining sector.

4. Support regional efforts to improve local content and value added.

5. Implement strategies for continuity in mining operations.

This would help with the transformation of minerals on the African continent as a viable way to spur economic growth and industrialization.[164] In particular, African governments have increasingly expressed interest in the value-added transformation of minerals, as shown by the Ghanaian government's interest in establishing an aluminum industry to capitalize on its bauxite deposits.[165] However, an immediate shift to transforming minerals on the African continent will not automatically drive development, as Africa currently lacks much of the infrastructure needed for these processes. The mining sector as a whole is a huge consumer of electricity, accounting for about 53.6 percent of consumption in the Central African copper belt.[166]

Additional minerals processing activities will only add to the electricity burden from this sector, while many Africans still suffer from insufficient access to electricity. In 2018, nearly half of all Africans lacked access to electricity, and frequent electricity disruptions caused economic losses for about 80 percent of Sub-Saharan African companies.[167] To make African countries competitive compared with other countries for value-added minerals transformation, significant investments need to be made in infrastructure, particularly in electricity access. Even after these investments, however, the value added in mineral transformation is often unstable. Transformation typically results in another product that can also suffer from commodity price shocks, as seen in the case of bauxite and aluminum. As a result, promoting mineral transformation should not be the sole or most important strategy employed to underpin long-term socioeconomic development on the continent.

The mining and natural resource sector is an important player in the overall economic development of African countries. Institutional strength is exceptionally important for the mining sector; this chapter has outlined both the risks and benefits of growing the natural resource sector amid both strong and weak institutions. Credibility and accountability are essential to encourage further investment in and exploration of Africa's vast mineral and natural resource wealth, which has the potential to boost the continent's economies for decades.

Notes

1. NRGI (2022).
2. NRGI (2022).
3. Zero Carbon Analytics (2024).
4. Zero Carbon Analytics (2024).
5. Chen et al. (2024).
6. IEA (2019, 28).
7. Invest Africa (2024).
8. Afreximbank (2023).
9. Chen et al. (2024).
10. UNCTAD (2019c, 44).
11. S&P Global (2024).
12. Chen et al. (2024).
13. Chen et al. (2024).
14. Banrejee et al. (2014, 11); Bermúdez-Lugo (2012, 1, 3).
15. African Union (2009, 5).
16. African Union (2009, 13).
17. Elliot et al. (2012).
18. Campbell (2013); Bermúdez-Lugo (2012, 1–2).
19. NRGI (2015). See Auty (2001) for an in-depth discussion of the impact of the "resource curse."
20. EITI (2020, 1).
21. See EITI's list of member countries at https://eiti.org/countries.
22. AfDB (2012).
23. USGS (2020); Brown et al. (2020).
24. IEA (2019, 202).
25. See "Ores and Metal Exports (Percent of Merchandise Exports): Sub-Saharan Africa," https://data.worldbank.org/indicator/TX.VAL.MMTL.ZS.UN?locations=ZG.
26. Banerjee et al. (2014, 11).
27. USGS (2020).
28. Matsika (2010).
29. Bermúdez-Lugo (2016).
30. Benton (2020).
31. Bermúdez-Lugo (2016, 1–2).
32. Deloitte (2024).
33. Deloitte (2024).
34. Abe (2022).
35. World Gold Council (2021).
36. OECD (2008).
37. Gylfason, Herbertsson, and Zoega (1999).
38. Nyamwaya (2013).

39. AfDB (2012).

40. Ashraf et al. (2015).

41. Addison and Roe (2018, 62).

42. Addison and Roe (2018, 62).

43. PwC (2012c).

44. Albertin, Devlin, and Yontcheva (2021).

45. Albertin, Devlin, and Yontcheva (2021).

46. Deloitte (2015).

47. Deloitte (2015).

48. Albertin, Devlin, and Yontcheva (2021).

49. World Gold Council (2015, 1).

50. World Gold Council (2015, 1).

51. Chuhan-Pole, Dabalen, and Land (2017, 67–68).

52. Cassim, Goodman, and Rajagopaul (2019).

53. Cassim, Goodman, and Rajagopaul (2019).

54. Cassim, Goodman, and Rajagopaul (2019).

55. PwC Australia–Africa Practice (2019, 11); Department of Foreign Affairs and Trade (2019).

56. AfDB (2012).

57. AfDB (2012).

58. Basov (2015).

59. Vedie (2017).

60. IDE-JETRO (2009).

61. Basov (2015); Vedie (2017).

62. See the statistics at https://www.statista.com/statistics/1322183/share-of-diamond-exports-from-africa-by-country/.

63. PR Newswire (2020). See Debwana's site: https://www.debswana.com/.

64. USGS (2020, 51).

65. IEA (2019, 28).

66. EITI (2023, 37).

67. EITI (2023, 37).

68. Brightmore (2020).

69. Brightmore (2020).

70. Rashotte (2019).

71. Oxford Business Group (2019).

72. Oxford Business Group (2019).

73. Brightmore (2020).

74. Brightmore (2020).

75. Brightmore (2020).

76. PwC Australia–Africa Practice (2019, 11).

77. PwC Australia–Africa Practice (2019, 11).

78. Global Business Reports & Mining Indaba (2019, 3, 92).

79. Global Business Reports & Mining Indaba (2019, 121).

80. Stancu (2020).

81. Global Business Reports and Mining Indaba (2019, 122–25).

82. Global Business Reports and Mining Indaba (2019, 102, 109).

83. RioTinto (n.d.).

84. Ford (2024).

85. World Bank (2016b).

86. Deloitte (2015, 7). See the Mines and Minerals Development Act No. 7 of 2008, Mines and Minerals Development (General) Regulations of 2008: https://faolex.fao.org/docs/pdf/zam133579.pdf; and Mines and Minerals Development (Prospecting Mining and Milling of Uranium Ores and Other Radioactive Mineral Ores) Regulations 2008 at https://faolex.fao.org/docs/pdf/zam133724.pdf.

87. KPMG (2013, 24–25); See the website https://www.worldometers.info/coal/zambia-coal/.

88. KPMG (2013, 4).

89. Chamber of Mines (2016).

90. KPMG (2013, 4).

91. Leith and Lofchie (1993); Ayee et al. (2011, 13).

92. Ayee et al. (2011, 13).

93. Ayee et al. (2011, 12); Mensah et al. (2015).

94. These are Goldfields Ghana Ltd (Tarkwa and Abosso mines), Anglo Gold Ashanti (Obuasi and Iduapriem mines), Central Africa Gold (formerly, AngloGold Ashanti Bibiani Mines), Golden Star Resources (Bogosu/Prestea and Akyempim mines), and, recently, Redback Mining Ltd (Chirano mine) and Newmont Ghana Gold Ltd (Ahafo and Akyemmines). See Amponsah-Tawiah and Dartey-Baah (2011, 2).

95. Besta (2020).

96. Ghana Business News (2017).

97. See Deloitte (2015, 7).

98. Ayee et al. (2011, 5).

99. PwC (2016b, 5).

100. PwC (2016b, 5); Policy Center for the New South and CyclOpe (2019, 221).

101. PwC (2016b, 8); Policy Center for the New South and CyclOpe (2019, 235).

102. PwC (2016b, 12).

103. Policy Center for the New South and CyclOpe (2019).

104. Policy Center for the New South and CyclOpe (2019, 209).

105. World Bank (2020f).

106. EARF (2018).

107. Yager (2013).

108. Abe (2022).

109. Deloitte (2015, 7).

110. International Trade Administration (n.d.-a).

111. International Trade Administration (n.d.-a).

112. Deloitte (2015, 24).

113. Bungane (2015).

114. McKinsey & Company (2020).

115. Laing (2020, 580); McKinsey & Company (2020).

116. Laing (2020, 580).

117. EITI (2020a, 6, 37).

118. EITI (2020a, 181).

119. Heiberg (2020).

120. Intergovernmental Forum on Mining, Mineral, Metals, and Sustainable Development (2020, 6).

121. Laing (2020, 581); Hall (2020).

122. Intergovernmental Forum on Mining, Mineral, Metals, and Sustainable development (2020, 6); Hall (2020).

123. EITI (2020b, 33, 36).

124. EITI (2020a, 6).

125. Ahadjie et al. (2021).

126. Auty (2001); Gelb (1988); Gylfason, Herbertsson, and Zoega (1999, 6); Nyamwaya (2013).

127. Gylfason, Herbertsson, and Zoega (1999, 6); Nyamwaya (2013); OECD (2009, 18).

128. OECD (2009, 18).

129. African Union (2009, 27); Gylfason, Herbertsson, and Zoega (1999); Corden (1984).

130. OECD (2009, 18).

131. Deloitte (2015, 24).

132. Veiga and Beinhoff (1997); Warhurst (1994, 1999); Akabzaa (2001).

133. Amponsah-Tawiah and Dartey-Baah (2011, 6); Chiaro and Joklik (1998, 13–206).

134. Aragón and Rud (2013).

135. Chuhan-Pole, Dabalen, and Land (2017, 20); Amponsah-Tawiah and Dartey-Baah (2011, 5); Aragón and Rud (2013).

136. AfDB (2012).

137. Africa Union (2009, 28–29).

138. Deloitte (2015, 7).

139. Banerjee et al. (2014).

140. Bungane (2015).

141. Intergovernmental Forum on Mining, Minerals, Metals, and Sustainable Development (2019).

142. Intergovernmental Forum on Mining, Minerals, Metals, and Sustainable Development (2019).

143. Policy Center for the New South and CyclOpe (2019).

144. Ramdoo (2017).

145. Ramdoo (2017).

146. Adedji et al. (2016).

147. Adedji et al. (2016).

148. *Financial Times* (2021).

149. World Gold Council (2015, 1).

150. Africa Union (2009, 27–28).

151. Africa Union (2009, 27–28).

152. IEA (2019, 3).

153. IEA (2019, 28, 157).

154. Cassim, Goodman, and Rajagopaul (2019, 8).

155. Hall (2020).

156. Hall (2020).

157. See the University of Witwatersrand's 'DigiMine' (2020) site: https://www.wits.ac.za/wmi/digimine/.

158. Cassim, Goodman, and Rajagopaul (2019, 6).

159. EY (2018).

160. UNCTAD (2019c, 48).

161. UNCTAD (2019c, 48).

162. World Gold Council (2015, 1).

163. World Gold Council (2015, 14).

164. Gudyanga (2020).

165. UNOGOZI Institute (2017).

166. Imasiku and Thomas (2020).

167. IEA (2019).

Six

Africa's Insurance Potential
TRENDS, OPPORTUNITIES, CHALLENGES, AND STRATEGIES

Amid an expanding middle class, enabling regulatory reforms, increasing digitization, and a growing knowledge of the benefits of insurance, the insurance industry is poised for significant growth. By 2032, the African insurance market is expected to reach $153.9 billion, with a compound annual growth rate of 6.3 percent between 2024 ad 2032.[1] By 2050, business spending in banking and insurance could exceed $640 billion.[2] Unlocking Africa's insurance[3] potential is critical, given its connections with promoting economic growth, development, and gender equality.[4] For example, by 2030, female customers will contribute $1.7 trillion to the global insurance industry, half of which will come from emerging markets.[5]

The total insurance penetration rate in Africa, measured as premiums as a percentage of gross domestic product (GDP), is under 3 percent, which is less than half the global average. Also in Africa, premiums per capita are about 11 times lower than the global average.[6] Yet, given the growth in African economies, there is immense potential for the market to expand amid growing financial entrepreneurship and cross-sectoral projects across the continent.[7]

Seven African countries host 83 percent of the roughly $68.15 billion total value of the insurance market.[8] South Africa, Kenya, Egypt, Nigeria, Algeria, Namibia, and Tunisia are the continent's largest insurance markets, but South Africa independently leads the life insurance market, with 85 percent of the market share.[9] South Africa is the continent's largest insurance market, accounting for over 69 percent of all premiums. It is followed by

Morocco (6.6 percent), Kenya (3.3 percent), Egypt (2.8 percent), and Nigeria (2.4 percent). These collectively represent 84.1 percent of the market.[10]

The insurance market is bound to expand, with greater participation by traditional insurance companies, and it can expand exponentially when reinsurance companies enter the market to accommodate increased risk. Reinsurance, which is an extension of the insurance market whereby an insurance company seeks to arrange a contract with a reinsurer for potential losses incurred from already-issued insurance policies, is set to expand on the continent.[11] The growth of the rest of the African countries as emerging markets has made an impact on the demand for insurance and has shifted the interest of global investors and insurance companies toward the continent. Despite fluctuations in insurance premium values in different African countries, the insurance market is continually developing alongside global trends toward digital integration and reinsurance resurgence. For example, social distancing regulations during the COVID-19 pandemic forced many insurance companies to rapidly digitize their operations, and this process has the potential to bring long-term benefits of efficiency and profitability.[12]

Changing risk assessments of the viability of African markets has forced the insurance sector to adapt and re-engage with domestic and international stakeholders. South Africa accounts for 44 percent of the continent's non–life insurance premium volume.[13] Countries like Namibia, Zambia, Ghana, Nigeria, and Tanzania have become new targets for insurance companies hoping to serve growing markets, particularly infrastructure development and industrialization processes that require insurance contracts to mitigate risk for investors and those with limited recovery capital. Changing climates and shifting patterns of development are increasing the risk to private investors, and insurance companies are poised to capitalize on the opportunities growing on the African continent.

Background Facts and Trends

The insurance sector contains three components: life insurance, nonlife insurance, and reinsurance. Life insurance—which includes savings, pensions, and health insurance—is generally considered the most beneficial for the low-income stratum of the population, and thus the most important for driving social and economic development. Africa's GDP share of life insurance premiums was second only to South and East Asia among emerging markets; but in 2019, insurance premiums accounted for only 2.65 percent

Table 6-1. Total Insurance Premiums in the Largest African Markets, 2019 (million dollars)

Country	Non–Life Premiums	Life Premiums	Total Premiums	World Ranking
South Africa	9,368	37,725	47,093	19
Kenya	1,283	956	2,239	58
Egypt	1,029	870	1,899	60
Nigeria	840	796	1,636	63
Algeria	1,128	120	1,243	75
Namibia	267	1,038	1,300	74
Tunisia	653	177	1,300	84
Total	14,568	41,682	56,710	—

Sources: Swiss Re Institute (2020, 26–30); author's calculations.

of the continent's total GDP, a clear decline in the volume and value of insurance premiums in relation to economic growth and development.[14] In 2018, African economies experienced GDP expansion of 3.5 percent, which was slightly below the global average, but their insurance premiums expanded ahead of GDP, at 4.9 percent.[15] People will not start long-term savings plans until their immediate needs have been met, which exacerbates the stagnation of life insurance in the majority of nations. This stands in stark contrast to the global life insurance market, which accounts for 55 percent of all premiums from emerging markets.[16]

Insurance has concentrated on non–life insurance because consumers have placed a higher priority on insurable assets like vehicles as economic development in Africa has increased and more households have risen to the middle class.[17] Non–life insurance includes property, transportation, and trade insurance, including insuring motor vehicles and international contracts. Here, Africa was top among emerging markets in insurance premium share of GDP in 2005, at 1.5 percent, although the rate is roughly like that of Latin America, South Asia and East Asia, and the Middle East, all of which exhibit ratios between 1.2 and 1.46 percent. In contrast, the premium share of GDP is more than twice as high in the developed world: 3.2 percent in Western Europe and 5 percent in North America.[18] With penetration rates of nearly 14 percent, South Africa continues to dominate the sector.[19] Table 6-1 shows the total life and non–life premiums in Africa's largest insurance markets and their world rankings.

As shown in table 6-1, both the life and non–life insurance markets in Africa are dominated by South Africa. South Africa has more life premiums that non–life premiums. However, in Kenya, Egypt, Nigeria, and Tunisia, non–life insurance premiums tend to dominate the insurance market. This means that,

Figure 6-1. Insurance Penetration Rates in Africa, 2021–22 (percent)

Country	2022 penetration rate			2021 penetration rate			2021–22 evolution		
	Life	Non–life	Total	Life	Non–life	Total	Life	Non–life	Total
South Africa	9.1	2.2	11.3	10.0	2.2	12.2	–9.0	0.0	–7.4
Namibia	5.8	2.0	7.8	5.1	2.0	7.1	13.7	0.0	9.9
Morocco	1.8	2.1	3.9	1.8	2.2	4.0	0.0	–4.5	–2.5
Kenya	1.1	1.2	2.3	1.0	1.2	2.2	10.0	0.0	4.5
Tunisia	0.6	1.6	2.2	0.5	1.6	2.1	20.0	0.0	4.8
Côte d'Ivoire	0.5	0.7	1.2	0.5	0.7	1.2	0.0	0.0	0.0
Algeria	0.1	0.5	0.6	0.1	0.6	0.7	0.0	–16.7	–14.3
Egypt	0.3	0.3	0.6	0.3	0.4	0.7	0.0	–25.0	–14.3
Nigeria	0.2	0.2	0.4	0.2	0.2	0.4	0.0	0.0	0.0
Ghana	–	–	–	0.5	0.6	1.1	–	–	–
Africa average	1.6	0.8	2.4	1.9	0.8	2.70	–15.8	0	–11.1

Source: *Atlas Magazine* (2022).

overall, more effort and resources are perhaps needed to expand the life insurance sector in Africa. Africa's total insurance premium volume increased from $65.2 billion in 2017 to $68.15 billion in 2019.[20]

However, African countries grew at different paces, and these diverse growth patterns are merely indicative of the need to target certain markets and discover the opportunities blossoming in Africa's new era of infrastructure development, rising incomes, and investment in new technologies and structural transformations. Due to the limited disposable income among the general population, the insurance penetration rate is still very low for African countries,[21] and this presents a big untapped market opportunity for companies interested in providing affordable insurance products suitable for the mass market.

As shown in figure 6-1, South Africa and Namibia have the highest total insurance penetration rates, of 13.40 and 10.44 percent, respectively. Most African markets have a penetration rate below 2 percent. The average total insurance penetration of the entire continent is estimated to be 2.98 percent.[22] This shows that South Africa, which constitutes about 85 percent of the total insurance market in Africa, brings up the average for the continent. In comparison, the average total insurance penetration rate in the United States is 11.40 percent, while other advanced countries like the United Kingdom, France, and Denmark have total penetration rates of 10.30, 9.21, and 10.68 percent, respectively.[23] South Africa is the continent's largest insurance market, accounting for over 69 percent of all premiums.[24] A study by Asongu Simplice, which investigated the role of insurance on economic growth, found that a total insurance penetration rate of 4.149 percent of GDP is the minimum threshold required for Africa to start experiencing positive spillover economic effects from the insurance industry.[25] Therefore, it is imperative for Africa to increase its overall insurance penetration rates to capture the maximum socioeconomic impact. Africa's low insurance penetration rates are one of the largest opportunities for investors.

In the past, foreign insurance companies investing in Africa have tended to focus on South Africa, since it has one of the continent's largest economies and has its most developed financial market.[26] The first African reinsurance company was founded in 2014, suggesting recent acknowledgment of the continent's growing insurance market and a need for further expanding risk. Reinsurance, in addition to expanding the spread of risk in the market, increases insurance companies' ability to write insurance, stabilizes financial results for all contract owners, protects against catastrophic loss, and finances growth.[27]

Put together, however, Africa's seven largest insurance markets are currently worth roughly $56 billion in premiums each year—83 percent of the total value of Africa's insurance sector.[28] Again, South Africa is the continent's largest insurance market, accounting for over 69 percent of all premiums. It is followed by Morocco (6.6 percent), Kenya (3.3 percent), Egypt (2.8 percent), and Nigeria (2.4 percent). This represents 84.1 percent of the market.[29] Life insurance accounts for roughly two-thirds of total market value. Due to its size and saturation, South Africa's insurance market is now growing relatively slowly, at just 1 percent (inflation adjusted) in 2014, compared with the sustained, rapid growth now witnessed in emerging markets like Kenya, Morocco, and Ghana. Certain subsectors, such as marine cargo insurance and life insurance, were the most profitable in 2019, while small business and motor insurance—which tends to be compulsory in Africa—are the fastest-growing markets.[30]

However, it is important to note that economic disruptions caused by the COVID-19 pandemic may slow down economic growth in the near term and also possibly in the long term if companies do not find ways to quickly adapt and stay in business. Such disruptions include rising unemployment, which is causing many customers to default on payments of insurance premiums, and historically low interest rates, which are decreasing profitability from investments and raising the likelihood of a global recession.[31] Regardless of the potential near-term economic slowdown, the increasing harmonization of cross-border finance and trade regulations in Africa's subregions is likely to further raise revenue potential for these subsectors in coming years.

The Insurance Sector's Importance for Africa's Development

Insurance plays a critical role in inclusive economic development. In fact, insurance provides guarantees against capital investment and credit and lengthens time horizons, thereby increasing the willingness of banks and investors to take on risk, which might be especially important in economic sectors that are at early stages of development.[32] At the national level, the insurance sector is embedded in indicators of macroeconomic volatility and fragility due to its impact on trade, inflation, exchange rates, and—as described above—national development objectives. Das, Podpiera, and Davies outline six specific mechanisms through which insurance positively affects growth: by improving financial stability for business and households; by mobilizing savings for public and private investment; by relieving pressure on government to provide public goods like pensions; by encouraging trade and entrepreneurship; by mitigating risk and enhancing diversification; and by improving social living standards and stability.[33] The unprecedented economic losses, health risks, and death caused by the COVID-19 pandemic further showed the importance of the insurance industry in building resilience.[34]

Although there have been few studies of the specific role of the insurance sector in African countries, the handful that do exist tend to support these claims.[35] Akinlo and Apanisile find a significant positive relationship between insurance premium levels and economic growth in Sub-Saharan Africa between 1986 and 2011.[36] In their within-country, time-series analyses of Nigeria, Yinusa and Akinlo show this positive effect holds over both the short and long terms.[37] Despite the small size of the African insurance market, the region's prospects for economic development are intrinsically linked to this sector's growth.

The African insurance market is far from saturated, and profitability is likely to continue increasing in coming decades, due primarily to rising demand from African households and governments. In a survey of African insurers conducted by EY, rising income levels associated with sustained growth was the top factor cited by respondents (41 percent) as exacerbating rising insurance premiums in Africa.[38] Before the COVID-19 pandemic started, sectorial analysts and insurance executives alike expected that the impressive rates of economic growth witnessed over the past decade would continue into the near future. Although the pandemic undermined these positive predictions in the short run, especially affecting preexisting weaknesses that many African countries face in the insurance industry and making it even more challenging for weak companies to grow, the post-COVID recovery will offer numerous opportunities for accelerated development in the coming decade.[39]

Key Drivers

At present, there is an abundance of remaining market capacity in Africa's insurance sector. At 3 percent of GDP, African insurance premiums per capita are lower than those of other emerging markets, such as India and Thailand. In addition to Africa's economies, its population has been growing and urbanizing at an extraordinary rate since the turn of the century—faster than any other world region at any other time in history. This pattern is also projected to continue and is likely to surpass that of India and China in the next ten years. These economic and demographic growth patterns are combining to create a rapidly expanding urban middle class in Africa—a segment that is increasingly aware of the value of insurance in supporting their households and small- and medium-sized businesses.[40] Thus, from a demand perspective, the growth of Africa's insurance market will be driven by the rapid increase in the level of disposable income and tax revenues on the continent, which translates to more spending—both private and public—on insurance products like pensions, property, and health insurance.

Meanwhile, cost efficiencies for insurance investors are likely to improve dramatically due to improvements in the regulatory climate, linkages with other financial subsectors, and technological innovation.[41] First, increasing regional and subregional integration in Africa is helping to coordinate financial regulatory frameworks, promote cross-border exchanges, and broaden market size beyond national borders. Despite the challenges faced during the COVID-19 pandemic with selective restriction measures to protect citizens,[42] it is unlikely that future policy reforms that are relevant to the insurance sector will be protectionist, since insurance is one of the economic sectors in which African governments and development organizations recognize the need for the technical expertise and accumulated capital of foreign firms.[43]

Second, enhanced distribution and diversification of insurance products are occurring, first, through partnerships and cross-collaboration with other markets, such as banks and telecoms companies—a driver of growth cited by

75 percent of survey respondents.[44] Over the past fifteen years, insurers and banks have been increasingly collaborating for mutual benefit. This synergistic relationship is a vital foundation for a robust financial system, as creditors and insurers work together to reduce the risk of lending and investment and to generate economies of scale and higher revenues in both sectors.[45] Bancassurance partnerships formed between banks and insurance companies are already common in the developed world and have begun to emerge in countries like Nigeria.[46]

Moreover, insurance services are becoming increasingly disaggregated and specialized. The nascent stage of the insurance sector means that African countries will have the potential to capture specific submarkets—such as marketing, claim settlement, accounting, and fund management—depending on a country's unique endowments, comparative advantages, and policy incentives. Education, productivity, dependency, inflation, and income, along with the independent variables of insurance penetration, were found to have a cointegrating and short-run significant relationship. This further demonstrates that over time, insurance penetration in West Africa is being determined by factors such as education, productivity, reliance, inflation, and income.[47]

Around the world, the insurance services market is changing rapidly due to digitization and technological progress, which produce gains in cost, time, and information.[48] Cost efficiency is improving due to the more rapid underwriting, purchase and payments, and claims processing to online and mobile platforms.[49] The COVID-19 pandemic created near-term urgency for digitization, and as a result, accelerated digitization trends as insurance companies suddenly had to adopt remote work.[50] In light of the challenge of analyzing and quantifying risk in a region where the majority of the population has had very limited exposure to formal financial services, insurance companies working in Africa view innovations in digital underwriting algorithms and premium quotations as particularly promising.

Meanwhile, in the developed world, nanotechnologies like embedded devices and sensors are being developed to anticipate and mitigate the risk associated with real-time events—environmental, behavioral, technological, or geopolitical—that affect insured individuals or property.[51] Within the next 10 years, more data will be generated by sensors and digital devices than are currently collected from all sources, and this will increasingly be complemented by informal data sources, such as from social media, real-time videos, and live blogs.[52]

Although gaps in technical infrastructure remain a challenge, Africa has already demonstrated its capacity to leapfrog latent technologies in a rapid and context-specific process of modernization, as demonstrated by the spread of mobile banking and money transfers.[53] In twenty years, the insurance industry will look nothing like it does today—as technologies become more affordable and internet and mobile phone penetration continue to spread, the potential for increasing cost efficiencies and profit margins in Africa's insurance sector is enormous. Progressive insurance companies will capitalize on opportunities to roll out new products and technologies and to expand their presence in Africa's rapidly growing insurance sector.[54]

Key Players

Over the past few decades, the global insurance services market has been transformed by interrelated processes of liberalization and consolidation. In Africa, the spread of neoliberal norms and economic liberalization stemmed from a series of structural adjustment reforms imposed by international financial institutions as conditions for receiving aid and debt relief. These reforms were necessary in overcoming the systemic financial crisis that plagued almost every country on the continent in the 1980s. The subsequent process of privatization and market deregulation led to new competition, followed by a series of mergers and acquisitions. This ultimately resulted in increased consolidation and stability of the financial market, including banking and insurance, leaving fewer, more efficient, capital-rich companies.[55]

As these processes have stabilized, and given the large amount of space for growth, analysts expect that foreign insurance investors will continue growing and increasing their market share in Africa's insurance sector.[56] AXA, one of France's largest insurance companies, made plans to invest about $87.27 million in the Africa Internet Group to become the largest provider of insurance products offered through online services like Jumia and other AIG platforms.[57] The French insurer AXA and online retailer Africa Internet Group announced their agreement, whereby AXA will provide AIG with all its insurance needs and will invest $84 million to acquire an about 8 percent interest in AIG.[58] This increases the awareness of insurance providers and the means of attaining the best services. Other firms, such as Old Mutual and Sanlam, are expanding up from South Africa and gaining footholds in almost every country on the continent.

There is a substantial market for reinsurance in Africa, as in other developing countries. Of the largest reinsurance companies working in the region, the top performers in recent years have been RGA Re and General Re, which reported 8 and 7 percent returns on investments, respectively, in 2015.

Due to their high capital-adequacy ratios—4.6 and 5.9, respectively—these companies have been successful at diversifying their investment portfolios. Other reinsurance companies working in Africa reported investment returns between 4 and 6 percent, including cash and equivalents, which is markedly low compared with the average ten-year government bond yield of 9.77 percent. Returns on reinsurance do appear to be increasing, though with substantial variation across companies caused by differences in investment strategy and risk. According to the latest survey data, the most profitable lines of reinsurance business are marine insurance, engineering insurance, and liability insurance because these segments have fewer, highly specialized players and low numbers of insurance claims per year.[59]

The least profitable lines of business are motor insurance, health insurance, and energy insurance, and these also tend to experience the slowest growth rate in premiums.[60] Although it was the top performer in 2014, Africa Re reported a 43 percent decrease in investment income in 2015; this is not surprising, as the strategy of investing 20 percent in equity instruments is likely to result in short-term volatility. In contrast, Scor reported a 93 percent increase in investment income the same year, and the overall average for the sector was a 2 percent increase in returns from the previous year.[61]

Opportunities

Considering the increasing demand for insurance and the relatively low levels of market penetration in Africa, opportunities for investment in the sector are abundant, as shown in table 6-2. The life insurance market in Africa is particularly ripe for growth. Most Sub-Saharan African markets are dominated by non–life insurance—premium income from non–life insurance accounts for 85.6 percent in Tanzania, 73.23 percent Uganda, 60 percent in Zambia, and 57.7 percent in Kenya.[62] In 2014, income from non–life insurance premiums accounted for 71 percent of the total, on average (excluding South Africa).[63] To date, the unique challenges of working in the region demand specialized risk management capacities and heavy investment in security and information gathering, which has led the sector to have significant foreign investment.[64] A number of recent developments and insurance product innovations present new opportunities for investment in Africa that have the potential to benefit first movers, whether global or domestic insurers.

Even though the COVID-19 pandemic undermined these new opportunities in the near term, the pandemic also created opportunities to solve challenges within the African insurance sector. One such possibility is

Table 6-2. Summary of Opportunities and Risks in Africa

Opportunities	Risks
Growing middle class	COVID-19 pandemic (increases likelihood of a global recession)
African Continental Free Trade Agreement	Global trade tensions
Declining growth in advanced economies (can increase foreign direct investment inflows to Africa)	Declining commodity prices
Increasing urbanization	Mounting debt in some countries
Population growth	Security
New technologies (digitization and Fourth Industrial Revolution)	Policy uncertainty
COVID-19 pandemic (potentially higher demand for insurance)	Low interest rates
	Climate change
	Dearth of skilled insurance workers
	Political instability

Sources: Schanz, Alms Company (2019); author's calculations; Swiss Re Institute (2020); EY (2016).

solving the problem of fragmentation.[65] The pandemic offered the opportunity for consolidation of the fragmented insurance sector by forcing unsustainable and inefficient players out of business.[66] If regulators took the initiative in monitoring and assisting insolvent insurers with the shutdown processes and implementing regulations to protect customers during this crisis, then the instability and disruption caused by small-player shutdowns was minimized. In the long run, the resulting consolidation of the insurance sector will be beneficial in facilitating innovation, healthy competition, and better coverage.[67]

A few African countries, including Botswana and Mauritius, have established offshore financial centers to attract investment by offering tax incentives, high-quality infrastructure, and a liberalized and well-regulated business environment.[68] Following the Irish model, the number of offshore operations increased worldwide by nearly 40 percent in 2003–4, and though they have traditionally been effective at attracting banking and credit institutions, insurance companies are increasingly recognizing the benefits of this model as well. Despite the fact that microcredit has become an extremely common financial service in Africa over the past fifteen years, the concept of microinsurance is only starting to emerge. These small-scale, low-cost, and low-risk products are ideal for accessing Africa's rising middle class.

One success story is the microfinance venture MicroEnsure, which has partnered with telecommunications providers to offer basic health and life insurance coverage as a free add-on to mobile phone service. In doing so, the company has been more effective in identifying customers for more comprehensive services and in creating a client base by increasing brand familiarity and awareness about insurance services more generally. In its first year, more than 1 million Ghanaians signed up for the service, and it now serves more than 8 million people across the region.[69] The International Finance Corporation unveiled an agreement in 2014 to extend micro health insurance to Senegalese with low incomes and sporadic employment. The pilot program sought to offer 108,000 consumers low-cost health microinsurance products. Through their mobile phones, Jamii Africa targets Tanzania's low-income people. The firm, founded in 2015, handles all of an insurer's administrative tasks and gives customers access to affordable insurance starting at just $1 a month. According to Jamii Africa, it has raised over $1 million and has over 20,000 active users and over 400 registered hospitals.[70]

This strategy of partnering with telecommunications companies while providing inexpensive and simply packaged products has proven to be an effective one for companies working in Africa, regardless of sector. In a microinsurance partnership between Kenya's Safaricom, Britam, and Changamka, a program called Linda Jamii provides yearly health coverage through the M-PESA mobile payment system.[71] In agriculture, the largest and most productive sector in most African economies and the primary source of income for the majority of African households, there is enormous potential for insurance products that help to protect farmers against loss caused by environmental or other shocks. In Kenya, APA provides livestock insurance coverage based on whether each animal has access to enough food, using satellite imagery to measure area of healthy forage. And in another example of mobile product innovation, UAP Old Mutual Group has launched a program called Kilimo Salama (Safe Agriculture) in partnership with Safaricom, which uses weather data to anticipate loss based on rainfall variation, providing compensation based on crops' unique rainfall needs.[72] In light of the factors identified as driving growth in Africa's insurance sector more generally, certain countries offer particularly attractive investment opportunities.

In Zambia, for example, the insurance market is currently small, with just $304 million in premium value in 2019. Additionally, 45 percent of all Zambians live in cities, a population that is already relatively urban compared with other African countries.[73] Considering the overall trend of diversification away from the economy's reliance on copper mining, Oxford economists projected annual growth in the insurance sector to exceed 11 percent between 2014 and 2018, with per capita premium density increasing from $18.20 in 2014 to $24.50 in 2018.[74] However, the primary constraint on growth in Zambia, as identified by local insurers, is the availability of human capital, especially qualified agents and marketing staff.[75]

Ghana, conversely, is characterized by a well-educated and professional workforce and political stability. President Nana Akufo-Addo, who came to power in 2017, committed to creating more employment by building factories in each district of the nation in addition to improving its fiscal balance. In 2018, President Akufo-Addo launched the seven-year Coordinated Programme of Economic and Social Development, aiming to improve Ghana's economic development through aspects like increasing the level of financial inclusion in the country.[76] Perhaps because of these developments, Ghana has experienced substantial growth in its banking sector, which can positively affect its insurance market in the future.[77] Still, only 6 percent of Ghanaians have insurance of any kind, excluding health insurance.[78]

Unlike more consolidated markets like Zambia, the insurance market in Ghana remains extremely fragmented—with roughly 54 insurance companies, 70 brokers, and 6,000 agents operating in the country, compared with 38 brokers and 222 agents in Zambia. There were 29 non–life companies, 95 brokerage firms, 22 life firms, 3 reinsurance firms, and 7,000 agents in 2021.[79] Insurers in Ghana have been capitalizing on the intense competition among telecommunications companies by including free coverage add-ons. Insurance premium growth was substantial between 2004 and 2014 in West Africa, but this growth slowed down between 2015 to 2017, due a fall in commodity prices, partially caused by the Ebola crisis in West Africa. This reduced Ghana's growth rate to only 5 percent in the past two years.[80]

Apart from this brief economic slowdown, regulatory conditions have been cited as the primary constraint for insurers, although Ghana's business environment is generally perceived as favorable and there have been positive indications that Ghana's National Insurance Commission is committed to improving market conditions through policies and Ghana's Ministry of Finance has recognized the significance of the insurance sector for the country's development and, as a result, the ministry initiated an insurance and pensions improvement plan to expand insurance penetration and develop capital markets.[81] For example, a previously required 17.5 percent value-added tax on financial services was removed in 2017. If policymakers in Ghana continue to make new, favorable policies, its insurance market will be a highly attractive destination for investors who are committed to long-term growth and impact. Despite growing urbanization and mobile connectivity, investors interested in Ghana should note that about 75 percent of Ghanaian adults are employed in the informal sector, and therefore coming up with innovative approaches to serve the informal sector is required.[82]

Since 2007, the number of Nigerians with insurance coverage has increased more than threefold. Like Zambia, the growth projections for Nigeria's insurance market are more than 10 percent per year, with annual premiums likely to increase from $1.8 billion in 2014 to $2.6 billion in 2018, or $10 to $13.2 in premium density per capita. Much of the market is concentrated in property and motor insurance, with low penetration of personal coverage, including health and life insurance. As of 2015, the market was unconsolidated and undercapitalized, which implies that a high degree of risk aversion, coupled with high premiums, were driving down demand.[83]

At the same time, however, product innovation via telecommunications partnerships has proved successful in Nigeria, as in Ghana and Zambia. MicroEnsure has entered the Nigerian market with a program that allows customers to make a monthly payment for phone credit that, depending on the amount of credit purchased, provides a certain level of coverage for hospital stays. In Nigeria, out-of-pocket spending for health care increased from 60.2 percent in 2000 to 77 percent in 2019. Due to the challenges of budgeting for an out-of-pocket payment when 40 percent of the population lives on less than $1.90 a day, a micro health insurance plan across the nation would provide greater access to health care.[84] There is massive potential for further uptake of coverage in other areas. For example, less than one-seventh of registered motor vehicles in Nigeria are adequately insured, and the government had plans to implement a policy making insurance compulsory, which could result in an increase of more than 6 million motor insurance policies.[85] Thus, the growth prospects are robust in Nigeria, but unlike in Zambia and Ghana, the uncertain regulatory and political climate in Nigeria also implies a high level of investment risk.

In 2016, high growth rates in Tanzania led experts at Oxford Economics to project high growth in insurance premiums—up to 7.9 percent in the subsequent years.[86] The domestic insurance market is still recovering from a period of almost exclusive public ownership of land and property, but the market capitalization reached roughly $400 million in annual premiums in 2018.[87] Technology adoption throughout the country is driving insurance premiums while simultaneously increasing overall growth rates, which average about 7 percent annually. Tanzania's high growth, relative to global averages, has yet to translate into concurrent growth of insurance in relation to GDP, which hovers below 1 percent.[88] Still, Dar es Salaam, the country's most populous city, is considered one of the fastest-growing cities in Africa and is steadily accumulating interest from investors hoping to offer insurance and capital to the city's urbanizing population. Tanzania, much like the other countries mentioned, is poised to become a growing insurance market, through which multinational and domestic firms can access unfulfilled demand in the coming years.

Risks and Challenges

Investing in the insurance sector in Africa requires a deep understanding of the complex risks and challenges specific to the continent or the countries of interest. These include decentralized cross-country markets with regulatory barriers, the regulatory clarity on e-signatures, major gaps in regulatory enforcement, the shortage of technical human capital, the low demand for insurance, market volatility, and climate change. As illustrated by the COVID-19 pandemic and discussed below, some challenges could even be turned into opportunities.

The COVID-19 Pandemic

The insurance industry in particular has been brought into the spotlight as a result of the risks that businesses and individuals faced during the COVID-19 crisis.[89] It is impossible to accurately predict the long-term impact of the pandemic on the insurance industry, but in the near term, insurance claims can be expected to rise significantly. Insurance companies will face the challenge of managing these claims and staying solvent to meet customer needs. Insurance premiums were included in the list of 'unnecessary" expenses that consumers were compelled to reduce, which will have an effect on insurance providers and the industry at large.[90]

On the positive side, the COVID-19 pandemic reemphasized the need for life insurance, and this could lead to all-time high demand for life insurance in the next decade.[91] Insurance companies are currently facing high levels of regulatory uncertainty, but this should not stop companies from strategically making long-term investments. Focusing on managing short-term disruptions will limit companies' ability to leverage opportunities created by the pandemic. For example, record low interest rates, increased market volatility, and uncertainty create opportunities to potentially obtain favorable merger-and-acquisition deals.[92] Implications of the COVID-19 pandemic are still unfolding, and the insurance industry will need to adapt accordingly in the future.

COVID-related innovations in Africa include:

—One South African insurer had a preexisting digitization plan that was intended to take effect over a three-year period when COVID-19 began. At the start of the pandemic, they were able to carry out this strategy in just three weeks.

—Prudential Life, which has operations in eight Sub-Saharan nations, has created a new, complimentary COVID-19 life insurance policy for both current and potential customers as well as staff members nationwide.

—For a period of six months, Hollard Zambia provided a free COVID-19 rider benefit to its life insurance contract.

—The insurance sector in Nigeria created a group life policy for front-line health care professionals. An insurance pool with a stop loss has been established by insurers, and the amount paid out is only as much as the premiums they collected.

—In South Africa, Naked Insurance automatically lowered auto insurance rates, and Discovery used telematics to offer savings to clients who drove less due to lockdown measures.

—In collaboration with One Acre Fund, MicroEnsure, which offers health and death insurance to Kenyan farmers, modified the way it handles claims by allowing farmers to fill out the paperwork by hand, photograph it, and submit it to the claims department.[93]

Because COVID-19 enabled digital payments to be quickly adopted, more people can now be covered because they can pay their fees more conveniently. An excellent example is Rwanda. As consumer behavior and readiness to use digital payments change, insurers in Rwanda now have the chance to transition from a conventional approach to a digital approach for premium collection and claims payments. However, compared with other financial service providers, the industry still lags in adopting digital processes.[94]

Decentralized Cross-Country Markets with Regulatory Barriers

Unlike in other financial sectors, Africa's insurance markets are characterized by a high level of fragmentation and diversity. Several challenges have prevented growth in the industry to date. The regulatory climate remains unwieldy at both national and regional levels, with four of five insurance executives citing the difficulty of meeting various reporting and capital requirements as a major impediment to doing business.[95] Meanwhile, cross-border business is hampered by the limited harmonization across countries.

The recent adoption of the African Continental Free Trade Area Agreement offers a unique opportunity to solve this challenge and boost intracontinental trade and investment in Africa.[96] The Inter-African Conference of Insurance Markets (CIMA) is a positive example of the increasing push for coordination and rationalization of policies affecting the sector, but much more progress is needed to implement policies that will encourage recapitalization and consolidation.[97]

Regulatory Clarity on E-Signatures

Although the use of electronic signatures increased during the COVID-19 pandemic, regulators should nonetheless note this area of ambiguity. E-signatures are permitted in some nations, such as Ghana and Nigeria, but regulators have not yet made this clear to the insurance industry, leaving room for confusion. The lack of a regulation requiring the incorporation of e-signatures in Zambia renders this alternative impractical for business leaders. These situations have hindered innovation and the adaptation of digital sales.

The primary insurance distribution channels, agents and brokers, were unable to transact business due to COVID-induced lockdowns and restrictions. To maintain their company, several corporations swiftly adopted a digital strategy. E-signatures were swiftly approved in Uganda to give citizens digital insurance. This is a strong, creative answer that ought to be adopted by other nations and made a permanent standard. The insurance sector would be better able to weather the storm and move closer to sustainable long-term development if regulators and the industry were more adaptable and were prepared for emerging threats. These risks, which can be easily controlled and prepared for, include but are not limited to climate change, natural disasters, political risk, and cyberattacks.[98]

One of the most potential ways to increase awareness of insurance goods is through digitization, which would make the products more appealing and affordable, especially for younger Africans. There are obstacles because there are not enough domestic businesses and insurance brokers who can use these digital goods and software, but they may be overcome. Personal lines business, particularly automobile and health, are the first items to be digitized. At 70 percent of the premium volume in most African markets, these are common, easily mass-produced, and cover a substantial portion of the market. They require less point-of-sale consultation because they are more general. Access to more desirable middle-class insurance clients—who are younger, more mobile, tech-savvy, and open to innovation and consumption—is made possible by technology.[99]

Major Gaps in Regulatory Enforcement

Even where improvements have been made, significant gaps remain at the level of implementation. Regulators often lack the capacity and credibility to punish companies that fail to meet industry standards—a problem that has been especially apparent in Ghana.[100] Moreover, the current push to reform Africa's financial sector, with governments under pressure from the African Development Bank and major international financial institutions, has generated uncertainty in the market about the nature and pace of imminent regulatory changes.[101]

The Shortage of Technical Human Capital

From the supply side, insurers working in the region note the shortage of technical and human capital as a major impediment to growth. Education gaps and the resulting deficiency of a high-skilled workforce means that there is a shortage of both talented and experienced professionals needed to staff an insurance office. Executives surveyed in countries as varied as Kenya, Nigeria, and Uganda repeatedly cite the difficulty of finding and retaining qualified employees, especially in the key areas of marketing, sales, and technology.[102] Beyond limiting the ability to grow a business, a major consequence of this shortage of human capital has been the lack of innovation in the industry, resulting in insufficient product differentiation.

Low Demand for Insurance

Conversely, demand for insurance has been relatively low in Africa. This is not only due to the low levels of disposable income, but more importantly also to the general lack of awareness of both the availability of insurance products and the potential benefits of those that are available.[103] An "insurance culture" does not yet exist in Africa, as most people have not been exposed to services that would credibly protect them against future loss. Moreover, despite notable improvements in macroeconomic stability in most countries, risk perceptions remain high, and consumers tend to have short time horizons.[104] Research indicates that most Africans do not trust either the financial ability or the willingness of insurance companies to follow through with claims settlements.[105]

Market Volatility

In fact, given the infancy of Africa's insurance sector, market volatility is a concern for insurers themselves. In Kenya, underwriting capacity and the economic outlook of the sector are leading concerns cited by executives. The possibility that macroeconomic indicators, or individual or environmental risk factors, could change substantially between the time of quoting and selling an insurance product and the time that a claim is made generates negative perceptions about the profitability of an insurance venture. Insurers are also concerned about fraudulent claims from customers, a problem exacerbated by a lack of data and technological oversight.[106] Overall, high levels of social trust and stable, long-term time horizons are an important prerequisite for the growth of a viable insurance industry. In figure 7-9 (see chapter 7 below), Ernst & Young presents an opportunity risk matrix analysis for investors and firms seeking to enter the market or expand their reach in the countries studied in this report.

Climate Change

Risks from flooding and drought predominate. Floods and droughts are the two most common climate risks for insurance markets, according to senior executives—including insurers, reinsurers, and brokers—operating in Africa questioned in a 2022 poll in "Africa Insurance Pulse," a report from Faber Consulting.[107] African countries' disaster risk profiles are changing as a result of increased urbanization, going from predominantly rural areas where food security and drought are the primary problems to urban areas where floods, cyclones, and earthquakes are the main dangers.

Climate disasters are occurring more frequently and with greater severity. Nearly all respondents to the poll reported that there has been a noticeable rise in the frequency of climatic threats, particularly tropical cyclones (especially in Mauritius, Madagascar, and Mozambique), floods in West and East Africa, forest fires in North Africa, and hailstorms in South Africa. Extreme weather occurrences, particularly floods and tropical storms, have become more severe in the same period. Additionally, respondents noted a dramatic growth in urban property values, which has an impact on the rise in disaster-related damage expenses. Higher demand has not yet been reflected by greater awareness. Experts in the insurance industry said that awareness of the hazards brought on by climate change is usually on the rise. Government is the sector with the highest awareness, followed by business and consumers. Higher levels of awareness, however, have not yet resulted in a major rise in demand among price-conscious African customers. Due to a combination of accessibility, price, and awareness, demand for commercial insurance is higher than that for private insurance, which is low or extremely low. There are also increased costs, marginally increased capacity, and tougher rules. The majority of respondents have noticed a rise in weather risk premiums in African markets over the last three years and anticipate one more rise in the coming year. Conditions have tightened while capacity has expanded for primary insurers and stayed mostly steady for reinsurers.

Regulation of climate change and environmental, social, and governance norms are gaining traction. Most interviewees concurred that climate change is intensifying and has become a significant concern for their local or regional insurance regulators and supervisors. Discussions of climate risk, however, have not yet resulted in new laws backing the insurance industry. Similar to that, environmental, social, and governance is a hot topic in Africa right now, but it has yet to receive the attention it needs.[108]

Investment Strategies

Considering remaining market volatility, insurers currently working in Africa must be aware of their access to reinsurance. Since one of the most essential elements of reinsurance is risk assessment, which requires a high level of technical sophistication and data gathering, the success of the insurance sector therefore depends on investing in human capital and information technologies.[109] Companies must first be prepared to invest substantial resources in the training and development of qualified staff. According to Matt Lilley, the chief executive officer of Prudential Africa, "The insurance industry will only grow as fast as the number of decently trained insurance advisers grows"[110]—his company trained 1,000 new agents in Ghana over an 18-month period.

Moreover, data sharing—both across companies and with regulatory agencies—will be vital to building the necessary databases and analytical capacity to effectively price products and manage risk. In building these digital capacities, insurers should consider investing in consultancy and outreach efforts in cooperation with policymakers at both national and regional levels to influence beneficial policy reforms. This includes ensuring that liberalization and privatization reforms are appropriately sequenced and that regulatory and oversight capacities are improved.[111]

As macroeconomic and regulatory climates continue to change over the coming years, businesses will need to adapt their investment strategies. In Africa, as elsewhere, developing a coherent capital strategy and continuously monitoring its progress are vital strategies for profitability and growth in insurance. Access to additional corporate funding will likely be important, as will—perhaps even more so—forging effective and innovative business partnerships.[112] For insurers, this means building linkages within the financial sector and across sectors, such as mobile and online technologies. A bancassurance partnership with one of the emerging pan-African banks, for example, offers an interesting opportunity to simultaneously ride the coattails of these banks to increase the credibility and distribution of insurance products. Such partnerships will be essential for improving product differentiation and overcoming the existing barriers to supply, as well as increasing awareness to generate demand. Innovation within the insurance sector is one area that deserves attention from international investors.

Looking to the Future

Around the world, the insurance industry is undergoing a sea of changes that are likely to transform traditional business models.[113] On one hand, distribution systems are changing due to the impact of analytics and digital technologies. The number of internet-connected sensors and devices in use is likely to surpass 50 billion by 2020, which will exponentially increase the availability of real-time information and its efficient use for estimating risk and managing loss.[114] The COVID-19 pandemic highlighted the need for insurance services; but its aftereffects continue to create unprecedented economic pressure for insurers to manage.[115]

On the other hand, global economic, demographic, and environmental transformations are rapidly increasing demand for insurance services, especially in low-penetration markets. Meanwhile, Africa's emerging markets have been among the most rapidly growing in the world since 2010—a trend that is likely to continue. Insurance density and penetration rates are exceedingly low on the continent, except in South Africa. These trends and statistics signal a massive potential for growth in the sector.[116] The biggest insurance markets in Africa will not necessarily be the best markets to invest in, if current stagnation trends observed in South Africa and Nigeria persist.[117] Investors could benefit more by investing in smaller emerging insurance markets on the continent that are experiencing double-digit growth of insurance premiums, and these countries include Namibia, Uganda, and Côte d'Ivoire.

Investors should expect to see increased alignment and coordination on insurance procedures by African countries in light of the importance of preventing environmentally caused damage and invigorating development amid global climate change. Currently, fourteen countries in Francophone Africa are governed by the CIMA Code.[118] Established in 1992, this code is one of many on the continent intended to consolidate legal and regulatory provisions on insurance and reinsurance. Coordinated policies ensure that premiums are kept within the countries of operation and encourage regulatory capital to established insurance companies. Risk placement and company compliance are monitored through CIMA Code protocols and similar regulations across Africa, which will become more relevant to new companies entering the insurance and reinsurance markets. Given the recent adoption of the African Continental Free Trade Area Agreement, investors should anticipate seeing even higher degrees of coordination of policy across African countries in the near future.

Insurance companies that capitalize on opportunities to improve their margins will command enormous market share in Africa as the sector continues to develop. Doing so will require increasing information and data, developing innovative and context-specific products, recapitalizing and consolidating investment, and moving first to roll out new technologies as they become affordable.[119] Even more significantly, companies that successfully pursue these strategies will help to create the insurance culture that is currently lacking in the region, and they will benefit from having their brands recognized as pioneers of credible and convenient insurance services in Africa.

Notes

1. Imarc (2024).
2. Signé (2020).
3. Insurance is often defined as the contractual arrangement between two parties on the defined amount to be paid to the policyholder in the event of a specific loss and assuming the policyholder's regular payments of a premium. Per the General Agreement on Trade in Services' Annex on Financial Services, insurance and insurance-related services include "(i) direct insurance (including co-insurance): (A) life, (B) non–life; (ii) reinsurance and retrocession; (iii) insurance intermediation, such as brokerage and agency; (iv) services auxiliary to insurance, such as consultancy, actuarial, risk assessment and claim settlement services." See https://www.wto.org/english/tratop_e/serv_e/10-anfin_e.htm.
4. In 2018, Rewendé found that the impact of insurance on economic growth is most significant in low-income countries with high-quality institutions and legal structures. In a 2019 study of the BRICS countries, Devarakonda annd Chittineni (2019) concluded that expanding the insurance sector should be considered a necessity because it increases the long-term investment potential for countries. Michael Ojo Oke (2012) found a weak causal relationship between expansion of insurance and economic growth for Nigeria due to a lack of conducive structural factors. However, he still argued that insurance can boost a country's available funds for capital-intensive projects which brings positive development impact, especially in the long run.
5. International Finance Corporation (2024b).
6. African Business (2024a).

7. Africa Insurance Organization (2020).
8. Swiss Re Institute (2020, 24).
9. Dr. Schanz, Alms & Company (2019, 18).
10. Africa Insurance Organization (2020).
11. Raim and Langford (2007, 40).
12. Beyers et al. (2020, 7).
13. Dr. Schanz, Alms & Company (2019, 18).
14. Dr. Schanz, Alms & Company (2019, 19).
15. Dr. Schanz, Alms & Company (2019, 7).
16. Africa Insurance Organization (2019).
17. Africa Insurance Organization (2019).
18. UNCTAD (2007, 26).
19. Swiss Re Institute (2020, 32). However, it was also relatively high in Namibia (10.44 percent) in 2019.
20. Dr. Schanz, Alms & Company (2019, 14); Swiss Re Institute (2020, 24).
21. Dr. Schanz, Alms & Company (2019, 18).
22. Dr. Schanz, Alms & Company (2019, 52).
23. Swiss Re Institute (2020, 32).
24. African Insurance Organization (2020).
25. Asongu and Odhiambo (2020a, 4).
26. Dr. Schanz, Alms & Company (2019, 19).
27. Raim and Langford (2007, 40).
28. These countries are South Africa, Morocco, Egypt, Nigeria, Kenya, Algeria, Angola, Namibia, Tunisia, and Mauritius.
29. African Insurance Organization (2020).
30. African Insurance Organization (2019).
31. PwC (2020a).
32. This is referred to by Patrick (1966) as the "supply-leading" relationship between insurance and growth, which is especially important in the causality pattern witnessed in developing countries.
33. Das, Podpiera, and Davies (2003).
34. Schlemmer, Rinehart-Smit, and Gray (2020, 10).
35. Olayungbo and Akinlo (2016, 6).
36. Akinlo and Apanisile (2014).
37. Yinusa and Akinlo (2013).
38. EY (2016b, 4–10).
39. Beyers, Scribante, and Gray (2020, 8).
40. EY (2016b, 4–10).
41. Dr. Schanz, Alms & Company (2016, 6).
42. Beyers, Scribante, and Gray (2020, 7).
43. Dr. Schanz, Alms & Company (2016, 6).
44. EY (2016b, 4–10); Dr. Schanz, Alms & Company (2016, 6).

45. UNCTAD (2007).

46. EY (2016b, 40).

47. Olarewaju and Msomi (2021).

48. Santenac and Manchester (2020).

49. EY (2016b, 4–10).

50. Schlemmer, Rinehart-Smit, and Gray (2020, 6).

51. PwC (2015a, 24).

52. KPMG (2016a, 79); PwC (2012b, 5).

53. EY (2016b, 4–10).

54. PwC (2015a, 22).

55. UNCTAD (2007).

56. Dr. Schanz, Alms & Company (2016, 6).

57. Reuters (2016).

58. Reuters (2016).

59. Swiss Re Institute (2020, 52–55).

60. Swiss Re Institute (2020, 52–55).

61. KPMG (2016b, 141).

62. EY (2016b, 4–10); IRA (2019).

63. Dr. Schanz, Alms & Company (2016, 17).

64. Dr. Schanz, Alms & Company (2016, 6).

65. Beyers, Scribant, and Gray (2020, 9).

66. Beyers, Scribant, and Gray (2020, 9).

67. Beyers, Scribant, and Gray (2020, 9).

68. UNCTAD (2007, 22–23); Deloitte (2005).

69. Dr. Schanz, Alms & Company (2016).

70. Adepoju (2021).

71. Dr. Schanz, Alms & Company (2016, 17).

72. Dr. Schanz, Alms & Company (2016).

73. See the population statistics at https://data.worldbank.org/indicator/SP.URB.TOTL.IN.ZS?locations=ZM.

74. EY (2016b, 36).

75. EY (2016b, 36).

76. Beyers et al. (2018b, 7).

77. Beyers et al. (2018b, xi).

78. Beyers et al. (2018a, 4).

79. KPMG (2021).

80. Dr. Schanz, Alms & Company (2019, 11).

81. Beyers et al. (2018a, 2).

82. Beyers et al. (2018a, 2).

83. PwC (2015b).

84. Adepoju (2021).

85. EY (2016b, 40).

86. EY (2016b, 32).
87. EY (2016b, 32).
88. EY (2016b, 32).
89. Beyers, Scribant, and Gray (2020, 9).
90. Deloitte (2020).
91. Bernard et al. (2020).
92. PwC (2020a).
93. Rinehart-Smit and Janse van Vuuren (2021).
94. Rinehart-Smit and Janse van Vuuren (2021).
95. EY (2016b, 13–15).
96. Dr, Schanz, Alms & Company (2019, 13).
97. Olayungbo and Akinlo (2016, 16); Dr. Schanz, Alms & Company (2016, 6).
98. Beyers, Scribante, and Gray (2022).
99. Faber Consulting (2020).
100. EY (2016b, 13–15).
101. EY (2016b, 13–15).
102. EY (2016b, 13–15).
103. Dr. Schanz, Alms & Company (2016, 6).
104. Olayungbo and Akinlo (2016, 16).
105. EY (2016b, 13–15).
106. EY (2016b, 13–15).
107. African Insurance Organization (2022).
108. Africa Insurance Organization (2022).
109. UNCTAD (2007, 26).
110. EY (2016b, 18).
111. UNCTAD (2007, 15).
112. EY (2016b, 13–15).
113. Deloitte (2015, 10).
114. PwC (2012b, 5).
115. Schlemmer, Rinehart-Smit, and Gray (2020, 10).
116. Olayungbo and Akinlo (2016, 16(; EY (2016, 4).
117. Swiss Re Institute (2020).
118. See the CIMA's website: https://cima-afrique.org/les-etats-membres/?lang=en.
119. PwC (2015a, 22); Olayungbo and Akinlo (2016, 16).

Seven

Africa's Investment, Private Equity, and Venture Capital Potential

TRENDS, OPPORTUNITIES, CHALLENGES, AND STRATEGIES

Emerging markets accounted for half of global gross domestic product (GDP) in 2023 and two-thirds of the global GDP growth over the past decade (2013–23).[1] Yet despite this reality, only 5 percent of the $1.3 trillion of assets under management in global private credit has gone to emerging markets, including less than 0.3 percent to Africa,[2] which showcases the lucrative opportunities that exist for investors on the continent. After peaking in 2021, more than doubling the amount in 2020 when investment was disrupted by the COVID-19 pandemic, foreign direct investment (FDI) in Africa declined in 2022 and 2023 as the continent continued to bounce back from economic and global shocks.[3] Yet despite FDI's decline, it remains higher ($53 billion) than it was before the pandemic.[4] Venture capital has rapidly accelerated in Africa. Over the 10-year period 2013–23, a total of $20 billion was raised in Africa—68 percent of which was raised in the last 3 years (2020–23), indicating how quickly venture capital is evolving on the continent.[5]

Before the pandemic, Africa's FDI accelerated rapidly. Natural resources were the main draw for foreign investors in the region, accounting for roughly one-third of the total, with fossil fuels and renewable energies receiving a combined $27.9 billion in investment in 2015. Thus, investments in Africa remained relatively concentrated, with a large average project size ($70.1 million per project in 2013, up nearly 15 percent from 2012), due to the dominance of oil and mining among investment projects.[6] However, while the value of

FDI to resource-rich African countries peaked in 2008, investment to non-resource-rich countries has continued to increase steadily.[7] These investments can be difficult to track as individual private equity or venture capital investments, because most countries report private equity and venture capital as part of the broader category of FDI. Yet the growth of nonindustrial firms and innovative start-ups, particularly as the Fourth Industrial Revolution expands across the continent, are indicative of the increase in private equity and venture capitalism. Clean tech became the leading FDI sector in 2022, offering important opportunities and high-value investments, including five greenfield megaprojects valued at over $5 billion in 2023.[8]

Foreign and domestic investors are taking advantage of higher returns on investments. Population growth, urbanization, and digital transformation are driving interest to Africa, while simultaneously providing the resources to ensure that investments are well appropriated. African markets are emerging on a global scale, and they need financial support in both the short and long terms to generate sustainable growth and innovation. Global private equity levels remain low in Africa, and large funds determine the areas of high returns, which can discourage smaller private equity firms from exploring other opportunities. However, Africa is rife with high-return opportunities, as evidenced by the increasing amounts of investment on the continent.

Current Global Shocks

The trends discussed in this chapter related to investment, private equity, and venture capital were disrupted greatly due to the COVID-19 pandemic and ongoing geopolitical conflicts. While Africa experienced a major decrease in investment levels compared with previous years, this decline was experienced around the globe, following a similar trend in other developing regions. According to the data so far, some countries have been able to recover from this shock more quickly than others, particularly countries such as South Africa that are less dependent on energy prices and that rely more on their service sectors.[9] Egypt experienced a significant decrease, but the Gulf States accelerated their investment in FDI in different sectors across Egypt, including $27.4 billion from the United Arab Emirates in 2022.[10]

Despite so far experiencing slower growth in FDI inflows since its decrease during the COVID-19 pandemic, Africa more than doubled its private capital flows from 2020 to 2021.[11] According to the African Private Capital Activity Report, the total value of private capital deals through private equity and venture capital reached its record high in 2021, at $7.4 billion, a 118 percent increase from 2020. This record year nearly doubled the five-year average of about $4 billion, with the report claiming this increase was due to the desire of investors and fund managers to resume after a year of limited activity during the pandemic, showcasing the desirability of African markets to investors. Now, due to an overall decrease in international project finance deals, each subregion faced FDI decreases (Central Africa faced the biggest decrease, at 17 percent) between 2022 and 2023, yet they did well attracting greenfield projects.[12] The ongoing conflicts will continue to bring challenges; however, the trends, drivers, opportunities, and strategies discussed in this chapter remain relevant to the overall development of African economies.

The Basics of Private Equity, Venture Capital, and Investment Banking

The private equity market includes all platforms that provide equity capital to firms that are privately owned and operated. Private equity is long-term funding for a determinate period to start a business, move a start-up to a more stable stage of operation, or assist in restructuring formerly publicly held firms to be more efficient. The venture capital market is made up of financial intermediaries that primarily invest in privately owned, early-stage companies that have strong potential for growth. For most companies funded by venture capital, other financing sources are inaccessible due to the high uncertainty, nonliquid assets, and risk associated with their business. For most, venture capitalism is a subset of the broader private equity investment space.[13] Conversely, investment banks primarily work to issue new securities across parties with asymmetric information in the market, provide expertise on mergers and acquisitions, and provide money management services for clients.[14]

In African countries, the private equity, venture capital, and investment banking markets have become increasingly important for economic development, because of unreliable foreign aid, fickle commodity prices, and a boom in entrepreneurial innovation that portends to create numerous jobs. These investments can be difficult to track as individual private equity or venture capital investments because most countries report private equity and venture capital as part of the broader category of FDI. However, the growth of nonindustrial firms and innovative start-ups—particularly as the Fourth Industrial Revolution expands across the continent—are indicative of the increase in private equity and venture capitalism.

In the decades after independence from colonial rule, most African countries adopted state-led, inward-oriented economic policies with the goal of igniting industrialization and developing export sectors that would be able to compete in the global economy. As a result, private investment was suppressed, a problem that became heightened by the crash in global commodity prices and mounting debt across the continent in the 1980s. This fiscal crisis—combined with pressure from the international financial institutions tasked with "filling the gap" to prevent the region's economic collapse—resulted in a period of rapid macroeconomic and structural reform, including the dismantling of state-led development institutions and a shift to an outward-oriented policy framework. Governments quickly divested from and privatized state-owned enterprises, dissembled marketing boards and price-setting commissions, eased restrictions on imports and foreign exchange, and restructured public services and utilities.[15]

The benefits of these reforms were felt almost immediately, with economic growth and productivity beginning to accelerate rapidly in the early 1990s and average inflation decreasing from 22 to 8 percent between 1990 and 2000. In Sub-Saharan Africa, FDI grew from $1.690 billion in 1990 to $31.595 billion in 2018. This places the region above Europe, Latin America and the Caribbean, Northern Africa, and Oceania, and only behind Asia in percentage growth of FDI inflows in the period. Foreign investment on the continent, however, responded much more slowly due to persistent fears about macroeconomic and political risks.[16] The region's share of the global economy continued to decline, from supplying 5.9 percent of world exports in 1980 to just 2.3 percent in 2003.[17] FDI inflows increased threefold, from $1.9 billion in 1983–87 to $6 billion in 1993–97, yet Africa's share of total FDI to developing countries actually declined from 11 percent to 4 percent over the same period.[18] Capital markets in African countries were not sufficiently capable of attracting private equity investments, and capital exchange fluctuations complicated the transition from state-driven investment to private ownership and investment growth.

In the mid-1990s, investment in Africa began to increase steadily, owing to increases in foreign exchange earnings through privatization, as well as improving political stability, democratization, and the resolution of civil wars.[19] Natural resources continued to constitute the majority of FDI to the continent, with minerals accounting for two-thirds of all FDI in 2004. However, investment began to diversify to tertiary sectors in the early-2000s, including to sectors like banking, telecommunications, and tourism.[20] Between 2000 and 2010, Africa experienced its most rapid period of economic growth, with real gross domestic product (GDP) increasing at an annual average rate of 4.9 percent—twice the rate of the preceding two decades. While resources generated just

32 percent of this growth, FDI's inward stock increased more than threefold, while remaining constant as a proportion of GDP.[21]

By 2008, Africa's collective GDP had surpassed that of other major emerging markets, like Brazil and Russia, and FDI inflows had reached their highest historical level, at more than $50 billion. Despite a slowdown in new FDI projects caused by the global financial crisis and political instability in North Africa, the value of FDI inflows continued to increase, especially in Sub-Saharan Africa, where capital investment increased by nearly 13 percent in 2013 and an impressive 65 percent in 2014, when it was valued at $87 billion.[22] In 2019, its collective GDP was ranked eighth, and it surpassed Brazil, Italy, Canada, and Russia. In 2021, FDI hit a record in Africa, at $83 billion. With FDI seeing a slight decrease after the COVID-19 pandemic, Africa's FDI still remains strong and higher than prepandemic levels, at $53 billion in 2023.[23]

Sub-Saharan African countries are now transitioning from official development assistance (ODA) to private equity funds, short-term venture capital investments, and long-term public bonds or other forms of investment banking. Volatile levels of ODA are no longer reliable, and Africa's market potential is attracting ever-increasing levels of global private investment. Venture capital and private transactions are funding services, value-added production, and the diversification of businesses in both intra-African markets and global trade. This chapter covers the different types of private investment—including venture capital, private equity, and investment banking—for investors, entrepreneurs, and policymakers to better explain the current conditions for investment and the potential for future returns.

Background Facts and Trends

Sub-Saharan African countries are the new market for long-term private investments in businesses, services, and innovation. After decades of growth based on overwhelming natural resource wealth and high commodity prices, the continent is transitioning to complex production and infrastructure development, which is fueling its growth. Resources now account for only about one-third of African countries' economic growth.[24] African governments are increasingly sourcing funding for infrastructure from their fiscal budgets, limiting their countries' fixed capital growth to the availability of government finances. This transition helps avoid a reliance on donor aid and external borrowing and opens Sub-Saharan African markets to investors looking to expand into Africa's growing and profitable markets.

Investment Sources

Given their colonial history, France and the United Kingdom were once Africa's primary sources of investment, together accounting for more than half of all FDI inflows until 1995.[25] As of 2022, the Netherlands, France, the United States, the United Kingdom, and China took the top five spots for FDI stock (figure 7-1).[26]

Although major FDI donor countries have not transitioned their political or diplomatic focus from ODA, Africa's investment markets are opening further to private equity and venture capital investments. International firms and individual investors are transitioning from developed markets, where returns have become increasingly smaller, to emerging markets that offer higher returns on investments. Even rising foreign direct investors, such as China, are diversifying their investment types in Africa due to the rapid expansion of investment banking and the burgeoning entrepreneurial movement.

Although Chinese investment in Africa initially focused on the procurement of primary materials to supply its domestic industries and households—especially hydrocarbons, copper, and iron—rising production costs have led Chinese firms to look to emerging African markets, such as textiles manufacturing in Ethiopia, Kenya, and Rwanda.[27] Chinese FDI to Africa fluctuated from $75 million in 2003 to an explosive $5 billion in 2021 before falling back down to $1.8 billion in 2022.[28] By 2016, China was the largest exporter to Africa, and the country accounted for a significant 17.5 percent of African imports.[29] In 2020, there was an important distinction in China's investment in Africa: it invested $2.96 billion, up 9.5 percent from 2019. In 2021 and 2022, China contributed to Africa's FDI in a much smaller proportion compared with previous years.[30]

Meanwhile, intra-African investment nearly tripled the share of FDI projects in the region, from 8 percent in 2003 to roughly 23 percent in 2013, and as high as 40 percent of total FDI inflows in Rwanda.[31] In 2022, intra-African investment accounted for 15 percent of total FDI, and it is higher in services than in selected manufacturing industries. [32] South Africa was the largest source of intra-African investment, and was second only to China on the list of developing countries that are FDI sources in Africa.[33]

Investment Recipients

Nearly all countries in Africa are benefiting from positive trends in capital investment, despite variation across the continent. Although 75 percent of

Figure 7-1. Africa's Top Ten Investor Economies by Foreign Direct Investment Stock, 2018 and 2022 (billions of dollars)

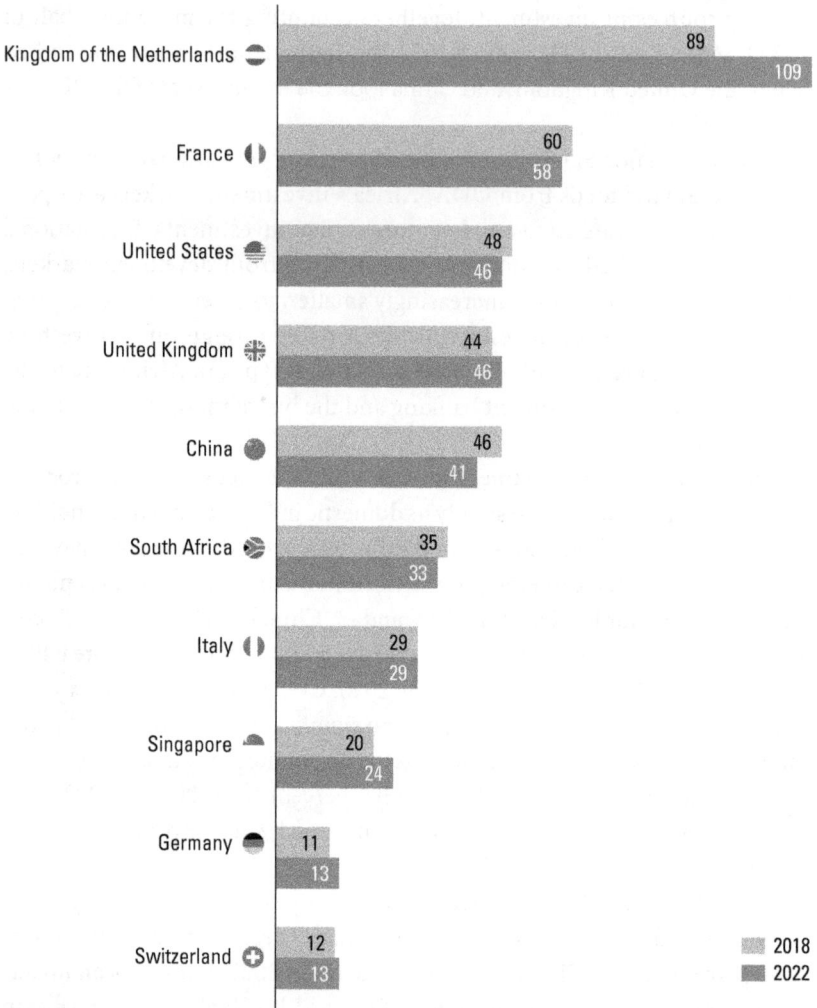

Source: UN Conference on Trade and Development, FDI/MNE database.

total capital investment is concentrated in the ten largest African markets, figure 7-2 shows that each region, except for Central Africa, is represented among the top ten recipients, to varying degrees.

North Africa has historically received the lion's share of Africa-focused investment, despite total investment decreasing after 2013 by 15 percent due to political instability in Libya and Tunisia.[34] Investment in Egypt remained relatively unscathed by the events related to the Arab Spring, holding its place as the largest single African market in investment value, and was the top recipient in Africa as of 2022, overtaking South Africa.[35]

North Africa's share of total FDI has declined markedly, especially since the mid-2000s, as investment in Sub-Saharan Africa has increased— by as much 33 percent in Central Africa and 11 percent in East Africa in 2014, even as the global volume of FDI declined by 16 percent that year.[36] Despite the increase, Central Africa continues to receive the smallest share of Africa's FDI inflows, and the value of investment in the subregion is largely dominated by Congo's oil sector.[37] Although South Africa's dominance in the region is declining, it still accounts for the highest number of FDI projects. The volume of FDI for Nigeria has also declined in recent years, due especially to divestment by the multinational oil giants Shell and Chevron early this century and more recently due to an unfavorable investment climate as a result of political risk and production increases in 2023.

Investment by Sector and Type

There is a specific focus on targeting small and medium-sized enterprises (SMEs) and investments in key areas such as tech innovation, climate adaptation, the digital economy penetration, innovation, and women's entrepreneurship.[38] Extractive industries accounted for 31 percent of capital flows between 2016 and 2020, but accounted for less than a quarter of the total projects. The continent has gradually become less dependent on these industries and more focused on technology, manufacturing, and service sectors. In 2020, business services had the most FDI projects, while the telecommunications sector had the highest capital investment, of about $8.5 billion.[39] Service-related sectors—including technology, media, and telecoms; business and professional services; financial services; consumers; and health sciences and wellness—accounted for over half of total projects (51.6 percent) as of 2022, while extractives only accounted for 4.3 percent of projects (figure 7-3).[40]

Figure 7-2. Ten Largest Recipients of Foreign Direct Investment Ranked by Score, 2022

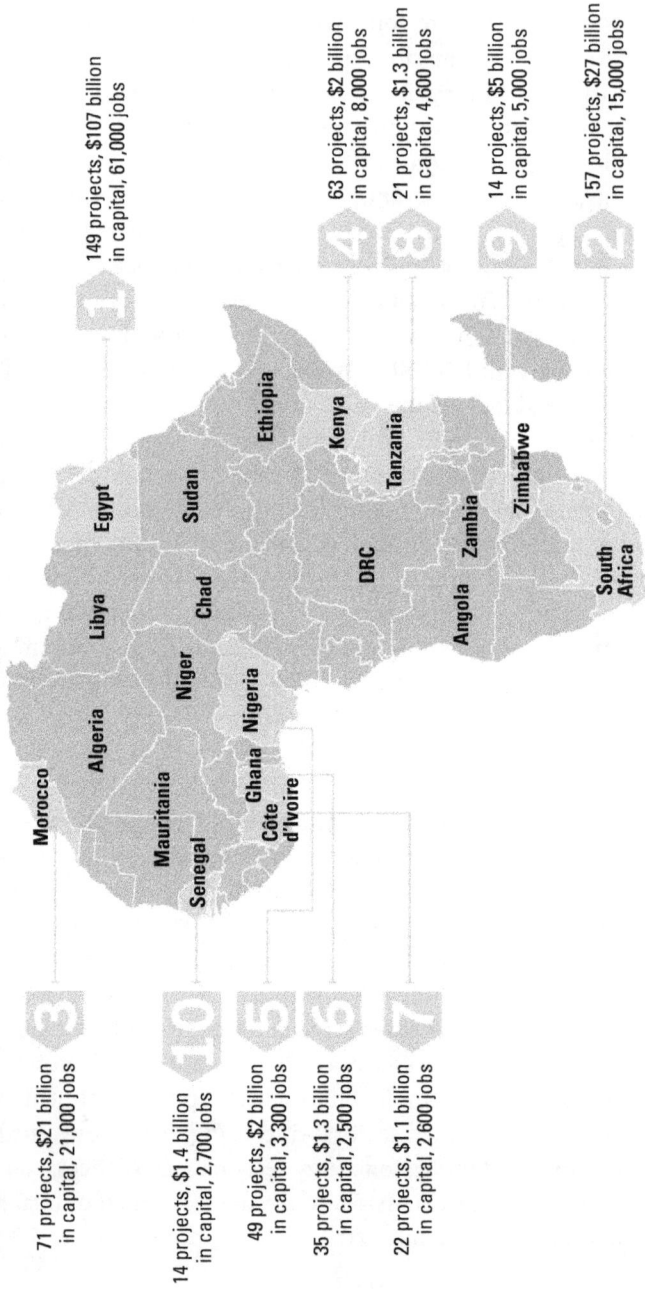

1 — 149 projects, $107 billion in capital, 61,000 jobs

4 — 63 projects, $2 billion in capital, 8,000 jobs

8 — 21 projects, $1.3 billion in capital, 4,600 jobs

9 — 14 projects, $5 billion in capital, 5,000 jobs

2 — 157 projects, $27 billion in capital, 15,000 jobs

3 — 71 projects, $21 billion in capital, 21,000 jobs

10 — 14 projects, $1.4 billion in capital, 2,700 jobs

5 — 49 projects, $2 billion in capital, 3,300 jobs

6 — 35 projects, $1.3 billion in capital, 2,500 jobs

7 — 22 projects, $1.1 billion in capital, 2,600 jobs

Source: EY (2023, 7).

Figure 7-3. Percentage Share of Foreign Direct Investment in Africa by Source, 2016–20

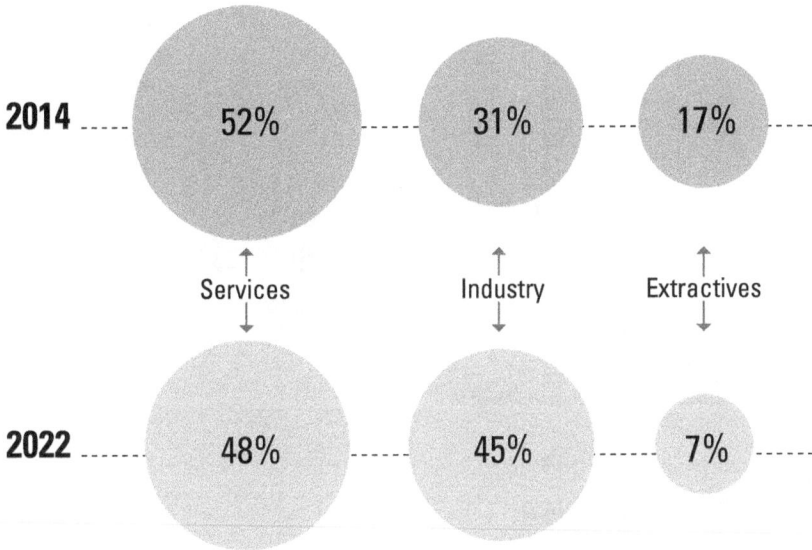

2014 ---- 52% ---- 31% ---- 17% ----

↑ Services ↓   ↑ Industry ↓   ↑ Extractives ↓

2022 ---- 48% ---- 45% ---- 7% ----

Source: EY (2023).

Clean technology dominated Africa's FDI sectors, followed by technology and mobility services in 2022. That year, the United Arab Emirates and France led the way, followed by India and the United Kingdom, together accounting for $77 billion on the continent, with Egypt, Morocco, and South Africa receiving over $110 billion.[41]

Although investment in the sector is continuing to grow across the region, only a few African countries have seen a substantial share of investment targeted to manufacturing to date, including Ethiopia, Kenya, and Nigeria. Compared with resource-dependent markets like Egypt and Nigeria, investment in countries like South Africa, Kenya, and Morocco tends to be more diversified toward less capital-intensive sectors, like real estate and financial services.[42] These countries have also led the way in the development of a domestic private equity market, with South Africa's market considered as sophisticated as that of many developed countries.[43]

Africa's venture capital has also skyrocketed in the past few years, to reach $3.4 billion across 545 deals in 2023 (not including the $0.9 billion in venture capital debt), after experiencing a gradual increase the decade prior and a record-setting number in 2022 (figure 7-4).[44]

Figure 7-4. Venture Capital Deal Volume by Year in Africa, 2014–23

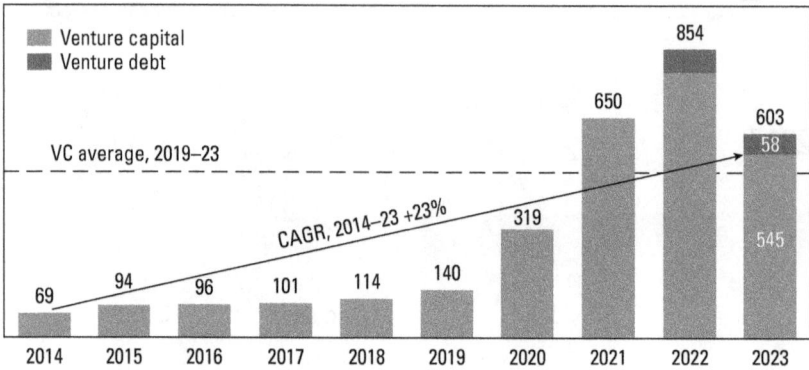

Source: AVCA (2024).
Note: CAGR = compound annual growth rate.

The Sector's Importance

Although the African continent survived the global financial crisis of 2007–8 relatively unscathed compared with other regions, in part due to its countries' low levels of financial integration, which shielded them from direct impact, the subsequent decline in official development assistance has negatively affected public spending, which has the potential to jeopardize countries' development goals and the continued improvement of the livelihoods of African households. Recent trends in the West have indicated that Africa's emerging economies can no longer count on ODA inflows as a market stabilizer, but that there is ample room for private capital to step in and keep the region on the path to sustainable development.[45]

Private capital and technical support to the public sector will be key in the transition from ODA to FDI-led infrastructure projects and service delivery. FDI to value-added industries, such as manufacturing, is a powerful multiplier of growth and indicates the growing rewards available for willing investors. Almost every African country has recently benefited from the wave of private equity fundraising and investment that is spreading across the continent. Capital investment is on the cusp of transitioning, if it has not already transitioned, from sole investments in the oil and natural gas sector to other important sectors that drive economic growth. This transition reinforces the short- and long-term potential for growth in Africa—Africa needs to continue to capitalize on this transition, especially focusing on high-potential

Figure 7-5. Foreign Direct Investment Inflows to Africa and Share of World Inflows, 2013–23 (billions of dollars and percent)

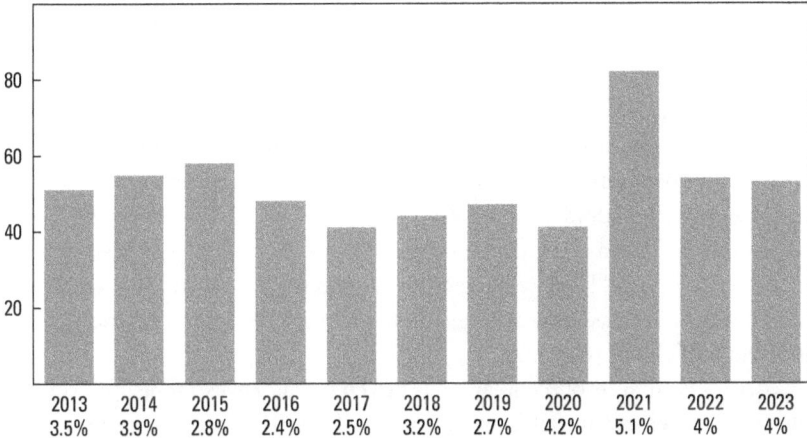

	2013	2014	2015	2016	2017	2018	2019	2020	2021	2022	2023
	3.5%	3.9%	2.8%	2.4%	2.5%	3.2%	2.7%	4.2%	5.1%	4%	4%

Source: UNCTAD (2024a).
Note: The value for each year represents the share of total inflows. Data exclude financial centers in the Caribbean and special-purpose entities in reporting countries.

sectors such as renewable energy, e-commerce and logistics, sustainable tourism, and the circular economy.[46]

Private equity and capital investment are two primary means by which global investors can access markets in Sub-Saharan Africa. Every sector requires short-term capital and long-term funding through equity investments to overcome start-up costs and maintain operational and innovation costs in ever-changing markets. Africa's global emerging markets—including in manufacturing, data, and energy—are receiving higher levels of investment, yet the majority are still considered small by international standards. Figure 7-5 indicates the relatively stable level of FDI through 2023, indicating its continued relevance.

Globally, FDI dominates the cash market in services. In Africa, the services sector received the largest share of foreign capital flows in 2014, at $37.5 billion, accounting for 48 percent of total FDI.[47] Yet a growing population and growing demand has led to Africa's investment needs for service delivery and infrastructure to be estimated at between $130 billion and $170 billion a year, presenting the notion of an insurmountable barrier that investors will need to overcome.

Another sector in significant need for investment growth is in the clean technology and renewable energy space. Africa will host much of the negative environmental effects associated with climate change in the near and long-term future, thus creating a new avenue by which investors can contribute to the continent's development and growth. Firms in all sectors can become more energy efficient and environmentally friendly, so there is ample opportunity for investment in high-return clean technology. To meet the demand for the increasing population, the International Energy Agency estimates that investments must increase to $120 billion annually by 2040.[48] This fourfold increase from current investment levels presents a large opportunity for investors. Already, global venture capital investments in clean energy start-ups have increased almost sixfold, from $1.9 billion in 2019 to $12.3 billion in 2022, and Africa should increasingly be viewed as a viable destination for these investments and impact.[49] Renewable energy investments on the continent will help meet the current need and may reform the current trajectory of African states in the face of climate challenges.

Africa's natural resource wealth has driven private investments for decades, but the changes in Sub-Saharan African markets to a greater focus on manufacturing, agro-processing, consumer markets, information and communication technologies, tourism, and banking indicate the need for new strategies for private investors. More private-equity-funded businesses in these markets will provide a bridge between mid-sized and large enterprises and the public market. There is a large gap in investment knowledge in African markets, and more could be done to support the continent in this area. Greater private investment support will allow domestic institutions, such as African governments and the African Development Bank (AfDB), to expand their portfolios and strengthen more assets.

Key Drivers

Several key aspects of African markets, government regulatory protocols, and changing consumerism drive investment from domestic and international firms, pushing the continent closer to achieving its targets and substantially encouraging Africa's structural transformation. These key drivers create an impetus for increased investment within the most profitable sectors or markets, while also creating a sense of security for firms looking to enter the African market for the first time. Sub-Saharan Africa is primed for investments at all levels—from large-scale infrastructure projects to SME creation—and private equity investments are the most reliable method of doing so.

The COVID-19 pandemic had a significant impact on FDI, and there was a stark contrast after the pandemic, when Africa's FDI fell sharply, by 50 percent. Thus, it was the hardest-hit region globally; however, there was significant adaptation, and extractives brought new opportunities. Africa's overall GDP contracted by 2.4 percent in 2020, yet it grew by 2.9 percent in 2023, and 3 percent growth was projected in 2024.[50]

Natural Resources

Natural resource wealth throughout the continent has driven FDI and private equity expansion for decades. New discoveries over the past two decades have allowed for steady investment in small infrastructure projects and rural adaptation to mining and extractive services. In 2007, the discovery of oil off the coast of Ghana spurred a flurry of interest and investment in the country's natural resource sector.[51] More recent oil, natural gas, and mineral discoveries in Tanzania, Mozambique, Egypt, Algeria, Angola, and Nigeria have attracted a large proportion of FDI capital to these countries. China has driven a large portion of overall investment in African countries' capital-intensive extractive sectors. Chinese companies contributed $112.34 billion in greenfield FDI and $24.6 billion in merger-and-acquisition deals between 2000 and 2022, two-thirds of which went to resource-rich countries, including Algeria, the Democratic Republic of Congo, Egypt, Ghana, Guinea, Morocco, Nigeria, Niger, Zambia, and Zimbabwe.[52]

Despite Africa's infrastructure challenges, the continent maintains relatively low exploration costs, which undoubtedly attracts investors in the short term. Many natural-resource-based projects require private equity to become viable in the long run, and investors are increasingly seeing African companies as worthy of long-term investment. A total of 99 percent of China's equity to nonenergy mining and processing projects was focused on the exploration and extraction of minerals and metals.[53] A notable example of long-term private equity investment in natural resources is Helios Investment Partners' $115 million investment in Oando Gas and Power in Nigeria.[54] Additionally, Africa holds the largest portion of arable land in the world, and it is home to 30 percent of the world's mineral reserves, 12 percent of the world's oil, and 8 percent of the world's natural gas reserves.[55] The potential long-term returns on agricultural products—considering rising urbanization, population explosions, and climate change effects on current production around the world—give Africa a competitive advantage on which investors would now be wise to capitalize.

Technology Adoption

Since commodities are affected by short-term fluctuations, private equity investors have expanded into the technology, financial services, and infrastructure sectors. Financial technology and technological adaptations in manufacturing are lifting African markets amid the global Fourth Industrial Revolution, ensuring that these markets remain competitive. Mobile services and technology already contribute greatly to Africa's GDP—8.1 percent of its value added in 2022—which is continuing to spur investments in other technology-based sectors.[56]

Improved Macroeconomic Policies

Improvements in economic policies follows the UN Sustainable Development Goals' intention of maximizing macroeconomic performance and attaining higher economic growth. These improvements can be seen through the differences in ease-of-doing business rankings. Sub-Saharan Africa scored 51.8 in 2020, well below the Organization for Economic Cooperation and Development's high-income economy average of 78.4 and the global average of 63.[57] African governments are increasingly adapting their regulatory systems to global macroeconomic shifts and are promising to install welcoming environments for global and intraregional investment. In 2023, Africa adopted more investment policy measures than any other region in the world, indicating its intentional effort to improve its environments.[58]

The unpredictability of aid flows to the continent has encouraged institutions to seek public–private partnerships and higher domestic savings plans that will attract more competitive investment. More consistent macroeconomic policies, such as better control of government budgets and debt relief strategies, are also responsible for proving political stability and administrative efficiency. Investors are generally motivated by access to resources, access to markets, efficiency gains, and acquisition of strategic assets. Therefore, both FDI and private equity are beginning to achieve similar efficiency gains in African markets, as well as in other emerging markets. Empirical evidence has shown that an enabling business environment increases FDI overall and intraregionally and, based on changes in policies and recent investment data, private equity investors are encouraged by African countries' improved fiscal policies, which facilitate the entry and exit of capital investments.[59]

Investment Hubs

Even during the pandemic, major FDI hubs emerged, with South Africa as the key hub in the Southern region, Kenya in the East, Nigeria and Ghana in the West, Angola in the Central Region, Morocco and Egypt in the North, and Côte d'Ivoire in Francophone Sub-Saharan Africa. These investment hubs reflect country and regional growth, particularly in Eastern Africa, where the dismantling of intraregional barriers to trade and investment inspires foreign investors to enter these markets. Investment hubs across Africa are commensurate with growth in digital technology adoption, primarily in large cities, as digitization and a broader understanding of digital banking have facilitated capital movement and the expansion of capital markets. Mobile communications are transforming the financial services sector so significantly that African investors can access markets regionally and continentally through their cellphones. Mobile banking and investment users are building on the momentum of first movers, or those who took the risks to be the first investors in a community and often receive the highest rates of return on their initial investments.

In 2022, Southern Africa attracted the second-highest number of investment projects, with capital investment of $36 billion; meanwhile, Northern Africa remains an FDI hub, especially thanks to Egypt, which received a record number of investments in 2022 (187 percent more than 2021), accounting for 60 percent of North Africa's total, with over $100 billion in capital.[60] Countries like Côte d'Ivoire, Uganda, Kenya, and Tanzania have all received substantial increases in FDI in recent years. Another key marker is the openness of one's economy—how easy it is to conduct business and attract outside investors. The degree of openness of the economy resulted in a positive and significant impact on private investment. This suggests that fostering an open, inclusive environment plays a critical role in the financial development and growth of the private sector in Côte d'Ivoire, Uganda, Kenya, and Tanzania.

Changing Entrepreneurship

The rise of investment and innovation hubs is partially attributable to Africa's growing population and urbanization. Half of all Africans are under the age of twenty years now and are increasingly moving to cities, driving the rate of urbanization to almost 40 percent of Africans living in urban areas.[61] By 2033, more Africans will live in urban areas than in rural ones, reaching 60 percent by 2050.[62] Changing consumer demands are driving entrepreneurship and investment in SMEs. SMEs, particularly those that are mobile or are digitally based, are undervalued among foreign investors in Africa. However, a larger middle class provides promise of future returns on firms supplying household goods and services. Consumer business is driving the reach of foreign investment and private equity to SMEs, entrepreneurial training institutes, and related markets.

Figure 7-6. Top Source Countries for Foreign Direct Investment Projects, 2022

2022	Projects	Capital Investment (US$b)	Jobs created ('000)	FDI score
Total	733	194.3	154.3	360.5
US	93	6.8	13.3	37.7
France	78	26.5	17.2	40.6
UK	64	19.2	13.0	32.1
UAE	60	49.9	18.6	42.8
Switzerland	44	2.2	3.1	16.4
Germany	37	1.2	4.1	14.1
China	21	2.6	9.4	11.0
Kenya	21	0.5	3.2	8.2
Canada	20	5.1	7.0	10.7
Nigeria	20	0.5	1.4	7.3
India	20	22.2	9.0	17.1

Source: EY (2023).

Key Players

Relatively high rates of return on FDI and private equity investment in Africa have led to increasing interest from other countries, particularly the United States, the United Kingdom, France, India, and the United Arab Emirates. These key players have become reliable factors for existing investors in Africa and are beginning to attract new investments. As the continent transitions from dependency on ODA to FDI, venture capital, and private equity investments, international firms are outpacing foreign governments' investments in African resources and markets (see figure 7-6).

Falling returns in Western markets have led to rising levels of FDI in Africa by private international firms and government-owned finance corporations. The Overseas Development Institute stated that UK companies have made more profit investing in Africa than any other developing region in the world.[63] The United States and the United Kingdom have both developed initiatives in recent years to boost government-led and private corporations' investments in Africa. Internationally headquartered investment firms and domestic management companies are responsible for driving private equity investments, and for ensuring positive promotions of the continent's potential to foreign investors.

Africa-Based Firms

Africa's share of global FDI has increased significantly since 2000, and continues to grow more rapidly than any other world region, but remains the

Figure 7-7. Largest Intraregional Investors in Africa, 2022

Africa's largest investing nations Three largest destinations	Projects	Capital Investment (US$m)	Jobs created ('000)	FDI score
Kenya	**21**	**474**	**3.232**	**8.2**
Tanzania	4	77	1.740	1.9
South Africa	3	15	27	1.0
Ghana	2	200	404	0.9
Nigeria	**20**	**470**	**1.423**	**7.3**
Ghana	7	123	220	2.4
Kenya	5	146	522	1.9
Egypt	3	81	540	1.2
South Africa	**17**	**701**	**1.232**	**6.3**
Egypt	4	85	115	1.4
Kenya	3	89	449	1.2
Nigeria	3	41	45	1.0
Mauritius	**16**	**1074**	**1.774**	**6.3**
Kenya	4	99	708	1.6
South Africa	4	484	219	1.6
Zimbabwe	2	217	140	0.8
Tunisia	**10**	**74**	**608**	**3.6**
Nigeria	3	21	123	1.0
Algeria	1	16	288	0.4
South Africa	1	7	41	0.3

Source: EY (2023).

source of just 12 percent of all FDI inflows in the developing world and only 5.2 percent of inflows globally; and intraregional greenfield projects represented 15 percent of all projects in Africa, but only 2 percent in terms of value in 2022.[64] There is a growing crop of private equity and financing firms in Africa that are exploring the benefits of intra-African investment and project development. Most of this investment targets the services sector, though some does flow into manufacturing and primary sector businesses. Intra-African investment in financial services, which received 70 percent of all deals made in services, has a compounding effect on attracting additional investment and encouraging economic growth through all sectors' efficient use of an improved financial services sector.[65] Kenya and Nigeria are the largest intraregional investors in Africa, achieving high levels of projects, FDI amounts, and job creation—as pictured in figure 7-7—and overtaking South Africa, which was once the region's largest intraregional investor by a large margin.

Figure 7-8. Percentage Share of Foreign Direct Investment by Source in Africa, 2016–20

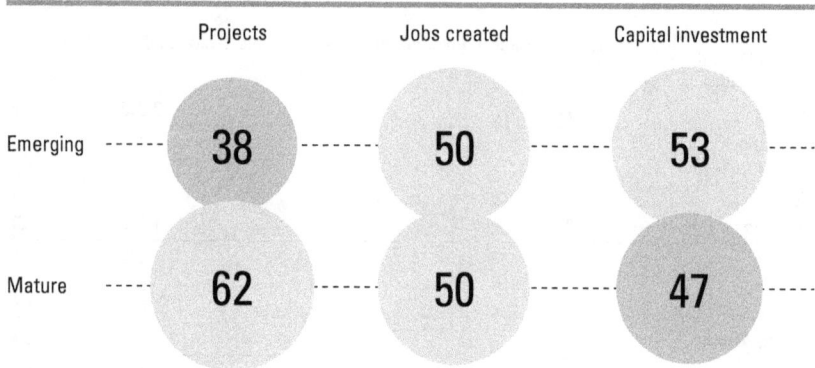

	Projects	Jobs created	Capital investment
Emerging	38	50	53
Mature	62	50	47

Source: EY (2021).

Some notable firms responsible for driving intraregional investment include Aureros Capital (Mauritius), Banco Africano de Investimentos (Angola), East African Capital Partners (Kenya), Ethos Private Equity (South Africa), and Helios Investment Partners (Nigeria).[66] With the creation of the African Continental Free Trade Area (AfCFTA), there is now a new opportunity for Africa to harness regional trade links, which are lacking. AfCFTA will enable economies to innovate and grow together by removing intraregional, artificial trade barriers; it has the expected goal of providing a $450 billion income gain for Africa by 2035.[67]

Emerging Economies

In addition to intra-African investment among the emerging economies on the continent, those economies around the world are increasingly seeking out African markets for their investments. Figure 7-8 shows that between 2016 and 2020, emerging markets were the source of 38 percent of all projects, 50 percent of all jobs created, and 53 percent of the capital investment, revealing that projects from emerging markets compared with mature markets are more labor and capital intensive.[68]

India, with a cumulative FDI to the continent of $74 billion, is one of the top five investors on the continent, and this is projected to rise to $150 billion by 2030. Indian companies have been concentrated in agribusiness, pharmaceuticals, information and communications technology (ICT), and renewables, with Egypt receiving the largest portion in 2022.[69]

China has been perceived in recent years as the primary investor in African infrastructure projects, manufacturing, and energy production; however, China's share of FDI has fallen significantly, from 11 percent in 2018 to 2.9 percent in 2022.[70] There is an emerging narrative that Chinese investment is riddled with economic woes, labor abuses, risky loans, and too much imported labor. There is a belief that it is contributing little to employment generation and local skills development for the receiving countries. Though this is true, Chinese-financed business outcomes have positively influenced and provided new technology transfer and significantly bridged infrastructure gaps in countries, including $155 billion in major infrastructure in Sub-Saharan Africa in the past two decades.[71] Yet amid Africa's rising debt, China's investment in Sub-Saharan Africa for global infrastructure development dropped 55 percent in 2022, to $7.5 billion, as Chinese companies shifted to other areas.[72]

Moreover, roughly 50 percent of China's FDI in Africa is now focused on noncommodity sectors like construction, manufacturing, and banking.[73] As many as 1 million Chinese laborers have moved to Africa in recent years to work on construction projects or to manage the implementation of special economic zones (SEZs).[74] China also leads investment in consumer-related industries, such as pharmaceuticals and light manufacturing, taking the lead in capitalizing on domestic consumption and growing consumer markets in Africa. During the period 2016–22, China was fourth in number of projects and second in capital, but first in job creation.[75]

China and India are taking advantage of locales where the United States and United Kingdom are less ingrained in investment markets to expand their projects and returns. Chinese investment has had a direct impact on reducing poverty and increasing overall economic growth, thus encouraging higher levels of investment by Chinese firms and other international firms.

Gulf states massively increased their FDI in Africa in 2022 and 2023, including $60 billion across 83 projects in 2022 and $53 billion across 73 projects in 2023, with the United Arab Emirates and Saudi Arabia accounting for most of it.[76] The increase is focused in decarbonization technologies—including hydrogen projects in Kenya, Mauritania, and Egypt; renewables in Morocco; and solar parks in South Africa. The United Arab Emirates has accelerated its FDI in Africa, contributing $50 billion in 2022 which is seven times more than the United States.[77] The United Arab Emirates' investment is significantly concentrated in Egypt and South Africa, which were the recipients of 95 percent of the Emirates' 2022 African FDI, now becoming Egypt's largest investor. The Emirates' investment is focused on clean tech, sustainable infrastructure, energy, oil, tourism, and agriculture.

Opportunities

South Africa, Nigeria, Egypt, and Kenya are, by now, well-known hubs for investment, business, and consumer demand. These countries are the most attractive to foreign investors, in part due to the depth of institutions and services available to their investors. They are important to watch in the short term, as FDI levels continue to increase and private equity firms expand in Africa. The recently instituted AfCFTA provides ample investment opportunities and access to intraregional markets to facilitate global economic growth, which is opening up opportunities for more countries to take the lead.

South Africa

Across a range of analyses, South Africa has been consistently identified as the most attractive investment destination in Africa, both in terms of its domestic market and as a gateway to the rest of the continent.[78] In addition to boasting one of the largest economies in Africa, South Africa has a robust and rapidly growing middle class, a wealth of natural resources—such as coal, gold, iron ore, platinum, manganese, uranium, and chromium, as well as oil and natural gas—and the best-developed national infrastructure on the continent.[79]

In fact, South Africa is the only one of Africa's emerging markets to be included as one of the BRICS economic powerhouses, putting it on par with Brazil, Russia, India, and China. Even as it has become a major investment hub—it received the largest share of FDI projects on the continent in 2022, with 23 percent of the total, demonstrating an impressive compound annual growth rate in FDI—South Africa remains a relatively cost-efficient location for doing business.[80] It is also the only country in Africa to offer an efficient financial market and a sophisticated stock exchange, and it is considered one of the most open jurisdictions for FDI in the world, with robust and independent legal protection of property rights and contracts. Beyond the range of direct investment incentives offered by the government and the increasingly liberalized trade policies in effect since the mid-1990s, South Africa's International Headquarters Company system makes the country an especially appealing location for multinationals looking for a hub for their African operations.[81]

Despite a decline in its overall attractiveness rating in recent years due to reduced growth projections, political corruption scandals, and problems with the rand, South Africa's position as the darling of investment in Africa is unlikely to change anytime soon. It continues to climb the World Economic Forum's Global Competitiveness rankings, driven largely by the impressive uptake of

ICT, growth in internet bandwidth, and corresponding improvements in innovation.[82] Business services and technology were the top FDI sectors as of 2022, with telecommunications receiving double the number of projects in 2022. The United Kingdom, United States, and United Arab Emirates led the way, with projects—including a $20 billion investment in a sustainable city, made by a Dubai-based company; a $750 million investment in the construction of a second data center, from a US-based company; and a $408 million investment in the second phase of the development of a mine by a UK-based company.[83] Looking to the future, South Africa's BRICS Business Council has identified the top five sectors for optimally targeted investment in the country: insurance, agriculture, electricity generation and transmission, ICT connectivity, and the North–South Development Corridor.

Egypt

Although Egypt has faced political turbulence related to the "Arab Spring," perceptions about the potential that violent uprisings and military intervention might threaten returns on investment, and currency depreciations, it was the largest destination for FDI in Africa in 2022. Increasing by 187 percent from 2021, Egypt received $100 billion in capital, boosted by investments from the top contributor—the United Arab Emirates—and others, including India, Saudi Arabia, and the United Kingdom.[84] In 2014, at the height of Egypt's political uncertainty, a survey of private investors listed Cairo as the second-most-appealing city in North Africa, after Casablanca, and Goldman Sachs continued to classify Egypt as among its NEXT 11 and CIVETS markets with the highest investment potential.[85] In fact, Egypt has remained the largest single market for FDI capital investment, worth $100.5 billion, over the past decade.[86]

Throughout changes in leadership and political uncertainty, the Egyptian government has maintained a technocratic approach to economic policy and a high level of commitment to its top priority of promoting investment. This has been done by cutting fuel subsidies by 30 percent and devaluing the national currency. It has continued to uphold its international treaties, trade agreements, and domestic financial laws.[87] In March 2015, Egypt's Economic Development Conference was convened in Sharm El-Sheikh to present the government's reform agenda. At the close of a three-day summit, the prime minister, Ibrahim Mahlab, announced that the country had signed deals worth $36.2 billion in investment—largely in energy, real estate, agriculture, and manufacturing—and a further $18.6 billion in construction contracts. British Petroleum alone agreed to invest $12 billion in natural gas extraction,[88] while investments from US companies included Coca-Cola ($500 million), Kellogg ($144 million), GE, and First Solar.

Egypt offers a relatively open environment for investment, by African standards. Although certain restrictions apply in special cases—such as the need for military approval for investments on the Sinai Peninsula and the ban on new licenses in the banking and insurance sector—there are no legal differences in the regulations applied to domestic and foreign investors in many sectors. Thus, while Egypt ranked just 118 out of 185 economies on the World Bank's Ease of Doing Business Index in 2020, this ranking is likely to improve markedly in coming years as the political environment stabilizes and as envisioned reforms succeed in enhancing transparency and stream-lining bureaucracy.[89]

One of the largest single opportunities for investment in Egypt lies in its planned construction of a new capital city, located between Cairo and the Suez Canal, at a total estimated cost of $45 billion. This city will require housing infrastructure to support 5 million inhabitants, government bodies and administration, and a financial district. Two other major projects connected to the Suez Canal are a national industrial and logistics hub, which will require $15 billion to be invested in utilities, and construction of a second, parallel waterway that will potentially double the canal's trade traffic.

Given Egypt's historical and cultural endowments and proximity to Europe, tourism and related industries also offer a notable opportunity for investment in the country. Recent moves that signal growth in the tourism sector include IHG Hotels & Resorts' decision to build two new hotels in Cairo. Also, EgyptAir's fleet is being expanded by Boeing to meet growing demand, and Egypt plans to double Cairo International Airport's passenger capacity.[90]

Morocco

Morocco boasts one of Africa's best-developed financial services sectors, which signals an appealing point of market entry for businesses seeking to establish a presence in the region.[91] In contrast to its North African neighbors, Morocco has managed to avoid much of the political instability related to the Arab Spring, and it has thus increased its regional market share of FDI. The government has capitalized on its robust infrastructure and favorable location,[92] combining these structural endowments with strategic macroeconomic policies and trade liberalization to become a regional manufacturing and export hub for multinational corporations.[93] In 2022, Morocco attracted $15.3 billion in capital investment across 71 projects, which is a 58 percent rise from 2021. The United States and United Arab Emirates invested the most across Morocco's leading sectors of clean tech, business services, and technology. Luxembourg invested $10 billion in a single renewable energy project in 2022, while a Chinese-German battery company invested $6.4 billion in an electric vehicle manufacturing facility in 2023. [94]

As an indication of its commitment to encourage investment, the Moroccan government has ratified 62 bilateral agreements on investor protection law and 51 agreements on eliminating overlapping taxation of corporate profits. It is also a signatory to the European Union Association Agreement, giving Morocco privileged access to the European market, and it has implemented its Investment Charter, which allows for the free movement of capital and investment returns.[95] The establishment of regional investment centers and SEZs across the country have helped to streamline investment procedures, while offering favorable tax exemptions, reduced trade barriers, targeted infrastructure improvements, and even monopoly rights.[96] According to potential investors, the greatest remaining constraint on investment in Morocco is the inefficiency of its commercial court system. The government is working to incorporate ICT to streamline and rationalize procedures and to reduce opportunities for corruption.

Considering Morocco's current incentive structures and economic trajectories, key sectors for investment in the country are consumer goods and retail, the automotive and aerospace industries, and electronics. Morocco already has the best-developed consumer market in Africa. In manufacturing, Morocco has emerged as Africa's leading producer of specialty, high-tech products—a signal of its highly skilled workforce, competitive costs, and strategic clustering of SEZs.[97] In aerospace alone, there are already more than 100 suppliers operating along the value chain.[98] Morocco and Egypt alike benefit from investor attraction as a result of their strategic geographic locations, strong manufacturing bases, and development plans.[99]

Nigeria

Nigeria received $2 billion across 49 projects in 2022, which is still below the FDI level before the COVID-19 pandemic, but still propels Nigeria to the rank of the top recipient in West Africa.[100] The Nigerian government has made substantial strides to attract foreign investment to its production and services industries. The Federal Ministry of Industry, Trade, and Investment has implemented a designation of "pioneer status" to eligible companies, which allows these firms to be exempted from the Companies Income Tax, the full claim of capital allowances on qualifying assets, and nontaxable dividends to company shareholders, as well as the ability to offset losses in subsequent tax years.[101] These incentives are important to encourage innovation and increased investments, as investors are insured against significant losses to the extent that they can return a firm to profitability within a few years. Nigeria has also engaged more with India, especially since the launch of the Nigeria India Business Council.

The government has also identified four priority subsectors for industrial development: metallurgical industries, engineering industries, chemicals/petrochemicals, and construction. These subsectors are critical for advancing the overall growth of Nigeria's entire industrial sector. Nigeria's growing population and rising rates of urbanization are driving the country's industrialization and expansion of its service industries.

Nigeria is a promising place for entrepreneurial expansion in the coming years and is likely to attract intra-African and foreign investment to finance its rapid expansion and growth. It was the top spot for venture capital deal volume from 2020 to 2023.[102] And it currently has one of the continent's largest economies, valued at $252.74 billion in 2024, which was Africa's biggest in 2022 and fourth-biggest in 2023.[103] Lagos is also often listed as one of the top five cities in which to invest throughout the continent, further proving the country's potential to produce high returns for investors, in addition to its attractive regulatory environment.

Kenya

The private sector in Kenya is more developed and is growing faster than that of any other country in East Africa. The service sector has been the largest contributor to Kenya's economic growth over the past decade. The country now boasts the leading market for technology and finance across East and Central Africa.[104] Since the creation of its Central Depository System in 2004 and the automation of its trading system in 2006, the Nairobi Securities Exchange now ranks among the most sophisticated and efficient in Africa. As of May 2024, Kenya's market capitalization is $13.4 billion, with 62 companies listed on the stock exchange.[105] Kenya has been among the top four nations for venture capital by deal volume for many years, and it is currently third in Africa, having jumped from $185 million in 2019 to $1.1 billion in 2022.[106]

Kenya's strong financial infrastructure has created a robust foundation for innovation-driven growth. Home to 97 percent of the country's start-ups, Nairobi is a leading tech city in Africa.[107] The country is now ranked number one in the world for mobile money services, owing in large part to the impressive uptake of ICT and relatively high mobile penetration rates. Most

Kenyans report having used M-PESA, the flagship mobile banking product launched in 2007 that has affected 40 million users.[108] The crowdsourcing app Ushahidi has become a major international tech firm, with applications in more than twenty countries. Its success led to the establishment of the iHub innovation center in Nairobi. Recognizing Kenya's potential, several major multinational tech companies have already established their regional headquarters in Nairobi, including Google, Microsoft, and Intel.[109] Now, the tech sector accounts for 1.1 percent of Kenya's econnomy.[110]

The Kenyan government has actively supported innovation as part of its commitment to investment-driven growth, which is the foundation for its "Digital Kenya 2030" strategy. The success of M-PESA, for example, is largely attributable to the Central Bank's concession that legal regulation of mobile banking would follow product development. As far back as the Foreign Investors Act of 1964 and the establishment of the Capital Markets Authority in 1990—which aims to protect investors by ensuring proper licensing and regulatory procedures to promote market development through innovation—the government has demonstrated the political ability to encourage investment through policy.[111] In 2021, Kenya's government passed the Startup Bill 2021, which included tax incentives for investors. Kenya has been among the most progressive governments in Africa in the implementation of nature conservation laws, for example, which has been effective in promoting tourism-related investment.

The Kenyan state has also ratcheted up efforts to improve national infrastructure in recent years, in cooperation with major private sector partners, as demonstrated by the completion of the TEAMS undersea fiber-optic cable network and the expansion of the Standard-Gauge Railway project.[112] Public–private partnerships with Chinese companies, in particular, have allowed a number of megaconstruction projects to progress in spite of gaps in funding from Western donors and regional development banks. Chinese investment has also helped Kenya lead the way in the establishment of SEZs intended to encourage investment in targeted sectors, including textiles and pharmaceuticals.[113]

Challenges and Risks

Among foreign investors, the common perception of the African region is often negative, shaped by the political and macroeconomic crises of the past. To be sure, political turmoil—including ethnic conflict, protests, and election-related violence—continues to threaten returns on investment in many parts of the continent, as the events related to North Africa's Arab Spring and South Africa's violent mining strikes have put into stark relief in recent years. Also, on average, the region has had a relatively low performance across a range of economic indicators, such as productivity, human capacity, supply chains, and unemployment levels.[114]

However, the African continent also contains a diverse mix of markets, which vary in both opportunities and risks. Investment challenges also vary significantly, depending on the economic sector in question, and these sector-specific risks are made apparent in this book's separate chapters. Here, we attempt to identify some of the most common challenges for investing in Africa's emerging markets, which are likely to apply to varying degrees across sectors and countries.

Regulatory Climate

Any survey or analysis of doing business in African markets is likely to highlight that investment growth is often constrained by legal uncertainty, bureaucratic red tape, and corruption.[115] A study by the World Economic Forum revealed that less than one-third of companies working on the continent believe that administrative and regulatory processes are dealt with efficiently, or that the particular national policy framework is generally supportive of investment.[116] Although the macroeconomic risks of investing in Africa were improved to a large degree by the reform programs of the 1990s, the process of privatization and liberalization actually exacerbated corruption levels in the region.[117] As of 2023, just four African countries broke into the top fifty countries in the world on Transparency International's Corruptions Perceptions Index: Seychelles (20), Cabo Verde (30), Botswana (39), and Rwanda (49).[118]

In the past, many foreign investors have exhibited a willingness to over-look public sector corruption when the returns on investment are sufficiently high or are guaranteed, as in Africa's natural resource sector. In fact, resource-seeking investors generally have little choice but to invest where resources are available, eventually coming to perceive corruption as akin to an unavoidable business "tax."[119] Where these patterns have become entrenched, however, it is more difficult to encourage investment in sectors where returns are less lucrative or certain, as in manufacturing and services. Increasingly, private equity firms in Africa prefer to make their business investments in sectors that have only a minimal amount of government involvement or interaction.[120]

At present, regulatory uncertainty is also heightened by ongoing regional integration negotiations. Although the obvious goal of integrating Africa's regional economic communities is to improve the harmonization and rationalization of trade and investment regulation, there appears to be a lack of political capacity to recognize common problems, to compromise and achieve agreement on policy solutions, and to implement the agreed-upon reforms at the national level.[121] Beyond this, many of Africa's smaller and poorer countries lack the technical, financial, and human capacity to enforce compliance consistently, or to punish political officials who engage in rent-seeking behavior.

The Early Stage of Structural Transformation

Despite remaining optimism among foreign observers, Africa's take-off in productivity has not yet begun. More efficient production would allow for significant gains on investment in sectors like manufacturing and agriculture, for example. Efficiency and productive gains are generally inhibited by a lack of structural transformation, which impedes value chain development and productive collaborations among big firms to implement infrastructure projects and industry-wide adoption of technology. To achieve an industrial state, FDI must be a significant catalyst for its tendency to attract both technological and managerial know-how, thus, ensuring promotion, adaptation, and access to regional and world value chains, enhanced efficiency, significant investment flows, and heightened productivity.[122]

Macroeconomic resilience is a signal of successful structural transformation. Figure 7-9 correlates investment attractiveness with GDP growth, revealing that those countries that are industrially and infrastructurally developed—such as South Africa, Egypt, and Morocco—are the most attractive to investors. Other countries invoke too much uncertainty. Underdevelopment is a deterrent for potential investors; however, some countries may be capable of bypassing the necessity of structural transformation by adopting new energy markets and ICT.

Commodity Market Volatility

As Africa waits for its structural transformation, many of its top investment markets remain overly dependent on primary commodities and have thus been adversely affected by the recent decline in global commodity prices. To a large extent, this decline has been driven by the slowdown of China's economic growth trajectory, and those markets that are China's main suppliers of primary products—like oil and natural gas, copper, and iron ore—are the most likely to be affected. Surging commodity prices had spurred much of Africa's economic success story since 2000; as a result, many African

Figure 7-9. Africa Investment Attractiveness Matrix

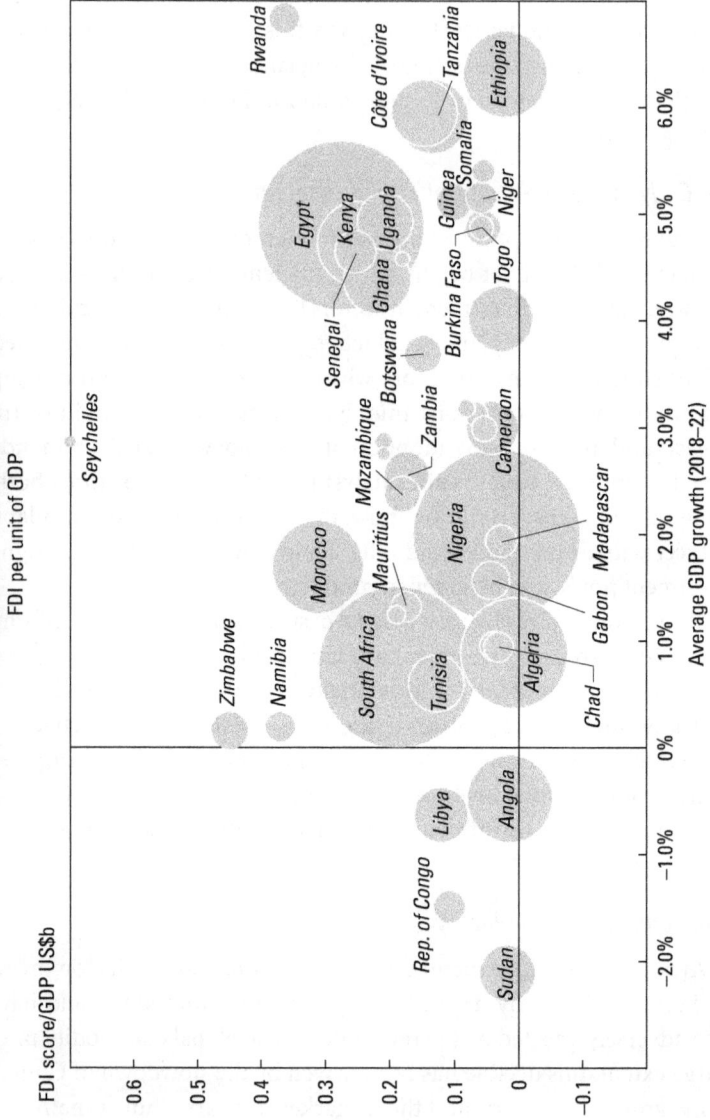

Faster-growing economies tend to attract larger FDI inflows

FDI per unit of GDP

FDI score/GDP US$b

Average GDP growth (2018–22)

Source: EY (2016a, 4).

economies have become even more dependent on commodity exports over the past fifteen years, making them particularly vulnerable to recent market volatility. UNCTAD estimates that 83 percent of African countries are highly dependent on commodities.[123] Geopolitical shocks are having and will continue to have effects on Africa's commodity volatility. According to a range of development organizations, filling Africa's infrastructure gap should be the first priority for encouraging investment and economic diversification on the continent.

Absorptive Capacities

FDI is a significant source of the money required for growth in underdeveloped nations. However, the absorptive capacities of the host country determine how much FDI will have an impact on growth. An interesting study found that the growth effect of FDI might be deceptive if economic freedom and the role of fragility in the emergence of the financial system are not taken into account.[124] The findings show that increased economic freedom stimulates growth, while the brittleness of the financial system inhibits it. Thus, a sound financial system and increased economic freedom are necessary for FDI to have a positive growth impact. The financial systems of developing nations, and Sub-Saharan Africa in particular, are weak. As a result, macroeconomic and development policies must be developed and put into practice by decision-makers to create a sound financial system that can withstand shocks. Additionally, governments must protect citizens' rights to liberty and freedom, because doing so may lead to increased economic growth. Thus, a sound financial system and increased economic freedom are necessary for FDI to have a positive growth impact.

As a result, the stock markets of many emerging nations have dramatically changed to support economic activities, and they are now more integrated with the rest of the world. Bekaert and Harvey report that the association between stock markets and international links may frequently rise as a result of capital market liberalization.[125] This will encourage interdependencies among regions, and also trade and economic links between markets. In turn, the influx of foreign money and resulting gains from diversification would not only promote economic growth but also ensure that shocks to the availability of bank credit do not have disproportionate consequences for that growth. The movement of their stock market indexes will be a key indicator of internal or external economic vulnerability as developing markets continue to develop and go through a considerable change in adopting market-oriented policies. Conversely, with FDI inflows of $45 billion in 2023, Africa has emerged as a significant recipient of foreign investment.[126]

Additional focused financial and institutional reforms are required, including improvements in the electronic payment system, excellent governance, more transparency, effective contract enforcement, and business process simplification. These changes are required to create a favorable climate and increase market effectiveness.[127]

Africa was the hardest-hit region globally in 2020, during the COVID-19 pandemic, with its FDI dropping by half. It lagged behind all other emerging markets as well as the two major mature regions, North America (–19 percent) and Europe (–23 percent). Only the fall in the Asia-Pacific region was close (–43 percent). This is partly attributable to its sizable resource-exporting economies, which experienced a recession due to falling commodity prices and fast declining demand, particularly from China. FDI decreased significantly in 2020, yet this only tells part of the tale. Long-term growth is becoming more sustainable because of increased investment in businesses other than the conventional extractive ones. The proportion of FDI going into the service sectors is quickly increasing, enabling long-term job growth in industries like business services, telecommunications, media and technology, financial services, and consumer goods and services.

Strategies for Investment

African policymakers' and entrepreneurs' dedication to Africa's growth and development are positive signposts for investors looking to the continent for the first time. First-time investors to African countries should focus on the diversity of their portfolio to mitigate the impact of most countries' continuing overall growth, which is sometimes beset by market fluctuations. African markets should no longer be underestimated.

In 2005, there was a boost in private equity after the Kuwait-based Mobile Telecommunications Company, later renamed Zain, acquired pan-African telecommunications provider Celtel International for a total value of $3.4 billion.[128] This move was one of the first to point to the high returns possible in African countries. This trend has proven the road to success for new entrants to African markets, while existing firms should seek to reinvest their profits to grow returns and African industries. Before choosing to invest, firms can use the "eclectic paradigm" conceptualized by Dunning, who considers "three types of advantages: ownership (O), location (L), and internalization (I)" (figure 7-10).[129]

Finally, one strategy for investing in Africa that is less commonly discussed is knowledge acquisition. Both domestic and foreign investors should be well

Figure 7-10. Ownership–Location–Internalization Framework for Investment Decisions

	Ownership	*Location*	*Internalization*
Advantages	Property rights/ patents	Labor advantages	Reducing uncertainty and transaction costs
	Expertise	Natural resources	Efficiency
	Access	Trade barriers that restrict imports	Avoidance of tariffs, foreign exchange controls, subsidies, etc.
		Gains in trade costs	

Source: Anyanwu and Yaméogo (2015, 7–9).

versed on the business practices of the target region, adapting their models for the benefit of local enterprises and substantial returns on their investments. Most private equity investments in Africa still originate from large global firms that have an extensive capacity to expand into Africa. Smaller private equity funds must recognize that markets on the continent are often characterized by large informal sectors, a lack of standardized practices, and minimal distinctions among investors and entrepreneurs. There is less of a taboo in African markets in terms of investing in public services like education and health care. Smaller private equity funds might seek to develop the social infrastructure throughout Africa. For social investors and smaller funds, Africa's large portion of informal markets are an important destination to incur social good and contribute to economic development in higher-risk areas.

Looking to the Future

Population growth, urbanization, and digital transformation are driving interest to Africa, while simultaneously providing resources to ensure that investments are well appropriated and succeed. African markets are emerging on a global scale and are in need of financial support in both the short and long terms for sustainable growth and innovation. Global private equity levels remain low in Africa, and large funds determine the areas of high returns, which can discourage smaller private equity funds from exploring other opportunities. However, Africa is rife with high-return opportunities, as evidenced by the increasing investment in firms on the continent.

Rising consumer demand is fueling Africa's industry and consumer markets, boosting the potential for high returns for both current and future investors. Government regulatory reforms, through the implementation of favorable tariff programs and efficient administration, have all worked to improve African countries' business environments. African firms can achieve high-quality growth with the support of private equity in growing firms, venture capital for the increasing number of start-up firms in investment hubs, and improved investment banking practices that facilitate the promotion of Africa's capital markets on a global scale. Digital transformation and technology adoption are changing the growth trajectory of African institutions and firms, and global investors might consider the extensive benefits of being first movers in these burgeoning sectors on the continent.

Given its young population and abundant natural resources, Africa has immense potential for growth and innovation, but these will require massive investments in various economic sectors, including infrastructure, education, health care, and the development of digital skills. Strong resilience strategies, an improved business climate, and speedy implementation of AfCFTA are all necessary for the continent to advance quickly—along with a new social contract whereby government and business form a partnership to create and carry out successful investment and economic plans.[130]

Notes

1. World Economics (2024).
2. Ninety One (2024).
3. UNCTAD (2022a).
4. UNCTAD (2024a).
5. Partech (2023).
6. EY (2014a, 6).
7. *Economist* (2015).
8. UNCTAD (2024a).
9. EY (2021).
10. EY (2023).
11. Collins (2022).
12. UNCTAD (2024a).
13. See Söderblom (2012, 12) for a definition of EVCA.
14. Sirri (2004, 24); see background note.
15. African Development Bank (2011).
16. Leke et al. (2010).
17. Dupasquier and Osakwe (2005, 1).
18. UNCTAD (1999, 1).
19. Oxford Policy Management (2002, 21–22); McKinsey & Company (2010).
20. Twimukye (2006, 3); Dupasquier and Osakwe (2005).

21. McKinsey & Company (2010).
22. EY (2014a, 6); Fingar (2015).
23. UNCTAD (2024a).
24. McKinsey & Company (2010).
25. Michalowski (2012).
26. UNCTAD (2024c).
27. Gamache, Hammer, and Jones (2013, 1).
28. Johns Hopkins School of Advanced International Studies (2022).
29. Jones, Ndofor, and Li (2022).
30. UNCTAD (2024a).
31. Diop et al. (2015); UNCTAD (2013, 6); EY (2014b, 7).
32. EY (2023); UNCTAD (2024c).
33. AfDB (2011, 48); Michalowski (2012, 626).
34. Fingar (2015).
35. Trends Research & Advisory (2024).
36. Loots and Kabundi (2012, 130–33).
37. Anyanwu and Yaméogo (2015, 6).
38. European Investment Bank (2021).
39. EY (2021).
40. EY (2023).
41. EY (2023).
42. EY (2014b, 6).
43. Andrianaivo and Yartey (2010, 395); Babarinde (2012, 67).
44. AVCA (2024).
45. UNDP (2015, IV).
46. Gwenge and Adhikari (2021).
47. UNCTAD (2015).
48. Barry and Adoh (2021).
49. Fritz et al. (2023).
50. UNCTAD (2024b).
51. KPMG (2015).
52. Moses (2024).
53. Moses (2024).
54. *Oando* (2016).
55. UNEP (n.d.)
56. Trustonic (2024).
57. AUDA-NEPAD (2020).
58. UNCTAD (2024c).
59. ECMR (2020).
60. EY (2023).
61. African Development Bank (n.d.–c).
62. Bos (2023).

63. Ridgewell (2020).
64. KPMG (2016a); UNCTAD (2022a, 2023b).
65. UNCTAD (2023b).
66. Babarinde (2012).
67. World Bank (2020d).
68. EY (2021).
69. EY (2023).
70. EY (2023).
71. Ofosu and Sarpong (2022).
72. EY (2023).
73. Diop et al. (2015); Chen, Dollar, and Tang (2015, 6).
74. Dollar (2016, ix).
75. EY (2023).
76. Irwin-Hunt (2024).
77. EY (2023).
78. RMB (2015, 5); EY (2016a, 4).
79. Department of Trade, Industry, and Competition (n.d.).
80. EY (2014, 24).
81. PwC (2012a).
82. Pennington (2023).
83. EY (2023).
84. EY (2023).
85. Moore (2012); EY (2014c, 8).
86. EY (2016a, 4).
87. US Department of State (2015, 3).
88. Reed (2015).
89. World Bank (2018, 4); World Bank (2016a).
90. IHG (2024); Ahram Online (2023); Ahram Online (2024).
91. PwC (2015c, 3).
92. In 2007, at the height of Morocco's FDI boom, when FDI volume reached nearly $2.5 billion, more than half of total FDI into the country came from France and Spain; US Department of State (2021).
93. US Department of State (2015, 3).
94. EY (2023); UNCTAD (2024a).
95. US Department of State (2015, 4).
96. US Department of State (2023).
97. Fauozi (2024).
98. McBain (2021).
99. EY (2021).
100. EY (2023).
101. KPMG (2016a, 81–85).
102. AVCA (2024).

103. See the data at https://www.imf.org/external/datamapper/profile/NGA; Vanek (2024); and https://www.howwemadeitinafrica.com/wp-content/uploads/2017/05/Africas-largest-economies.jpg.

104. Kimenyi and Kibe (2014).

105. See Kenya's market capitalization data at https://www.ceicdata.com/en/indicator/kenya/market-capitalization. See Kenya's list of companies on the stock exchange at https://www.cdsckenya.com/investor-education/listed-companies.

106. AVCA (2024); Fourrage (2024).

107. Fourrage (2024).

108. Fourrage (2024).

109. Kimenyi and Kibe (2014).

110. Fourrage (2024).

111. Kimenyi and Kibe (2014).

112. Yieke (2024).

113. UNCTAD (2005, 2).

114. African Development Bank (2024c).

115. EY (2014); Emery et al. (2000).

116. Gray (2016).

117. Oxford Policy Management (2002, 21–22).

118. See the 'Corruptions Perception Index" data at https://www.transparency.org/en/cpi/2023.

119. OECD (2002).

120. Emery et al. (2000).

121. AfDB (2007, 130).

122. Oduola, Bello, and Popoola (2021).

123. UNCTAD (2023a).

124. Kwablah and Amoah (2022).

125. Bekaert and Harvey (1997).

126. EY (2015).

127. Ahmed and Huo (2018).

128. Minney (2011, 22).

129. Dunning (1977, 1993).

130. EY (2021).

Eight
Africa's Capital Markets Potential
Trends, Opportunities, Challenges, and Strategies

In the past two decades, African stock markets have developed rapidly, with their combined market capitalization growing from $260 billion in 2000 to $1.6 trillion in 2024.[1] This impressive growth started as Africa grew along with global developing markets in the early 2000s. Higher market capitalization has allowed financial services sectors throughout Africa to diversify their financing opportunities, despite not achieving the market's fullest potential.

African capital markets rebounded quickly after the 2008–9 financial crisis and 2016 commodity price collapse, offering the potential to global investors to improve risk/return trade-offs in this period of global growth. The number of countries with stock exchanges has now grown rapidly, from just 8 in 2002 to 38 in 2024.[20]

Stock return volatility has declined substantially in the last decade, showing that the risks associated with African markets are manageable. Stock exchanges and bond markets make up the majority of these marketplaces. On the continent, securities markets are significant complements to banking, with most governments issuing bonds and few large companies being listed on domestic stock exchanges. In the majority of African nations, corporate bonds make up a very small portion of the capital markets. By utilizing the enormous financial resources of institutional investors, African capital markets can grow their investor base.[3]

Many African nations still have weak financial institutions, which places restrictions on credit—particularly for small and medium-sized businesses—resulting in low investment rates. As a result, it has been deter-mined that a lack of money is the biggest barrier to doing business in Africa. It is a significant barrier for both business sectors and start-up businesses and corporate innovation.[4] Due to this, Africa has a significantly lower investment rate (24 percent) than other growing economies like China (40 percent), South Asia (28 percent), and East Asia and the Pacific (32 percent).[5]

There is cause for optimism, nevertheless, as the number of stock exchanges on the continent increased significantly and steadily, from 5 in 1989 to 29 (in 38 different nations) as of 2024, along with the volume of shares listed and traded. The capitalization of African stock markets expanded tenfold, from $113 billion to over $1.6 trillion, between 1992 and 2021. As of 2024, the Johannesburg Stock Exchange is the largest, with over $1 trillion in market capitalization, followed by the Nigerian Stock Exchange, at over $40 billion, and the Egyptian Stock Exchange, at over $30 billion.[6] Despite these encour-aging developments in the bond and stock markets, Africa's financial markets are still in their infancy.

Africa's financial sector has only recently grown, with the inception of mobile banking. Mobile banking and traditional banking services continue to dominate financial markets, offering high interest rate margins and high returns on equity and assets. These incentives benefit the insurance and pri-vate equity markets; however, the growth of capital markets is being hin-dered, with the limited capital and capacity of the banking sector to be an intermediary in stock exchanges, debt markets, and capital markets. Free-flowing capital on the continent is hard to come by, and financial services firms are often strapped to expand their lending habits to stimulate broad growth. Still, Africa's reality as an emerging market is slowly eclipsing its reputation as a risky location for lending and borrowing. Africa's banking sector and financial services sector can coexist and cooperate to expand risk-sharing and the existence of long-term financing and short-term capital in both the public and private sectors.

Côte d'Ivoire and Zimbabwe are two cases emblematic of the growth of Sub-Saharan Africa's capital markets. The Abidjan-based BRVM stock exchange for West African countries, including Côte d'Ivoire, contributed to an increase in gross domestic product of 75 percent over the first ten years of its existence.[7] There is neither a direct nor sole correlation between the exchange's existence and growth in gross domestic product, but BRVM and capital flows helped Côte d'Ivoire maintain high levels of growth during the 2016 commodity price collapse.[8] Meanwhile, Zimbabwe's stock exchanges have pulled the country through periods of growth and decline since 1896.

The stock exchange's market liquidity only grew between 2000 and 2009, performing exceptionally well during the period by achieving a total increase from 3.8 percent in 2000 to 16.1 percent in 2009.[9] The Zimbabwe Stock Exchange is currently looking to expand its activities to incorporate more collaborative work with the Zimbabwean government and the Reserve Bank of Zimbabwe to create a high-functioning market for government and corporate bonds.[10] Capital markets have alleviated stress in Zimbabwe and Côte d'Ivoire, representing the relative success already achieved in African capital markets and the potential for growth throughout Sub-Saharan Africa.

Africa's capital markets have equivalent potential to achieve growth and stability, as with other emerging markets. This chapter first discusses the background underpinning African capital markets and their changing trends over time, which then informs conclusions about the sector's importance, the key aspects driving market growth, and key players. Then, an overview of the opportunities and strategies to advance the reach of capital markets expands the conversation about capital market potential on the continent. The chapter concludes with ideas for engaging additional stakeholders and resources in the future.

Background Facts and Trends

The number of private equity funds working in the region has proliferated, from just 12 in 1997 to more than 200 today, with a collective portfolio worth more than $30 billion. The year 2014–15 witnessed the largest single year of capital formation targeting Africa, with $7 billion raised, including the first billion-dollar Sub-Saharan funds: Helios Investors III and Equatorial Guinea Co-Investment Fund.[11] The year 2023 was a solid one for private equity in Africa after the COVID-19 pandemic, reaching $7.47 billion across 331 transactions.[12] Public funds, especially those from European development finance institutions, such as France's Proparco and the British International Investment, also represent increasingly important sources of capital investment in Africa.[13] Capital markets, though relatively young on the continent for the most part, have always been important mediums by which private equity investment and other capital flows have expanded in the region. Sub-Saharan African countries developed national and regional markets at different times, thus creating a conglomeration of varying capital markets throughout the continent. These capital markets operate at different levels, according to the degree of implementation, resources, and access to foreign markets.

African markets are beginning to welcome international investors to their equity markets, and trade in domestic and foreign debt in international markets has also accelerated. Fifteen countries had issued at least 1 Eurobond by 2021, and more African issuers are entering the market as of 2024, as economies recover and rates are expected to go lower. For example, in 2024, Côte d'Ivoire issued 2 Eurobonds worth a combined $2.6 billion, Benin issued $750 million in 14-year Eurobonds, and Kenya issued a $1.5 billion 7-year Eurobond.[14]

Before 1989, only five stock markets existed in Sub-Saharan Africa, and three in North Africa. By 2010, this number had grown to more than twenty stock exchanges, including the established exchanges in Lagos and Johannesburg.[15] Most of these stock exchanges, excluding those in South Africa, doubled their market capitalization between 1992 and 2002 and achieved a total market capitalization of $244.7 billion. Before the 2008 financial crisis, African stock exchanges attracted international confidence in the market potential and public interest for African-listed initial public offerings (IPOs), such as Safaricom and Celtel. Now, as of 2024, 29 stock exchanges across 27 countries are active, with a combined market capitalization of $1.6 trillion as of 2022.[16]

Figure 8-1 shows the trend in IPO offerings and their relative value between 2017 and 2021 in African markets. Following a sharp fall over the previous four years (2017–20), IPO activity in 2021 saw an increase in value and volume, by 43 percent and 14 percent, respectively, compared with 2020. African companies have conducted seventy-one IPOs over the past five years on both domestic and foreign exchanges, raising $8.1 billion.[17]

Politically, African capital markets have been beholden to international influence and, in some cases, operation. As early as 1953, the London Stock Exchange recognized the Nairobi Securities Exchange (NSE) as an overseas stock exchange. The NSE was established in 1954 with the listing of forty-six companies, acting as a voluntary association of stockbrokers. However, the NSE was not immediately recognized among African stakeholders, and Africans were not allowed to trade in securities until after independence in 1963.[18]

Historically, Nigeria's first capital market represents similar experiences in other African countries, where liberalization, privatization, and stabilization have only slowly progressed over the past few decades.[19] Only recently have Africa's financial markets seen a significant increase in international investment and capital formation. By 2014, over $7 billion in capital had been raised for investment in Africa by over 200 private equity funds managing almost $30 billion.[20] Africa, along with other emerging markets, attracted

Figure 8-1. Trends in Initial Public Offerings, 2017–21

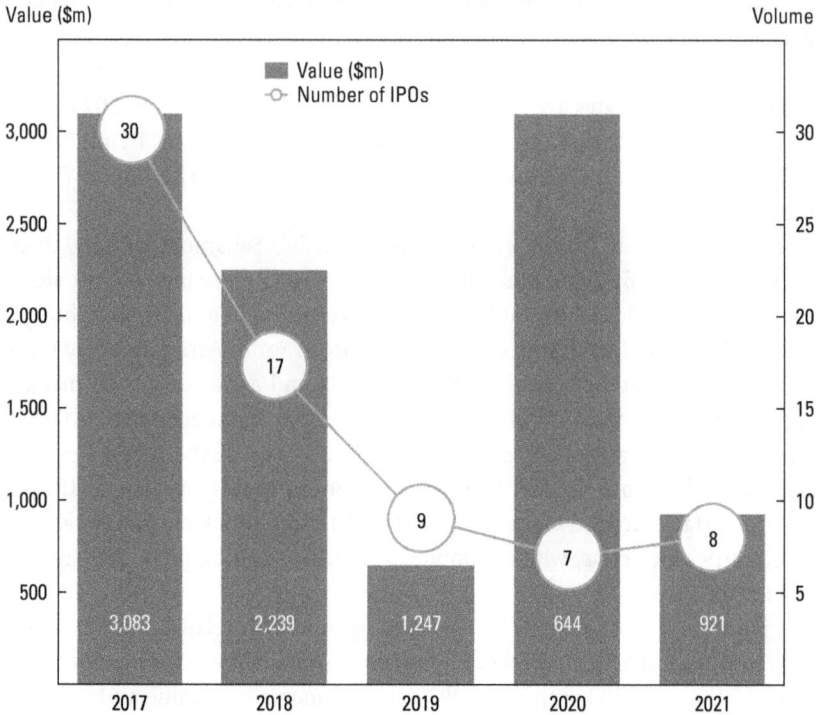

Source: PwC (2022d).

extensive interest in the aftermath of the 2008 financial crisis, due to the high levels of growth potential that was unattainable in more established international markets, with disastrous losses during the crisis. Africa's domestic exchanges have become more liquid as political and foreign exchange risk has decreased, increasing the number of exit paths for private equity funds. Financial depth throughout Sub-Saharan Africa has only increased since the early 2000s, as the continent's banking systems have become more stable and governments have become increasingly capable of providing credit to struggling banks.[21]

Government and bank cooperation have helped Africa's capital markets mature and develop into highly attractive exchanges. For example, the value of national pension funds, a nascent industry in most African countries, is growing exponentially and is projected to reach $7 trillion by 2050. As of 2022, about $206 billion was held by African pension funds, while $120–$130 billion was believed to be the value of the assets of the fifteen African sovereign wealth funds.[22] Market-friendly policies, improving investment environments, and outreach to foreign investors are stimulating upward movement in private sector credit growth, private equity funds, and foreign and domestic investment. Specifically, improved sovereign risk profiles of credit issues, fiscal stability and national economic growth, and large-scale debt relief have combined to grow Africa's regional capital markets. Institutional investors and emerging market hedge funds are seeking refuge on the continent, where African debt markets offer higher yields and high potential for capital gains.

The Sector's Importance

Africa's capital markets have grown along with global emerging markets in the aftermath of the global economic crisis. Africa's markets compare relatively well with other emerging markets, such as those in Latin America, the Middle East and North Africa region, and the Central and Eastern Europe / Russia region. While still behind Asia, particularly in shares of private equity funds, of which Sub-Saharan Africa hosts 7 percent and Asia hosts 58 percent, Sub-Saharan African markets have proven to be reliable mediums to conduct capital transfers, provide credit, and act as financial intermediaries among domestic and international buyers and sellers. Figure 8-2 shows the value of private capital deals from 2016 to 2021.

These high-growth markets can mobilize resources for investment throughout Africa. Continued exchange rate liberalization will only increase these markets' capacity to attract private investment and capital accumulation.[23] A decline in global economic growth in 2016 and after 2020 affected African capital markets, but they have shown resilience compared with those in other regions.

Stock markets are indispensable to credit markets and private investment. Africa's banking sector has received much of the financial attention given to emerging markets in recent years, but the growth and stabilization of Africa's credit markets are essential for investment-led development and Africa's emergence as a competitive market for international investment and capital formation. Mergers and acquisitions among domestic and international firms will continue to foster private sector investment and global exposure to the potential in Africa's public funds as sources of capital for domestic and international economic activity.

Similar to other regions, Africa has faced challenges in the years since the COVID-19 pandemic due to high inflation and market volatility, which have led to a decrease in private equity deals. Yet despite this decrease, Africa had 450 deals

Figure 8-2. Value of Private Capital Deals in Africa by Year, 2016–21

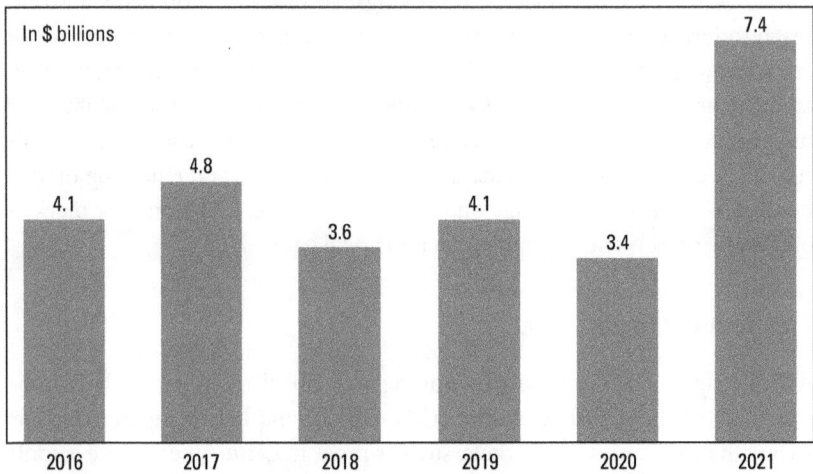

Source: Collins (2022).

in 2023 worth $5.9 billion—a major increase from the 198 deals in 2019.[24] These large-scale investments, while significantly smaller than deals in developed countries, are clear indicators of the potential within Africa's capital markets.

Financial and consumer discretionary companies dominated African IPO markets from 2017 to 2021, making up 52 percent of new listings, but technology and telecommunications industries were also on the rise.[25] Limited liquidity is just one aspect holding back African capital markets, though there have been improvements in recent years that hint at the potential growth of these markets in domestic and international spheres. Figure 8-3 shows the 2021 distribution of stock exchanges on the continent, based on the value of market capitalization.

According to the Absa Africa Financial Markets Index,[26] the top-performing markets in Africa in 2023 were South Africa (1st), Mauritius (2), Nigeria (3), Uganda (4), and Namibia (5).[27] See figure 8-4.

The distribution of stock market listings will only change with a systemic push by other African countries to reform their monetary policies and incentivize companies to engage with African stock exchanges and investors. Stock markets are part of the equation to enhance African countries' development, by acting as a platform for companies to access external capital funds and for holders of ownership certificates to trade in secondary markets. Most countries have the structure and political ability to focus on the growth

Figure 8-3. Overview of African Stock Exchanges, 2021

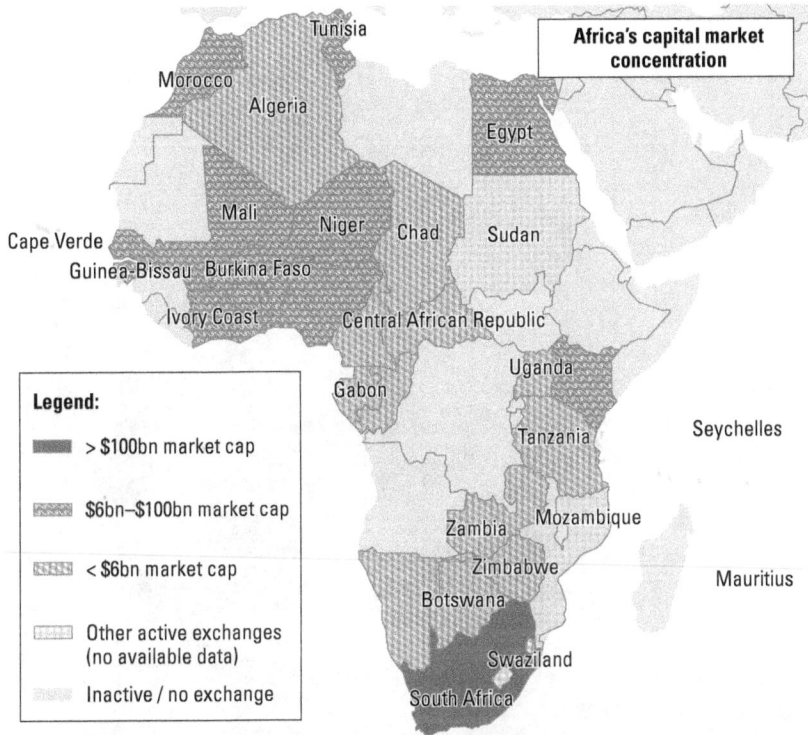

Source: Gopaldas (2021).

of capital markets for the sake of economic growth; in fact, "since 1995 there has been at least one African stock market in the top ten best-performing markets in the world."[28] Despite this, challenges remain, and there are several lessons to be learned from around the continent as to how to proceed in this new era of African capital markets.

Key Drivers of Growth

Productivity gains on the continent cannot occur without the existence and ready supply of capital. Insurance and pensions industries' growth on the continent, which have buttressed Western capital markets for decades, are key indicators of the uptake of support for capital market expansion in emerging markets. African countries are increasingly seeking the steady support

Figure 8-4. Absa Africa Financial Markets Index: Top Performers in 2023

Rank 2023	Rank 2022	Country	Score 2023	Score 2022	Comments
1	1	South Africa	88	89	Lower pension assets in dollar terms weigh on score
2	2	Mauritius	77	77	Rise in sovereign and corporate credit ratings
3	3	Nigeria	67	68	Foreign exchange shortages and rising inflation reduce score
4	4	Uganda	63	64	Fall in foreign exchange (FX) reserves and liquidity
5	5	Namibia	63	63	Large pension assets but decline in fixed-income market
6	8	Botswana	59	58	New incentives for environmental, social, and governance (ESG) asset issuance lifts score
7	6	Kenya	59	60	Lower FX reserves and market liquidity
8	10	Morocco	58	57	New climate stress testing and higher FX liquidity
9	7	Ghana	58	59	Deterioration in FX reserves and price stability
10	12	Tanzania	55	55	Improved product diversity with sukuk bond issuance
11	9	Egypt	55	58	Weaker FX reserves and macroeconomic outlook
12	11	Zambia	55	55	Reduction in external debt after restructuring
13	13	Malawi	49	49	Surge in market capitalization but liquidity remains low
14	14	Eswatini	46	46	Higher pension fund assets but limited market activity
15	15	Seychelles	46	45	Jump in value of pension fund assets
16	-	Cabo Verde	45	-	New framework and issuance of blue bonds
17	16	Rwanda	44	43	Stronger ESG market framework with support of international bodies
18	19	Zimbabwe	43	42	New climate risk management guidelines lift score
19	-	Tunisia	43	-	Macroeconomic vulnerabilities constrain score
20	17	Angola	43	42	Improvement in inflation and external debt
21	18	Côte d'Ivoire	40	42	Fall in FX reserves reduces score
22	21	Cameroon	40	40	Market size and liquidity remain relatively low
23	20	Senegal	38	40	Rise in external debt-to-GDP ratio
24	22	Mozambique	37	36	Strong growth prospects from liquefied natural gas boost
25	23	DRC	35	34	Improvement in monetary policy reporting
26	24	Lesotho	34	34	Limited market activity and high tax rates
27	25	Madagascar	31	32	Fall in FX reserves coverage
28	26	Ethiopia	29	27	Moving closer to launching a securities exchange

Source: OMFIF (2021, 7).

of capital markets to fund infrastructure projects and long-term development. African markets also present high potential for liquidity and increasing demand for consumer-related and communications sector goods that have specifically brought more attention to private equity markets.[29] This demand has been driven by Africa's population growth that is enabling predictions of a necessary explosion of investment and production in coming years.[30] These factors are encouraging African governments, financial institutions, and individual stakeholders to focus on improving capital markets' bandwidth and ensuring they are capable of handling potentially high investments and private equity's future growth.

Debt Capital Markets

Foreign currency debt has played a large role in African countries in the long term, due to a reliance on multilateral funding through external markets.[31] Local-currency debt, which had typically only covered short-term credit needs, is becoming better able to stabilize debt issuance and develop instruments to coordinate access to liquid capital and monitor necessary benchmarks. African debt markets from 2000 to 2020 included 7,400 loans and bonds from over 50 different public and private external lenders with a total volume of $790 billion,[32] and these markets are seeing an increase in interest and depth from investors.[33] While available bank debt remains low on the continent, government bonds and corporate issuance of credit are sufficiently buoying Sub-Saharan Africa's capital markets. The region is increasingly seen as a source of returns.

Regional Collaboration and Risk Sharing

African economies are in the process of greater regional integration as a result of decades of effort to promote intra-African trade, investment, and financial risk-sharing among economies at relatively similar stages. Stock market development is often inconceivable without external support in debt cancellation, technical capacity building, or strengthening countries' banking systems. Where these types of assistance have been lacking, African countries have instead implemented risk-sharing initiatives to improve their resource allocation and encourage regional growth through the shared promotion of African markets' liquidity and safety for external investors. African governments have made increasing reforms to their market policies and investment rules, so as to present a unified face of high returns and high potential for long-term growth.[34] Political stability is increasing throughout the continent, and African governments are continuing to seek regionally appropriate measures to advance their economic policies and create a system of stable institutions for external investors.

Trade under the African Continental Free Trade Agreement has officially begun with significant political will from African governments and the private sector, which will further accelerate regional collaboration. Cross-border initiatives are also helping to stimulate trade and liquidity in African capital markets. One such initiative is the African Exchanges Linkage Project (AELP), which facilitates cross-border trading and listings between the Casablanca Stock Exchange, Egyptian Exchange, Johannesburg Stock Exchange, Nairobi Securities Exchange, Nigerian Exchange, Stock Exchange of Mauritius, and Bourse Régionale des Valeurs Mobilières (a stock exchange for the West African Economic and Monetary Union's eight countries). AELP will allow an investor in one country to trade securities in another through a single broker and trading system. The securities industry is optimistic that unlike other attempts to integrate markets, AELP has great potential to be successful.[35]

Technology Adoption

The digital revolution on the continent has made an impact on almost every sector in African markets. More recently, digital and technological innovation has been introduced to the financial systems to improve capital markets' operation and transform outdated systems for the future of financing. For example, in 2015, the Zimbabwe Stock Exchange (ZSE) introduced automated trading by connecting digital equity trading to settlements using a centralized computer depository system.[36] This system is the first step to improving confidence in the capacity of the ZSE and the security of trading.

The telecommunications industry is similarly aiding in the growth of African capital markets by creating more connected individuals, firms, and governments, and by increasing the level of awareness of capital and credit potential for interested parties. Mobile phone banking may quickly transition to mobile trading for more stakeholders. The telecommunications industry has also been a driver of investment on the continent, and Africa is the fastest-growing region of the world for mobile subscriptions. Investment in technological solutions in other industries will be important for African capital markets, by introducing new types of capital and increasing the interest of foreign investors in expanding their financial trading on the continent. The COVID-19 pandemic also accelerated this digital transformation. For example, in 2020, the Egyptian Exchange created a digital voting system that allowed companies to continue corporate activities during the pandemic.[37]

A 2016 study revealed that by enabling Kenyan households to save more and manage their money more effectively, the mobile payment system M-PESA enhanced consumption and financial resilience. According to the study's authors, the adoption of M-PESA may have helped elevate about 200,000 Kenyan households out of poverty. The availability of less expensive, more effective financial services as a result of digitization can also be of disproportionate advantage for small and medium-sized enterprises (SMEs), allowing them to stimulate economic growth. To reach out to smaller enterprises, for instance, banks may find it more cost-effective as administrative costs decline, and lenders may feel pressured to do the same when they face competition from new funding sources like crowdfunding platforms. The financial sector's digitization can also have larger, favorable implications for growth and development—for instance, by assisting in the formalization of small businesses and thus enhancing governments' ability to generate income. Additionally, by enabling more focused service delivery and increasing the transparency and traceability of monetary transactions, it can aid financial institutions in becoming more efficient.

Conversely, the digitization of financial services increases or creates a variety of new hazards. These include hazards for people and households, which must be handled through proper consumer protection, the possibility that a digital divide may develop if access to these services is unequal, and risks at the systemic level, which are covered in more depth below. Digitization is high on the policy agenda in Africa due to its catalytic role in increasing financial access and sustainable development as well as the necessity for regulatory action and collaboration to prevent hazards. Despite broad access to traditional banking services, mobile money is becoming more and more popular in many nations. In some countries, however, mobile money is making up for a lack of access to traditional lenders.[38]

These three drivers are integral to the growth of African capital markets and other industries' growth through the security of capital movements and credit lending. Each of these factors has originated on the continent, and they play a significant role in elevating Africa's capital markets to the global stage.

Key Players

There are several key players in Africa's capital markets. Some are domestic to the continent, while others influence the investment and funding fields from international or multinational firms.

Foreign Financial Institutions

Foreign financial institutions have been important for Africa's monetary systems since before African countries achieved their independence. The banking sector has long been controlled by state-owned banks with foreign credit or by a few large, multinational banks. Large formal firms dominate banking and credit scenarios because they are the best equipped to over- come any challenges that might arise. Private firms contribute significantly to capital markets, including production and investment, at the same level in Africa as in developing countries.[39] Particularly in resource-rich countries, foreign financial institutions are major players in growing lines of credit and accelerating resource development with increasing investment. Development financial institutions are also instrumental to Africa's private equity industry, through fundraising and taking on investment opportunities by providing seed money to public and private projects. In early 2012, the African Develop- ment Bank—which, though domestic to the continent, is primarily financed by foreign credit—had a total equity portfolio of more than $1 billion.[40] In 2018, private equity fundraising in Africa totaled $2.7 billion, an increase of 10 percent over 2017. After the COVID-19 pandemic, Africa mirrored global downward trends, but has been starting to recover since 2023, when the private equity fundraising (total value of final closed funds) was $1.9 billion.[41] The African bond market is likewise expanding, with a $500 billion total market value in 2019.[42] The African Development Bank, along with other financial institutions, are on track to support Africa's still-growing bond markets and introduce new financial instruments for development and economic growth.

International Fund Managers

In addition to the general role of international financial institutions, much can be said for the specific role of international fund managers in Africa's stock markets. These managers are responsible for offering investment vehicles for firms to access and thrive in African markets. While Africa's stock mar- kets perform well and generate high returns, international fund managers have been responsible for bringing significant attention to the potential of these markets. Most of the largest listings in these markets are also listed in other stock markets, such as Ashanti Goldfields Ltd. and Ecobank Trans- national, which increases the role of fund managers to ensure investors are inclined to seek out more opportunities on the continent or through African firms.[43]

Private Sector Firms and Investors

Between 1996 and 2008, private sector firms accounted for over two-thirds of total investment in and three-fourths of total credit supplied to African economies.[44] Creating jobs and providing credit to opportunities in the private sector creates a unique value-added chain for industries and employment. Private companies benefit greatly from advancing financial systems and have relied on bank credit and equity finance to supply their needed capital and investment funding. In low-income countries, the private sector accounts for a higher proportion of jobs than in middle-income countries.[45] The expanding banking sector in African countries has allowed these private equity markets to compete with those in Latin America and the Middle East.[46] Private equity and private investors who take a long-term view of development in the region are important for overall growth and development through capital-heavy projects, such as infrastructure transformation. Currently, large private equity funds are managing the African Infrastructure Investment Fund's projected portfolio of $1 billion for toll roads, thermal power, wind power, ports, and social infrastructure and the Pan Africa Infrastructure Development Fund's fifteen-year, $630 million commitment.[47] These and other privately managed funds are critical for African economies' development.

African Pension Funds

By utilizing the large financial resources that African sovereign wealth funds and pension funds have on deposit, African capital markets might expand their investor base. Sub-Saharan African sovereign wealth funds are estimated to have assets worth $16.4 billion, and African pension funds owned about $700 billion in total as of 2022.[48] The liquidity of several African exchanges and bond markets would increase if these monies were directed to the region's domestic capital markets. Although some markets have made substantial progress while others have made much less, this would require suitable market mechanisms (e.g., a strong regulatory framework, transparent management structures, and a safe business environment), which do not yet fully exist. Even so, projections are optimistic—by 2030, Africa's assets in pension funds and sovereign wealth funds could reach $1 trillion.[49]

African Governments

African governments have played a pivotal role in deregulating their markets and increasing incentives for investment. Governments were also critical in opening the telecommunications, financial, and real estate sectors to foreign competition and ownership, thereby elevating these sectors to higher levels of investment and attention from equity funds.[50] Improving governance measures has had a similar effect on attracting investment and private enterprises to expand their operations on the continent and contribute to infrastructural, institutional, and capital market development. African governments are also responsible for growing Africa's national pension funds, which are projected to surpass $7 trillion by 2050, assuming the continuation of the current trajectory of capital accumulation and distribution.[51] It has been shown that much of the domestic issuance of capital through pension funds is done to provide securities for market development.[52] This fact suggests a growing maturity of African governments' handling of accumulated capital and their intention to build Africa's development through capital market growth.

Debt market growth has brought together many of these key players to collaborate on expanding the depth of Africa's capital markets to accommodate new investors and existing players seeking to advance their role. Domestic credit and bond issuance are receiving stronger demand interest from international investors, and both developed and emerging market funds are looking to the region as a source of returns.

Opportunities

In addition to the more-established regional markets in Nigeria and South Africa, several African countries are becoming real competitors among the continent's capital markets. Ghana, Kenya, Zambia, and Egypt are becoming popular locations for private equity investment, capital formation, and credit allowances. These four countries represent the growing interest in African capital markets and the potential for African stock exchanges, creditors, and investors to become global players. South Africa is no longer the sole reliable location for international investors, as improved macroeconomic policies around the continent are encouraging investors to look elsewhere for high returns with equal levels of risk. Ghana, Kenya, and Nigeria are increasingly connected to global markets and represent the new era of African economies capable of operating in global currencies.[53]

Ghana

Trading on the Ghana Stock Exchange in Accra began in 1990 as part of broader economic objectives of privatization and mobilizing savings. Operations were slow to gain momentum amid accusations that listed companies provided misleading information about liquidity. However, by 2024, there were 37 listed companies with the market capitalization reaching a record high at GH¢80.2 billion.[54] As of 2019, the exchange was dominated by companies working in the manufacturing, banking, and beverage sectors, although major recent investments include Tullow Oil and other companies attracted to Ghana's oil and gas sector.

New products have also been introduced in recent years to increase liquidity through investment, as an alternative to equity. The Ghana Alternative Market, for example, provides SMEs with access to capital by eliminating listing and application fees and reducing the listing restrictions that exist on the primary market. The Ghana Fixed Income Market was created for trading fixed income instruments and other securities, which should help to increase participation in the market by improving understanding and experience with trading among the broader population.[55] In 2007, on the heels of a debt relief package, Ghana became the first African country to issue dollar bonds. Since then, 10 other countries have followed suit.[56] In September 2016, Ghana completed a five-year bond offering worth $750 million, which offered a 9.25 percent yield. Interest from investors was so strong that the offer was oversubscribed to the tune of more than $4.3 billion in orders.[57] For use in stores, the Central Bank of Ghana introduced a universal quick response code payment option linked to clients' bank accounts.[58]

A few market barriers to private equity and venture capital do exist in Ghana, nevertheless. Most developing nations face some of these obstacles, like the challenges associated with investing in SMEs. In Ghana, there is essentially no legal or regulatory framework for venture capital and private equity. Alternative asset classes are not governed by the Securities and Exchange Commission, despite promises to do so with a new draft law that must be approved by the Parliament.[59]

Kenya

According to a survey by Deloitte, nine out of ten private equity firms looking to invest in East Africa prefer Kenya over other countries in the region, citing its vibrant private sector, ease of doing business, and growing middle class.[60] In comparison, just 50 percent of firms reported that they would consider investing in Uganda or Tanzania, and just 38 percent in Ethiopia. This is particularly striking in light of the fact that equity firms are looking increasingly to East Africa, in part due to negative growth and currency devaluations in West Africa, especially in Nigeria.[61] Increasing integration, market diversification, short-term economic growth projections of 6 percent or more, and relative ease of market entry and exit make East Africa's emerging markets an increasingly attractive investment option compared with the rest of the continent.[62]

Of the total private equity deals and development finance institution investments recorded between 2013 and the first half of 2023, Kenya accounted for 69 percent.[63]

As an indication of the progressive approach to capital markets and positive long-term outlook in Kenya, the government led the way in Africa by issuing a twenty-five-year bond in 2010. In addition to simplifying the system, the National Treasury has actively moved to involve SMEs and small-scale investors by lowering the minimum threshold for investment in government bills and bonds to just Ksh3,000, roughly $31.[64] Meanwhile, a joint venture between the NSE and the Central Bank of Kenya has led to the establishment of an automated trading system for fixed-income securities, which was launched in September 2014. The system is integrated into the national Electronic Payment and Settlement System, which guarantees delivery of payments and mitigates risk to investors and supports trading in different currencies.

Although it is still developing, Kenya's stock exchange, the NSE, is among the most developed and sophisticated in the Sub-Saharan African region— only South Africa's and Zimbabwe's are older, established in 1886 and 1896, respectively.[65] The NSE was established in 1954 with 46 listed companies, and by the end of the colonial period, this number had already risen to 63 companies.[66] Economic downturn and market stabilization programs in the late twentieth century resulted in undersubscription of IPOs and delistings, and by 2005 the number of listed companies had fallen to 50. While market capitalization stands at roughly 50 percent, which is low compared with the ratio of 155 percent typically exhibited by high-income countries, the NSE has already rebounded to its previous height in investment saturation, owing largely to the entry of firms working in new and growing sectors, including information technology.[67] By leading the way in innovation and incentivizing investment regionally, the NSE is poised to become the central trading floor of the East African Community after increased regional integration.[68]

Kenya has a reputation for having a "private sector-led economy, a strong entrepreneurial culture, and relative regulatory stability" and serving as the social, cultural, and economic "powerhouse" of East Africa. Due to Kenya's participation in the East African Community, investors can use it as a jumping off point for international investments. Due to its position, Kenya is now the leading deal-maker for regional capital market activity. Despite these advantages, Kenya still needs to fix structural issues with its legal, regulatory, and fiscal framework for Private Equity Venture Capital (PEVC) funds. PEVC funds still choose to register offshore rather than set up shop in Kenya, despite the efforts of the Kenyan authorities to provide incentives for investors to do so. The main legal and regulatory issues for PEVC funds operating in Kenya, in the absence of a comprehensive legal and regulatory framework, are (1) the structural inefficiency of the available legal forms; (2) the time and resource burdens imposed by multiple (i.e., regional and national) competition systems; and (3) the regulatory and structural barriers to domestic institutional investment in the asset class, despite pension funds now being permitted to invest up to 10 percent of their assets in this asset class.[69]

Zambia

The Zambian economy is heavily dependent on copper exports and, as a result, was negatively affected by the global financial crisis of 2008–9 and the crash in global commodity prices after 2014.[70] Since a decline in export earnings has the unfortunate side effect of reducing liquidity and profitability in the financial sector, the response of commercial banks has been to further diminish loans to the private sector.

The Lusaka Stock Exchange (LuSE) has been operational since 1993, with substantial technical and financial support from the World Bank, the United Nations Development Program, and the Zambian government.[71] Today, it is owned by ten shareholders and is incorporated as a private, nonprofit limited liability company, and its listed products include government and corporate bonds and twenty-three equities. Since its founding, twenty-one companies have been listed for trading, the first of which was the Lafarge Cement Company (formerly Chilanga Cement), which has exhibited a 40,000 percent increase in share price since its initial listing.[72] The first bond was issued on the LuSE by the PTA Bank in 2000, and over the next seven years, roughly $12 million in bonds were traded in support of various developments, such as parks, shopping centers, and infrastructural improvements in energy and education. The government bond market has continued to grow in Zambia over the past decade, even as global performance has declined.[73]

Zambia has been relatively resilient amid the global shocks over the past few years, which in part is due to their relative political stability and natural resource endowment. In fact, Zambia's capital market's total savings increased from $3.46 billion in 2021 to $3.74 billion as of mid-2023.[74]

Egypt

Established in 1888 in Alexandria and 1903 in Cairo, the Egyptian Stock Exchange (ESE) is the second oldest on the continent, after South Africa's, and is now one of the largest in trading volumes and market capitalization.

Although trading slowed in the 1950s due to centralized market planning, the turn to free market policies led to the rapid expansion of Egypt's capital markets. In the early 1990s, the government viewed capital market restructuring as a key component of its economic reform program, resulting in an overhaul of legislation governing the securities industry. The new law replaced outdated legislation, aimed to protect investors, and increase the role of commercial banks in stimulating capital markets, especially through the establishment of mutual funds.[75] Combined with macroeconomic stabilization and improvements in institutional procedures, the reforms proved successful, and by the turn of the century there were more than 1,100 companies listed on the ESE, with market capitalization valued at $26.2 billion.[76] In 2022, the Stock Exchange announced the creation of Africa's first voluntary carbon market—AFRICARBONEX.[77]

South Africa

In the World Economic Forum's *Global Competitiveness Report 2013–14*, South Africa was ranked at the top globally for the regulation of securities exchanges and has since maintained its status as a well-regulated, well-managed exchange. The 2011 decision to amend South Africa's inward listing regulations to permit foreign-domiciled firms to be classed as domestic listings is another legislative shift that could have broad ramifications. Despite the fact that foreign companies have been permitted to be listed on the Johannesburg Stock Exchange (JSE) since 2004, there were prior restrictions on the quantity of these stocks that local investors could hold due to foreign exchange rules. The removal of these restrictions marks a significant regulatory turning point for the exchange and enhances the JSE's appeal as a location for listings.

The wider privatization dilemma in Africa is typified by South Africa's refusal to sell off or privatize underperforming state assets. The state supports loss-making companies like airlines and electricity generation firms with public funding or bond issuances rather than divesting them through IPOs. The market forces that produce efficiency are weakened by the government's lack of support. The merits of this position are outside the purview of this chapter, but it is obvious that policymakers can do much more to promote both local and international private sector engagement in African capital markets.[78]

Challenges and Risks

African capital and financial markets have grown upon improved macroeconomic stability and declining political risk in most African countries. However, several challenges remain for investors and institutional leaders to overcome obstacles to capital accumulation, issuance for economic growth and development, and investment to promote long-term sectoral transformations. Government prioritization and private sector interest are necessary to make African countries more investor friendly overall, and to catapult these countries to the forefront of emerging markets for capital market action. The success of these initiatives requires the continuous improvement of the business environment, the establishment of sound and reliable regulatory frameworks, financial literacy, and management structures that do not yet fully exist in many African countries.[79]

The Difficulty of Market Entry and Exit

Effectively buying and selling businesses tends to be impeded by the general lack of data and information in Africa, including credit histories, risk indicators, market research, and especially the storage and sharing of relevant information via information and communications technology.[80] Moreover, market entry is directly undermined by the lack of access to commercial private credit.

Two of the most common practices of private equity firms also tend to be more difficult in Africa. Overloading a newly acquired business with debt to maximize returns can be hard due to market volatility. Another difficulty is selling a company after a few years of expansion and improved efficiency. In this case, given the relatively low level of investment in Africa compared with other markets and the underdeveloped nature of local stock markets, it is often difficult to find a buyer, especially for the larger and valuable companies that tend to be the focus of private equity firms. And even when a new investor is found, local partners are often less willing to sell.[81]

Low Liquidity

Stock market liquidity, measured by the ease with which investors can buy and sell securities at given prices, is not particularly a characteristic of African markets. African markets have a low turnover ratio, suggesting that though market performance has been increasing, most African stock markets are rather illiquid. Only the markets of Zimbabwe, Egypt, and South Africa have been measured to have higher levels of turnover and liquidity of securities.[82] Low liquidity undermines "equity price discovery," which hinders economic performance.[83] On the cause side of illiquidity, it is important to note that nascent markets are driven by a lack of market culture, high levels of fear of loss, insufficient investor protections, and high listing costs.[84] Each of these factors determines the level of illiquidity in African markets, and represents the major challenges that remain to transform African stock markets into high-functioning liquid markets where domestic and international investors can thrive.

Low liquidity is also purported to be caused by a lack of "equity culture," poor government regulations, and a lack of maturity in the market. In Tanzania, some people are entirely unaware of the products and services available in the Dar es Salaam Stock Exchange.[85] This lack of public awareness does not inform political stakeholders of the needs of investors and suppliers. Meanwhile, governments often do not require foreign businesses to list in domestic stock markets, failing to capitalize on investment in the region for greater economic performance and the growing maturity of stock markets. African governments are known for state-owned enterprises, which do not necessarily bring significant investment to the private sector or generate outsized employment opportunities for local people. In Ghana, the sale of Ghana Telecom to Vodafone is an example of government failure to improve the liquidity of the market, despite most studies indicating that "share issue privatization has a positive effect on local market liquidity."[86]

Low liquidity is more than a result of poor policies and insufficient privatization procedures. It is representative of broader challenges in African capital markets, including difficulty trading, spreading awareness of the opportunities within these markets, and enabling fund managers to efficiently operate in African markets. High documentation costs and banking fees also represent the intersection of immature markets with insufficient government policies. For example, the fees for a current account across African countries amounted to more than 4 percent of monthly income, while other non-African developing countries see fees of less than 3 percent.[87] High fees and low awareness lead to stagnant markets that are less than attractive to potential new investors or stakeholders with higher aversions to risk.

Costs Associated with Capital Market Entry

Brokerage commission fees make up a major portion of the cost of trading in all African markets, with the exception of Kenya, Nigeria, Seychelles, and South Africa. For example, Uganda and Rwanda have 4.1 percent and 3.4 percent of the value of trade fees, respectively, compared with other developing markets that have below 1 percent.[88] The low amount of trading on most African exchanges, which drives brokers to raise the fees on each deal to meet their costs, and the small number of regulated brokers, which limits competition among them, are both exacerbating factors for the excessive fees charged by brokers.[89]

Global Disruptions

As African countries become more integrated into the global economic system, they are exposed to more opportunities but also more risks due to global disruptions. The world has had its fair share of global disruptions the past few years, from the COVID-19 pandemic and the war in Ukraine to the rising tensions between the United States and China. These economic, political, geopolitical, and social issues have wide-ranging ramifications for capital markets, with each country and region uniquely affected. Yet despite the complex disruptions occurring simultaneously, Africa has shown notable resilience in some areas, which is an encouraging sign for future investors. African markets recovered more slowly in 2021 than they did in the second half of 2020, but gains were dispersed throughout all four quarters. The pandemic's recovery was also visible in the higher amounts of nonlocal corporate, governmental, and supranational debt issued during the year (2021: 94 issuances / $47.5 billion; 2020: 81 issuances / $28.5 billion).[90] Budget deficits in African countries were and continue to be a concern; however, global investors did not seem to be as affected by these, as was perhaps anticipated, with several issuances being oversubscribed by three times and several sovereigns attaining a better interest rate than their previous issuances. One area that is not as encouraging is the decline in IPOs and capital raising in 2021 compared with 2020, which was also a trend the past five years and could be due to low valuations and high costs of corporate actions.[91]

The economic repercussions of the COVID-19 pandemic have boosted African nations' ambition in expanding their domestic capital markets and shifting their attention more toward environmental, social, and governance (ESG) norms. Several African nations, including Ghana, are now planning to issue green and social bonds to raise money as part of the recovery. These nations must ensure that the bond framework and associated procedures comply with global ESG norms. Investors who are interested in these instruments should work with issuers to make sure that bond proceeds are transparently allocated to the ESG initiatives that were initially proposed. They should also collaborate with regulators to establish the necessary regulatory framework that encourages the issuance of these kinds of instruments.[92]

The financial markets in Africa are moving toward a new post-COVID-19 phase, where past market performance is no longer a good predictor of future results. Africa today has a significant opportunity to hasten the growth of its capital markets sector because of the irreversible changes taking place in world markets. This trend is especially important because traditional finance options are becoming increasingly limited as a result of the complicated interaction between already-heavy debt loads, changing ESG investment requirements, and a realignment of global politics.[93]

To re-price its debt and invest in the development-promoting infrastructure required to assure sustained long-term growth, Africa must take advantage of the current low interest rate environment and abundant market liquidity. Africa has already taken the lead in the development of Islamic, blue, and green finance. The capital markets are poised to play a big role in diversifying Africa's funding systems, even though much more must be done.

The path to the market must be altered for both the public and private sectors, shifting from greater accountability to greater monitoring and better cooperation. Market turmoil is still very much ongoing. There has never been a better time for Africa to increase its finance base through a combination of bondholders, local and foreign currencies, tenor (debt maturity), and privatization (equity, both local and foreign). Global disruptions will continue to be a challenge for African capital markets, but the defenses against extreme consequences are also becoming stronger and more resilient, with regionalization and market development.

Strategies for Investment

The overwhelming opportunities incumbent in Africa's capital markets indicate that there is a significant potential to overcome the existing challenges and risks to investment and capitalize on these growing markets. Global sovereign debt crises and financial crises are leading international private equity managers to seek out new emerging markets—Africa is that new market. Diasporic Africans are assisting in spreading awareness about the opportunities on the continent, and simultaneously building a talent pool of capable investors and fund managers with the market knowledge to further grow international interest and build Africa's capital markets.[94]

Global private equity firms should undoubtedly look to the continent for the growing opportunities in Egypt, Kenya, Zambia, and Ghana, in addition to other emerging African markets with budding capital markets. Any efforts that governments make to open up capital markets and pass new policies that prioritize investors should be capitalized on in the short term and taken as signals of long-term potential. These efforts would stimulate capital markets and the banking sector, providing sufficient indications of market maturation.

African governments should take the lead in stimulating investment and capital accumulation on the continent. They should prioritize the selling of state-owned enterprises to strategic investors that are willing to list these firms in domestic markets and contribute to capital movement through the region's capital markets.[95] Governments can also provide direct incentives for listed companies and interested investors. Specifically, governments can exempt capital gains and dividends from "the newly introduced 1 percent withholding tax on investment income," which will have the immediate effect of encouraging further investment and the expansion of private equity funds. The banking sector will be critical for this tax exemption strategy, as governments will need to make up the losses in tax revenue with a money market investment tax.[96]

Governments can be the primary motivators of bringing depth to public debt markets. Issuing infrastructure and municipal bonds will be strategic moves that encourage investment and help navigate the infrastructure deficits currently plaguing African countries. As Oja and Pillay explain, "Issuance of infrastructure via government agencies (e.g., electricity and water/utility companies), with implicit guarantees from the central government will (1) inject a great deal of sizable issues into these markets in ways that will attract both institutional and foreign investors, (2) expand investor base, and (3), importantly, shift government use of this market away from funding budget deficits— which are mainly for recurrent expenditure—to production of economic infrastructure," expanding the production base of the economy.[97] Debt management can be accomplished with good governance and policies that consider how to mitigate the risks and engender long-term debt sustainability.

African markets have the increasing potential to improve risk/return trade-offs that global investors are looking to overcome in other markets. African equities provide attractive returns and offer the added benefit of portfolio diversification for international investors. Private investment activity in Africa increased by 136 percent in 2013, reaching a total market capitalization value of $3.2 billion, compared with $1.46 billion in 2012.[98] Africa's equity markets are diverse and growing in total market capitalization, posing a great opportunity for international investors to diversify their portfolios with minimal risk to fluctuations due to global tensions. In this case, African markets' limited connections to developed markets prove to be beneficial for investors with minimal bandwidth to accommodate risk.

International funds are also important factors in building bond markets for infrastructure and housing construction purposes. Domestic bond markets are integral to creating more fiscal stability and extending the duration of debt for job creation, construction, and employment. Infrastructure investments and bonds for private sector growth are critical tools that can have resounding effects on the vitality of Africa's capital markets.

Regionalization and integration should be closely followed to determine the markets with the most beneficial regulations and procedures for low costs, high returns, and identifiable cash flow funds that will buttress the credit and debt markets.[99] New markets are projected to open in Anglophone West Africa and in East Africa, providing new platforms for investment to the broader region and not just the major markets of Nigeria, Uganda, and South Africa. Firms should scout out the opportunities for cross-border listings and strategies to capitalize on regional integration and regionalization of African stock markets. The East African Community has already started the process of interlinking its payment systems, which portends significant potential for investors seeking more efficient transfer systems.[100]

Looking to the Future

Digitization, the rapid adoption of advanced technologies, increasing regionalization, and expected population growth throughout Africa are markers of the potential to advance African capital markets into a successful future. There is evidence that mounting financial flows are translating into real economic growth by advancing the financial intermediation capability of local banking institutions. Governments must ensure that macroeconomic and fiscal policies are reformed to provide for long-term sustainable growth. The financial sector still requires significant support and stabilization policies.

Private sector growth will occur in keeping with the growth of capital markets, and existing operations have the potential to expand across borders and into new, growing markets. Capital markets are helping firms break into new products and sectors. By 2063, Africa will be one of the highest-performing regions in the world for capital markets, and strategies of inclusive growth will be critical for developing these markets and ensuring that financial services are stable enough to support the growth of agricultural production, technological innovations, employment, and social service systems.

Notes

1. AFSIC (2024).
2. Oxford Business Group (2022); See the number of stock exchanges at https://www.africanviews.org/focus/economics/african-stock-exchanges.
3. Soumaré, Kanga, and Raga (2021).
4. Ayyagari, Demirgüç-Kunt, and Maksimovic (2011); Gorodnichenko and Schnitzer (2013).

5. Soumaré, Kanga, and Raga (2021).
6. Spratt (n.d.).
7. Nguimeya and Breton (2013).
8. Deloitte (2016).
9. Ishioro (2013).
10. African Business (2015).
11. Barry and Eseonu (2017).
12. Ecofin Agency (2024b).
13. Dickinson (2008).
14. Landers and Martinez (2024).
15. World Bank (2011).
16. Oxford Business Group (2022).
17. PwC (2022).
18. Nyasha and Odhiambo (2014).
19. World Bank (2011).
20. Barry and Eseonu (2017).
21. Honohan and Beck (2007).
22. Mo Ibrahim Foundation (2024).
23. Adjasi, Biekpe, and Osei (2011).
24. AVCA (2023).
25. Oxford Business Group (2022).
26. The Absa Africa Financial Markets Index is calculated based on six pillars: market depth; access to foreign exchange; market transparency, tax, and regulatory environment; capacity of local investors; macroeconomic environment and transparency; and legal standards and enforceability.
27. OMFIF (2023).
28. Ncube and Mingiri (2015).
29. Dickinson (2008).
30. African Business (2015).
31. Blommstein and Horman (2007).
32. Kiel Institute for the World Economy (2023).
33. Kuramo Capital Management (2023).
34. Dickinson (2008).
35. Standard Chartered (2022).
36. African Business (2015).
37. Oxford Business Group (2022).
38. European Investment Bank (2021).
39. African Development Bank (2011).
40. Babarinde (2012).
41. AVCA (2023).
42. UNECA (2020b).
43. Allen, Otchere, and Senbet (2011).

44. African Development Bank (2011).

45. African Development Bank (2011).

46. Andrianaivo and Yartey (2009).

47. World Economic Forum (n.d.).

48. Climate Policy Initiative (2022).

49. Oxford Business Group (2022).

50. Babarinde (2012).

51. Babarinde (2012).

52. Blommestein and Horman (2007).

53. Sy (2014).

54. GroConsult (2024).

55. Gvozdanovic and Baning-Osafo (2016).

56. These countries are Cameroon, Côte d'Ivoire, Ethiopia, Gabon, Kenya, Namibia, Nigeria, Rwanda, Senegal, and Zambia.

57. Raber (2016).

58. European Investment Bank (2021).

59. Divakaran, Schneider, and McGinnis (2018).

60. *Nation* (2016).

61. RisCura and EAVCA (2016).

62. Deloitte (2016).

63. Mwaniki (2023).

64. *East African* (2015).

65. Parkinson and Waweru (2008); Nyasha and Odhiambo (2014).

66. Nyasha and Odhiambo (2014).

67. Nyasha and Odhiambo (2014).

68. Oxford Business Group (n.d).

69. Divakaran, Schneider, and McGinnis (2018).

70. Maimbo et al. (2011).

71. Maxfield (2009).

72. LuSE (n.d.).

73. LuSE (n.d.).

74. Sayila (n.d.).

75. Omran (2006).

76. Simons and Laryea (2006).

77. Abdel-Razek (2024).

78. Raubenheimer (2019).

79. Soumaré et al. (2021).

80. Essa (2016).

81. *Economist* (2015).

82. Ncube and Kapingura (2015).

83. Jun and Shawky (2003); Chordia and Subrahmanyam (2008); Lesmond (2005); Collins and Abrahamson (2006); Ntim et al. (2011).

84. World Bank (2011).
85. Maselle et al. (2015).
86. Gvozdanovic and Baning-Osafo (2016).
87. Honohan and Beck (2007).
88. Oxford Business Group (2022).
89. UNECA (2020b).
90. PwC (2022).
91. PwC (2022).
92. Milken Institute (2021).
93. Gopaldas (2021).
94. Babarinde (2012).
95. Gvozdanovic and Baning-Osafo (2016).
96. Gvozdanovic and Baning-Osafo (2016).
97. Ojah and Pillay (2009).
98. EY (2014c).
99. Ojah and Pillay (2009).
100. Wajid (2015).

Nine
Conclusion
STRATEGIES FOR SUCCESS IN REALIZING AFRICA'S POTENTIAL— FOCUSING ON THE PRIVATE AND PUBLIC SECTORS

Building from the trajectory of *Unlocking Africa's Business Potential*, this book has continued to make the case for the immense economic potential found on the African continent across countries and sectors, from health care and mining to venture capital and the creative industries. The ongoing transformation on the continent is opening new opportunities and new challenges—both of which can be strategically leveraged by new and existing investors. Understanding the trends, opportunities, and challenges for each industry, both historically and within the current context, is critical for generating new interest and gathering important information. Despite their complex diversity, most of the countries and companies which have outperformed their peers, share unique characteristics and have adopted winning strategies to successfully achieve their aspirations. The next section focuses on the strategies for success in realizing Africa's potential for businesses and is followed by a section on strategies for the public sector.

Strategies for the Private Sector to Realize Africa's Potential

To take the next step in realizing Africa's potential, companies should astutely use this knowledge to develop unique strategies for their engagements with African countries. While a one-size-fits-all approach to doing business in African countries will surely be inadequate and ineffective, especially for a continent as diverse as Africa, there are still important general lessons to be learned both from the ongoing debates between scholars and business consultants and directly from companies that are already operating on the continent, especially those in the industries discussed in this book.

Companies such as Novartis, United Bank for Africa, African Finance Corporation, Sanlam Allianz, Coca-Cola, DHL, Agility, DP World, Our Next Energy, Volkswagen, and Yara International, as partners with the World Economic Forum, have already found success by investing in African countries. Each has carved its own path, filled with challenges and successes, and each credits its success to a multitude of strategies and external factors that will be of interest and assistance for new investors considering business expansion, relocation, or creation in Africa. These strategies are explored in the next sections of this chapter.

Strong Partnerships and Trust with Governments and with Communities

One key difference between developed and emerging markets is the role of the informal sector and informal social institutions. Compared with developed economies, emerging economies are more influenced by informal institutions and social contracts than by formal contracts and rules.

Scholars have emphasized the importance of formal and informal networks in entrepreneurship and business expansion in emerging economies. Informal networks have played a role in facilitating cooperation between firms and in the internationalization of small entrepreneurial firms.[1] A 2017 study suggested that in resource-rich, landlocked African countries (Botswana, Zambia, and Zimbabwe) in particular, international companies should differentiate themselves from competitors by emphasizing informal networks and cultural attributes.[2] Informal networks often provide awareness of foreign market opportunities, even more so than formal market research. For small firms in particular, networks provide the opportunity to internationalize and compete with bigger firms.[3] Strengthening these informal networks has been shown to deepen collaboration between informal and formal firms.[4]

Beyond networks, a more recent approach is the "business ecosystem" perspective, which considers the establishment and evolution of various relationships, including a company's relationship with industrial players, governments, and other stakeholders.[5] This perspective has been used to understand how multinational companies have been successful in expanding into institutionally weak host countries by leveraging a company's relationships with governments and other companies to first emerge, as well as the need to establish networks with partners that have specialized capabilities, as this will strengthen the overall business ecosystem as it evolves.[6] Success has often been attributed to how large a company's professional network is.[7]

An example of building relationships with local governments can be found in the experience of Novartis, a global pharmaceutical company that credits its success in Africa to its robust partnerships, including with African governments. The company has managed to work collaboratively with African governments to expand access to generic medicines through data sharing and by focusing on mutual goals. For example, Novartis and the Ghanaian government worked together closely to reimburse sickle cell disease treatments through the country's national health plan as well as to expand access to generic medicines. The company has also worked with governments to advance an innovative cancer treatment through a freedom-to-operate license agreement that allows generic manufacturers in middle-income countries— including Egypt, Morocco, and Tunisia—to independently manufacture generic versions of treatment for chronic myeloid leukemia. The goal is to tailor approaches to intellectual property, in close collaboration with governments.

As an example of the importance of building relationships with local communities, one study that included interviews with fourteen African fintech companies found that working with local people and customers to develop a marketing strategy is critical, especially during intra-African expansion.[8] This includes directly involving customers in the marketing process, adapting communication and pricing strategies, and segmenting customers by geography. At the core is the relationship with customers; for these companies, a bottom-up, value-proposition approach to marketing has worked well in navigating this particular emerging market context.[9]

Prioritizing Local Partners That Understand the Distinct Challenges and Complexities of Each Individual Country and Community

Strategic management theories can provide important tools for company strategies; however, they have been criticized for their reliance on Western-influenced theories due to a lack of management theories that incorporate the nuances of the African continent in particular.[10] Indigenous management theories attempt to include these nuances, as well as "cultural, social, political, and environmental factors" into management principles, similar to how indigenous knowledge has been infused into other areas, such as sustainability and medicine.[11] This field of research is growing, which provides opportunities for information gathering through extensive market research or local partners.

Local partnerships are critical for business expansion because they can guide new companies to better understand both the "hard" and "soft" elements of doing business and can help expedite the growth of a company's professional network. Local partnerships can be developed through employing local employees, acquiring local companies, or working together with local players. Novartis, for example, works extensively with local health care providers and foundations to reach more people. In 2022, Novartis used its local partners to tailor its Healthy Family program to each country's health care goals, reaching more than 90,000 people with community education and services for reproductive health and family planning. It has also partnered with religious and community organizations, such as the Uganda Protestant Medical Bureau and the Uganda Catholic Medical Bureau, as well as the Tropical Health Education Trust in Ethiopia, which have helped it reach and build trust with local communities.[12]

Aligning the Needs of Companies, Governments, and Communities Where Possible to Overcome Infrastructure and Human Capital Challenges

Another key strategy for success is aligning the needs of companies, governments, and communities and turning needs into opportunities. A lack of infrastructure has long been cited as a key deterrent for new investors. However, several successful companies have been able to turn this deterrent into an opportunity. Rather than shying away from challenges such as infrastructure, human capital, poverty, and the like, some companies have been able to expand their business by investing in solutions as well. For example, Shoprite, Africa's largest supermarket retailer, invested in its own water supply through boreholes and purification plants in some areas and invested in electric generators in others when it first entered these markets.[13]

The mining sector in particular has several opportunities to align needs to benefit country and company alike by building schools, roads, and local clinics. A Deloitte study found that inclusive solutions are critical for a comprehensive strategy for mining companies in particular. This is partially due to needing a "social license to operate" within mineral deposits by actually providing value in the local community. Often, value can be provided by engaging third-party partners to deliver solutions on behalf of the company through agreements with local governments. To develop inclusive solutions that will be embraced by local communities and governments, mining companies should consider both internal factors (shareholder expectations, management and employee views, and current internal policies) and external factors (the social context, leading examples, and relevant regulations).[14]

Given Africa's youthful population, youth talent has the potential to become the driver of African economies for decades to come. However, without improvements in education and job opportunities, this potential may be stifled. The private sector, alongside governments, can play a leading role in developing Africa's human capital through skill-building, on-the-job training, and a relevant educational curriculum.[15] Some companies have found success partnering with local universities. OCP, for example, partners with Mohammed VI Polytechnic University to develop job-training programs, house 80 percent of the company's research and development, and provide African students with multidisciplinary vocational and technical training.[16] The company also embeds human capital development more broadly through its product and service offerings by training the farmers themselves in productive and sustainable farming practices. Yara International also launched MBA-style leadership academies in Kenya for micro, small, and medium-sized enterprises across the entire agricultural value chain.[17] As the digital transformation continues to transform necessary workforce skills, companies will likely need to take a proactive approach when considering their talent acquisition and development strategies.[18]

Aligning Strategies with Future Trends and Demand in Intra-African Trade

As mentioned throughout this book, important and ongoing economic, political, and social trends around the globe and in Africa specifically will be critical for understanding and guiding companies to success in the future. One of these trends is continuing regional integration. The African Continental Free Trade Agreement (AfCFTA) is reducing trade barriers between African countries, as countries are looking to strengthen local value chains in the wake of global economic disruptions. One major strategy of businesses in Africa today has been to align products, services, and overall business strategies with this future trend that signals greater intra-African trade.

The United Bank for Africa (UBA), African Finance Corporation (AFC), and DP World have all understood the ongoing needs of local communities and sought to add value and bridge gaps, especially in areas that will only continue to grow in demand in the future. As discussed in the World Economic

Forum's report *A New Era for Global Business and Investment*, these companies have focused on investing for the long term in things that will accelerate intra-African trade.[19]

UBA, for example, has centered its customer-centric strategy on three key levers—people, process, and technology—leading it to invest in areas critical to Africa's future demand: job creation, e-commerce, and infrastructure. UBA is helping to create jobs by assisting small businesses to overcome traditional barriers by offering business formalization, access to credit, and taxation support. The company is also leading the charge for digital solutions for payment and currency conversion issues. UBA has been a leader in deploying the Pan-African Payment and Settlement System, which facilitates cross-border payments and transactions, and has also created its own digital products, such as Leo, Africa's largest chat banking platform.[20] UBA is also partnering directly with AfCFTA through its credit fund, which focuses on infrastructure finance in the private sector, attracting local and foreign partners to deliver capital.[21] Overall, UBA's strategy to align its goals with future trends and local needs in intra-African trade has proven successful.

AFC is also focusing on meeting the need for logistics infrastructure, recognizing the role of high-quality infrastructure in accelerating intra-African trade. Already, AFC has led or contributed to about $4 billion in sovereign facilities for power, roads, water, and other infrastructure.[22] Similarly, DP World, a global logistics provider that has been operating in Africa for twenty years, has focused on investing in ports as a way to improve logistics, particularly given the anticipated increase in demand due to AfCFTA increasing intra-African trade. In Kigali, Rwanda, DP World has helped significantly increase exports through a one-stop-shop logistics hub that connects the landlocked country to markets in Europe, the United States, and the Middle East. In Somaliland, DP World invested more than $440 million to transform Berbera Port into a main maritime gateway in the Horn of Africa. The company is also investing in a nearby economic zone to attract other logistics, warehousing, and manufacturing companies. This is not only a lucrative business opportunity but also a way to invest in the future as Africa continues to integrate regionally and grow trade relationships.[23]

Leveraging Digital Tools and Digital Transformation

A common misconception about African countries as a whole and within the business context is that the majority are technologically weak.[24] As a result, social media and digital channels are currently underutilized in Africa. Yet this assumption ignores the fact that several countries are technologically advanced, from South Africa to Egypt, Nigeria, Kenya, and Ghana. Despite the upward trend of internet connectivity and mobile phone usage, businesses have yet to harness the immense potential of social media and digital channels, which connect customers directly to products and can help not only sales but also improvement and feedback on products and services.[25] However, some creative industries—such as music, comedy, and design—have begun to leverage social media platforms. Creative technology companies—such as Kenya's Black Rhino VR, which uses virtual reality for education, tourism, and health—are working to strengthen the regulatory ecosystem across the continent, and African Digital Heritage uses technology to archive African heritage digitally.[26] These companies are able to combine creative pursuits with technologies to enter new markets. Mobile money platforms can further facilitate the monetization of creative industries.

In addition to creative industries, leveraging the digital transformation and advanced technologies is a critical strategy for the insurance industry. Since insurance companies typically cite their employees and agents as the foundation for success, agents' productivity and skills are a key focus. Technology is already changing how insurance policies are sold, and will continue to do so as advanced technologies evolve. Insurance agents must leverage technology to remain agile and customer-centric.[27] However, implementing technology can be costly and may come with challenges such as data security and the lack of a skilled workforce. One way that some companies have chosen to overcome such challenges is by forming joint ventures to increase sales. One example is the Sanlam Allianz joint venture, which joined one of the largest insurance companies in Africa with an international company based in Germany that operates in 170 countries, creating one of the largest nonbanking financial services companies.[28]

Embracing digital technologies also goes hand-in-hand with tailoring strategies and products to the local context through the power of data. According to Neurotech Africa, unlocking data as an asset could add $750 billion in value across Africa by 2025.[29] To do so, companies should embrace a data-centric business strategy that lays out how and which data will be collected, stored, managed, and used for the short and long terms. Data scarcity across Africa has been a problem, making it necessary and strategic for some companies to build and own proprietary data analytics.[30]

Beyond data, embracing advanced digital technologies where possible can help increase productivity and add value to the extractive industry, for example, or create a better product. OCP Africa, a fertilizer company based in

Morocco, leverages artificial intelligence to provide customized fertilizer and farming solutions, which has helped improve the productivity of African crops by 20–40 percent over six years.[31] The digital transformation is also a way to reach more customers, develop more efficient supply chains, and incorporate sustainable business practices. Yara International, a Norwegian fertilizer company that has been operating in Africa since 1990, uses online environments to connect smallholder and commercial farms to investors and to understand challenges and administer agricultural advice to improve farm productivity in a sustainable way.[32] In 2020, Yara used digital technologies to track the fertilizer's distribution route from port to farmers in East Africa in order to better understand and adapt its supply chain and distribution systems.[33]

Considering Different Types of Diversification Based on Company Strengths, Industry Characteristics, and Local Needs

Another common, and often necessary, strategy is for businesses or start-ups to become vertical stack operators, meaning that they develop both a product/service and the infrastructure that enables it.[34] To deliver their core products, companies often must expand into areas beyond the core product or service due to a lack of outsourcing options. This strategy typically leads to a larger number of employees and a wider portfolio of specializations. One of the major benefits of a vertically stacked firm is that the lack of outsourcing builds resilience and reduces dependency on the broader environment and shelters a company from its various risks.[35]

Coca-Cola has had first-hand experience with vertical stacking. Employing more than 50,000 people with 30 bottling partners and 130 bottling plants, Coca-Cola has managed to successfully operate across Africa since 1970.[36] When the company first expanded to Africa, it realized that it needed to bring with it its own investment in infrastructure, including setting up its own power generation facilities and sewage systems.[37] The company also managed its own logistics system, creating innovative distribution systems to reach people by bike or foot when trucks cannot reach them.[38] Having successfully operated in every country in Africa, the company continues its investment in Africa now, not just out of necessity but also out of its commitment to the continent. One example is Coca-Cola's Replenish Africa Initiative, which has provided more than 6.7 million people across forty-one countries in Africa access to safe water, sanitation, and hygiene.[39]

Similarly, Tolaram, now one of Africa's biggest food companies employing 16,000 people across fifteen countries and bringing in about $1.2 billion in annual revenues, began its experience with vertical stacking in Africa in 1995 when it moved its manufacturing production to Nigeria.[40] Driven by lower costs and lowering dependency on external forces, Tolaram's manufacturing strategy had always been about backward integration. When the company first moved its manufacturing production to Nigeria, out of necessity, it brought with it significant infrastructure, from electricity, water, and waste management to in-house employee training and education.[41] Tolaram's CEO, Sajen Aswani, explains how one of the company's largest brands, Indomie—an instant noodle brand making up about a quarter of the company's gross revenue—really took off after manufacturing was moved to Nigeria. The move made it possible to localize production, which was important for both the company and its customers, and reduce supply chain lengths. Key to Tolaram's strategy is ensuring that it is able to source raw materials locally wherever possible, manufacture at a competitive price, distribute efficiently, and ensure people have the skills to produce.[42] Now, Tolaram continues to invest in infrastructure for both immediate and long-term gain. Already, the company has brought in its own logistics systems, and it now has plans to build a $1 billion deep-sea port off the coast of Lagos to address trade bottlenecks. The project is a huge investment that entails partnering with various stakeholders, including state and federal governments, the port operator and builders, Chinese financiers, and licensing agencies.[43]

Companies have also successfully implemented horizontal diversification. Building horizontally has significant benefits, helping companies expand profitability, improve competitive positioning, and capture more of a nascent market.[44] Successful horizontal build-outs typically have come when a company extends into a different product line that self-reinforces its other lines. For example, fintech companies have expanded beyond payment services to offer other financial services, such as insurance, loans, and savings accounts. Kuda, a digital banking service, has expanded its services in Nigeria to tap into horizontal markets such as loans. This horizontal move helps increase market share and takes advantage of its network and the relevance of its services to its customers.[45]

While they are valuable when leveraged strategically, vertical and horizontal integration can also be costly and slow agility. Now that certain markets have matured, some companies have found success by incorporating more specialization and partnerships rather than having to do everything in house. For example, ROAM, an electric motorcycle manufacturer in East Africa, and M-KOPA, an asset finance company, have partnered, drawing on their respective strengths. ROAM designs and manufactures the motorcycles, while M-KOPA boosts sales through its experience in internet-of-things devices and its pay-go asset financing.[46] Through this partnership, they have successfully reduced operational costs by over 70 percent for motorcycle taxi and delivery entrepreneurs and have increased their daily incomes by 50 percent.[47]

Overcoming Internal Corporate Challenges

It is clear from the management literature that there is no universally accepted management process that guides high-performance firms. This lack of a one-size-fits-all approach is even more pronounced in the African context, given the gaps in research on management processes in the region specifically. Yet the existing research, as well as the experiences of successful firms so far, can shed light on a few clear principles to consider in overcoming corporate challenges.

Corporate Governance

First, strong corporate governance is key for resilience, capital raising, and scale. About 76 percent of family businesses in Africa do not have succession plans, and 19 percent deliberately decided not to. In Nigeria, 50 percent of family businesses had no governance policies.[48] Academic studies have highlighted that across Africa, leadership has been more prone to deploy reactive and ineffective risk management rather than preemptive and strategic risk management.[49] A strategic board for governance that has diverse knowledge and networks is critical. The nonexecutive board can be leveraged as well, to include diverse characteristics that will consider different aspects as companies evolve, including things like human resources planning and codes of conduct. Companies should also make sure that the governance structure and its various roles are clearly defined so that each stakeholder has a clear understanding of its role in creating an impartial governance process.[50] Tinuade Awe, CEO of NGX Regulation, a regulatory subsidiary of the Nigerian Exchange Group, highlights that principles-based corporate governance allows flexibility and scalability while also indicating her belief that both the youth and the democratic creation of technology will be huge factors for corporate governance in the future.[51]

Financial Management

Financial and resource management should be a foundational pillar, as it can help companies and start-ups absorb internal and external shocks, which is especially important within more volatile environments.[52] Dedicated leadership for resource management is critical to be able to balance both short-term, and, more importantly, long-term goals that continuously evolve as a business enters different stages of growth. Appointing a CFO or financial director who can provide informed strategic financial advice to leadership and use data-centric tools to help guide decision-making is one way to prioritize this type of management.[53]

Carefully Consider When to Scale Up

Premature scaling up has been cited as the main factor for failure of a majority (74 percent) of high-growth start-ups globally. Understanding the most effective scaling-up pathway for a start-up or company is always a key consideration, but even more so in the African context, where a "growth at all costs" model may not be the most effective.[54] One major obstacle is the lack of timely business data related to product feedback and development. Companies may need to prioritize data collection and analysis, leveraging digital tools to overcome data bottlenecks.

Concluding Thoughts for the Private Sector

The experiences of these African and international companies are a testament to current and future business potential across the continent, showcasing how companies can overcome challenges and seize opportunities. Each company has had its own unique internal and external factors that have guided its strategy, yet companies' experiences reveal commonalities and themes that have led to their success. Understanding future trends and opportunities among sectors—including mining, health care, creative industries, and all the other sectors explored in this book—will help guide companies in creating their own strategies for entering or expanding into African countries, with the potential for extremely lucrative opportunities for companies and countries alike.

The unprecedented growth of African business opportunities offers Africa an incredible opportunity to unlock prosperity by creating quality jobs, raising incomes, reducing inequalities, and lifting millions out of poverty. Yet the realization of these opportunities is not guaranteed and requires the strategic leadership of the public sector to usher in an era of African investment in a way that contributes to the sustainable, inclusive, and resilient development of African countries. To capture the benefits of the enormous business opportunities that lie ahead for Africa, the public sector has a key role to play.

Figure 9-1. Key Strategies for the Public Sector

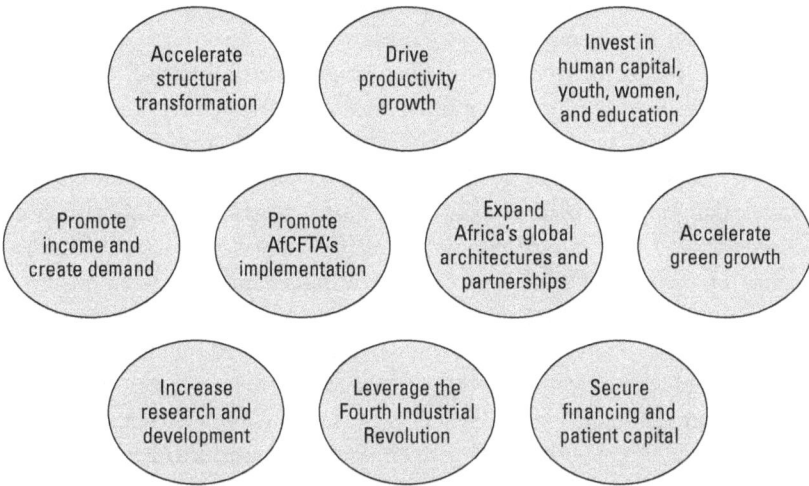

Strategies for the Public Sector to Realize Africa's Potential

Given the diversity, heterogeneity, and complexity of the 54 African economies and contexts, there is no one-size-fits-all solution for all African governments. However, outperformers on the continent can offer valuable insights for underperformers based on their successes. While each government will face its own contexts, the public sector should consider the strategies outlined here to effectively partner with the private sector and ensure that increased investment translates to structural transformation. Figure 9-1 highlights these strategies, and then I discuss each one in some detail.

The process of structural transformation of African economies and diversification of sources of growth is a condition for setting the continent on a journey to prosperity and accelerating the process of global income convergence. Africa's lack of diversification of sources of growth and trade has been an important driver of its excess growth in volatility and recurrent balance-of-payment crises that amplify its risk perception. The impressive performance achieved by the region during the first decade of the twenty-first century (2000–10) was due to the commodity supercycle in a region that is home to almost half of all commodity-dependent countries in the world.[55] Growth decelerated sharply after the 2014–15 adverse commodity terms-of-trade shock, and further after the COVID-19 pandemic downturn, which only highlighted the region's vulnerability to global volatility. Africa's prosperity relies on overcoming the colonial development model of resource extraction, which for decades has been the bane of African economies, to achieve the African Union's Agenda 2063 vision that emphasizes Africa's agency as the key driver of its own destiny.

To do so, the public sector should design and successfully implement robust policies that drive productivity growth, including through the promotion of investment, capital formation, competition, innovation, technology, and market efficiency, as well as investing in infrastructure, mechanization, and human capital (skills) and increased scale of production. Outperforming African economies do better than others in these areas. The public sector should focus on increasing labor market efficiency and creating a conducive business environment through measures such as fewer regulatory and tax barriers to business, stronger property rights and rule of law, improved regulatory quality, and the implementation of special economic zones. Regulatory sandboxes and other mechanisms that allow governments to pilot programs before scaling them up have been effective for emerging economies to create enabling policies that work within their unique context. Emerging economies that have outperformed others are those that attract large, competitive firms that often invest in research and development (R&D), do skills training for employees, and invest in assets which can spillover to smaller firms.[56] Some outperforming economies have supported their competitive domestic companies through measures such as low-cost loans, low tax rates, R&D subsidies, and preferential exchange rates.[57] African countries should also ensure that investment in productivity is not limited to high-tech firms, but includes a focus on improving productivity for the informal sector that often dominates African labor markets through investments in education and digital inclusion, requiring public sector leaders to straddle the dual challenge of innovation and inclusion when it comes to policies that drive productivity growth.[58]

The public sector should also invest in Africa's human capital, youth, women, and education. By 2063, Africa will be home to half of the global working age population,[59] making it the fastest-growing youth population in the world. In contrast to countries like Japan and Italy that are battling declining and aging populations, Africa will be home to half the world's young consumers and workers and half the young people who will be at the forefront of solving global issues and responding to global crises, while also fueling and shaping art, music, and culture. This seismic demographic shift requires strategic investment from the public sector in human capital development to ensure that working age Africans (15–65 years of age) (whose population will hit 1 billion by 2030[60]) are equipped with high-quality education and skills, and that African labor markets are well developed to provide quality jobs. The African Union's declaration of 2024's theme of "Educate and Skill Africa for the 21st Century" is a powerful signal of the key role education will play, but it must be met with a wealth of investment and action to make sure that gains in educational attainment are met with stronger labor markets ready to absorb African talent.[61] Unemployment and insecure employment pose a huge threat to the flourishing of the youth population. The proportion of African young adults not in the employment, education, or training (NEET) population hit 21.9 percent in Sub-Saharan Africa in 2023, and three of five of the young NEETs were women.[62]

Additionally, three out of four young adult workers held jobs that are deemed "insecure."[63] The public sector will play a key role in implementing a youth employment strategy, including investing in demand-driven education and skills development, elevating youth voices in policymaking, and investing in labor and social protection aimed at promoting high-quality jobs.[64] Policymakers should adjust education curricula to match skills needed for future industries, and should promote entrepreneurship and on-the-job skills training. Specific strategies and policies must be put in place to ensure that girls and women are supported in education, labor markets, and entrepreneurship. Already, African women are leading the way with small and medium-sized enterprises, with a quarter of these enterprises on the continent being led by women, and Sub-Saharan Africa being home to the highest proportion of women entrepreneurs globally.[65] Despite their entrepreneurial spirit, only 1.5 percent of funds raised by African start-ups were allocated to women-led businesses between 2019 and 2023.[66] The public sector must lead the way in elevating women's voices among leadership positions, steering investments toward women-led companies and entrepreneurs, targeting education and skills investment to reach women specifically, and promoting policies that will help transition women out of vulnerable or informal jobs toward high-quality jobs with social benefits. The public sector must take the lead in removing barriers to gender equality, as there can be no African prosperity without the prosperity of women.

The public sector should also develop strong policies that promote income and create demand, nationally, regionally (African Continental Free Trade Area), and globally. Realizing Africa's potential requires not just leaving no one behind but also increasing both household income and middle-class finances through higher wages, also obtained through generating high-quality jobs.[67] The stability and growth of Africa's middle class will drive demand and can facilitate import substitution in key industries where Africa relies heavily on imports.[68] For example, the government of Rwanda has made its "Made in Rwanda" initiative, which is meant to promote the manufacturing of and consumption of local products, a cornerstone of its Second National Strategy for Transformation for 2024–29.[69] The campaign so far has approached this issue with many policy approaches. For example, in the textile industry, the "Made in Rwanda" campaign worked to improve the perception of Rwandan-made textiles in the local market while also putting in place a policy to phase out second-hand clothing by raising tariffs on imported used clothes, giving room for domestic companies to capture more of the local market. The number of new fashion businesses has risen since "Made in Rwanda's" inception,[70] and now, looking ahead, the country is focusing on creating complementary policies to make sure that local manufacturers fill the gap. On the continental and global levels, demand can be promoted by accelerating the implementation of AfCFTA, creating a single continental market for goods and services. The public sector must lead the way, in partnership with the private sector, in boosting local demand and creating a policy environment that promotes competitive domestic companies that create high-quality jobs.

The public sector should also lead the way in promoting Africa's regional integration by supporting and accelerating the implementation of AfCFTA. As trade begins under AfCFTA, much work remains to implement the trade agreement, harmonize regulations across all the countries, and put the infrastructure in place to support the acceleration of intra-African trade. African countries must work to remove nontariff barriers and remove import barriers in order to open themselves up to African imports and the development of regional value chains.[71] The African public sector should take a leading role by prioritizing its participation in national implementation committees (NICs). These can help coordinate implementation policies across ministries, monitor and evaluate projects and objectives, coordinate donor activities and capacity building opportunities, raise awareness among the private sector, ensure inclusiveness, and act as a liaison between the AfCFTA Secretariat and state parties.[72] Countries such as Ghana, Nigeria, and Côte d'Ivoire have been prioritizing NICs since AfCFTA's inception and have begun trade under the Guided Trade Initiative, meanwhile countries such as the Democratic Republic of the Congo, Tunisia, and Comoros have just recently approved NICs in law.[73] The public sector should also take the lead in steering investment and attracting partnerships for developing trade-enabling infrastructure, including that related to transportation, to reduce the cost of doing business across the continent. Overall, the implementation of AfCFTA—which relies on resources, compliance, and strategic leadership—should be a leading priority at the national, subregional, and continental levels, as Africa works to unlock the benefits of one of the continent's most transformational opportunities.

The public sector should also expand Africa's role in global economic, financial, and political architectures and its global partnerships to ensure that decisions affecting the continent better represent its perspective and are more aligned with realizing Africa's potential. African countries have found success elevating their concerns on the global stage by speaking with one voice, earning a spot in the Group of Twenty and support from countries like the United States in gaining two seats on the UN Security Council. African countries should continue to elevate their concerns across global institutions and push for representation that accurately reflects their demographic present and future. This is particularly true for Africa's representation in global financial institutions, where African countries face disproportionately low voting power and resource allocation. African countries and the African Union should continue to push for their important priorities, including finding real solutions to the debt crisis, increasing grant and concessional money to Africa, and rechanneling special drawing rights to African financial institutions.[74]

The public sector should also accelerate green growth and transformation, including by leveraging the global energy transition and making Africa's critical minerals work for the continent. The public sector should lead the way in accelerating green growth, both domestically, as Africa works to close its energy deficit, and internationally, where demand for clean energy solutions is high. Africa's high supply of critical minerals for powering the renewable energy transition, from lithium to cobalt to manganese, offers a powerful opportunity for African countries to lead the way in competitive areas and develop green value chains. For example, the Democratic Republic of Congo, accounting for 89 percent of global cobalt exports, could become a leader in the production of lithium-ion batteries, moving the value chain to the continent that can link to other industries like automotives.[75]

Investing in value-adding activities, whether in processing minerals or in other areas such as solar and wind energy production, will be key to capture the benefits and to create green regional value chains within different niches. For example, in Nigeria, the government's energy plan outlines its strategy to bolster domestic solar panel manufacturing; in Senegal, the government is hosting Africa's first utility-scale wind farm, positioning itself for associated industrial growth;[76] and in Namibia, the government is forging ahead with a $10 billion green hydrogen project in collaboration with the private sector as the first step to becoming a leading exporter of green ammonia and developing the country's green hydrogen industry.[77]

To lead in the green growth transformation, Africa needs new, additional, and consistent resources. African countries could explore carbon taxation, pricing, or credits to generate resources coupled with strategies to protect vulnerable populations from price impacts, to leverage their natural endowments.[78] The public sector should also support green financing products by promoting green investment banks while also working to lower investment risk in Africa by encouraging multilateral development banks to utilize innovative instruments, funds, and facilities to provide better risk modeling to lower the cost of capital for Africa.[79] Leading the way in the green growth transformation could help create 3.8 million net new jobs,[80] while acting as a catalyst for new innovations and industries to spur on the continent.

The public sector should also increase the capacity of research institutions to participate in research and development (R&D) activities and protect intellectual property.[81] R&D investments, including in the public and private sectors and universities, have positive effects on economic growth by encouraging the development of new knowledge, techniques, and technologies that improve productivity.[82] Currently, South America and Africa combined are responsible for less than 5 percent of total global R&D, despite having more than 20 percent of the world's population.[83] Indeed, Africa itself falls short of the 1.7 percent R&D global average, with many African countries only investing 0.42 percent of their total GDP.[84] To improve participation in R&D, governments can provide incentives to research organizations, such as by allowing companies to commercially exploit technology developments arising from government-funded research; build pools of researchers and innovators by providing scholarships and investing in human capital and education; increase the capacity of research institutions to undertake high-quality research by providing funding; and encouraging diaspora scientists, engineers, and innovators to return.

The public sector should leverage the power of the Fourth Industrial Revolution to unlock prosperity. The Fourth Industrial Revolution's (4IR's) advanced technologies can help governments deliver public services more efficiently, whether delivering medicines via drone technology or drastically reducing barriers to trade through advanced automation and data storage. These 4IR technologies can play an important role in improving the competitiveness of domestic industries that can substitute for imports by improving quality and processes. To leverage the 4IR, African policymakers should put the 4IR at the forefront of its leadership by crafting dedicated national strategies for embracing the 4IR—one that considers input from a range of stakeholders from private companies, government agencies, nonprofits, and community groups.[85] Morocco has led by example through its government's support for advanced technology research, its creation of networks of innovators, and its proactive approach in coordinating the public and private sectors as well as foreign investors for 4IR investment.[86] The public sector plays a key role in 4IR preparedness, and countries like Mauritius and Kenya lead the way in key indicators. Mauritius, for example, is ranked number one in the world for ensuring widespread access to internet in schools and in e-commerce legislation.[87] Meanwhile, Kenya outperforms countries with a similar income level in entrepreneurship, attitudes toward risk, and business dynamism, ranking 18th in the world in providing users access to online financial accounts.[88] Through robust government support in driving partnerships, competitiveness, innovation, entrepreneurship, and the promotion of digital skills, these countries have been able to emerge as leaders on the continent, with lessons for economies performing less well, as discussed in the book *Africa's Fourth Industrial Revolution.*[89]

Finally, financing and patient capital need to be secured for long-term economic performance. The expansion of manufacturing industries needed to broaden the fiscal space and expand opportunities to set the continent on the right development path relies on the injection of large-scale, patient capital. Yet for decades, access to affordable, patient capital has been a major binding constraint on growth and economic development in the region. The limited fiscal space associated with the deficit of diversification of sources of growth affects both infrastructure development and structural transformation. The chronic deficit of infrastructure undermines the process of structural transformation, and the economic consequences of financial repression are even broader and have confined the region to a vicious cycle of intergenerational poverty.

The scale of financing required for economic transformation is such that only well-capitalized regional development banks could rise to the challenge where sustained investments preclude commercial viability. More than de-risking the financial ecosystem, regional development banks will crowd in more financing, including from venture capitalists and private equity funds, to further expand prosperity during upturns and extend countercyclical financing to soften economic blows during downturns. Development banks can provide credit enhancements and subordinate debt, which can accelerate much-needed private capital for the continent.[90]

Concluding Thoughts for the Public Sector: Strengthening Government Effectiveness and Bridging the Implementation Gap

Perhaps most important, to successfully implement these strategies and effectively translate Africa's burgeoning economic opportunities into tangible outcomes that unlock its prosperity, the public sector needs agile, effective, and accountable leadership.[91] Strengthening governments' effectiveness and economic management capacity, including their ability to efficiently govern a fast-growing economy, should be at the forefront.

Effective leadership requires the commitment and strategy to bridge the gap between policy goals and implementation outcomes. Policymakers should structure the mechanisms of implementation with institutional designs that ensure the highest level of accountability and transparency.[92] Richard Matland offers a useful model that systematizes the policy implementation process by connecting the levels of policy conflict and policy ambiguity within each context.[93] By doing so, policymakers can ensure the successful implementation of an economic policy at its conception by designing it based on the particular city's, nation's, or region's unique dynamics among actors and the convergence between ideational (economic paradigms) and strategic (interest, power, and funding) variables. This will require visionary and strategic leadership across all levels of government.

Taken together, these strategies for both the private and public sectors will accelerate Africa's journey to economic transformation, which will drastically improve livelihoods in one of the most promising regions of the world.

Notes

1. Dana and Ratten (2017).
2. Dana and Ratten (2017).
3. Dana and Ratten (2017).
4. Koto (2017).
5. Parente et al. (2019).
6. Parente et al. (2019).
7. Department of Planning, Monitoring, and Evaluation (2013).
8. Hammerschlag, Bick, and Luiz (2020).
9. Hammerschlag, Bick, and Luiz (2020).
10. Iguisi (2014); Inyang (2008); Thomas et al. (2016).
11. Team Conyach (2023).
12. World Economic Forum (2023).
13. Coetzee, Bezuidenhout, and Mhonyera (2020).
14. Lane and Reggio (2013).
15. Kuyoro et al. (2023).
16. World Economic Forum (2023).
17. World Economic Forum (2023).
18. ETK Group (2021).
19. World Economic Forum (2023).
20. World Economic Forum (2023).
21. World Economic Forum (2023).
22. World Economic Forum (2023).
23. World Economic Forum (2023).

24. Coetzee, Bezuidenhout, and Mhonyera (2020).
25. *ALN* (2023).
26. Ochai (2021).
27. Roy (2023).
28. Roy (2023).
29. Charles (2022).
30. Kuyoro et al. (2023).
31. World Economic Forum (2023).
32. World Economic Forum (2023).
33. See Yara's website: https://www.yara.com/this-is-yara/our-history/.
34. African Scalecraft (n.d.).
35. African Scalecraft (n.d.).
36. World Economic Forum (2023).
37. Coca-Cola Company (2021).
38. ETK Group (2021).
39. World Economic Forum (2023).
40. Amosun and Geller (2021).
41. African Scalecraft (n.d.).
42. Amosun and Geller (2021).
43. Amosun and Geller (2021).
44. African Scalecraft (n.d.).
45. African Scalecraft (n.d.).
46. Hill et al. (2022).
47. Hill et al. (2022).
48. Hill et al. (2022).
49. African Scalecraft (n.d.).
50. Irokosu (2022).
51. Better Boards Admin (2023).
52. Better Boards Admin (2023).
53. African Scalecraft (n.d.).
54. African Scalecraft (n.d.).
55. UNCTAD (2023c).
56. McKinsey & Company (2018).
57. McKinsey & Company (2018).
58. Fox and Signé (2022).
59. African Development Bank (2023d).
60. African Development Bank (2019).
61. African Union (2024b).
62. International Labour Organization (2024).
63. International Labour Organization (2024).
64. International Labour Organization (2024).
65. Mojela and Ndhlazi (2024).

66. African Business (2024b).

67. Fox and Signé (2022).

68. United Nations (2023b).

69. Republic of Rwanda (2024).

70. Fashion Revolution and the British Council (2021).

71. Mold and Mangeni (2024).

72. Habte and Willem te Velde (2023).

73. Habte and Willem te Velde (2023).

74. African Union (2024a).

75. Songwe and Adam (2023).

76. UNDP (2024b).

77. Creamer (2024).

78. Songwe and Adam (2023).

79. UNDP (2024a).

80. Bouchene et al. (2021).

81. This recommendation is an excerpt from Signé (2022b).

82. Yazgan and Yalcinkaya (2018).

83. Heney (2020).

84. Conversation (2021).

85. Signé (2023).

86. Signé (2023).

87. Network Readiness Index (2023a).

88. Network Readiness Index (2023b)

89. Signé (2023).

90. UNDP (2024a).

91. Signé (2017a, 2017b, 2018c).

92. Signé (2017c).

93. Top-down policy implementation models provide an authoritative starting point for identifying the traceability of the problem and structure for implementation, as well as nonstatutory variables affecting implementation. Such models advise policy-makers to adopt clear and consistent goals, to limit the extent of change necessary, to place responsibility for implementation in an agency sympathetic with the policy's goals, and regularly to neglect prior context and political aspects—as if the implementation process were only a matter of administrative function that depends solely on the availability of resources. Bottom-up policy implementation models instead view policy from the perspective of the target population and the service deliverers. These models are based on the belief that central decision-making is poorly adapted to local conditions and that flexibility is important for reaching goals. They are usually criticized as overemphasizing local autonomy and favoring administrative account-ability rather than democratic processes and policy leaders' ability to structure local behaviors. Between the two extremes, Loyola University professor Richard Matland (1995) proposes a hybrid model that systematizes the policy implementation process by connecting levels of policy conflict and policy ambiguity.

References

Abdel-Razek, Sherine. 2024. "A Promising Year on the Stock Exchange." https://english.ahram.org.eg/News/515017.aspx.

Abe, Oyeniyi. 2022. "Between Control and Confrontation: The Pitfalls and Potential of Corporate-Community Participatory Development in Africa's Energy and Extractive Industries." *Extractive Industries and Society* 11: 101095.

Abisuga, Oluwayemisi Adebola, and Mziwoxolo Sirayi. 2018. "The Role of Creative Industries as a Driver for a Sustainable Economy: A Case of South Africa." *Creative Industries Journal* 11. no. 3: 225–44.

Adams & Adams. No date. "State of The Art: Africa's Creative Industries in the New Millennium." https://www.adams.africa/insights/africas-creative-industries-millennium/#:~:text=African%20film%2C%20music%2C%20art%20and, investment%20from%20foreign%20entertainment%20giants.

Addison, Tony, and Alan Roe, eds. 2018. *Extractive Industries: The Management of Resources as a Driver of Sustainable Development.* Oxford University Press.

Adedji, Niran Abdulkabir, Shaufique Fahmi Sidique, Azmawani Abd Rahman, and Siong Hook Law. 2016. "The Role of Local Content Policy in Local Value Creation in Nigeria's Oil Industry: A Structural Equation Modeling (SEM) Approach." *Resources Policy* 49: 61–73.

Adedokun, Adebayo. 2018. "The Effects of Oil Shocks on Government Expenditures and Government Revenues Nexus in Nigeria (with Exogeneity Restrictions)." *Future Business Journal* 4, no. 2: 219–32. https://doi.org/10.1016/j.fbj.2018.06.003.

Adegoke, Sope. 2011. "Intellectual Property Rights in Sub-Saharan Africa." CMC Senior Thesis. http://scholarship.claremont.edu/cmc_theses/289.

Adepoju, Paul. 2021. "Small-Scale Health Insurance for a More Secure Future." *Re:solve*, December 1. https://www.re-solveglobalhealth.com/post/small-scale-health-insurance-for-a-more-secure-future.

Adjasi, Charles Komla Delali, Nicolas Biekpe, and Kofi A. Osei. 2011. "Stock Prices and Exchange Rate Dynamics in Selected African Countries: A Bivariate Analysis." *African Journal of Economic and Management Studies* 2, no. 2: 143–46.

AfCFTA (African Continental Free Trade Area). 2021. "AfCFTA Private Sector Engagement Strategy, 2022–2032." AfCFTA Secretariat.

———. 2022. "AfCFTA Secretariat and Afreximbank Sign an Agreement for the Management of the AfCFTA Adjustment Fund." https://www.afreximbank.com/afcfta-secretariat-and-afreximbank-sign-an-agreement-for-the-management-of-the-afcfta-adjustment-fund/.

———. 2023. "African Trade Report 2023." https://media.afreximbank.com/afrexim/AFRICAN_TRADE_REPORT_2023.pdf.

———. 2024. "Trade and Economic Outlook Report 2024." https://media.afreximbank.com/afrexim/Afreximbank-African-Trade-and-Economic-Outlook-2024_compressed-1.pdf.

Afreximbank. 2020. "Afreximbank Announces $500-Million Creative Industry Support Fund as CAX WKND Opens—African Export-Import Bank." https://www.afreximbank.com/afreximbank-announces-500-million-creative-industry-support-fund-as-cax-wknd-opens/.

Africa Legal Network. 2022. "Agriculture Under the African Continental Free Trade Area." https://aln.africa/insight/agriculture-under-the-african-continental-free-trade-area-afcfta/?utm_source=Mondaq&utm_medium=syndication&utm_campaign=LinkedIn-integration.

African Business. 2014. "African Creative Industries: Art coming in out of the cold." https://african.business/2014/01/technology-information/african-creative-industries-art-coming-in-out-of-the-cold.

———. 2015. "Zimbabwe Stock Exchange Goes Automatic." https://african.business/2015/09/economy/zimbabwe-stock-exchange-goes-automatic.

———. 2016. "Comment: Investing in Africa's Healthcare Sector." https://african.business/2016/11/economy/comment-investing-africas-healthcare-sector.

———. 2024a. "Race for East Africa's Insurance Market Heats Up." https://african.business/2024/08/finance-services/race-for-east-africas-insurance-market-heats-up.

———. 2024b. "More Sustainable Investments Needed to Boost Women-Led Businesses in Africa." https://african.business/2024/07/partner-content/more-sustainable-investments-needed-to-boost-women-led-businesses-in-africa.

African Development Bank. 2007. "2007 AEC—Regional Economic Communities within Nepad: What Prospects for Sustainable Economic and Social Development in Africa?" https://www.afdb.org/en/documents/document/2007-aec-regional-economic-communities-within-nepad-what-prospects-for-sustainable-economic-and-social-development-in-africa-8480.

———. 2011. "The Role of the Private Sector in Africa's Economic Development." In *African Development Report 2011.* www.afdb.org/sites/default/files/documents/publications/african_development_report_2011.pdf.

———. 2012. "Mining Industry Prospect in Africa." https://blogs.afdb.org/fr/afdb-championing-inclusive-growth-across-africa/post/mining-industry-prospects-in-africa-10177

———. 2013. "Health in Africa over the Next 50 Years." https://www.afdb.org/fileadmin/uploads/afdb/Documents/Publications/Economic_Brief_-_Health_in_Africa_Over_the_Next_50_Years.pdf.

———. 2018a. "Africa's Infrastructure: Great Potential but Little Impact on Inclusive Growth." https://www.afdb.org/fileadmin/uploads/afdb/Documents/Publications/2018AEO/African_Economic_Outlook_2018_-_EN_Chapter3.pdf.

———. 2018b. "African Economic Outlook (AEO) 2018." https://www.afdb.org/en/documents/document/african-economic-outlook-aoe-2018-99877.

———. 2019. "African Economic Outlook 2019." https://www.afdb.org/fileadmin/uploads/afdb/Documents/Publications/2019AEO/AEO_2019-EN.pdf.

———. 2021. "Infrastructure Development." https://www.afdb.org/en/knowledge/publications/tracking-africa's-progress-in-figures/infrastructure-development.

———. 2022a. "Africa Investment Forum 2022: Medical and Vaccines Transactions Expected to Draw Healthy Investor Interest During Market Days Event." https://www.afdb.org/en/news-and-events/africa-investment-forum-2022-medical-and-vaccines-transactions-expected-draw-healthy-investor-interest-during-market-days-event-55874.

———. 2022b. "Diaspora's Remittances, Investment and Expertise Vital for Africa's Future Growth, Say Participants at African Development Bank Forum." https://www.afdb.org/en/news-and-events/press-releases/diasporas-remittances-investment-and-expertise-vital-africas-future-growth-say-participants-african-development-bank-forum-57024.

———. 2022c. "Financing a Just Transition in Africa: Challenges and Opportunities." https://www.afdb.org/sites/default/files/2022/12/09/financing_a_just_transition_in_africa-challenges_and_opportunities_final_1_2.pdf.

———. 2023a. "Second International Summit on Food Production in Africa to Open in Dakar." https://www.afdb.org/en/news-and-events/press-releases/second-international-summit-food-production-africa-open-dakar-58210.

———. 2023b. "Africa Must Tackle Huge Infrastructure Gap to Unlock Opportunities for Transformation—Report." https://www.afdb.org/en/news-and-events/press-releases/africa-must-tackle-huge-infrastructure-gap-unlock-opportunities-transformation-report-65734.

———. 2023c. "Public-Private Partnerships Needed to Bridge Africa's Infrastructure Development Gap." https://www.afdb.org/en/news-and-events/public-private-partnerships-needed-bridge-africas-infrastructure-development-gap-65936#:~:text=He percent20noted percent20that percent20the percent20African,been percent20primary percent20investors percent20in percent20infrastructure.

———. 2023d. "Leveraging Potentials of the Youth for Inclusive, Green and Sustainable Development in Africa." https://www.afdb.org/sites/default/files/2023/08/11/setting_the_scene_presentation_for_g-cop_on_youth_s_.pdf.

———. 2024a. "New Africa Sustainable Development Report Shows Critical Importance of Scaled-Up Development Financing." https://www.afdb.org/en/news-and-events/press-releases/new-africa-sustainable-development-report-shows-critical-importance-scaled-development-financing-72773#:~:text=%E2%80%9CFinancing%20remains%20a%20challenge%20for,commitments%20and%20Nationally%20Determined%20Contributions.

———. 2024b. "$4 Trillion Is New Annual Financial Target to Save Sustainable Development Goals, Says African Development Bank's Adesina." https://www.afdb.org/en/news-and-events/press-releases/4-trillion-new-annual-financial-target-save-sustainable-development-goals-says-african-development-banks-adesina-70346.

———. 2024c. "African Economic Outlook 2024." https://www.afdb.org/sites/default/files/2024/06/06/aeo_2024_-_chapter_2.pdf.

———. No date–a. "Investing in the Creative Industries: Fashionomics." https://www.afdb.org/fileadmin/uploads/afdb/Documents/Generic-Documents/Fashionomics_creative_industries_executive_summary_brochure.pdf.

———. No date–b. "Final External Report: Feasibility Study for the Development of the Fashionomics Platform." https://www.afdb.org/fileadmin/uploads/afdb/Documents/Generic-Documents/Final_Report_AFDB_Fashionomics_-_Investing_in_the_African_Creative_Industries_for_the_Continent_s_Inclusive_Growth.pdf.

———. No date-c. "Human Development." https://www.afdb.org/en/knowledge/publications/tracking-africa%E2%80%99s-progress-in-figures/human-development.

African Insurance Organization. 2019. "Africa Insurance Barometer 2019." https://faberconsulting.ch/files/faber/pdf-pulse-reports/Africa_Insurance_Barometer_19_full_E.pdf.

———. 2020. "Africa Insurance Pulse: Growth Perspective of African Re-/Insurance Markets." https://faberconsulting.ch/files/faber/pdf-pulse-reports/Africa_Insurance_Pulse_Growth_e_2020.pdf.

———. 2022. "Africa Insurance Pulse 2022: Climate Change and Its Impact on the African Insurance Sector." *African Insurance Pulse*, June. https://faberconsulting.ch/files/faber/pdf-pulse-reports/2022_AIO_AIP_Climate_EN.pdf.

African Scalecraft. No date. "Growth & Management Strategies." https://www.africanscalecraft.com/management-strategy.

African Union. 2009. "Africa Mining Vision." https://docs.igihe.com/IMG/pdf/africa_mining_vision_english.pdf.

———. 2021a. "The African Union Plan of Action on Cultural and Creative Industries: Development and Promotion of The Creative Economy on the Continent." *AU Echo.* https://au.int/sites/default/files/documents/42796-doc-AUEcho_2021_Digital_Version.pdf.

———. 2021b. "34th AU Summit Strives to Ensure That, as a Continental Body, No Country Is Left Behind in the COVID-19 Responses 'as We Enhance Integration.'"

https://au.int/en/pressreleases/20210206/34th-au-summit-strives-ensure-continental-body-no-country-left-behind-covid.

———. 2024a. "Presidential Dialogue on African Union Financial Institutions; Reforms of the Global Financial Architecture; and the Launch of the Africa Club." https://au.int/en/newsevents/20240217/presidential-dialogue-african-union-financial-institutions-reforms-global.

———. 2024b. "Theme of The Year 2024: Educate and Skill Africa for the 21st Century." https://au.int/en/theme/2024/educate-african-fit-21st-century.

———. No date. "Revised African Union Plan of Action on Cultural and Creative Industries (Draft)." 7th draft. https://ocpa.irmo.hr/resources/docs/AU_Plan_of_Action_Cultural_and_Creative_Industries-en.pdf.

African Union Development Agency. No date. "Who We Are." https://amrh.nepad.org/amrh-microsite/who-we-are.

AFR-IX Telecom. 2022. "African Growth and the Rising of African Middle Class." https://afr-ix.com/african-growth-and-the-rising-of-african-middle-class/.

AFSIC. 2024. "Stock Market in Africa." https://www.afsic.net/stock-market-stocks-in-africa/.

Agarwal, Prachi, Anthony Black; Alberto Lemma, Vuyiswa Mkhabela, and John Stuart. 2022. "The African Continental Free Trade Area and the Automotive Value Chain." *ODI*, July. https://cdn.odi.org/media/documents/VVC_paper_final___.pdf.

Ahadjie, Jerry, Ousman Gajigo, Danlami Gomwalk, and Fred Kabanda. 2021. *Impact of COVID-19 on Mining: Case Study of Four African Countries*. African Development Bank, Working Paper 357. Abijdan: African Development Bank.

Ahmed, Abdullahi D., and Rui Huo. 2018. "China–Africa Financial Markets Linkages: Volatility and Interdependence." *Journal of Policy Modeling* 40, no. 6: 1140–64. https://doi.org/10.1016/j.jpolmod.2018.05.002.

Ahram Online. 2023. "EgyptAir to expand fleet with 18 new Boeing aircraft." https://english.ahram.org.eg/NewsContent/1/1235/512163/Egypt/Urban--Transport/EgyptAir-to-expand-fleet-with--new-Boeing-aircraft.aspx.

———2024. "Egypt Plans to Double Capacity of Cairo International Airport." https://english.ahram.org.eg/News/515768.aspx.

Ajayi-Dopemu, Y. 1985. "Educating Through Television in Nigeria." *Journal of Educational Television* 11, no. 2: 115–21.

Akabzaa, Thomas, and Abdulai Darimani. 2001. "Impact of Mining Sector Investment in Ghana: A Study of the Tarkwa Mining Region." *South African Population Research Infrastructure Network*. http://www.saprin.org/ghana/research/gha_mining.pdf.

Akan, Joey. 2022. "Nollywood's streaming romance." UNESCO. https://courier.unesco.org/en/articles/nollywoods-streaming-romance.

Akinlo, Taiwo, and Olumuyiwa Tolulope Apanisile. 2014. "Relationship between Insurance and Economic Growth in Sub-Saharan African: A Panel Data Analysis." *Modern Economy*, 5 no. 2: 120–27.

Akinsola, Wunmi. 2022. "The State of Nigeria's Fashion Industry." *Stears*, November 18. https://www.stears.co/article/the-state-of-nigerias-fashion-industry/.

Alaoui M'Hammdi, Nezha, and Larabi Jaïdi. 2023. "The Cultural and Creative Industries in Africa and Latin America." Policy Center for the New South. https://www.policycenter.ma/sites/default/files/2023-09/Report%20-%20The%20Cultural%20and%20Creative%20Industries%20in%20Africa%20and%20Latin%20America_0.pdf.

Albertin, Giorgia, Dan Devlin, and Boriana Yontcheva. 2021. "Countering Tax Avoidance in Sub-Saharan Africa's Mining Sector." IMF. https://www.imf.org/en/Blogs/Articles/2021/11/05/blog-countering-tax-avoidance-sub-saharan-africa-mining-sector.

Alcorn, Keith. 2024. "Almost Two-Thirds of New HIV Cases Occur Outside Southern and Eastern Africa." *AIDSmap*, March 26. https://www.aidsmap.com/news/mar-2024/almost-two-thirds-new-hiv-cases-occur-outside-southern-and-eastern-africa.

Allen, Franklin, Isaac Otchere, and Lemma W. Senbet. 2011. "African Financial Systems: A Review." *Review of Development Finance* 1, no. 2: 79–113. https://www.sciencedirect.com/science/article/pii/S1879933711000042.

Allen, Tim, and Suzette Heald. 2004. "HIV/AIDS Policy in Africa: What Has Worked in Uganda and What Has Failed in Botswana?" *Journal of International Development* 16, no. 8: 1141–54. https://onlinelibrary.wiley.com/doi/abs/10.1002/jid.1168.

Alliance for Affordable Internet. 2020. "The Affordability Report 2020." Web Foundation. https://a4ai.org/wp-content/uploads/2020/12/Affordability-Report-2020.pdf.

ALN. 2023. "Trends and Opportunities for Businesses in Africa in 2023." January 5. https://aln.africa/news/trends-and-opportunities-for-businesses-in-africa-in-2023/.

Amosun, Adedoyin, and Laura W. Geller. 2021. "Tolaram's Diversified Strategy for Growth in Africa." PwC. https://www.strategy-business.com/article/Tolarams-diversified-strategy-for-growth-in-Africa.

Amponsah-Tawiah, Kwesi, and Kwasi Dartey-Baah. 2011. "The Mining Industry in Ghana: A Blessing or a Curse?" *International Journal of Business and Social Science* 2, no. 12. https://www.researchgate.net/publication/280557496_The_Mining_Industry_in_Ghana_A_Blessing_or_a_Curse. 294.

Amref. No date. "Re-engineering the Health Workforce in Sub-Saharan Africa." https://amref.org/position-statements/re-engineering-the-health-workforce-in-sub-saharan-africa/.

Andersen, Birgitte, Zeljka Kozul-Wright, and Richard Kozul-Wright. 2000. "Copyrights, Competition and Development: The Case of the Music Industry." UN Conference on Trade and Development, Discussion Paper 145. https://unctad.org/system/files/official-document/dp_145.en.pdf.

Anderson, Daniel R., and Kaveri Subrahmanyam. 2017. "Digital Screen Media and Cognitive Development." *Pediatrics* 140 (Supplement 2): S57–S61. https://doi.org/10.1542/peds.2016-1758c.

Andersson, Åke E., and David Andersson. 2006. *The Economics of Experiences, the Arts and Entertainment*. Cheltenham, UK: Edward Elgar.

Andrianaivo, Mihasoniriana, and Charles Amo Yartey. 2009. "Understanding the Growth of African Financial Markets." International Monetary Fund, Working

Paper 2009/182. https://www.imf.org/en/Publications/WP/Issues/2016/12/31/Understanding-the-Growth-of-African-Financial-Markets-23209.

Anyanwu, John, and Nadège D. Yaméogo. 2015. "Regional Comparison of Foreign Diret Investment to Africa: Empirical Analysis." *African Development Review* 27, no. 4: 345–93.

APA News. 2020. "Nigeria's Fashion Industry Rakes in Over N2tn Revenue Annually—Minister." October 12. http://apanews.net/en/news/nigerias-fashion-industry-rakes-in-over-n2tn-revenue-annually-minister.

Aragón, Fernando M., and Juan Pablo Rud. 2013. "Natural Resources and Local Communities: Evidence from a Peruvian Gold Mine." *American Economic Journal: Economic Policy* 5, no. 2: 1–25.

Ashraf, Muhammad Aqeel, Maliha Sarfraz, Rizwana Naureen, and Mohamedreza Gharibreza. 2015. "Mining and Economic Development: Mining and Environmental Problems." In *Environmental Impacts of Metallic Elements, Environmental Earth Sciences*, ed. James W. LaMoreaux. Singapore: Springer Singapore.

AsokoInsight. 2023. "Trends in Africa's Pharmaceutical Production." https://www.asokoinsight.com/content/market-insights/trends-in-africa-pharmaceutical-production-market.

Asongu, Simplice, and Nicholas Odhiambo. 2020a. "Insurance Policy Thresholds for Economic Growth in Africa." *European Journal of Development Research* 32, no. 3: 672–89.

Asongu, Simplice A., and Nicholas M. Odhiambo. 2020b. "Foreign Direct Investment, Information Technology and Economic Growth Dynamics in Sub-Saharan Africa." *Telecommunications Policy* 44, no. 1: 101838. https://doi.org/10.1016/j.telpol.2019.101838.

Assembly of the African Union. 2019. "Decisions and Declarations." 12th Extraordinary Session of the Assembly, Ext/Assembly/AU/ Decl.1, XIII. https://au.int/sites/default/files/decisions/37553-ext_assembly_au_dec_1-3_xii_e.pdf.

Atlas Magazine. 2022. "Africa: Insurance Penetration Rates in 2022." https://www.atlas-mag.net/en/category/tags/pays/africa-insurance-penetration-rate.

AUDA-NEPAD. 2020. "World Bank's ease of doing business 2020: Headwinds in many African economies." https://www.nepad.org/news/world-banks-ease-of-doing-business-2020-headwinds-many-african-economies.

Augoye, Jayne. 2023. "Nigerian Artistes Generated over N11 billion in Revenue on Spotify in 2022—Report." *Premium Times Nigeria.* https://www.premiumtimesng.com/entertainment/music/615526-nigerian-artistes-generated-over-n11-billion-in-revenue-on-spotify-in-2022-report.html?tztc=1.

Augustine, Calvin. 2024. "African Continental Free Trade Area." South African Government. https://www.gov.za/blog/african-continental-free-trade-area-0.

Auty, M. Richard. 2001. "The Political Economy of Resource-Driven Growth." *European Economic Review* 45, nos. 4–6: 839–46.

AVCA. 2023. "2023 Private Capital Activity in Africa." https://www.avca.africa/data-intelligence/research-publications/2023-african-private-captial-activity-report/

#:~:text=450%20reported%20deals%20in%202023,a%20significant%2048%25
%20YoY%20decline.

———. 2024. "Venture Capital in Africa Report." https://www.avca.africa/media/
o5makqy5/avca234-19-vc-report_4.pdf.

Awases, Magda, Akpa Gbary, Jenniger Nyoni, and Rufaro Chatora. 2004. "Migration
of Health Professionals in Six Countries: A Synthesis Report." World Health Organization Regional Office for Africa.

Ayee, Joseph, Tina Søreide, G. P. Shukla, and Tuan Minh Le. 2011. "Political Economy in
the Mining Sector in Ghana." World Bank, Policy Research Working Paper 5730.
Washington: World Bank.

Aykut, Dilek, and Monika Blaszkiewicz-Schwartzman. 2018. "Shaping the Future of
Africa: Markets and Opportunities for Private Investors." International Finance
Corporation. https://www.ifc.org/content/dam/ifc/doc/mgrt/africa-ceo-forum-
report-fin3-web-lores.pdf.

Ayo-Odewale, Bouluwatife. 2023. "Gaming Industry of Nigeria, South Africa and
Egypt to Hit Combined Value of $2B by 2023." *Technext.* https://technext24.com/
2023/09/18/gaming-egypt-south-africa-nigeria-video/.

Ayyagari, Meghana, Asli Demirgüç-Kunt, and Vojislav Maksimovic. "Firm Innovation
in Emerging Markets: The Role of Finance, Governance, and Competition." *Journal
of Financial and Quantitative Analysis* 46, no. 6: 1545–80.

Babarinde, Olufemi. 2012. "The Private Equity Market in Africa: Trends, Opportunities,
Challenges, and Impact." *Journal of Private Equity*, 56–73.

Banerjee, Ghosh Sudeshna, and Elvira Morella. 2013. "Africa's Water and Sanitation
Infrastructure Access, Affordability, and Alternatives." World Bank.

Banerjee, Ghosh Sudeshna, et al. 2014. *The Power of Mine: A Transformative Opportunity for Sub-Saharan Africa.* Washington: World Bank.

Barry, Ken and Oji Adoh. 2021. "Private equity in Africa: Trends and opportunities
in 2021." White & Case. https://www.whitecase.com/insight-our-thinking/private-
equity-africa-trends-and-opportunities-2021#:~:text=The%20International%20
Energy%20Agency%20estimates,a%20rising%20proportion%20from%20PE.

Barry, Kenneth, and Ndidi Eseonu. 2017. "Private Equity in Africa: Emerging Trends."
Capital Markets in Africa. https://www.capitalmarketsinafrica.com/private-equity-
in-africa-emerging-trends/.

Basov, Vladimir. 2015. "The Chinese Scramble to Mine in Africa." *Mining,* December 15.
https://www.mining.com/feature-chinas-scramble-for-africa/.

Bekaert, Geert, and Campbell R. Harvey. 1997. "Emerging Market Volatility." *Journal
of Financial Economics* 43, no. 1: 29–77. https://doi.org/10.1016/S0304-405X(96)
00889-6.

Benton, Dale. 2018. "South Africa Mining Industry Prepared for R220 Billion Investment in 2018." *Mining Digital,* May 17. https://www.miningglobal.com/supply-
chain-and-operations/south-africa-mining-industry-prepared-r220-billion-
investment-2018.

Bermúdez-Lugo, Omayra. 2016. "The Mineral Industry of Sierra Leone." In *2013 Minerals Yearbook*. Washington: US Geological Survey. https://d9-wret.s3.us-west-2. amazonaws.com/assets/palladium/production/mineral-pubs/country/2013/myb3-2013-sl.pdf.

Bernard, Pierre-Ignace, Kweilin Ellingrud, Jonathan Godsall, et al. 2020. "The Future of Life Insurance: Reimagining the Industry for the Decade Ahead." https://www. mckinsey.com/industries/financial-services/our-insights/the-future-of-life-insurance-reimagining-the-industry-for-the-decade-ahead.

Besta, Shankar. 2020. "Top Five Gold Mining Countries of Africa from Ghana to Burkina Faso." NS Energy. https://www.nsenergybusiness.com/news/top-gold-mining-countries-africa/.

Betterboards Admin. 2023. "Governance Challenges in Africa." https://better-boards. com/governance-challenges-in-africa/.

Beyers, Nichola, Karien Scribante, and Jeremy Gray. 2020. "How Are Insurance Regulators in Sub-Saharan Africa Being Affected by, and Responding to, COVID-19?" *FSD Africa*, August. https://www.fsdafrica.org/wp-content/uploads/2020/08/ Insurance-regulators-COVID-19-28.08.20.pdf.

———. 2022. "Insurance Regulators' Response to COVID-19: Learnings on Efficacy." *Cenfri*, March. https://www.fsdafrica.org/wp-content/uploads/2022/05/Insurance-regulators-response-to-COVID-19_March-2022.pdf.

Beyers, Nichola, Jeremy Gray, Kate Rinehart, et al. 2018a. "The Role of Insurance in Inclusive Growth: Ghana in Brief." *Cenfri*, December. https://cenfri.org/wp-content/ uploads/2019/02/The-role-of-insurance-in-inclusive-growth_-Ghana-in-brief-Note-2.pdf.

———.2018b. "The Role of Insurance for Inclusive Growth: Ghana Diagnostic." *Cenfri*, December. https://cenfri.org/wp-content/uploads/2019/02/The-role-of-insurance-in-inclusive-growth_-Ghana-diagnostic.pdf.

Blommestein, Hans J., and Greg Horman. 2007. "Government Debt Management and Bond Markets In Africa." *Financial Market Trends* 2007, no. 1 (2007): 217–244.

Bloom, David, and David Canning. 2008. "Population Health and Economic Growth." Commission on Growth and Development, Working Paper 24. https://documents1. worldbank.org/curated/en/599491468151504321/pdf/475880NWP0REPL101 PUBLIC10gcwp024web.pdf.

Bloom, David E., David Canning, Rainer Kotschy, Klaus Prettner, and Johannes Schünemann. 2019. "Health and Economic Growth: Reconciling the Micro and Macro Evidence." National Bureau of Economic Research Working Paper No. 26003.

Bloomberg. 2020. "Africa's Largest Pay-TV Firm to Add Sport to Streaming Service." https://www.bloomberg.com/news/articles/2020-07-07/africa-s-largest-pay-tv-firm-to-add-sport-to-streaming-service.

Bluestorage. No date. "CanalOlympia, Where Culture Vibrates in Africa !" https://blue-storage.com/en/our-references/the-canal-olympia-concept/.

Bonsundy-O'Bryan, Tom, and Josefina Bonsundy-O'Bryan. 2024. "It's Time to Invest in the African Creatives Shaping the Trends." Atlantic Council. https://www.atlantic

council.org/blogs/africasource/its-time-to-invest-in-the-african-creatives-shaping-global-trends/.

Bos, Jean-Michel. 2023. "Africa Drives Global Urbanization." *DW*, May 17. https://www.dw.com/en/africa-drives-global-urbanization/a-65653428.

Bouchene, Lyes, Kartik Jayaram, Adam Kendall, and Ken Somers. 2021. "Africa's Green Manufacturing Crossroads: Choices for A Low-Carbon Industrial Future." McKinsey Sustainability. https://www.mckinsey.com/capabilities/sustainability/our-insights/africas-green-manufacturing-crossroads-choices-for-a-low-carbon-industrial-future.

Boughin, Jacques, Musta Chironga, Georges Desvaux, Tenbite Ermias, et al. 2016. "Lions on the Move II: Realizing the Potential of Africa's Economies." McKinsey Global Institute. https://www.mckinsey.com/featured-insights/middle-east-and-africa/lions-on-the-move-realizing-the-potential-of-africas-economies.

Breedon, Robert. 2016. "Maximizing the Return on Healthcare Investment in Africa." Gowling WLG International Limited. https://gowlingwlg.com/en/insights-resources/articles/2016/maximising-the-return-on-healthcare-investment-in/.

Brightmore, Daniel. 2020. "Ghana Beats South Africa to Continent's Gold Production Crown." *Mining Digital*, May 17. https://www.miningglobal.com/automation-and-ai/ghana-beats-south-africa-continents-gold-production-crown.

Brixi, Hana, Rawlings, Laura B. Rawlings, and Elizabeth Koechlein. 2021. "Unleashing Women and Girls' Human Capital: A Game Changer for Africa." International Monetary Fund. https://www.imf.org/en/Publications/fandd/issues/2021/12/Africa-Unleashing-Women-Girls-Human-Capital.

Broadband Commission Working Group on Broadband for All. 2019. "Connecting Africa Through Broadband: A Strategy for Doubling Connectivity by 2021 and Reaching Universal Access by 2030." https://www.broadbandcommission.org/Documents/working-groups/DigitalMoonshotforAfrica_Report.pdf.

Brown, T. J., N. E. Idoine, C. E. Wrighton, et al. 2019. "World Mineral Production 2014–2018." Keyworth, UK: British Geological Surve. https://nora.nerc.ac.uk/id/eprint/534466/1/WMP_2014_2018.pdf.

Bryan, Lowell, Michael Conway, Tineke Keesmaat, Sorcha McKenna, et al. 2010. "Strengthening Sub-Saharan Africa's Health Systems: A Practical Approach." McKinsey & Company. https://www.mckinsey.com/industries/healthcare/our-insights/strengthening-sub-saharan-africas-health-systems-a-practical-approach.

Buckingham, David, and Margaret Scanlon. 2000. "That Is Edutainment: Media, Pedagogy, and the Market Place." Paper presented to International Forum of Researchers on Young People and the Media, Sydney.

Building Design. 2021. "WA100 2021: The Big List." https://www.bdonline.co.uk/wa100-2021-the-big-list/5109915.article.

Bungane, Babalwa. 2015. "The Top 10 Issues Facing Mining Companies in 2016: Deloitte." *Mining Review Africa*, December 4. https://www.miningreview.com/news/the-top-10-issues-facing-mining-companies-in-2016-deloitte/.

Buse, Ribio Nzeza Bunketi. 2020. "COVID-19 and Culture in Africa: A Comparative Analysis of Economic Impact Studies." Arts Management Network—State of the Arts, August 27. https://www.artsmanagement.net/Articles/COVID-19-and-culture-in-Africa-A-comparative-analysis-of-economic-impact-studies,4184.

Business Wire. 2020. "Publishing of Books & Other Publications in South Africa—2019—ResearchAndMarkets.com." February 7. https://www.businesswire.com/news/home/20200207005345/en/Publishing-of-Books-Other-Publications-in-South-Africa---2019---ResearchAndMarkets.com.

———. 2023. "South Africa TV Broadcasting Markets, Forecasts, Competition & Opportunities, 2018–2023 & 2024–2028: Pay TV Subscribers and Local Content Driving Market Expansion Amidst Challenges from Piracy—ResearchAndMarkets.com." September 8. https://www.businesswire.com/news/home/20230908025941/en/South-Africa-TV-Broadcasting-Markets-Forecasts-Competition-Opportunities-2018-2023-2024-2028-Pay-TV-Subscribers-and-Local-Content-Driving-Market-Expansion-Amidst-Challenges-from-Piracy---ResearchAndMarkets.com#:~:text=According%20to%20MultiChoice%20Group%20Ltd,in%20South%20Africa%2C%20in%202022.

Byaruhanga, Janet. 2020. "How Africa Can Manufacture to Meet Its Own Pharmaceutical Needs." *Africa Renewal*, September 4. https://www.un.org/africarenewal/magazine/september-2020/how-africa-can-manufacture-meet-its-own-pharmaceutical-needs#:~:text=A percent20pooled percent20procurement percent20mechanism percent20will,Local percent20Pharmaceutical percent20Production percent20(LPP).

Calderon, Cesar, Albert G. Zeufack, Gerard Kambou, et al. 2020. "Africa's Pulse, no. 22, October: An Analysis of Issues Shaping Africa's Economic Future." World Bank, October 7.

Campbell, Keith. 2013. "China's Interest in Africa Picking Up as Its Economy Recovers." *Mining Weekly*, February 22. https://www.miningweekly.com/article/chinas-interest-in-africa-picking-up-as-its-economy-recovers-2013-02-22-1.

Cassim, Ziyad, Stewart Goodman, and Agesan Rajagopaul. 2019. "Putting the Shine Back into South African Mining: A Path to Competitiveness and Growth." McKinsey & Company. https://www.mckinsey.com/~/media/McKinsey/Featured%20Insights/Middle%20East%20and%20Africa/Putting%20the%20shine%20back%20into%20South%20African%20mining/McK-Putting-the-shine-back-into-South-African-mining-A-path-to-competitiveness-and-growth.pdf.

Cavallito, Matteo. 2022. "Deforestation in the Congo Basin Is Growing at an Alarming Rate." Re Soil Foundation. https://resoilfoundation.org/en/environment/deforestation-congo-basin/#:~:text=During percent2021 percent2C percent20the percent20-Congo percent20Basin,in percent20a percent2012 percent2Dmonth percent20period.

Center for Global Development. 2012. "Africa: Exodus of Doctors, Why Rwanda's Story Is Different (AllAfrica)." https://www.cgdev.org/article/africa-exodus-doctors-why-rwandas-story-different-allafrica.

Chamber of Mines of Namibia. 2016. "Annual Review 2016." https://chamberofmines. org.na/wp-content/uploads/2020/06/2016-Chamber_of_Mines_Annual_Review_ Web_Final.pdf.

Chand, Smriti. No date. "7 Most Influential Factors Affecting Foreign Trade." http:// www.yourarticlelibrary.com/foreign-trade/7-most-influential-factors-affecting- foreign-trade/5938." *Your Article Library.* https://www.yourarticlelibrary.com/ foreign-trade/7-most-influential-factors-affecting-foreign-trade/5938.

Charles, Innocent. 2022. "The Guide to Data Strategy for African Businesses." Neurotech Africa. https://blog.neurotech.africa/the-guide-to-data-strategy-for- african-businesses/.

Chatora, Rufaro. 2003. "An Overview of the Traditional Medicine Situation in the African Region." *African Health Monitor* 4, no. 1: 4–7.

Chen, Wenjie, David Dollar, and Heiwai Tang. 2015. "Why Is China Investing in Africa? Evidence from the Firm Level." The World Bank Economic Review, 32(3), 2018, 610–632 doi: 10.1093/wber/lhw049.

Chen, Wenjie, Athene Laws, and Nico Valckx. 2024. "Harnessing Sub-Saharan Africa's Critical Mineral Wealth." https://www.imf.org/en/News/Articles/2024/04/29/cf- harnessing-sub-saharan-africas-critical-mineral-wealth.

Chen, Wenjie, and Roger Nord. 2018. "Reassessing Africa's Global Partnerships." In *Foresight Africa 2018*, Brookings. https://www.brookings.edu/research/reassessing- africas-global-partnerships/.

Chordia, Tarun, Richard Roll, and Avanidhar Subrahmanyam. 2008. "Liquidity and Market Efficiency." *Journal of Financial Economics* 87, no. 2: 249–68.

Chuhan-Pole, Punam, Andrew L. Dabalen, and Bryan Christopher Land. 2017. "*Mining in Africa: Are Local Communities Better Off?*" Africa Development Forum Series. Washington: World Bank. https://openknowledge.worldbank.org/bitstream/handle/ 10986/26110/9781464808197.pdf?sequence=6&isAllowed=y.

Cirisano, Tatiana. 2020. "A&R In Africa: The Next Wave Of Superstars." Billboard. https://www.billboard.com/pro/africa-next-wave-superstars-ar-trend/.

Clausen, B. Lily. 2015. "Taking on the Challenge of Healthcare in Africa." Stanford Business. https://www.gsb.stanford.edu/insights/taking-challenges-health-care- africa.

Climate Policy Initiative. 2022. "The State of Climate Finance in Africa: Climate Finance Needs of African Countries." https://www.climatepolicyinitiative.org/wp- content/uploads/2022/06/Climate-Finance-Needs-of-African-Countries-1.pdf.

Coca-Cola Company. 2021. "RAIN Marks a Milestone: Replenish Africa Initiative Positively Impacts 6 Million Lives." https://www.coca-colacompany.com/media- center/rain-marks-6-million-milestone.

Coetzee, Zihné, Henri Bezuidenhout, and Gabriel Mhonyera. 2020. "Effective Strat- egies Followed by Multinational Enterprises Expanding into Africa." *Journal of Economic and Financial Sciences* 13, no. 1.

Collins, Daryl, and Mark Abrahamson. 2006. "Measuring the Cost of Equity in African Financial Markets." *Emerging Markets Review* 7, no. 1: 67–81.

Collins, Tom. 2022. "Private Capital Flow into Africa More Than Doubled from 2020 to 2021." *Quartz*, April 25. https://qz.com/africa/2158408/private-capital-flow-into-africa-more-than-doubled-from-2020-to-2021.

Conversation. 2021. "African Countries Must Muscle Up Their Support and Fill Massive R&D Gap." https://theconversation.com/african-countries-must-muscle-up-their-support-and-fill-massive-randd-gap-161024.

Conway, Michael, Tania Holt, Adam Sabow, and Irene Yuan Sun. 2019. "Should Sub-Saharan Africa Makes Its Own Drugs?" McKinsey & Company. https://www.mckinsey.com/industries/public-sector/our-insights/should-sub-saharan-africa-make-its-own-drugs.

Cooperative Logistics Network. 2021. "The African Continent Free Trade Agreement: How It Will Be a Game Changer for the Transportation and Logistics Industry." https://www.thecooperativelogisticsnetwork.com/blog/2021/05/25/theafrican-continent-free-trade-agreement-how-it-will-be-a-game-changer-for-the-transportation-and-logistics-industry/.

Corden, W. Max. 1984. "Booming Sector and Dutch Disease Economics: Survey and Consolidation." *Oxford Economic Papers* 36: 359–80. https://www.jstor.org/stable/2662669?seq=1.

Creamer, Martin. 2024. "$10-Billion Namibian Green Hydrogen Project Receives Major German Boost." *Mining Weekly*. https://www.miningweekly.com/article/10-billion-namibian-green-hydrogen-project-receives-major-german-boost-2024-03-22.

Dakora, Edward. 2019. "Fashionomics: Emerging Issues and Opportunities in Africa." Sol Plaatje University, PowerPoint presentation, March 13. https://www.google.com/url?sa=t&rct=j&q=&esrc=s&source=web&cd=&cad=rja&uact=8&ved=2ahUKEwiRg5rpq5XwAhXOAp0JHQkBBEwQFjARegQIChAD&url=https%3A%2F%2Fwww.southafricanculturalobservatory.org.za%2Fdownload%2F426&usg=AOvVaw3CIdlttzcF_fqBzSI6zcJ5.

Dana, Léo-Paul, and Vanessa Ratten. 2017. "International Entrepreneurship in Resource-Rich Landlocked African Countries." *Journal of International Entrepreneurship* 15: 416–35.

Dangote, Aliko. 2019. "Doing Business in Africa: My Experience." In *Foresight Africa 2019*, Brookings. https://www.brookings.edu/blog/africa-in-focus/2019/02/01/doing-business-in-africa-my-experience/.

Das, S. Udaibir, Richard Podpiera, and Nigel Davies. 2003. "Insurance and Issues in Financial Soundness." IMF Working Paper 2003/138. International Monetary Fund, July. https://www.imf.org/en/Publications/WP/Issues/2016/12/30/Insurance-and-Issues-in-Financial-Soundness-16524.

Deaton, Angus S., and Robert Tortora. 2015. "People in Sub-Saharan Africa Rate Their Health and Health Care Among Lowest in the World." *Health Aff. (Millwood)* 34: 519–27. doi: 10.1377/hlthaff.2014.0798.

Deloitte. 2005. "2005 Insurance Outlook: Top Ten Issues."

———. 2015. "State of Mining in Africa." https://www2.deloitte.com/content/dam/Deloitte/za/Documents/energy-resources/za_state_of_mining_africa_09022015.pdf.

———. 2016. "2016 Africa Private Equity Confidence Survey." https://www.africacapitaldigest.com/2017/11/26/private-equity-confidence-in-africa-up-deloitte-survey-finds/.

———. 2020. "Insurance Outlook Report 2020/21: East Africa." https://www2.deloitte.com/content/dam/Deloitte/ke/Documents/financial-services/EA%202020%20Insurance%20Outlook%20Report.pdf.

———. 2021. "The Future of the Creative Economy." https://www2.deloitte.com/content/dam/Deloitte/uk/Documents/technology-media-telecommunications/deloitte-uk-future-creative-economy-report-final.pdf.

———. 2024. "Tracking the Trends 2024." https://www2.deloitte.com/content/dam/Deloitte/global/Documents/Energy-and-Resources/us-trend-3.pdf.

Department of Planning, Monitoring, and Evaluation. 2013. "KPA 1: Strategic Management." In *KPA 1 Case Stories 2013.* https://www.dpme.gov.za/keyfocusareas/mpatSite/Case%20Studies/KPA%201%20CASE%20STORIES%202013.pdf.

Department of Sports, Arts, and Culture. 2020. "Strategic Plan 2020–2025." Republic of South Africa. https://www.dsac.gov.za/sites/default/files/2022-10/Strategic%20Plan%202020%20-%202025.pdf.

Department of Trade and Industry and Invest South Africa. 2020. "Investing in South Africa's Clothing, Textile, Footwear and Leather Sector." Invest South Africa. http://www.investsa.gov.za/wp-content/uploads/2021/03/FACT-SHEET_TEXTILES_2020.pdf.

Department of Trade, Industry, and Competition. No date. "Why Invest in South Africa?" Republic of South Africa. https://www.thedtic.gov.za/sectors-and-services-2/1-4-2-trade-and-export/investment-promotion/why-invest-in-sa/.

Devarakonda, S., and J. Chittineni. 2019. "Does Insurance Promote Economic Growth? Evidence from BRICS Countries." *Journal of Applied Management and Investments* 8, no. 3: 135–46.

Dickinson, Thomas. 2008. "Private Equity: An Eye for Investment under African Skies?" *Policy Insights* 60 (OECD Publishing), April. https://www.oecd-ilibrary.org/docserver/240271262764.pdf?expires=1719934976&id=id&accname=guest&checksum=9F5D70FB3A1D1726D47C23720EB1EB6F.

Digital TV Research. 2021a. "African OTT to generate $1.7 billion." https://digitaltvresearch.com/wp-content/uploads/2021/01/Africa-OTT-TV-and-Video-Forecasts-2021-TOC_toc_306.pdf.

———. 2021b. "Africa to reach 51 million pay TV subs." https://digitaltvresearch.com/wp-content/uploads/2021/01/Africa-Pay-TV-Forecasts-2021-TOC_toc_305.pdf.

Diop, Makhtar, Yuan Li, Li Yong, and Ato Ahmed Shide. 2015. "Africa Still Poised to Become the Next Great Investment Destination." World Bank, June 30. https://www.worldbank.org/en/news/opinion/2015/06/30/africa-still-poised-to-become-the-next-great-investment-destination.

Divakaran, Shanthi, Sam Schneider, and Patrick McGinnis. 2018. "Ghana Private Equity and Venture Capital Ecosystem Study." World Bank, Policy Research Working Paper 8617. https://papers.ssrn.com/sol3/papers.cfm?abstract_id=3269615.

Dollar, David. 2016. "China's Engagement with Africa From Natural Resources to Human Resources." Brookings Institution, July 13. https://www.brookings.edu/wp-content/uploads/2016/07/chinas-engagement-with-africa-david-dollar-july-2016.pdf.

Dr. Schanz, Alms & Company. 2016. "Africa Reinsurance Pulse 2016." https://faberconsulting.ch/files/faber/pdf-pulse-reports/Africa%20Reinsurance%20Pulse%202016_final.pdf.

———. 2019. "Africa Reinsurance Pulse 2019: An Annual Market Survey." https://faberconsulting.ch/files/faber/pdf-pulsereports/Africa_Reinsurance_Pulse_2019.pdf.

Dundee & Angus Chamber of Commerce. 2022. "E-Tariff Book and Rules of Origin Manual Key to African Trade." https://www.dundeeandanguschamber.co.uk/news/article/21251/e-tariff-book-and-rules-of-origin-manual-key-to-african-trade.

Dunning, J. H. 1977. "Trade, Location of Economic Activity and the MNE: A Search for an Eclectic Approach." In *The International Allocation of Economic Activity*, edited by B. Ohlin, P. O. Hesselborn, and P. M. Wijkman. London: Palgrave Macmillan. https://doi.org/10.1007/978-1-349-03196-2_38.

———. 1993. *Multinational Enterprises and the Global Economy*. Wokingham, UK: Addison Wesley.

Dupasquier, Chantal, and Patrick N. Osakwe, United Nations. Economic Commission for Africa, United Nations. Economic Commission for Africa. 2005. "Foreign Direct Investment in Africa: Performance, Challenges and Responsibilities." African Trade Policy Centre, no. 21. https://repository.uneca.org/handle/10855/12601.

EARF (East Africa Research Fund). 2018. "Economic Contributions of Artisanal and Small-Scale Mining in Kenya: Gold and Gemstones." https://assets.publishing.service.gov.uk/media/5a392bb8e5274a79051c9d7c/Kenya_case_study.pdf.

East African. 2015. "Small, Retail Investors to Gain Access to the Bond Market under New Rules." June 20. https://www.theeastafrican.co.ke/tea/business/small-retail-investors-to-gain-access-to-the-bond-market-under-new-rules--1337412.

EBCAM. 2020. "The Automotive Industry in Africa: Domestic Production for Local Job Creation and Safe, Climate-Friendly Mobility." https://www.ebcam.eu/images/EBCAM-AAAM_Automotive_Africa_-_Position_Paper.pdf.

ECMR. 2020. "Intra-African Foreign Direct Investment (FDI) and Employment: A Case Study." African Development Bank, Working Paper 335.

Ecofin Agency. 2024a. "African Nations Expand Guided Trade Initiative within the AfCFTA Framework." https://www.ecofinagency.com/public-management/1801-45152-african-nations-expand-guided-trade-initiative-within-the-afcfta-framework.

———. 2024b. "Private Equity in Africa Sees a Dip in Early 2024 at $3.5 Billion, Despite Previous Highs." https://www.ecofinagency.com/public-management/

1704-45405-private-equity-in-africa-sees-a-dip-in-early-2024-at-3-5-billion-despite-previous-highs.

Economist. 2000. "The Hopeless Continent." May 13. https://www.economist.com/weeklyedition/2000-05-13.

———. 2015. "A Sub-Saharan Scramble." January 22. https://www.economist.com/business/2015/01/22/a-sub-saharan-scramble.

EHS Africa Logistics. No date. "The 3 Trends Shaping the Future of Logistics in African Markets." https://ehsafricalogistics.com/the-3-trends-shaping-the-future-of-logistics-in-african-markets/.

EIB (European Investment Bank), Economics Department. 2021. "Finance in Africa: For Green, Smart, and Inclusive Private Sector Development." https://www.eib.org/attachments/publications/economic_report_finance_in_africa_2021_en.pdf.

EITI (Extractive Industries Transparency Initiative). 2020. "EITI Progress Report 2020." https://eiti.org/sites/default/files/attachments/eiti_progress_report_2020_english.pdf.

———. 2023. "Democratic Republic of the Congo 2020–2021 EITI Report." https://eiti.org/documents/democratic-republic-congo-2020-2021-eiti-report/.

Ekekwe, Ndubuisi. 2017. "How Digital Technology Is Changing Farming in Africa." *Harvard Business Review*, May 18. https://hbr.org/2017/05/how-digital-technology-is-changing-farming-in-africa.

Elliott, Lauri E., Hartmut Sieper, Nissi Ekpott, and Nwakego Eyisi. 2012. *Grow Rich in the New Africa: Navigating Business Opportunities on the Continent.* Brackenfell, South Africa: Conceptualee, Inc. at Smashwords.

Emery, James J., Melvin T. Spence, Jr. Louis T. Wells, Jr. and Timothy S. Buehrer. 2000. "Adminisrative Barriers to Foreign Investment." World Bank. https://documents1.worldbank.org/curated/es/681831468758122652/pdf/multi-page.pdf.

Enos, Michael. 2023. "Three New Categories Added for the 2024 Grammys: Best African Music Performance, Best Alternative Jazz Album & Best Pop Dance Recording." Grammys. https://www.grammy.com/news/three-new-categories-added-for-the-2024-grammys.

Erraji, Abdellah. 2023. "Moroccan Film Industry to Generate Record Profits in 2023." *Morocco World News*, June 27. https://www.moroccoworldnews.com/2023/06/356170/moroccan-film-industry-to-generate-record-profits-in-2023.

Essa, Al Sultan Tarek. 2016. "6 Reasons to Invest in Africa." World Economic Forum. https://www.weforum.org/agenda/2016/05/6-reasons-to-invest-in-africa/.

Esther, Glory Usoro. 2023. "More Screens, More Money for Nollywood." *Business Day*, January 20. https://businessday.ng/arts-and-life/article/more-screens-more-money-for-nollywood/#google_vignette.

ETK Group. 2021. "Identifying the Key Challenges of Doing Business in Africa." https://www.etkgroup.co.uk/identifying-the-key-challenges-of-doing-business-in-africa/.

Euromonitor International. 2021. "Apparel and Footwear in Nigeria." https://www. euromonitor.com/apparel-and-footwear-in-nigeria/report.

Exchange. 2023. "Investing in Africa's Human Capital." *Further Africa*, April 24. https://furtherafrica.com/2023/04/24/investing-in-africas-human-capital/.

Export.gov. 2019a. "Healthcare: Medical Devices and Pharmaceuticals." In *South Africa: Country Commercial Guide,* Washington: International Trade Administration. https://www.trade.gov/country-commercial-guides/south-africa-healthcare-medical-devices-and-pharmaceuticals.

EY (Ernst & Young). 2014a. "African Oil and Gas: Driving Sustainable Growth."

———. 2014b. "EY's Attractiveness Survey: Africa 2014."

———. 2014c. "2014 Africa Attractiveness Survey."

———. 2015. "Cultural Times: The First Global Map of Cultural and Creative Industries." https://unesdoc.unesco.org/ark:/48223/pf0000235710.

———. 2016a. "Navigating Africa's Current Uncertainties." https://assets.ey.com/ content/dam/ey-sites/ey-com/en_za/topics/attractiveness/reports/ey-aar-2016-navigating-uncertainties.pdf.

———. 2016b. "Waves of Change Revisited: Insurance Opportunities in Sub-Saharan Africa."

———. 2018. "Top Ten Business Risks Facing Mining and Metals in 2019–2020." https://assets.ey.com/content/dam/ey-sites/ey-com/en_gl/topics/mining-metals/ mining-metals-pdfs/ey-top-10-business-risks-facing-mining-and-metals-in-2019-20_v2.pdf.

———. 2021. "Reset for Growth: Fast Forward." https://assets.ey.com/content/dam/ ey-sites/ey-com/en_za/topics/attractiveness/reports/ey-aar-reset-for-growth-final.pdf.

———. 2023. "A Pivot to Growth." https://assets.ey.com/content/dam/ey-sites/ey-com/ en_za/topics/attractiveness/africa-attractiveness-2023/graphics/new-graphics/ ey-com-en-za-2023-ey-africa-attractiveness-report-nov.pdf.

European Investment Bank. 2021. "Finance in Africa: for Green, Smart and Inclusive Private Sector Development." https://www.eib.org/attachments/publications/ economic_report_finance_in_africa_2021_en.pdf.

Faber Consulting. 2020. "Africa Insurance Pulse: The Digitization of Africa's Insurance Markets." https://faberconsulting.ch/files/faber/pdf-pulse-reports/Africa_Insurance_ Pulse_e_2020_WEB_FINAL.pdf.

Fashion Revolution and British Council. 2021. "An Evaluation of Made in Rwanda: A Policy Dialogue on Standards, Quality and Sustainability." https://issuu.com/ fashionrevolution/docs/made_in_rwanda_policy_dialogue.

Fauozi, Adil. 2024. "Morocco's Aviation Industry Aiming to Become Africa's Manufacturing Hub." *Morocco World News*, April 25. https://www.moroccoworldnews. com/2024/04/362298/moroccos-aviation-industry-aiming-to-become-africas-manufacturing-hub.

Fayomi, Oluyemi O. 2015. "Transanational and Integrative Cultural Roles of Nollywood Entertainment Media in West Africa: The Case Study of Benin Republic and Ghana." *International Journal of International Relations, Media and Mass Communication Studies* 1, no. 1: 34–41. https://www.eajournals.org/wp-content/uploads/Transnational-and-Integrative-Cultural-Roles-of-Nollywood-Entertainment-Media-in-West-Africa1.pdf.

Fingar, Courtney. 2015. Foreign Direct Investment in Africa Surges. *Financial Times*, May 19. https://www.ft.com/content/79ee41b6-fd84-11e4-b824-00144feabdc0.

Fofack, Hippolyte. 2020. "Making the AfCFTA Work for 'the Africa We Want.'" Brookings. https://www.brookings.edu/articles/making-the-afcfta-work-for-the-africa-we-want/.

———. 2024. "The Future of African Trade in the AfCFTA Era." Brookings. https://www.brookings.edu/articles/the-future-of-african-trade-in-the-afcfta-era/.

Ford, Neil. 2024. "Simandou: Is Africa's biggest mining project finally ready to go?" African Business. https://african.business/2024/02/resources/simandou-is-africas-biggest-mining-project-finally-ready-to-go.

Fourrage, Ludo. 2024. "Inside Nairobi, Kenya's Thriving Tech Hub: Startups and Success Stories." *Nucamp*, June 5, 2024. https://www.nucamp.co/blog/coding-bootcamp-kenya-iken-inside-nairobi-kenyas-thriving-tech-hub-startups-and-success-stories.

Fox, Louise, and Landry Signé. 2022. "Technology and the Future of Jobs in Africa." Brookings. https://www.brookings.edu/articles/technology-and-the-future-of-jobs-in-africa/.

Freire, Clovis, and Anja Slany. 2023. "Realizing Product Diversification for Structural Change in African Countries." UNCTAD, Working Paper 5. https://unctad.org/publication/realizing-product-diversification-structural-change-african-countries.

Fritz, Thomas, Mark Pellerin, Leopold Zangemesiter, and Christopher Sohn. 2023. "Investment in Clean Energy Startup Booming." *Oliver Wyman*, May. https://www.oliverwyman.com/our-expertise/insights/2023/may/investment-in-clean-energy-startups-is-booming.html.

Frost & Sullivan. 2016. "African Pharmaceuticals Market Forecast 2020: Assessing Market Potential with a Focus on Kenya and Nigeria."

FurtherAfrica. 2022. "African Countries with the Highest Number of Mobile Phones." https://furtherafrica.com/2022/07/19/african-countries-with-the-highest-number-of-mobile-phones/.

Fusacchia, Ilaria, Jean Balié, and Luca Salvatici. 2022. "The AfCFTA Impact on Agricultural and Food Trade: A Value-Added Perspective." *European Review of Agricultural Economics* 49, no. 1: 237–84.

Gachara, George. 2020. "Policymakers Must Nurture Africa's Creative Economy." *African Business*, November 20. https://african.business/2020/11/trade-investment/policymakers-must-nurture-africas-creative-economy.

Galma, Kulé. 2022. "Here's How African Leaders Can Close the Climate Finance Gap." World Economic Forum. https://www.weforum.org/agenda/2022/11/heres-how-leaders-close-climate-finance-gap/.

Gamache, Lauren, Alexander Hammer, and Lin Jones. 2013. "China's Trade and Investment Relationship with Africa." *USITC Executive Briefings on Trade*, April. https://www.usitc.gov/publications/332/2013-04_China-Africa%28Gamache HammerJones%29.pdf.

Gavi Vaccine Alliance. 2022. "Expanding Sustainable Vaccine Manufacturing in Africa; Priorities for Support." https://www.gavi.org/news-resources/knowledge-products/expanding-sustainable-vaccine-manufacturing-africa-priorities-support.

Gbadamosi, Nosmot. 2020. "Is It Time to Repatriate Africa's Looted Art?" *Foreign Policy*, July 28. https://foreignpolicy.com/2020/07/28/time-repatriate-africa-looted-art-artifacts-cultural-heritage-benin-bronzes-nigeria-ghana-europe-british-museum/.

Gelb, Alan, et al. 1988. *Oil Windfalls: Blessing or Curse?* Oxford University Press. http://documents1.worldbank.org/curated/en/536401468771314677/pdf/296570 paper.pdf.

Ghana Business News. 2017. "Mining Sector Contributes GH¢1.6b to Ghana's Revenue in 2016." February 20. https://www.ghanabusinessnews.com/2017/02/20/mining-sector-contributes-gh%C2%A21-6b-to-ghanas-revenue-in-2016/.

Global Business Reports and Mining Indaba. 2019. "The Official Mining in Africa Country Investment Guide." https://www.gbreports.com/files/pdf/_2019/MACIG_2019_-_Web_Version.pdf.

Global HIV Prevention Coalition. 2023. "HIV Prevention: From Crisis to Opportunity." UNAIDS. https://www.unaids.org/sites/default/files/media_asset/2023-global-hiv-prevention-coalition-scorecards-key-findings_en.pdf.

Global Trade Staff. 2018. "Hapag-Lloyd Invests in Growing East African Market." *GlobalTrade*, September 12. https://www.globaltrademag.com/hapag-lloyd-invests-in-growing-east-african-market/.

Goedde, Lutz, Amanda Ooko-Ombaka, and Gillian Pais. 2019. "Winning in Africa's Agricultural Market." McKinsey & Company. https://www.mckinsey.com/industries/agriculture/our-insights/winning-in-africas-agricultural-market.

Goodfellow, Melanie. "Vivendi's Canal+ Group Makes Move To Acquire African Entertainment Giant MultiChoice." Deadline, February 1. https://deadline.com/2024/02/vivendi-canal-plus-group-acquire-african-entertainment-multichoice-1235810717/.

Google and IFC (International Finance Corporation). 2020. "E-conomy Africa 2020— Africa's $180 Billion Internet Economy Future." https://www.ifc.org/content/dam/ifc/doc/mgrt/e-conomy-africa-2020.pdf.

Gopaldas, Ronak. 2021. "Unlocking Africa's Capital Markets." Nanyang Technological University. https://www.ntu.edu.sg/cas/news-events/news/details/unlocking-africa-s-capital-markets#:~:text=Africa's percent20capital percent20markets percent20remain percent20concentrated, percent2C percent20Libya percent2C percent20 Rwanda percent20and percent20Seychelles.

Gorodnichenko, Yuriy, and Monika Schnitzer. 2013. "Financial Constraints and Innovation: Why Poor Countries Don't Catch Up." *Journal of the European Economic association* 11, no. 5: 1115–52.

Gouda, N. Hebe, Fiona Charlson, Katherine Sorsdahl, Sanam Ahmadzada, et al. 2019. "Burden of Non-communicable Diseases in Sub-Saharan Africa, 1990–2017: Results from the Global Burden of Disease Study 2017." *The Lancet Global Health* 7, no. 10: e1375–87. https://www.sciencedirect.com/science/article/pii/S2214109X19303742.

Gray, Alex. 2016. "African Farmers Need Investment—but These 6 Factors Stand in the Way." *World Economic Forum*, May 2. https://www.weforum.org/agenda/2016/05/6-challenges-to-investing-in-african-farmers/.

Grigorov, V. 2009. "Healthcare in Africa." *Cardiovascular Journal of Africa* 20, no. 5: 275–77. https://www.ncbi.nlm.nih.gov/pmc/articles/PMC3721597/#R05.

GroConsult. 2024. "Ghana Stock Exchange Reaches Record GH¢80 Billion Market Capitalization." https://groconsult.com/ghana-stock-exchange-reaches-record-gh%C2%A280billion/.

GSMA. 2020. "The Mobile Economy Sub-Saharan Africa 2020." https://www.gsma.com/mobileeconomy/wp-content/uploads/2020/09/GSMA_MobileEconomy2020_SSA_Eng.pdf.

Gudyanga, Francis. 2020. *Minerals in Africa: Opportunities for the Continent's Industrialisation.* London: Taylor & Francis.

Gvozdanovic, Igor, and Justice Seth Baning Osafo. 2016. "Challenges of Frontier Stock Markets with Low Liquidity: A Case Study of Ghana Stock Exchange." *International Journal of Economics & Management Sciences* 5, no. 4: 1–7. https://pdfs.semanticscholar.org/ae0f/ce62a69c0615a19557103ab99d6b468dd91e.pdf.

Gwenge, Sosten, and Ratnakar Adhikari. 2021. "Why Foreign Direct Investment Is Key to Africa's Sustainable Recovery." World Economic Forum, August 19. https://www.weforum.org/agenda/2021/08/foreign-direct-investment-key-africa-sustainable-recovery/.

Gyimah-Boadi, E., Landry Signé, and Josephine Appiah-Nyamekye Sanny. 2020. "US Foreign Policy toward Africa: An African Citizen Perspective." Brookings. https://www.brookings.edu/blog/africa-in-focus/2020/10/23/us-foreign-policy-toward-africa-an-african-citizen-perspective/.

Gylfason, Thorvaldur, Tryggvi Thor Herbertsson, and Gylfi Zoega. 1999. "A Mixed Blessing: Natural Resources and Economic Growth." *Macroeconomic Dynamics* 3, no. 2: 204–25.

Habte, Million, and Dirk Willem te Velde. 2023. "How Implementation Committees Are Moving the African Free Trade Area from Talks to Action." World Economic Forum. https://www.weforum.org/agenda/2023/04/moving-from-talks-to-implementation-of-the-african-free-trade-area-through-national-implementation-committees/.

Hackman, Bryanne. 2021. "The New Age of Agro-processing in Africa." *Future Africa Forum*, May 13. https://futureafricaforum.org/the-new-age-of-agro-processing-in-africa/.

Hall, Matthew. 2020. "COVID-19: Could the Coronavirus Pandemic Accelerate Autonomous Mining?" *Mining Technology*, March 19. https://www.mining-technology.com/features/coronavirus-autonomous-mining-projects/.

Hammerschlag, Zara, Geoff Bick, and John Manuel Luiz. 2020. "The Internationalization of African Fintech Firms: Marketing Strategies for Successful Intra-Africa Expansion." *International Marketing Review* 37, no. 2: 299–317.

Hattingh, Damian, Acha Leke, and Bill Russo. 2017. "Lions (Still) on the Move: Growth in Africa's Consumer Sector." McKinsey & Company. https://www.mckinsey.com/~/media/McKinsey/Industries/Consumer%20Packaged%20Goods/Our%20Insights/Lions%20still%20on%20the%20move%20Growth%20in%20Africas%20consumer%20sector/Lions-still-on-the-move-Growth-in-Africas-consumer-sector.pdf.

Heiberg, Tanisha. 2020. "S.Africa to allow mines to operate at 50% capacity during lockdown." Reuters. https://www.reuters.com/article/business/finance/s-africa-to-allow-mines-to-operate-at-50-capacity-during-lockdown-idUSKBN21Y2LI/.

Heney, Paul. 2020. "Global R&D Investments Unabated in Spending Growth." *R&D World*. https://www.rdworldonline.com/global-rd-investments-unabated-in-spending-growth/.

Hill, Katie, Chris Mitchell, Zoë Karl-Waithaka, Mills Schenck, et al. 2022. "Strategies for Scaling Africa's Green Ventures." BCG Global. https://www.bcg.com/publications/2022/scaling-green-ventures-in-africa.

Hivos. 2018. *The Status of the Creative Economy in East Afrrica*. https://www.hivos.org/assets/2018/09/ubunifu_report_1.pdf.

Holt, Tania, Mehdi Lahrichi, Jean Mina, and Jorge Santos da Silva. 2015. "Insights into Pharmaceuticals and Medical Products: Africa, A Continent of Opportunity for Pharma and Patients." McKinsey & Company. https://www.mckinsey.com/~/media/mckinsey/industries/life%20sciences/our%20insights/africa%20a%20continent%20of%20opportunity%20for%20pharma%20and%20patients/pmp%20africa%20a%20continent%20of%20opportunity%20for%20pharma.pdf.

Honohan, Patrick, and Thorsten Beck. 2007. *Making Finance Work for Africa*. Washington: World Bank.

Hruby, Aubrey. 2018. "Getting Creative About Development." Atlantic Council. https://www.atlanticcouncil.org/wp-content/uploads/2019/09/Getting_Creative_About_Development_092418.pdf.

———. 2020. "Africa's Creative Industries Are Ripe for US Investment." *Foreign Policy*, September 22. https://foreignpolicy.com/2020/09/22/africas-creative-industries-are-ripe-for-u-s-investment/.

Human Rights Watch. 2024. "African Governments Falling Short on Healthcare Funding." https://www.hrw.org/news/2024/04/26/african-governments-falling-short-healthcare-funding.

iAfrica. 2019. "African Continental Free Trade Agreement: Will the SA Beef Industry Benefit?" https://www.bilaterals.org/?african-continental-free-trade-40206&utm_source=dlvr.it&utm_medium=facebook.

IDE-JETRO. 2009. "China in Africa: A Strategic Overview." https://www.ide.go.jp/library/English/Data/Africa_file/Manualreport/pdf/china_all.pdf.

IEA (International Energy Agency). 2019. "African Energy Outlook 2019." In *World Energy Outlook Special Report*. https://iea.blob.core.windows.net/assets/2f7b6170-d616-4dd7-a7ca-a65a3a332fc1/Africa_Energy_Outlook_2019.pdf.

———. 2021. "The Role of Critical Minerals in Clean Energy Transitions: Executive Summary." https://www.iea.org/reports/the-role-of-critical-minerals-in-clean-energy-transitions/executive-summary.

———. 2022. "Africa Energy Outlook 2022." https://www.iea.org/reports/africa-energy-outlook-2022/key-findings.

———. 2024. "World Energy Investment 2024." https://www.iea.org/reports/world-energy-investment-2024/africa.

IFPI (International Federation of the Phonographic Industry). 2016. "Global Music Report: State of the Industry Overview 2016.", 2016.

———. 2019. "Music Listening 2019." https://www.ifpi.org/wp-content/uploads/2020/07/Music-Listening-2019-1.pdf.

———. 2020. "Global Music Report: The Industry in 2019." https://www.ifpi.org/wp-content/uploads/2020/07/Global_Music_Report-the_Industry_in_2019-en.pdf.

IFPMA (International Federation of Pharmaceutical Manufacturers and Associations). 2023. "Supporting Africa's Health Ecosystem." https://www.ifpma.org/areas-of-work/supporting-africas-health-ecosystem/.

Iguisi, Osaru. 2014. "Indigenous Knowledge Systems and Leadership Styles in Nigerian Work Organizations." *International Journal of Research in Business and Social Science* 3: 1–13.

IHG. 2024. "IHG Hotels & Resorts Strengthens Portfolio in Egypt with Two New Crowne Plaza Signings." IHG Hotels & Resorts, May 28. https://www.ihgplc.com/en/news-and-media/news-releases/2024/ihg-hotels-resorts-strengthens-portfolio-in-egypt-with-two-new-crowne-plaza-signings.

IIPA (Indian Institute of Public Administration). 2018. "2018 IIPA Special 301 Report on Copyright Protection and Enforcement." https://www.iipa.org/files/uploads/2018/02/2018_SPECIAL_301.pdf.

———. 2021. "IIPA Special 301 Report on Copyright Protection and Enforcement." https://www.iipa.org/files/uploads/2021/01/2021SPEC301REPORT.pdf.

Ijjasz-Vasquez, Ede, Jamal Saghir, and Morgan Richmond. 2024. "Finance for Climate Adaptation in Africa Still Insufficient and Losing Ground." Brookings. https://www.brookings.edu/articles/finance-for-climate-adaptation-in-africa-still-insufficient-and-losing-ground/.

Invest Africa. 2024. "Investing in Women for Sustainable Growth in Africa." https://www.investafrica.com/insights-/investing-in-women-for-sustainable-growth-in-africa.

Imarc. 2024. "Africa Insurance Market Report by Type (Life Insurance, Non–Life Insurance), and Country 2024–2032." https://www.imarcgroup.com/africa-insurance-market.

Imasiku, Katundu, and Valeria M. Thomas. 2020. "The Mining and Technology Industries as Catalysts for Sustainable Energy Development." *Sustainability* 12, no. 24: 10410. https://www.mdpi.com/2071-1050/12/24/10410.

IndustriALL Global Union. 2020. "Sub Saharan Africa Automotive Sector: Potential to Boost Manufacturing and Create Decent Jobs." https://www.industriall-union. org/sub-sahara-africa-automotive-sector-potential-to-boost-manufacturing-and-create-decent-jobs.

Integrated African Health Observatory and World Health Organization. 2024. "Climate Change Is Impacting Health in Africa." https://files.aho.afro.who.int/ afahobckpcontainer/production/files/iAHO_Climate_change_in_health_Fact_ Sheet-April_2024.pdf.

Intergovernmental Forum on Mining, Minerals, Metals, and Sustainable Development. 2019. "Local Content Policies in the Mining Sector: Scaling Up Local Procurement." International Institute for Sustainable Development. https://www.iisd.org/system/ files/publications/local-content-policies-mining.pdf?q=sites/default/files/ publications/local-content-policies-mining.pdf.

———. 2020. "The Impact of COVID-19 on Employment in Mining." International Institute for Sustainable Development. https://www.iisd.org/system/files/publications/ covid-19-employment-mining-en.pdf.

International Finance Corporation. 2000. "The Business of Health in Africa." World Bank. https://documents1.worldbank.org/curated/en/878891468002994639/pdf/ 441430WP0ENGLI1an10110200801PUBLIC1.pdf.

———. 2007. "IFC and Partners to Mobilize Up to $1 Billion to Strengthen Private Health Care in Africa—New Report Sees Huge Demand for Investment over Next Decade." https://pressroom.ifc.org/all/pages/PressDetail.aspx?ID=21294.

———. 2016. "The Business of Health in Africa." https://www.unido.org/sites/default/ files/2016-01/IFC_HealthinAfrica_Final_0.pdf.

———. 2019. "Digital Skills in Sub-Saharan Africa: Spotlight on Ghana." https:// www.ifc.org/content/dam/ifc/doc/mgrt/digital-skills-report-web-es.pdf.

———. 2022. "IFC Study: $100 Billion in Climate Change Adaptation Investment Opportunities in Africa by 2040." https://pressroom.ifc.org/all/pages/PressDetail. aspx?ID=27270.

———. 2024a. "Digital Opportunities in African Businesses." https://www.ifc.org/en/ insights-reports/2024/digital-opportunities-in-african-businesses.

———. 2024b. "Leadway Assurance: Innovating the Insurance Industry." https://www. ifc.org/en/insights-reports/2024/leadway-assurance-innovating-the-insurance-industry.

———. No date. "Creative Industries." https://www.ifc.org/en/what-we-do/sector-expertise/creative-industries.

International Labour Organization. 2024. "Global Employment Trends for Youth 2024." https://www.ilo.org/media/583636/download.

International Monetary Fund. 2017. "The Informal Economy in Sub-Saharan Africa." In *Regional Economic Outlook: Restarting the Growth Engine*. Washington: International Monetary Fund. https://www.imf.org/-/media/Files/Publications/REO/ AFR/2017/May/pdf/sreo0517-chap3.ashx.

International Trade Administration. 2022. "Healthcare: Medical Devices." In *Kenya: Country Commercial Guide.* Washington: International Trade Administration. https://www.trade.gov/country-commercial-guides/kenya-healthcare-medical-devices.

———. 2024. "South Africa: Country Commercial Guide—Healthcare: Medical Devices and Pharmaceuticals." https://www.trade.gov/country-commercial-guides/south-africa-healthcare-medical-devices-and-pharmaceuticals.

———. No date–a. "Mozambique: Mining and Mineral Resources." https://www.privacyshield.gov/ps/article?id=Mozambique-Mining.

———. No date–b. "Healthcare Resource Guide - Morocco." *International Trade Administration.* https://www.trade.gov/healthcare-resource-guide-morocco.

Invest Africa. 2024. "5 Trends Shaping Africa's Mining Industry 2024." https://www.investafrica.com/insights-/5-trends-shaping-africas-mining-industry-in-2024.

InvestSA. 2020. "Investing in South Africa's Agro-processing Sector." Department of Trade and Industry, Republic of South Africa. http://www.investsa.gov.za/wp-content/uploads/2021/03/FACT-SHEET_AGRO-PROCESSING_2020.pdf.

Inyang, Benjamin James. 2008. "The Challenges of Evolving and Developing Management Indigenous Theories and Practices in Africa." *International Journal of Business and Management* 3.

Ipsos. 2018. "Ipsos Affluent Survey Africa 2018." https://www.ipsos.com/en-nl/press-release-affluent-africa-2018-how-digital-driving-media-growth-africa.

IRA. 2019. "Annual Insurance Market Report." Insurance Regulatory Authority of Uganda. https://ira.go.ug/cp/uploads/Insurance%20Market%20report%202019.pdf.

Irokosu, Wale. 2022. "3 Strategies for Overcoming the Challenges of Business Partnerships and Succession Planning in Africa." *Business Insider Africa*, June 2. https://africa.businessinsider.com/local/careers/3-strategies-for-overcoming-the-challenges-of-business-partnerships-and-succession/t3rsxjw.

Isaac, Nkechi. 2019. "Nigeria Moves to Revive Its Textile Industry." Alliance for Science. https://allianceforscience.cornell.edu/blog/2019/04/nigeria-moves-revive-textile-industry/.

Ishioro, Bernard O. 2013. "Stock Market Development and Economic Growth: Evidence from Zimbabwe." *Ekonomska misao i praksa* 22, no. 2: 343–60.

Jackson, Tom. 2021. "African Tech Startup Funding Passes $700M in Record-Breaking 2020." *Disrupt Africa*, January 21. https://disrupt-africa.com/2021/01/21/african-tech-startup-funding-passes-700m-in-record-breaking-2020/.

Jaiyeola, Temitayo. 2023. "World Bank links Nigeria's ICT Growth to High Data Consumption." *Punch*, July 4. https://punchng.com/world-bank-links-nigerias-ict-growth-to-high-data-consumption/.

Joffe, Avril. 2021. "COVID-19 and the African Cultural Economy: An Opportunity to Reimagine and Reinvigorate?" *Cultural Trends* 30, no. 1: 28–39.

Johns Hopkins School of Advanced International Studies. 2022. "Chinese FDI in Africa." China Africa Research Initiative. https://www.sais-cari.org/chinese-investment-in-africa.

Jones, D. Carla, Hermann A. Ndofor, and Mengge Li. 2022. "Chinese Economic Engagement in Africa: Implications for US Policy." Foreign Policy Research Institute, January 24. https://www.fpri.org/article/2022/01/chinese-economic-engagement-in-africa/.

Jun, Sang-Gyung, Achla Marathe, and Hany A. Shawky. 2003. "Liquidity and Stock Returns in Emerging Equity Markets." *Emerging Markets Review* 4, no. 1: 1–24.

Kabanda, Patrick. 2014. "The Creative Wealth of Nations: How the Performing Arts Can Advance Development and Human Progress." World Bank, Policy Research Working Paper 7118. Washington: World Bank. https://documents1.worldbank.org/curated/en/512131468147578042/pdf/WPS7118.pdf.

Kaseje, Dan. 2006. "Health Care in Africa: Challenges, Opportunities and an Emerging Model for Improvement." Woodrow Wilson International Center for Scholars. https://www.wilsoncenter.org/sites/default/files/media/documents/publication/Kaseje2.pdf.

Kasilo, Ossy M. J. 2003. "Enhancing Traditional Medicine Research and Development in the African Region." *African Health Monitor* 4, no. 1: 15–18.

Katrina, Manson. 2015. "GE and Philips Scan Africa Medical Market." *Financial Times*, March 5.

Katz, Brigit. 2017. "Africa's Largest Contemporary Art Museum Opens in Cape Town." *Smithsonian Magazine*, September 26. https://www.smithsonianmag.com/smart-news/africas-largest-contemporary-art-museum-opens-cape-town-180965018/.

Kazeem, Yomi. 2020. "Netflix Is Betting on Boosting Growth in Africa with Mobile-Only Subscriptions." *Quartz*, October 6. https://qz.com/africa/1913770/netflix-is-testing-mobile-only-plans-in-africa/.

Kearney, Melissa S., and Phillip B. Levine. 2019. "Early Childhood Education by Television: Lessons from Sesame Street." *American Economic Journal: Applied Economics* 11, no. 1: 318–50. https://www.aeaweb.org/articles?id=10.1257/app.20170300.

Kiel Institute for the World Economy. 2023. "Sovereign Debt in Africa: Large Interest Rate Differences across Creditors." https://www.ifw-kiel.de/publications/news/sovereign-debt-in-africa-large-interest-rate-differences-across-creditors/.

Kimenyi, Mwangi S., and Josephine Kibe. 2014. "Africa's Powerhouse" Brookings Institution, January 6. https://www.brookings.edu/articles/africas-powerhouse/.

Kirigia, Muthuri Joses, and Saidou Pathe Barry. 2008. "Health Challenges in Africa and the Way Forward." *International Archives of Internal Medicine* 1, no. 1. https://www.ncbi.nlm.nih.gov/pmc/articles/PMC2615747/#B6.

Koigi, Bob. 2021. "Africa Bets on Creative Sector." *AB Magazine*, July. https://abmagazine.accaglobal.com/global/articles/2021/jul/business/africa-bets-on-creative-sector.html.

Koto, Senyo Prosper. 2017. "Is Social Capital Important in Formal-Informal Sector Linkages?" *Journal of Developmental Entrepreneurship* 22, no. 2: 1–16.

KPMG. 2013. "Zambia: Country Mining Guide." https://assets.kpmg/content/dam/kpmg/pdf/2013/08/zambian-country-guide.pdf.

———. 2015. "Oil and Gas in Africa." https://assets.kpmg.com/content/dam/kpmg/za/pdf/Oil-and-Gas-sector-report-2015.pdf.

———. 2016a. "Africa in a Changing Global Environment." https://assets.kpmg.com/content/dam/kpmg/za/pdf/2017/03/foreign-direct-investment.pdf.

———. 2016b. "Financial Services: The South African Insurance Industry Survey 2016." https://assets.kpmg/content/dam/kpmg/pdf/2016/07/2016-Insurance-Survey-v2.pdf.

———. 2021. "Insurance in the Land of Gold." https://assets.kpmg.com/content/dam/kpmg/za/pdf/2021/insurance-in-the-land-of-gold.pdf.

Kuramo Capital Management. 2023. "Sovereign Debt in Africa: Large Interest Rate Differences Across Creditors." https://www.ifw-kiel.de/publications/news/sovereign-debt-in-africa-large-interest-rate-differences-across-creditors/.

Kuyoro, Mayowa, Acha Leke, Olivia White, Lola Woetzel, Kartik Jayaram, and Kendyll Hicks. 2023. "Reimagining Economic Growth in Africa: Turning Diversity into Opportunity." McKinsey Global Institute. https://www.mckinsey.com/mgi/our-research/reimagining-economic-growth-in-africa-turning-diversity-into-opportunity.

Kwablah, Edmund, and Anthony Amoah. 2022. "Foreign Direct Investment and Economic Growth in Sub-Saharan Africa: The Complementary Role of Economic Freedom and Financial Market Fragility." *Transnational Corporations Review* 14, no. 2: 127–39.

Kwakwa, Victoria. 2024. "Celebrating Water Day: Why Access to Clean Water Is Vital for Africa." World Bank blog. https://blogs.worldbank.org/en/africacan/celebrating-water-day--why-access-to-clean-water-is-vital-for-af.

Laing, Timothy. 2020. "The Economic Impact of the Coronavirus 2019 (COVID-2019): Implications for the Mining Industry." *Extractive Industries and Society* 7, no. 2: 580–82. https://www.sciencedirect.com/science/article/pii/S2214790X2030126X.

Lakmeeharan, Kannan, Qaizer Manji, Ronald Nyario, and Harald Poeltner. 2020. "Solving Africa's Infrastructure Paradox." McKinsey & Company. https://www.mckinsey.com/~/media/McKinsey/Industries/Capital%20Projects%20and%20Infrastructure/Our%20Insights/Solving%20Africas%20infrastructure%20paradox/Solving-Africas-infrastructure-paradox.pdf.

Landers, Clemence, and Nico Martinez. 2024. "Is Sub-Saharan Africa's Credit Crunch Really Over?" Center for Global Development. https://www.cgdev.org/blog/sub-saharan-africas-credit-crunch-really-over.

Lane, Andrew, and Riccardo Reggio. 2013. "Mining in Africa: How Inclusive Solutions Can Mitigate Risk." Deloitte. https://www2.deloitte.com/content/dam/Deloitte/us/Documents/strategy/us-consulting-mining-in-africa.pdf.

Léautier, Frannie. 2021. "Why Pharma Investors Are Looking at Africa 'with New Eyes." Also by Alison Buckholtz. International Finance Corporation. https://www.ifc.org/wps/wcm/connect/news_ext_content/ifc_external_corporate_site/news+and+events/news/cm-stories/pharma-investors-looking-at-africa-with-new-eyes-en.

Leith, J. C., and M. F. Lofchie. 1993. "The Political Economy of Structural Adjustment in Ghana." In Political and Economic Interactions in Economic Policy Reform: Evidence from Eight Countries, edited by R. H. Bates and A. O. Krueger. Cambridge, MA, US: Basil Blackwell.

Leke, Acha Susan Lund, Charles Roxburgh, and Arend van Wamelen. 2010. "What's Driving Africa's Growth." McKinsey & Company, June 1. https://www.mckinsey.com/featured-insights/middle-east-and-africa/whats-driving-africas-growth.

Lesmond, David A. 2005. "Liquidity of Emerging Markets." *Journal of Financial Economics* 77, no. 2: 411–52.

Lewis, Noah. 2020. "A Tech Company Engineered Drones to Deliver Vital COVID-19 Medical Supplies to Rural Ghana and Rwanda in Minutes." *Business Insider*, May 12. https://www.businessinsider.com/zipline-drone-coronavirus-supplies-africa-rwanda-ghana-2020-5.

Lobaugh, Kasey, Bobby Stephens, and Jeff Simpson. 2019. "The Consumer Is Changing, but Perhaps Not How You Think." *Deloitte Insights*, May 29. https://www2.deloitte.com/us/en/insights/industry/retail-distribution/the-consumer-is-changing.html.

Loots, Elsabe, and Alain Kabundi. 2012. "Foreign Direct Investment to Africa: Trends, Dynamics and Challenges." *South African Journal of Economic and Management Sciences*, 1.LuSe. No date. "Our Story." https://www.luse.co.zm/our-story/.

Maimbo, Samuel Munzele, Issa Faye, and Thouraya Triki. 2011. *Financing Africa: Through the Crisis and Beyond*. Washington: World Bank.

Manlan, Carl. 2019. "This Is the Key to Boosting Economic Growth in Africa." World Economic Forum. https://www.weforum.org/agenda/2019/05/investing-in-africans-health/.

Mansouri, Amine. 2024. "2024 Healthcare Predictions for Africa." IQVIA. https://www.iqvia.com/locations/middle-east-and-africa/blogs/2024/01/2024-healthcare-predictions-for-africa.

Manyika, James, Michael Chui, Jacques Bughin, Richard Dobbs, Peter Bisson and Alex Marrs. (2013). "Disruptive technologies - advances that will transform life, business and the global economy." McKinsey Global Institute. https://www.mckinsey.com/capabilities/mckinsey-digital/our-insights/disruptive-technologies.

Marshall, Alex. 2021. "Germany Sets Out Plans to Return Benin Bronzes." *New York Times*, April 30. https://www.nytimes.com/2021/04/30/arts/design/benin-bronzes-germany.html.

Masaba, R., G. Woelk, S. Siamba, J. Ndimbii, M. Ouma, J. Khaoya, A. Kipchirchir, B. Ochanda, and G. Okomo. 2023. "Antiretroviral Treatment Failure and Associated Factors Among People Living with HIV on Therapy in Homa Bay, Kenya: A Retrospective Study." *PLOS Glob Public Health*, March 2. doi: 10.1371/journal.pgph.0001007.

Maselle, Jared, Casius Darroux, Henry Jonathan, and Xu Fengju. 2015. "Challenges Faced by Dar-es-Salaam Stock Exchange Market in Tanzania." *Research Journal of Finance and Accounting* 4, no. 15.

Matland, Richard E. 1995. "Synthesizing the Implementation Literature: The Ambiguity-Conflict Model of Policy Implementation." *Journal of Public Administration Research and Theory* 5, no. 2: 145–74.

Matsika, Batanai. 2010. "A Closer Look at Zimbabwe's Mining Sector." *How We Made It in Africa*, September 10. https://www.howwemadeitinafrica.com/a-closer-look-at-zimbabwes-mining-sector/.

Maxfield, Sylvia. 2009. "Stock Exchanges in Low- and Middle-Income Countries." *International Journal of Emerging Markets* 4, no. 1: 43–55.

Mbaku, John M. 2020. "Good and Inclusive Governance Is Imperative for Africa's Future." Brookings. https://www.brookings.edu/research/good-and-inclusive-governance-is-imperative-for-africas-future/.

McBain, Will. 2021. "Morocco's Aerospace Ecosystem Faces Up to COVID-19." *African Business*, April 23. https://african.business/2021/04/energy-resources/moroccos-aerospace-ecosystem-faces-up-to-covid-19.

McKee, Alan, Christy Collis, Tanya Nitins, et al. 2014. "Defining Entertainment: An Approach." *Creative Industries Journal* 7, no. 2: 108–20. http://dx.doi.org/10.1080/17510694.2014.962932.

McKinsey & Company. 2010. "Africa's Path to Growth: Sector by Sector." https://www.mckinsey.com/featured-insights/middle-east-and-africa/africas-path-to-growth-sector-by-sector.

———. 2018. "Outperformers: High-Growth Emerging Economies and the Companies That Propel Them." https://www.mckinsey.com/~/media/mckinsey/industries/public%20and%20social%20sector/our%20insights/outperformers%20high%20growth%20emerging%20economies%20and%20the%20companies%20that%20propel%20them/mgi-outperformers-full-report-sep-2018.pdf.

———. 2020. "Lessons from the Past: Informing the Mining Industry's Trajectory to the Next Normal." https://www.mckinsey.com/industries/metals-and-mining/our-insights/lessons-from-the-past-informing-the-mining-industrys-trajectory-to-the-next-normal.

Mensah, Albert, Ishmail O. Mahiri, Obed Owusu, et al. 2015. "Environmental Impacts of Mining: A Study of Mining Communities in Ghana." *Applied Ecology and Environmental Sciences* 3, no. 3: 81–94.

Mgbolu, Charles. 2024. "Nigerian Content Creators' Battle Against Piracy." *TRT Afrika*, January 23. https://trtafrika.com/lifestyle/nigerian-content-creators-battle-against-piracy-16752575.

Michalowski, Tomasz. "Foreign direct investment in Sub-Saharan Africa and its effects on economic growth of the region." Working Papers Institute of International Business University of Gdañsk 2012, no. 31. https://ekonom.ug.edu.pl/web/download.php?OpenFile=970.

Milken Institute. 2021. "Interview Megan McDonald: COVID-19 and African Capital Markets, and What Lies Ahead?" https://milkeninstitute.org/video/megan-mcdonald-covid-african-capital-markets.

Minney, Tom. 2011. "Funds flows into African private equity – $1.5bn in 2010." *African Capital Market News*. https://africancapitalmarketsnews.com/funds-flows-into-african-private-equity-1-5bn-in-2010/.

Mo Ibrahim Foundation. 2024. "Financing Africa: Where Is the Money?" Mo Ibrahim Foundation. https://mo.ibrahim.foundation/sites/default/files/2024-06/2024-forum-report.pdf.

Mojela, Louisa, and Nontobeko Ndhlazi. 2024. "Investing in Africa: Investing in Women." Henley & Partners. https://www.henleyglobal.com/publications/africa-wealth-report-2024/investing-africa-investing-women.

Mold, Andrew, and Francis Mangeni. 2024. "How to Catalyze AfCFTA Implementation in 2024." Brookings. https://www.brookings.edu/articles/trade-and-regional-integration-foresight-africa-2024/.

Moodley, Lohini, Mayowa Kuyoro, Tania Holt, Acha Leke, Anu Madgavkar, Mekala Krishnan, and Folakemi Akintayo. 2019. "The Power of Parity: Advancing Women's Equality in Africa." McKinsey Global Institute. https://www.mckinsey.com/featured-insights/gender-equality/the-power-of-parity-advancing-womens-equality-in-africa.

Moore, Elaine. 2012. "Civets, Brics and the Next 11." *Financial Times*, June 8. Mordor Intelligence. No date. "Africa Gaming Market-Growth, Trends, COVID-19 Impact, and Forecasts (2021–2026)." https://www.mordorintelligence.com/industry-reports/africa-gaming-market/market-size.

Moses, Oyintarelado. 2024. "10 Charts to Explain 22 Years of China-Africa Trade, Overseas Development Finance and Foreign Direct Investment." BU Global Development Policy Center, April 2. https://www.bu.edu/gdp/2024/04/02/10-charts-to-explain-22-years-of-china-africa-trade-overseas-development-finance-and-foreign-direct-investment/.

Moudio, Rebecca. 2013. "Nigeria's Film Industry: A Potential Gold Mine?" *Africa Renewal*, May. https://www.un.org/africarenewal/magazine/may-2013/nigeria's-film-industry-potential-gold-mine.

MTN Group Limited. 2020. "Sustainability Report for the Year Ended 31 December 2019." https://group.mtn.com/wp-content/uploads/2020/03/MTN-Sustainability-report.pdf.

Mulupi, Dinfin. 2012. "Penda Health Raises Nearly $100,000 for Expansion." *Ventures Africa*, August 14. https://venturesafrica.com/kenyan-clinic-raises-nearly-100000-for-expansion/.

Munyati, Chido, and Signé, Landry. "In Africa's Free Trade Area, Investment in Pharmaceuticals Means Impact and Profit." World Economic Forum, March 28.

Mutu, Kari. 2020. "Kenya's First Online Art Auction Almost Sells Out, Brings Big Relief to Industry." *East African*, December 3. https://www.theeastafrican.co.ke/tea/magazine/kenya-first-online-art-auction-almost-sells-out-3215518.

Mwaniki, Charles. 2023. "Kenya Outshines Her Neighbours in PE and Venture Capital Deals." *Business Daily*, September 13. https://www.businessdailyafrica.com/bd/

markets/capital-markets/kenya-outshines-her-neighbours-in-pe-and-venture-capital-deals--4367782.

Nation. 2016. "Nine Out of 10 Private Equity Firms Eyeing East Africa Prefer Kenya." June 29.

Naspers. 2020. "Integrated Annual Report 2020." https://www.naspers.com/~/media/Files/N/Naspers-Corp-V2/investor/results-reports-events/results-reports-and-events-archive/financial-results/full-year/2020/2020-annual-report.pdf.

Ncube, Gail, and Kapingura Forget Mingiri. 2015. "Stock Market Integration in Africa: The Case of the Johannesburg Stock Exchange and Selected African Countries." *International Business & Economics Research Journal* 14, no. 2: 367. https://core.ac.uk/download/pdf/268107974.pdf.

Ndukwe, Ijeoma. 2020. "Artisan Luxury's New Focus: Nigeria." *Vogue Business*, August 21. https://www.voguebusiness.com/fashion/artisan-luxurys-new-focus-nigeria.

Ndung'u, Njuguna, and Landry Signé. 2020. "The Fourth Industrial Revolution and Digitization Will Transform Africa into a Global Powerhouse." In *Foresight Africa 2020*, Brookings. https://www.brookings.edu/research/the-fourth-industrial-revolution-and-digitization-will-transform-africa-into-a-global-powerhouse/.

Ndwaru, James. 2022. "Africa: The African Diaspora Can Help Chart a Solid Economic Growth Path." *AllAfrica*, October 29. https://allafrica.com/stories/202210290050.html.

Network Readiness Index. 2023a. "Mauritius." https://download.networkreadiness index.org/reports/countries/2023/mauritius.pdf.

———. 2023b. "Kenya." https://networkreadinessindex.org/country/kenya/.

News24. 2021. "Jobs in South Africa's Film Industry Cut by 60% during Lockdown—with Little Gov't Relief." https://www.news24.com/news24/bi-archive/jobs-in-south-africa-film-industry-cut-by-covid-19-lockdown-2021-9.

Nex Media. 2023. "Africa's Entertainment and Media Industry Forecast to Grow Despite Cost-of-Living Challenges." https://www.nexmedia.co.za/2023/11/10/africas-entertainment-and-media-industry-forecast-to-grow-despite-cost-of-living-challenges/#:~:text=Kenya's%20E%26M%20market%20saw%20revenue,fastest%2Drising%20segments%20in%20Kenya.

Nielsen. 2014. "Why Marketing to Consumers, Not the Masses, Is the Key to Brand Success in Africa." https://www.nielsen.com/ssa/en/insights/article/2014/why-marketing-to-consumers-not-the-masses-is-the-key-to-brand-success-in-africa/.

Ninety One. 2024. "Notes from the Road: Africa Private Credit | Top Five Questions from Institutional Investors." https://ninetyone.com/en/united-kingdom/insights/africa-private-credit-top-five-questions-from-us-institutional-investors.

Niohuru, Ilha. 2023. "Disease Burden and Mortality." Healthcare and Disease Burden in Africa, March 19. https://link.springer.com/chapter/10.1007/978-3-031-19719-2_3.

NRGI (National Resource Governance Institute). 2015. "The Resource Curse: The Political and Economic Challenges of Natural Resource Wealth." https://resource governance.org/sites/default/files/nrgi_Resource-Curse.pdf

———. 2022. "Triple Win: How Mining Can Benefit Africa's Citizens, Their Environment and the Energy Transition." https://resourcegovernance.org/publications/triple-win-mining-africa-environment-energy-transition.

Ntim, Collins G., Kwaku K. Opong, Jo Danbolt, and Frank Senyo Dewotor. 2011. "Testing the Weak-Form Efficiency in African Stock Markets." *Managerial Finance* 37, no. 3: 195–218.

Nubong, Gabila F. 2021. "Africa's Industrialisation and Economic transformation within a Developmental Regionalism Paradigm." *European Journal of Economics, Law and Social Sciences* 5, no. 2. https://iipccl.org/wp-content/uploads/2021/06/616-638.pdf.

Nwora, Chiamaka. No date. "The Future of Digital Marketing in Africa," Whirlspot. https://whirlspotmedia.com/digital-frontier/future-of-digital-marketing-in-africa/.

Nyamwaya, Christabel. 2013. "Benefits Sharing on Extractive Natural Resources with Society in Kenya." Kenya Human Rights Commission. https://cegkenya.org/wp-content/uploads/2019/03/Benefits_Sharing_on_Extractive_Natural_Resources_with_Society_in_Kenya_2013.pdf.

Nyasha, Sheilla, and Nicholas M. Odhiambo. 2014. "The Dynamics Of Stock Market Development in Kenya." *Journal of Applied Business Research* 30, no. 1: 73. https://core.ac.uk/download/pdf/268105192.pdf.

Nzimande, Meluleki, Yael Shafrir, and Elisha Bhugwandeen. 2022. "Trading under the AfCFTA Becomes a Reality: Guided Trade Initiative Launched." *Polity*, November 3. https://www.polity.org.za/article/trading-under-the-afcfta-becomes-a-reality-guided-trade-initiative-launched-2022-11-03/searchString:Trading+Under+the+AfCFTA+Becomes+a+Reality+Guided+Trade+Initiative+Launched.

Oando. 2016. "Oando PLC Completes $115.8 Million Gas and Power Partial Divestment to Helios Investment Partners." December 20. https://www.oandoplc.com/press_release/oando-plc-completes-115-8-million-gas-and-power-partial-divestment-to-helios-investment-partners/.

Ochai, Ojoma. 2021. "Africa's Creative Industries on the Move, Breaking Barriers." *Africa Renewal*, December 7. https://www.un.org/africarenewal/magazine/december-2021/africas-creative-industries-move-breaking-barriers.

Oduola, Musa, Mustapha O.Bello and Rahmon Popoola. 2021. "Foreign Direct Investment, Institution and Industrialisation in Sub-Saharan Africa." https://www.semanticscholar.org/paper/Foreign-Direct-Investment%2C-Institution-and-in-Oduola-Bello/e521f2da44c5b0ff6133d0d4b37e348e8b2f5895.

OECD (Organization for Economic Cooperation and Development). 2002. "Foreign Direct Investment for Development: Maximising Benefits, Minimising Costs." https://www.oecd.org/investment/investmentfordevelopment/1959815.pdf.

———. 2008. "Growing Unequal?" https://www.oecd-ilibrary.org/social-issues-migration-health/growing-unequal_9789264044197-en.

———. 2009. *Natural Resources and Pro-Poor Growth*. DAC Guidelines and Reference Series. Paris: OECD Publishing. https://www.oecd.org/dac/environment-development/42440224.pdf.

Office of the United States Trade Representative. 2016. "Beyond AGOA: Looking to the Future of US–Africa Trade and Investment." https://ustr.gov/sites/default/files/2016-AGOA-Report.pdf.

Ofosu, George, and David Sarpong. 2022. "China in Africa: On the Competing Perspectives of the Value of Sino-Africa Business Relationships." *Journal of Economic Issues* 56, no. 1: 137–57. https://www.tandfonline.com/doi/full/10.1080/00213624.2022.2020025.

Ogbalu, Mike, III. 2022. "Boosting the AfCFTA: The Role of the Pan-African Payment and Settlement System." Brookings. https://www.brookings.edu/articles/boosting-the-afcfta-the-role-of-the-pan-african-payment-and-settlement-system/.

Ogunmilade, C. A. 1979. "Television, Politics, and Society: The Role of Television in National Development." Paper presented at NAVA Convention, Benin.

Ojah, Kalu, and Kishan Pillay. 2009. "Debt Markets and Corporate Debt Structure in an Emerging Market: The South African Example." *Economic Modelling* 26, no. 6: 1215–27.

Okan, Zühal. 2003. "Edutainment: Is Learning at Risk?" *British Journal of Educational Technology* 24, no. 3: 255–64.

Oke, Michael Ojo. 2012. "Insurance Sector Development and Economic Growth in Nigeria." *African Journal of Business Management* 6, no. 23. https://academicjournals.org/journal/AJBM/article-full-text-pdf/07376D538061.

Okillong, Philemon. 2024. "Road Fatalities Have Robbed Us of Our Future." Economic Policy Research Centre. https://eprcug.org/blog/road-fatalities-have-robbed-us-our-future/.

Olarewaju, Odunayo and Thabiso Msomi. 2021. "Determinants of Insurance Penetration in West African Countries: A Panel Auto Regressive Distributed Lag Approach." JRFM, MDPI, vol. 14(8), 1–15.

Olayungbo, D. O., and A. E. Akinlo. 2016. "Insurance Penetration and Economic Growth in Africa: Dynamic Effect Analysis Using Bayesian TVP-VAR Approach." *Cogent Economics & Finance* 4, no. 1. https://www.tandfonline.com/doi/full/10.1080/23322039.2016.1150390.

OMFIF. 2023. "Absa Africa Financial Markets Index 2023." Absa Group Limited and OMFIF. https://cib.absa.africa/wp-content/uploads/2023/10/AFMI-2023-Final.pdf.

Omondi, Gregory. 2020. "The State of Mobile in Ghana's Tech Ecosystem." GSMA. https://www.gsma.com/solutions-and-impact/connectivity-for-good/mobile-for-development/blog/the-state-of-mobile-in-ghanas-tech-ecosystem/.

Omran, Mohammed. 2006. "Structural Break in the Egyptian Stock Market: A Logistic Regression Analysis." *International Journal of Business* 11, no. 4: 403.

Onu, Stephen. 2023. Nollywood to generate $14.82 billion by 2025 – Report." Premium Times. https://www.premiumtimesng.com/entertainment/nollywood/647151-nollywood-to-generate-14-82-billion-by-2025-report.html.

Onyango, Conrad. 2022. "Streaming Wars Come to Africa." *Mail & Guardian*, May 31. https://mg.co.za/africa/2022-05-31-streaming-wars-come-to-africa/.

Oramah, Benedict. 2021. "Afreximbank in the Era of the AfCFTA." *Journal of African Trade* 8, no. 2: 24–25. https://www.atlantis-press.com/journals/jat/125966586/view.

Ossé, Lionel, and Matthias Krönke. 2024. "Health for Everyone, Everywhere?" *Afrobarometer*, April. https://www.afrobarometer.org/wp-content/uploads/2024/04/PP91-PAP12-Africans-rate-health-as-a-top-priority-for-government-action-Afrobarometer-3april24.pdf.

Owoo, Nkechi S., and Monica P. Lambon-Quayefio. 2018. "The Agro-Processing Industry and Its Potential for Structural Transformation of the Ghanaian Economy." In *Industries Without Smokestacks: Industrialization in Africa Reconsidered* (Oxford University Press).

Owusu-Gyamfi, Mavis. 2023. "Equal Power, Faster Progress: A Recipe for Africa's Transformation." Brookings. https://www.brookings.edu/blog/africa-in-focus/2023/03/08/equal-power-faster-progress-a-recipe-for-africas-transformation/.

Oxford Business Group. 2019. "Ghana's Mining Output Benefits from Increased Investment and Improved Regulation." https://oxfordbusinessgroup.com/overview/gold-standards-greater-investment-has-increased-production-across-sector-improved-regulation-set.

———. 2022. "African Stock Exchanges Focus Report."

———. No date. "Kenya's Bond Market Slowing Despite Improvements." https://oxfordbusinessgroup.com/reports/kenya/2016-report/economy/bonding-process-secondary-trading-has-been-slowing-despite-improvements-in-transparency-and-efficiency.

Oxford Policy Management. 2002. *"Agriculture and Rural Enterprise in Africa: Is There an Investment Gap?"; a Study for DFID*. Oxford: Oxford Policy Management.

Palladium. 2020. "The New Investment Case for Africa." https://thepalladiumgroup.com/downloads/b6546b05983f6352e82df8cb46534c5a.

Pan African Chamber of Commerce and Industry. No date. "Intra-African Trade Up 7.2 percent in 2023, Report Finds." https://www.pacci.org/intra-african-trade-up-7-2-in-2023-report-finds/#:~:text=Intra%2DAfrican%20trade%20increased%20by,Wednesday%2C%20June%2012%2C%202024.

Pareles, Jon. 2020. "The Legacy of Fela Kuti's Music of Resistance: Hear 15 Essential Songs." *New York Times*, June 10. https://www.nytimes.com/2020/06/10/arts/music/fela-kuti-afrobeat-playlist.html.

Parente, Ronaldo, Ke Rong, José-Mauricio G. Geleilate, and Everlyne Misati. 2019. "Adapting and Sustaining Operations in Weak Institutional Environments: A Business Ecosystem Assessment of a Chinese MNE in Central Africa." *Journal of International Business Studies* 50: 275–91.

Parikh, Nupur. No date. "Health Financing." *One.* https://data.one.org/topics/health-financing/.

Parkinson, John M., and Nelson M. Waweru. 2008. "The Nairobi Stock Exchange and New Equity Capital: 1998 to 2004." *Journal of International Business Research 7,* no. 2: 75.

Partech. 2020. "2020 Africa Tech Venture Capital Report." https://partechpartners.com/2020-africa-tech-venture-capital-report/#section-1.

———. 2023. "2023 Africa Tech Venture Capital Report." https://partechpartners.com/africa-reports/2023-africa-tech-venture-capital-report.

Paulson, Cole. 2012. "Marketers and Pirates, Businessmen and Villains." *St. Anthony's International Review 7,* no. 2: 51–68. https://www.jstor.org/stable/26228582.

Pennington, Steuart. 2023. "SA Climbs 7 Places in Global Competitiveness Report." South Africa: The Good News. https://www.sagoodnews.co.za/sa-climbs-7-places-in-global-competitiveness-report/.

Peter, Lanre. 2022. "AfCFTA: Why Is the Pan-African Payment and Settlement System Important?" *African Liberty,* June 20. https://www.africanliberty.org/2022/06/20/afcfta-why-is-the-pan-african-payment-and-settlement-system-important/.

Policy Center for the New South and CyclOpe. 2019. *Arcadia 2019: Africa and the Global Commodity Markets.*

PR Newswire. 2020a. "Botswana Mining Market Study 2020 with Profiles of 26 Players Including Debswana, Botswana Ash, Khoemacau Copper Mines, Lucara, Kukama and Efora Energy." https://www.prnewswire.com/news-releases/botswana-mining-market-study-2020-with-profiles-of-26-players-including-debswana-botswana-ash-khoemacau-copper-mines-lucara-kukama-and-efora-energy-301078736.html.

Prosper Africa. 2023. "African Healthcare Investment Opportunities Report." https://www.prosperafrica.gov/wp-content/uploads/2024/01/Prosper-Africa-Healthcare-Investment-Report_2023_vF_DIGITAL_C.pdf.

PwC. 2012a. "Africa Regional." In *International Transfer Pricing 2012.* https://www.pwc.com/gx/en/international-transfer-pricing/assets/south-africa.pdf.

———. 2012b. "Insurance 2020: Turning Change into Opportunity." https://www.pwc.com/gx/en/insurance/pdf/insurance-2020-turning-change-into-opportunity.pdf.

———. 2012c. "Corporate Income Taxes, Mining Royalties and Other Mining Taxes: A Summary of Rates and Rules in Selected Countries." https://www.pwc.com/gx/en/energy-utilities-mining/publications/pdf/pwc-gx-miining-taxes-and-royalties.pdf.

———. 2015a. "Africa Insurance Trends." https://www.pwc.com/ng/en/assets/pdf/nigeria-insurance-survey.pdf.

———. 2015b. "Insurance 2020 & Beyond: Necessity Is the Mother of Reinvention." https://www.pwc.com/gx/en/insurance/publications/assets/pwc-insurance-2020-and-beyond.pdf.

———. 2015c. "North Africa's unfinished revolution." Global Economy Watch. https://www.pwc.com/gx/en/issues/economy/global-economy-watch/assets/pdfs/gew-june-2015-north-africa.pdf.

———. 2016a. "PwC Entertainment and Media Outlook: 2016–2020." https://www.pwc.co.za/en/assets/pdf/enm/entertainment-and-media-outlook-2016-2020.pdf.

———. 2016b. "Highlighting Trends in the South African Mining Industry." In *SA Mine*, 8th edition. https://www.pwc.co.za/en/assets/pdf/sa-mine-2016.pdf.

———. 2017. "The Business of Entertainment Harnessing growth opportunities in entertainment, media, arts and lifestyle." https://www.pwc.com/ng/en/assets/pdf/the-business-of-entertainment-final.pdf.

———. 2018. "Entertainment and Media Outlook: 2018–2022: An African Perspective." https://www.pwc.co.za/en/assets/pdf/entertainment-and-media-outlook-2018-2022.pdf.

———. 2019. "Insights from the Entertainment and Media Outlook: 2019–2023 An African Perspective." https://www.pwc.co.za/en/assets/pdf/entertainment-and-media-outlook-2019-2023.pdf.

———. 2020a. "COVID-19 and the Insurance Industry: Issues and Actions to Consider." https://www.pwc.com/jg/en/issues/covid-19/covid-19-and-insurance-industry.pdf.

———. 2020b. "Perspectives from the *Global Entertainment and Media Outlook 2020–2024*: Pulling the Future Forward: The Entertainment and Media Industry Reconfigures Amid Recovery." https://www.pwc.com/gx/en/entertainment-media/outlook-2020/perspectives.pdf.

———. 2022. "Africa Capital Markets Watch 2021." https://www.pwc.co.za/en/assets/pdf/africa-capital-markets-watch-2021.pdf.

———. 2023. "Africa Entertainment and Media Outlook: 2023–2027." https://www.pwc.co.za/en/assets/pdf/pwc-africa-entertainment-and-media-outlook-2023.pdf.

———. No date. "Nigeria Will Be the World's Fastest-Growing E&M Market—PwC Report." https://www.pwc.com/ng/en/press-room/nigeria-will-be-the-worlds-fastest-growing-e-m-market-pwc-report.html#:~:text=According%20to%20the%20latest%20report,growing%20at%20a%201.7%25%20CAGR.

PwC Australia–Africa Practice. 2019. "Investment in Africa. Working Together to Maximise the Potential." https://www.pwc.com.au/industry/energy-utilities-mining/investing-in-africa-working-together-to-maximise-the-potential.pdf.

Raber, Henrik. 2016. "African's Bond Markets Boom with Good Demand from International Investors." *BusinessDay*, November 6. https://www.businesslive.co.za/bd/opinion/2016-11-06-africans-bond-markets-boom-with-good-demand-from-international-investors/.

Raim, M. Davis, and Joy L. Langford. 2007. "Understanding Reinsurance." In *Newtv Appleman on Insurance Law Practice Guide*.

Ramdoo, Isabella. "Local Content Policies in the Mining Sector: Lessons, Challenges and New Tools." PowerPoint presentation, IGF Annual General Meeting, Geneva, October 19. https://www.igfmining.org/wp-content/uploads/2018/09/Session-14-Local-content-policies-in-the-mining-sector-by-Isabelle-Ramdoo.pdf.

Rao, Pavithra. 2022. "AfCFTA's Guided Trade Initiative Takes Off, Set to Ease and Boost Intra-African Trade." *Africa Renewal*, October 12. https://www.un.org/africarenewal/magazine/october-2022/afcfta%E2%80%99s-guided-trade-initiative-takes-set-ease-and-boost-intra-african-trade.

Rashotte, Nicole. 2019. "Mining Gold in Africa: A Look at Ghana, Mali and Burkina Faso." Investing News Network. https://investingnews.com/daily/resource-investing/precious-metals-investing/gold-investing/africa-ghana-mali-burkina-faso-iamgold-roxgold-true-gold-randgold-perseus-askano/.

Raubenheimer, Heidi. 2019. "African Capital Markets: Challenges and Opportunities." CFA Institute Research Foundation. https://www.cfainstitute.org/-/media/documents/article/rf-brief/rf-african-capital-markets.pdf.

Reed, Stanley. 2015. "BP Signs \$12 Billion Deal to Develop Natural Gas in Egypt." *New York Times*, March 5. https://www.nytimes.com/2015/03/07/business/international/bp-signs-12-billion-deal-to-develop-natural-gas-in-egypt.html.

Reis, Fonseca Carla Ana, Andrea M. Davis, Edna dos Santos-Duisenberg, et al. 2008. "Creative Economy as a Development Strategy: A View of Developing Countries." Itaú Cultural. https://dlc.dlib.indiana.edu/dlc/bitstream/handle/10535/5519/ebook_eng.pdf?sequence=1.

Republic of Rwanda. 2024. "NST2 to Create Jobs, Boost Exports, Enance Skills Development, and Service Delivery." https://www.gov.rw/blog-detail/rwanda-announces-2nd-national-transformation-strategy.

Rickwood, Sarah, and Stefan Lutzmayer. 2023. "Africa's Next Chapter: A Continent of Opportunity." *IQVIA*, September 22. https://www.iqvia.com/blogs/2023/09/africas-next-chapter-a-continent-of-opportunity.

Ridgwell, Henry. 2020. "Report: Africa Delivers Largest Profits on Investment." VOA, February 5. https://www.voanews.com/a/economy-business_report-africa-delivers-largest-profits-investment/6183772.html.

Rinehart-Smit, Kate, and Pieter Janse van Vuuren. 2021. "COVID-19 Catalyses Insurance Innovation." *Cenfri*, April. https://cenfri.org/articles/covid-19-catalyses-insurance-innovation/.

RioTinto. No date. "Africa's Largest Mining and Related Infrastructure Project." https://www.riotinto.com/en/operations/projects/simandou.

RisCura and EAVCA. 2016. "East Africa Private Equity Deal Dashboard." https://www.riscura.com/wp-content/uploads/2016/03/RisCura-EAVCA-East-Africa-Private-Equity-Deal-Dashboard-1.pdf.

RMB. 2015. "Where to Invest in Africa 2015." https://www.rmb.co.za/campaign/where-to-invest-in-africa.

Rodrik, Dani. 2016. "Premature Deindustrialization." *Journal of Economic Growth* 21: 1–33.

Roxborough, Scott. 2022. "Why the Streamers Are (Finally) Investing in Africa." *Hollywood Reporter*, January 17. https://www.hollywoodreporter.com/business/business-news/netflix-disney-pus-streamers-investment-africa-1235073026/.

Roy, Shibani. 2023. "Strategies to Grow Your Insurance Business in Africa." Lead-Squared. https://www.leadsquared.com/industries/insurance/setting-up-insurance-teams-to-overachieve.

Russo, Giuliano, Gerald Bloom, and David McCoy. 2017. "Universal Health Coverage, Economic Slowdown and System Resilience: Africa's Policy Dilemma." *BMJ Global Health* 2, no. 3. https://gh.bmj.com/content/2/3/e000400.info.

SACO (South African Cultural Observatory). 2016. "The Economic Mapping of the Cultural and Creative Industries in South Africa 2022." https://www.southafrican culturalobservatory.org.za/download/comments/974/4311359ed4969e8401880e3 c1836fbe1/The+Economic+Mapping+of+the+Cultural+and+Creative+Industires+ in+SA+2022.

———. 2018. "The Impact of the 2016 National Arts Festival." https://assets.national artsfestival.co.za/wp-content/uploads/2017/05/NAF-social-impact-report.pdf.

———. 2020a. "Industry Highlights." https://www.southafricanculturalobservatory. org.za/industry-highlights.

———. 2020b. "The Economic Mapping of the Cultural and Creative Industries in South Africa 2020." https://www.southafricanculturalobservatory.org.za/assets/ reports/capstonereport.pdf.

———. 2022. "The SA Cultural Observatory: Measuring and Valuing SA's Cultural and Creative Industries." https://www.southafricanculturalobservatory.org.za/article/ the-sa-cultural-observatory-measuring-and-valuing-sa-s-cultural-and-creative- industries.

South African Government. 2010. "Research Report: Assessment of Visual Arts in South Africa." https://www.gov.za/sites/default/files/gcis_document/201409/research reportassessmentofvisualartsinsa-10.pdf.

Santenac, Isabelle, and Peter Manchester. 2020. "How Disruption from COVID-19 Can Help Insurers Accelerate Change." Ernst & Young, April 20. https://www.ey. com/en_bh/insurance/how-disruption-from-covid-19-can-help-insurers-accelerate- change.

Sarr, Felwine, and Bénédicte Savoy. 2018. "The Restitution of African Cultural Heri- tage. Toward a New Relational Ethics." *Philippe Rey*, November 21. https://www. unimuseum.uni-tuebingen.de/fileadmin/content/05_Forschung_Lehre/Provenienz/ sarr_savoy_en.pdf.

Sayila, Katutu. No date. "The Developing Country with a Positive Trajectory." World Finance. https://www.worldfinance.com/markets/zambia-the-developing-country- with-a-positive-trajectory.

Schaefer, Simon, and Ahmed Bulbulia. "Digital Commerce Acceleration: Increased Online Purchases Present New Opportunities for Digital Commerce Players." *Deloitte.Digital*, February. https://www2.deloitte.com/content/dam/Deloitte/za/ Documents/strategy/za-Digital-Commerce-Acceleration-2021-Digital.pdf.

Schlemmer, Lucia, Kate Rinehart-Smit, and Jeremy Gray. 2020. "Never Waste a Crisis: How Sub-Saharan African Insurers Are Being Affected by, and Are Responding to, COVID-19." *Cenfri*, July. https://www.fsdafrica.org/wp-content/uploads/2020/07/ Impact-of-COVID-19-on-insurers-10.07.201.pdf.

SES. 2019. "Delivering HD across Africa." https://www.ses.com/sites/default/files/ 2020-07/SES_CaseStudy_Canal%2BAfrique_A4_FINAL_WEB.pdf.

Sharma, Nidhi. 2022. "Africa Pharmaceutical Logistics Market Report 2022–2027: Industry Size, Share, Trends and Forecast." *LinkedIn*, May 14. https://www.linkedin. com/pulse/africa-pharmaceutical-logistics-market-report-2022-2027-nidhi-sharma.

Signé, Landry. 2017a. "Policy Implementation: A Synthesis of the Study of Policy Implementation and the Causes of Policy Failure." Policy Center for the New South. https://www.policycenter.ma/sites/default/files/OCPPC-PP1703.pdf.

———. 2017b. "Public Service Delivery: What Matters for Successful Implementation and What Can Policy Leaders Do?" Policy Center for the New South. https://www. policycenter.ma/sites/default/files/2021-01/OCPPC-PP1704.pdf.

———. 2017c. "Innovate or Fail: The Options open to Africa for Implementing the SDGs and Agenda 2063." Brookings. https://www.brookings.edu/articles/innovate-or-fail-the-options-open-to-africa-for-implementing-the-sdgs-and-agenda-2063/.

———. 2018a. "Capturing Africa's High Returns." Brookings. https://www.brookings. edu/opinions/capturing-africas-high-returns.

———. 2018b. "How Can the New African Free Trade Agreement Unlock Africa's Potential?" OECD. https://oecd-development-matters.org/2018/10/22/how-can-the-new-african-free-trade-agreement-unlock-africas-potential/.

———. 2018c. "Accountable Leadership: The Key to Africa's Successful Transformation." Brookings. https://www.brookings.edu/wp-content/uploads/2018/01/signe_african leadership_globalview.pdf).

———. 2020. *Unlocking Africa's Business Potential: Trends, Opportunities, Risks, and Strategies.* Brookings.

———. 2021a. "How to Restore US Credibility in Africa." *Foreign Affairs*, January 15. https://foreignpolicy.com/2021/01/15/united-states-africa-biden-administration-relations-china/.

———. 2021b. "US Trade and Investment in Africa: Before the Subcommittee on Africa and Global Health Policy of the Committee on Foreign Relations, 117th Cong."

———. 2022a. "Understanding the African Continental Free Trade Area and how the US can Promote Its Success." Brookings. https://www.brookings.edu/articles/understanding-the-african-continental-free-trade-area-and-how-the-us-can-promote-its-success/.

———. 2022b. "Harnessing Technology and Innovation for a Better Future in Africa: Policy Priorities for Enabling the 'Africa We Want.'" Brookings. https://www. brookings.edu/articles/technological-innovations-creating-and-harnessing-tools-for-improved-livelihoods/.

———. 2023. *Africa's Fourth Industrial Revolution.* Cambridge University Press.

Signé, Landry, and Ameenah Gurib-Fakim. 2019. "The High Growth Promise of an Integrated Africa." Brookings. https://www.brookings.edu/opinions/the-high-growth-promise-of-an-integrated-africa/.

Signé, Landry, and Chris Heitzig. 2022. "Effective Engagement with Africa: Capitalizing on Shifts in Business, Technology, and Global Partnerships." Brookings. https:// www.brookings.edu/wp-content/uploads/2022/04/Effective-engagement-Africa_ April-2022.pdf.

Signé, Landry, and Payce Madden. 2021. "Considerations for Rules of Origin Under the African Continental Free Trade Area." *Journal of African Trade* 8, suppl. 2: 77–87.

Signé, Landry, and Colette van der Ven. 2019. "Keys to Success for the AfCFTA Negotiations." Brookings. https://www.brookings.edu/research/keys-to-success-for-the-afcfta-negotiations/.

Simons, Daniel, and Samuel A. Laryea. 2006. "The Efficiency of Selected African Stock Markets." *Finance India* 20, no. 2: 553.

Sirri, Erik. 2004. "Investment Banks, Scope, and Unavoidable Conflicts of Interest." Federal Reserve Bank of Atlanta, *Economic Review* 89, no. 4. https://www.atlantafed.org/-/media/documents/research/publications/economic-review/2004/vol89no4_sirri.pdf.

Slavova, Mira, and Ekene Okwechime. 2016. "African Smart Cities Strategies for Agenda 2063." *African Journal of Management* 2, no. 2: 210–29.

Söderblom, Anna. 2012. "The Current State of the Venture Capital Industry." *Näringspolitiskt Forum*, January. https://entreprenorskapsforum.se/wp-content/uploads/2012/01/Rapport_Current-state-of-the-venture_webb.pdf.

Solutions for Youth Employment. 2021. "Unlocking Opportunities for Youth in the Orange Economy: Music in Africa." World Bank, Knowledge Brief Series Issue 15. https://www.s4ye.org/sites/default/files/2021-09/S4YE%20Knowledge%20Brief%20on%20Music%20Final_1.pdf.

Songwe, Vera, and Jean-Paul Adam. 2023. "Keys to Climate Action, Chapter 9: Delivering Africa's Great Green Transformation." Working Paper 180-9, Brookings. https://www.brookings.edu/wp-content/uploads/2023/10/Chapter-9.-Delivering-Africas-great-green-transformation.pdf.

Soumaré, Issouf, Désiré Kanga, Judith Tyson, and Sherillyn Raga. 2021. *Capital Market Development in Sub-Saharan Africa: Progress, Challenges and Innovations.* Working Paper 2. London: Overseas Development Institute. https://cdn.odi.org/media/documents/ODI_Working_Paper_2_Capital_markets_development_in_SSA_FINAL_clean.pdf.

Spratt, Annie. No date. "Analyzing the Performance of African Stocks." AFSIC. https://www.afsic.net/analyzing-the-performance-of-african-stocks/.

Stancu, Lorena. 2020. "Expanding Mining Frontiers in West Africa." *Global Business Reports*, October 2. https://www.gbreports.com/article/expanding-mining-frontiers-in-west-africa.

Standard & Poor's Global. 2024. "Africa Mining by the Numbers 2024." https://www.spglobal.com/marketintelligence/en/news-insights/research/africa-mining-by-the-numbers-2024.

Standard Chartered. 2022. "The Re-shaping of Africa's Capital Markets." https://www.sc.com/en/news/ccib/re-shaping-africas-capital-markets/.

Stanley, Andrew. 2023. "African Century." IMF. https://www.imf.org/en/Publications/fandd/issues/2023/09/PT-african-century.

Subrahmanyam, Kaveria, and Bhavya Renukarya. 2015. "Digital Games and Learning: Identifying Pathways of Influence." *Educational Psychologist* 50, no. 4: 335–48.

Swiss Re Institute. 2020. "World Insurance: Regional Review 2019, and Outlook." https://www.swissre.com/dam/jcr:864e8938-3d3c-48cc-a3d7-8682962971e7/sigma-4-2020-extra-complete.pdf.

Sy, Amadou. 2014. "Which African Countries Are at Risk from the Current Market Turmoil?" Brookings. https://www.brookings.edu/articles/which-african-countries-are-at-risk-from-the-current-market-turmoil/#:~:text=Although percent20it percent 20is percent20difficult percent20to,portfolio percent20reallocation percent20by percent20foreign percent20investors.

Tagholm, Roger. 2019. "Bookselling in Lagos and the Politics of Piracy." *Publishing Perspective*, June. https://publishingperspectives.com/wp-content/uploads/2019/06/Publishing-Perspectives-Magazine-African-Publishing-June-2019-Magazine.pdf.

Team Conyach. 2023. "Indigenous Knowledge: A Crucial Resource for Environment Preservation." https://conyach.scot/indigenous-knowledge-a-crucial-resource-for-environment-preservation/.

Thomas, Howard, Michelle P. Lee, Lynne Thomas, and Alexander Wilson. 2016. "Does Africa Need an 'African' Management Education Model?" *Global Focus: European Foundation for Management Development* 10: 58–63.

Torkington, Simon. 2024. "African Nations Have Agreed a Plan to Increase Locally Produced Vaccines. This Is How It Will Work." World Economic Forum, March 7. https://www.weforum.org/agenda/2024/03/africa-healthcare-vaccines-production/.

TRALAC. 2023. "Status of AfCFTA Ratification." TRALAC Trade Law Centre. https://www.tralac.org/resources/infographic/13795-status-of-afcfta-ratification.html.

Transparency International. 2022. "Corruptions Perceptions Index." https://www.transparency.org/en/cpi/2022.

Trends Research & Advisory. 2024. "Foreign Direct Investment in Africa: Trends and Prospect." May 1. https://trendsresearch.org/insight/foreign-direct-investment-in-africa-trends-and-prospects/.

Trisos, C. H., I. O. Adelekan, E. Totin, A. Ayanlade, J. Efitre, A. Gemeda, et al. 2023. "Africa." In *Climate Change 2022: Impacts, Adaptation and Vulnerability. Contribution of Working Group II to the Sixth Assessment Report of the Intergovernmental Panel on Climate Change*, edited by H. O. Pörtner, D. C., Roberts, M. Tignor, E. S. Poloczanska, K. Mintenbeck, A. Alegría, et al. Cambridge University Press. DOI: https://doi.org/10.1017/9781009325844.011.

Trustonic. 2024. "How Access to Smartphones is Transforming Lives and Economies in Africa." May 25. https://www.trustonic.com/opinion/how-access-to-smartphones-is-transforming-lives-and-economies-in-africa/.

Twimukye, Evarist. 2006. "An Econometric Analysis of Determinants of Foreign Direct Investment: A Panel Data Study for Africa." PhD diss., Clemson University. https://www.proquest.com/openview/76aded3cae78f9d7cd2632f08a78800c/1?pq-origsite=gscholar&cbl=18750&diss=y.

234 Media. 2018. "Framing the Shot: Key Trends in African Film." https://www.yumpu.com/en/document/read/61237774/framing-the-shot-key-trends-in-african-film.

Udoakpan, Nokuphiwa, and Robertson Khan Tengeh. 2020. "The Impact of Over-the-Top Television Services on Pay-Television Subscription Services in South Africa." *Journal of Open Innovation: Technology, Market, and Complexity* 6, no. 4: 139. https://doi.org/10.3390/joitmc6040139.

UNCTAD (UN Conference on Trade and Development). 1999. "Foreign Direct Investment in Africa: Performance and Potential." https://unctad.org/system/files/official-document/poiteiitm15.pdf.

——. 2005. "World Investment Report 2005." https://unctad.org/system/files/official-document/wir2005_en.pdf.

——.2007. "Trade and Development Aspects of Insurance Services and Regulatory Frameworks." https://unctad.org/system/files/official-document/ditctncd20074_en.pdf.

——. 2008. "Creative Economy Report 2008." https://unctad.org/system/files/official-document/ditc20082cer_en.pdf.

——. 2013. "Economic Development in Africa Report 2013." https://unctad.org/system/files/official-document/aldcafrica2013_en.pdf.

——. 2015. "World Investment 2015." https://unctad.org/system/files/official-document/wir2015_en.pdf.

——. 2019a. "Economic Development in Africa Report 2019." https://unctad.org/system/files/official-document/aldcafrica2019_en.pdf.

——. 2019b. "How the Creative Economy Can Help Power Development." https://unctad.org/news/how-creative-economy-can-help-power-development.

——. 2019c. "Commodities and Dependence, Climate Change and the Paris Agreement." In *Commodities and Development Report 2019*. https://www.developmentaid.org/api/frontend/cms/uploadedImages/2019/09/ditccom2019d3_en.pdf.

——. 2021a. "AfCFTA Could Boost Maritime Trade in Africa." https://unctad.org/press-material/afcfta-could-boost-maritime-trade-africa.

——. 2021b. "Creative Economy to Have Its Year in the Sun in 2021." https://unctad.org/news/creative-economy-have-its-year-sun-2021.

——. 2022a. "Investment flows to Africa Reached a Record $83 Billion in 2021." June 9. https://unctad.org/news/investment-flows-africa-reached-record-83-billion-2021.

——. 2022b. "Creative Economy Offers Countries Path to Development, Says New UNCTAD Report." https://unctad.org/press-material/creative-economy-offers-countries-path-development-says-new-unctad-report.

——. 2023a. "The Potential of Africa to Capture Technology-Intensive Global Supply Chains." https://unctad.org/system/files/official-document/aldcafrica2023_en.pdf.

——. 2023b. "Investment Flows to Africa Dropped to $45 Billion in 2022." July 5. https://unctad.org/news/investment-flows-africa-dropped-45-billion-2022.

——. 2023c. "State of Commodity Dependence 2023." https://unctad.org/system/files/official-document/ditccom2023d3_en.pdf.

——. 2024a. "Africa: Foreign Investment in Clean Energy Boosts Sustainability Momentum." June 20. https://unctad.org/news/africa-foreign-investment-clean-energy-boosts-sustainability-momentum.

——. 2024b. "Global Economic Growth Set to Slow to 2.6 percent in 2024, Just Above Recession Threshold." April 18. https://unctad.org/news/global-economic-growth-set-slow-26-2024-just-above-recession-threshold.

————. 2024c. "World Investment Report." https://unctad.org/system/files/official-document/wir2024_en.pdf.

UN DESA (United Nations, Department of Economic and Social Affairs), Population Division. 2019. "World Population Prospects 2019: Highlight." https://population.un.org/wpp/publications/files/wpp2019_highlights.pdf.

UNDP (UN Development Program). 2015. "Impact Investment in Africa: Trends, Constaints, and Opportunities." https://www.undp.org/sites/g/files/zskgke326/files/migration/africa/14aae1f27ec1834e6e96d4a6af4a75de5956e746f588c7accc93c84bde98d725.pdf.

————. 2023. "Accelerating Creative and Innovation in Africa." https://www.undp.org/ghana/blog/accelerating-creativity-and-innovation-africa.

————. 2024a. "Sahel Human Development Report 2023." https://www.undp.org/africa/publications/sahel-human-development-report-2023.

————. 2024b. "Africa Green Business and Financing Report." https://www.undp.org/africa/publications/africa-green-business-and-financing-report.

UNECA (UN Economic Commission for Africa). 2020a. "Creating a Unified Regional Market: Towards the Implementation of the African Continental Free Trade Area in East Africa." https://archive.uneca.org/publications/creating-unifiedregional-market-towards-implementation-african-continental-free-trade.

————. 2020b. "Economic Report of Africa 2020: Innovative Finance for Private Sector Development in Africa."

————. 2021. "Africa Private Sector Summit." https://www.uneca.org/events/apss2021#:~:text=The percent20Africa percent20Continental percent20Free percent20Trade,US percent2429 percent20trillion percent20by percent202050.

————. 2022. "Private Sector as the Backbone of the AfCFTA Implementation." Konrad-Adenauer-Stiftung, June 1. https://www.kas.de/documents/13332971/17139048/Policy+brief+-+Private+sector+as+the+backbone+of+the+AfCFTA+implementation.pdf/09f35ba4-326f-a283-bf48-5ee3965a1661?t=1655293939245.

UONGOZI Institute. 2017. "Enhancing Value Addition in the Extractive Sector in Africa." https://uongozi.or.tz/newsite/wp-content/uploads/2022/12/Enhancing-Value-Addition-In-the-Extractive-Sector-in-Africa.pdf.

UNECA, GBCHealth, and Aliko Dangote Foundation. 2019. *Healthcare and Economic Growth in Africa.* Addis Ababa: United Nations Economic Commission for Africa."

UNEP (UN Environment Program). No date. "Our Work in Africa." https://www.unep.org/regions/africa/our-work-africa.

UNICEF (UN International Children's Emergency Fund). 2023. "What Is the Average Life Expectancy in Africa?" https://data.unicef.org/how-many/what-is-the-average-life-expectancy-in-africa/.

UNIDO (UN Industrial Development Organization). 2018. "Africa: An Opportunity for Pharma and Patients." McKinsey & Company. https://www.mckinsey.com/~/media/McKinsey/Industries/Pharmaceuticals%20and%20Medical%20Products/Our%20Insights/Africa%20A%20continent%20of%20opportunity

%20for%20pharma%20and%20patients/Africa_a_continent_of_opportunity_
for_pharma_and_patients.pdf.

United Nations. 2009. "Nigeria Surpasses Hollywood as World's Second-Largest Film Producer." https://news.un.org/en/story/2009/05/299102-nigeria-surpasses-hollywood-worlds-second-largest-film-producer-un.

———. 2023a. "African Union-Led Peace Support Operations Need Predictable, Adequate, Sustainable Support, Speakers Stress to Security Council." https://press.un.org/en/2023/sc15294.doc.htm.

———. 2023b. "Growing Middle Class and Import Substitution Connecting the Dots to Unlock Made in Africa." https://www.un.org/osaa/sites/www.un.org.osaa/files/ads2023_policy_brief_2.pdf.

United States Trade Representative, Office of. 2024. "2024 Biennial Report on the Implementation of the African Growth and Opportunity Act." https://ustr.gov/sites/default/files/2024%20AGOA%20Biennial%20Report%206-27-2024%20PDF.pdf.

Universal Music Group. 2021. "Universal Music Group Announces Strategic Leadership Appointments within Africa." https://www.universalmusic.com/universal-music-group-announces-strategic-leadership-appointments-within-africa/.

US Department of State. 2015. "2015 Egypt Investment Climate Statement." https://2009-2017.state.gov/documents/organization/241756.pdf.

———. 2021. "2021 Investment Climate Statements: Morocco." https://www.state.gov/reports/2021-investment-climate-statements/morocco/.

———. 2023. "2023 Investment Climate Statements: Morocco." https://www.state.gov/reports/2023-investment-climate-statements/morocco/.

USGS (US Geological Survey). 2020. "Mineral Commodity Summaries 2020." https://pubs.usgs.gov/publication/mcs2020.

Vanek, Monique. 2024. "Nigeria's Economy, Once Africa's Biggest, Slips to Fourth Place." *Bloomberg*, April 18. https://www.bloomberg.com/news/articles/2024-04-18/nigeria-s-economy-once-africa-s-biggest-slips-to-fourth-place?embedded-checkout=true.

Vedie, Henri-Louis. 2017. "Chinese Mining Investments in Africa." OCP Policy Center. https://www.policycenter.ma/publications/chinese-mining-investments-africa.

Veiga, M. Marcello, and Christian Beinhoff. 1997. "UNECA Centers, a Way to Reduce Mercury Emissions from Artisanal Gold Mining and Provide Badly Needed Training." *Industry and Environment* 20, no. 4: 49–51.

Ventures Africa. 2021. "#AfricaDay: Celebrating Africa's Unfolding Film Story." May 25. https://venturesafrica.com/africa-day-celebrating-africas-unfolding-film-story/.

Virginia Economic Development Partnership. 2021. "Industry Report: Africa Healthcare/Life Sciences." https://exportvirginia.org/sites/default/files/2021-07/Africa_Healthcare_Report_July_21.pdf.

Vourlias, Christopher. 2017. "'Wedding Party' Fuels Record Nigerian Box Office Despite Ailing Economy." *Variety*, February 3. https://variety.com/2017/film/global/

wedding-party-fuels-record-nigerian-box-office-despite-ailing-economy-1201977878/.

Wajid, S. Kal. 2015. "Themes and Lessons from the Financial Sector Assessment Programs." In *The Quest for Regional Integration in the East African Community*. Washington: International Monetary Fund.

Warhurst, Alyson. 1994. "Environmental Best-Practice in Metals Production." In *Mining and Its Environmental Impact*, ed. R. E. Hester and R. M. Harrison, vol. 1. London: Royal Society of Chemistry.

Weil, David. 2014. "Health and Economic Growth." *Handbook of Economic Growth*, vol. 2, pp. 623–682.

WHO (World Health Organization). 2014. "The African Regional Health Report 2014: The Health of the People: What Works." https://www.afro.who.int/publications/african-regional-health-report-2014-health-people-what-works.

———. 2016. "Atlas of African Health Statistics 2016: Health Situation Analysis of the African Region." https://iris.who.int/bitstream/handle/10665/206547/9789290232919.pdf?sequence=1&isAllowed=y.

———. 2022a. "Atlas of African Health Statistics 2022: Health Situation Analysis of the WHO African Region."

———. 2022b. "Chronic Staff Shortfalls Stifle Africa's Health Systems: WHO Study." https://www.afro.who.int/news/chronic-staff-shortfalls-stifle-africas-health-systems-who-study.

———.2022c. "Kenya." https://data.who.int/countries/404.

———. 2023. "Africa Health Workforce Investment Charter." https://iris.who.int/bitstream/handle/10665/376689/9789290314998-eng.pdf.

———. 2024a. "World Health Statistics 2024: Monitoring health for the SDGs, Sustainable Development Goals." https://iris.who.int/bitstream/handle/10665/376869/9789240094703-eng.pdf?sequence=1.

———. 2024b. "Pioneering Charter to Drive Up Investment in Africa's Health Workforce." https://www.afro.who.int/news/pioneering-charter-drive-investment-africas-health-workforce.

Woldemichael, Andinet. 2020. "Closing the Gender Gap in African Labor Markets Is Good Economics." Brookings. https://www.brookings.edu/blog/africa-in-focus/2020/01/23/closing-the-gender-gap-in-african-labor-markets-is-good-economics/.

Wolken, Jordan. 2020. "Startup Acts Are the Next Form of Policy Innovation in Africa." Atlantic Council. https://www.atlanticcouncil.org/blogs/africasource/startup-acts-are-the-next-form-of-policy-innovation-in-africa/.

Workpay. 2022. "Skilled Workers Demand Is High, but There's a Shortage in Africa." https://www.myworkpay.com/blogs/skilled-workers-demand-is-high-but-theres-a-shortage-in-africa-.

World Bank. 2011. "Landscaping African Finance." https://documents1.worldbank.org/curated/en/633671468194645126/122290272_201503117033446/additional/646640PUB0fina00Box361543B00PUBLIC0.pdf.

————. 2016a. "Africa's Unexplored Potential of Trade in Services." https://www. worldbank.org/en/news/feature/2016/08/04/africas-unexplored-potential-of-trade-in-services#:~:text=A percent20burgeoning percent20services percent20 sector percent20is,promising percent20opportunities percent20for percent20export percent20diversification.

————. 2016b. "Zambia Mining Investment and Governance Review: Final Report."

————. 2018. "Doing Business 2018." https://www.doingbusiness.org/content/dam/ doingBusiness/media/Annual-Reports/English/DB2018-Full-Report.pdf.

————. 2020a. "Trade Pact Could Boost Africa's Income by $450 Billion, Study Finds." https://www.worldbank.org/en/news/press-release/2020/07/27/african-continental-free-trade-area.

————. 2020b. "The African Continental Free Trade Area." https://www.worldbank. org/en/topic/trade/publication/the-african-continental-free-trade-area.

————. 2020c. "The African Continental Free Trade Area: Economic and Distributional Effects." https://openknowledge.worldbank.org/handle/10986/34139.

————. 2020d. "The African Continental Free Trade Area." https://www.worldbank. org/en/topic/trade/publication/the-african-continental-free-trade-area.

————. 2020e. "Accelerating EITI Adoption." https://www.worldbank.org/en/news/ feature/2020/02/20/accelerating-eiti-adoption.

————. 2024. "Digital Opportunities in African Business." International Finance Corporation. https://openknowledge.worldbank.org/server/api/core/bitstreams/ e6f2cc1b-ad12-460f-9f17-ff95b69cb378/content.

World Economic Forum. 2017a. "The Africa Competitiveness Report 2017: Addressing Africa's Demographic Dividend." http://documents1.worldbank.org/curated/ en/733321493793700840/pdf/114750-2-5-2017-15-48-23-ACRfinal.pdf.

————. 2017b. "The Future of Jobs and Skills in Africa: Preparing the Region for the Fourth Industrial Revolution." https://www3.weforum.org/docs/WEF_EGW_FOJ_ Africa.pdf.

————. 2017c. "The Global Human Capital Report 2017." https://weforum.ent.box. com/s/dari4dktg4jt2g9xo2o5pksjpatvawdb.

————. 2023. "AfCFTA: A New Era for Global Business and Investment in Africa." https://www3.weforum.org/docs/WEF_Friends_of_the_Africa_Continental_ Free_Trade_Area_2023.pdf.

————. 2024. "An Action Plan to Accelerate Global Business and Investment in Africa." https://www3.weforum.org/docs/WEF_An_Action_Plan_to_Accelerate_ Global_Business_and_Investment_in_Africa_2024.pdf.

————. No date. "Harith General Partners." https://www.weforum.org/organizations/ harith-general-partners/.

World Economics. 2024. "Emerging Markets." https://www.worldeconomics.com/ Regions/Emerging-Markets/.

World Gold Council. 2015. "The Social and Economic Impacts of Gold Mining." https://www.gold.org/download/file/3823/the-social-and-economic-impacts-of-gold-mining.pdf.

World Mining Data. Various years. https://www.world-mining-data.info/?World_Mining_Data___PDF-Files.

WT Research. 2020. "Successes & Shortcomings Of Music Streaming In Africa—Mapping 25+ Platforms." *Wee Tracker*, May 13. https://weetracker.com/2020/05/13/music-streaming-africa/.

Yager, R. Thomas. 2013. "The Mineral Industry of Uganda." In *US Geological Survey Minerals Yearbook: 2013*. Washington: US Geological Survey. https://d9-wret.s3.us-west-2.amazonaws.com/assets/palladium/production/mineral-pubs/country/2013/myb3-2013-ug.pdf.

Yazgan, Sekip, and Omer Yalcinkaya. 2018. "The Effects of Research and Development (R&D) Investments on Sustainable Economic Growth: Evidence from OECD Countries (1996–2015)." *Review of Economic Perspectives* 18, no. 1: 3–23.

Yieke, Lennox. 2024. "Tanzania's Standard Gauge Railway Readies Launch of New Line." *African Business*, March 26. https://african.business/2024/03/trade-investment/tanzanias-standard-gauge-railways-readies-launch-of-new-line.

Yinusa, Olalekan, and Taiwo Akinlo. 2013. "Insurance Development and Economic Growth in Nigeria, 1986–2010." *Journal of Economics and International Finance* 5: 218–24. doi: 10.5897/jeif2013.0498.

Zeitz Museum of Contemporary Art Africa. 2019. "An Icon Opens Its Doors." https://zeitzmocaa.museum/wp-content/uploads/2019/07/Zeitz-MOCAA-Annual-review-year-1.pdf.

Zero Carbon Analytics. 2024. "Developing Africa's Mineral Resources: What Needs to Happen." https://zerocarbon-analytics.org/archives/netzero/developing-africas-mineral-resources-what-needs-to-happen.

Zhang, Ganyi. 2021. "AfCFTA: A More Integrated Africa in the Global Supply Chain." *Upply*, February 17. https://market-insights.upply.com/en/afcfta-a-more-integrated-africa-in-the-global-supply-chain.

Zogning Nguimeya, Félix, and Gaétan Breton. 2013. "Economic Growth and the Development of Financial Markets: Some African Evidence." *Lahore Journal of Business* 1, no. 2.

Index

International Intellectual Property
Alliance (IIPA), 78
International Monetary Fund (IMF), 23,
122, 123
intra-African trade and investment,
26–28, 31, 114–15, 179, 252
Africa-based firms, 190–92
aligning strategies with future
trends and demand in, 242–43
See also African Continental Free
Trade Area (AfCFTA)
investment, private equity, and venture
capital in Africa, 18
AfCFTA investment strategies,
41–46
background facts and trends, 178
basics of private equity, venture
capital, and investment
banking, 176–78
challenges and risks, 199–204
equity culture, 230
equity price discovery, 229–30
future directions, 205–6
importance of sector, 184–86
institutional investors, 15–16, 210
Investment Charter, 197
investor protection law, 197
joint venture partnerships,
112n61, 126–27, 244
key drivers, 186–89
key players, 190–93
negotiation procedures, 123
opportunities, 194–99
public-private partnerships, 107,
109, 139–40, 188, 199
recipients, of investment, 179–81,
182
sector and type, investment by,
181, 183–84
shocks, 25, 30, 39, 117, 134–35,
143, 174–76, 203, 227, 231–32,
247–49

sources of investment, 179, 183
strategies for investment, 204–5
technology investors, 8, 71–72
venture capitalism, 110, 174–76,
178–79, 183–84, 190, 225, 255
See also foreign investment;
private equity; private sector;
public sector
investment strategies in Africa
in capital markets sector, 232–34
in entertainment/creative sector,
72–78
in health care sector, 98–103,
106–9
in insurance sector, 168–69
in mining sector, 139–41
in public sector, 18, 249–56
See also private sector, strategies
for success
Inxeba (film), 75
Ipsos (consulting firm), 57
Ireland, 159

Jamii Africa, 160
Jihadism, 139
Johannesburg Stock Exchange (JSE),
211, 228
joint venture partnerships, 112n61,
126–27, 244
Joox, 62
Jumia, 157

Kenya, 77–78, 100–102, 109, 164,
166–67, 191, 225–27, 242, 244, 255
Central Bank of Kenya, 226
Department for Culture and
Heritage, 69
Digital Kenya 2030 strategy, 199
M-PESA digital payment
platform, 63–64, 160, 199, 221
Nairobi Securities Exchange
(NSE), 198–99, 213

About the Author

Landry Signé is a Senior Fellow in the Global Economy and Development program and with the Africa Growth Initiative at Brookings. He is a professor and executive director at the Thunderbird School of Global Management, a distinguished fellow at Stanford University, cochair of the World Economic Forum's (WEF's) Regional Action Group for Africa, cochair of the WEF's Friends of the African Continental Free Trade Area, and a member of the WEF's Global Future Council on the Future of Technology Policy. He is a disruptive global leader bridging ideas and actions to solve some of the world's most complex challenges, and he has won over eighty awards and distinctions globally for his academic, policy, business, and leadership accomplishments—including being recognized as a WEF Young Global Leader for "finding innovative solutions to some of the world's most pressing issues," one of "Apolitical's 100 Most Influential Academics in Government," one of the "100 Iconic African Leaders" worldwide, among the "Global Top 100 Most Influential Export and International Trade" leaders, one of the "100 Most Influential People of African Descent," one of the "100 Most Influential Africans" in the world, "Thought Leader Extraordinaire" by *New Africa Magazine*, an Andrew Carnegie Fellow for being one of the "most creative thinkers," a Desmond Tutu Fellow, a Rubenstein Fellow, and a Wilson Center Public Policy Fellow. He frequently advises top global leaders, including heads of state and cabinet ministers, heads of international organizations, and CEOs of global multinationals, and he often testifies before the US Congress, the US International Trade Commission, and other such bodies. His books include *Innovating Development Strategies in Africa* (Cambridge University Press, 2017); *African Development, African Transformation* (Cambridge University Press, 2018); *Unlocking Africa's Business Potential* (Brookings, 2020); and *Africa's Fourth Industrial Revolution* (Cambridge University Press, 2023).